CINDERELLA'S BIG SCORE

CINDERELLA'S BIG SCORE

Women of the Punk and Indie Underground

MARIA RAHA

SEAL PRESS

CINDERELLA'S BIG SCORE
Women of the Punk and Indie Underground

Copyright © 2005 by Maria Raha

Some photos and illustrations are used by permission and
are the property of the original copyright owners.

Published by
Seal Press
An Imprint of
Avalon Publishing Group, Incorporated
1400 65th Street, Suite 250
Emeryville, CA 94608

For permissions information, see page 342.

Library of Congress Cataloging-in-Publication Data

Raha, Maria.
  Cinderella's big score : women of the punk and indie underground / by Maria Raha.-- 1st ed.
    p. cm.
  Includes bibliographical references (p.   ), discography and index.
  ISBN 1-58005-116-2 (pbk. : alk. paper)
  1. Rock music--History and criticism. 2. Women rock musicians. I. Title.

ML3534.R34 2005
781.66'082--dc22

                                    2004026231

          ISBN 1-58005-116-2

          9 8 7 6 5 4 3 2 1

          DESIGNED BY PATRICK DAVID BARBER

Printed in the United States of America by Worzalla
Distributed by Publishers Group West

*To all the devil-may-care rebel cowgirls of the world
with stories to sing.
Without you, I would surely lose my mind.
And in memory of some super-duper stars:
Kurt Cobain, Kristen Pfaff, Wendy Orleans Williams,
and Mia Zapata*

TABLE OF CONTENTS

Introduction   IX

Part I: America in the 1970s

I Am Woman, Hear Me Whisper: Introduction   3

CHAPTER 1   *Babelogue*: Patti Smith   16

CHAPTER 2   *Queens of Noise*: The Runaways   22

CHAPTER 3   *The Girl in the Band*: Tina Weymouth   27

CHAPTER 4   *Girl Germs*: Lorna Doom and Nicole Panter   32

CHAPTER 5   *Woman Overboard*: Debbie Harry   38

CHAPTER 6   *The World's a Mess; It's in My Kiss*: Exene Cervenka   42

CHAPTER 7   *Married to Myself*: Penelope Houston   47

CHAPTER 8   *Bikini Girls with Gretsch Guitars*: Poison Ivy   52

Part II: Britain in the 1970s

No One's Little Girls: Introduction   59

CHAPTER 9   *Voodoo Dolly*: Siouxsie Sioux   73

CHAPTER 10   *Number One Enemy*: The Slits   79

CHAPTER 11   *The Day the Girls Turned Day-Glo*:
              Lora Logic and Poly Styrene   86

CHAPTER 12   *Shaved Women, Collaborate!*:
              Joy de Vivre and Eve Libertine   92

CHAPTER 13   *Shouting Out Loud*: The Raincoats   100

Part III: The 1980s

Cruel, Cruel Decade: Introduction   107

CHAPTER 14   *Conspiracy of Women*: Lydia Lunch   121

CHAPTER 15   *Stunt Priestess*: Wendy O. Williams   127

CHAPTER 16   *Sonic Force*: Kim Gordon   133

CHAPTER 17   *Fast Enough*: Kim Warnick and Lulu Gargiulo   140

CHAPTER 18   *New Year*: Kim Deal   144

Part IV: The 1990s

TRUEPUNKROCKSOULCRUSADERS: Introduction   151

CHAPTER 19   *Look Right Through Me*: Mia Zapata   165

CHAPTER 20   *Courage*: Jenny Toomey   170

CHAPTER 21   *Pretty on the Inside*: Hole   177

CHAPTER 22   *Smell the Magic*: L7   182

CHAPTER 23   *Butch in the Streets*: Tribe 8   186

CHAPTER 24   *Babysitters on Acid*: Lunachicks   193

CHAPTER 25   *50 FT Queenie*: PJ Harvey   198

CHAPTER 26   *Reject All American*: Bikini Kill   203

CHAPTER 27   *So Many Cowards and So Little Time*: Bratmobile   209

CHAPTER 28   *To the Enemies of Dyke Rock*: Team Dresch   215

Part V: The Late 1990s–Early 2000s

Feminists, We're Calling You. Please Report to the Front Desk: Introduction   223

CHAPTER 29   *I Wanna Be Your Joey Ramone*: Sleater-Kinney   234

CHAPTER 30   *The Galaxy Is Gay*: The Butchies   239

CHAPTER 31   *Hot Topic*: Le Tigre   243

CHAPTER 32   *Back It Up, Boys*: Peaches   247

CHAPTER 33   *Arkansas Heat*: The Gossip   252

CHAPTER 34   *Controlled Chaos*: Erase Errata   256

Girls Get Busy: Conclusion   261

APPENDIX   *Rock 'n' Roll Fight Songs:* Discographies   263

Notes   281

Bibliography   302

INDEX   324

INTRODUCTION

To me, that's what rock and roll should
always come down to—the unallowed.
—LEEE CHILDERS[1]

WRITING THIS BOOK WAS HARD FOR ME; NOT BECAUSE DIGGING
up some of these women was an arduous task, and not because I also worked
full time while writing it. It was hard because it's always difficult to betray a
community of people you love. All of the beautiful, strange mutations of the
indie underground are the only places I've ever felt solace, and where I've met
the smartest, most articulate, motivated, and creative people in my life. Its art
and music liberated me from the mundane trappings of a suburban upbringing; it was the backdrop against which I first fell in love, and the place where
I found the individuals who articulated the reasons I felt culturally starved by
mainstream America. It cured my boredom by offering me something more
exciting; it lifted the veil of apathy through which I viewed the world; it
allowed me to fall in love for the first time, not only with a man, but with art
and the world and with other people. It was the first place where I found
people like me, who found injustice as intolerable as our culture's compulsive
consumerism. Yet here I am, attempting to rip it apart from the inside.

It feels a bit traitorous to criticize a community in which I have invested
so much. Yet harder still is knowing that in the grand scheme of things, this
scene, for me and for a lot of other people, is still as good as it gets. It still

succeeds by providing room for people to grow and to experience art not intentionally marketed as product. Whether female; a person of color; a trans, gay, lesbian, or bi individual; a drug addict or drunk; a good artist; a bad writer; a weekend warrior; a former Catholic school girl; a frat boy; a suburbanite; a 'zine editor (or one whose music is bemoaned by 'zine editors); an activist; a vegan; a pacifist; poor; rich; or a hardcore music nerd, each of us has felt constrained by indie rock's boundaries and obstacles, machismo or homophobia, self-righteousness or apathy, yet there is something about this community and the culture it has produced that still makes us feel free.

Those of us who criticize it from the inside have been in the uncomfortable position of loving music and art that makes us, at times, feel marginalized, yet it's still what we most closely identify with, the art we are captured by, the music that possesses us. And that's why it's so important to hold it accountable. Indie rock is still too vital for too many outcasts to allow it to become mired in its own prejudices, spoiled by its own success, powerless to critique our society, or unable to hold the passion of its devotees.

And speaking of devotion, indie passion for music is as expansive as it is explosive. While readers may split hairs about who should or shouldn't be included in these pages, ponder the legitimacy of Courtney Love nestling near Kathleen Hanna, or argue the use of the words "punk," "indie," or "underground," those definitions and boundaries are loosely structured. As the Slits' Ari-Up and Tsunami's Jenny Toomey will tell you, subversive culture once had less distinct boundaries: Fans were joined only by what awakened their minds and what connected them with other misfits. Lovers of music (and the weird) still delve into what conveys the real and the raw, rather than the perfect—whether on vinyl, through an amplifier, or on an MP3. Underground music culture has always been about more than the specificity of its sound.

Some of the women I have chosen to profile may not fit into a preconceived notion of "punk rock" or the "independent music underground," as the terms are generally and most strictly defined. All of them did, however, help fans to find themselves, to write, to sing, to play, to become politicized, and to uncover other artists and voices that lead to further self-exploration. Beyond cultural definitions, these women are rooted in the same place: the shake-up of rock that punk started in the 1970s. Among all the aesthetic definitions that go along with it, the indie spirit is about accepting yourself and other people, loving unpolished art, and making a contribution, regardless of what pop culture holds in high esteem. This definition may be too broad for some, but scenes vary from town to country to commune to squat to college, and so do the definitions, beliefs, and aesthetics that have come to encompass them. These pockets, some with personalities as complex as the people who create them, aren't easily defined with one blanket word, but for the purpose of this book "punk," "indie," and "underground" will have to suffice.

Cinderella's Big Score is a tribute to the women who were, and are, instrumental in shaping punk and indie underground music. It is also the study of a community which proudly rejects societal and cultural norms, yet, that same community falls prey to those same traditional and confining notions of behavior in regards to gender and sexual identity. As I began the research for this book, I found one record review after another berating rock journalism that specifically categorizes "women in rock," and some bemoaning music that's heavily political and, in particular, feminist. Kristy Eldredge writes in an article entitled "Chicks Rock: No Shit, Sherlock" on the *Glorious Noise* website: "My first thought was: Oh boy, how obsolete can you get? Is there anything left to say about women's strong and exciting contributions to rock? I'd say they've *made* their place; they're in the rock world and there's nothing remarkable about that anymore."[2] The notion of treating women as rarities because they are at once musicians and female is obsolete—it's as archaic as the question posed to Sleater-Kinney singer and guitarist Carrie Brownstein in an interview by *Salon* writer Joe Heim: "How does it feel to be 'women in rock'?"[3] Brownstein refused to answer the question, and then hung up on Heim when he asked it a second time.

These are the kinds of sweeping generalizations and inane inquiries that with repetition cause frustrated sighs by critics and bands alike. The popular media is all too happy to link female musicians together, regardless of the group's divergent styles and genres. When Britney Spears, Mary J. Blige, and Alanis Morissette grace *Rolling Stone*'s 2002 "Women In Rock" issue, to consider and question the position of women in music and the popular media's portrayal of their contributions hardly seems irrelevant.

Yet it's no surprise that artists like Spears are honored by *Rolling Stone*, when women who employ a broader perspective in songwriting, like politics, are often dubbed musically "boring." In his book *England's Dreaming*, Jon Savage accused postpunk bands like the Raincoats of being so dogmatic, "the music was no fun at all."[4] *Punk 77*, a website that thoroughly documents British punk in the '70s, emblazoned its feature on Rock Against Racism and Sexism (connected, loose alliances of politicized, leftist punkers) with the headline "No Fun No Fun!! Politics."[5] (The website does feature extensive documentation of women in punk, however.) As we'll see, riot grrrl was put through the wringer for its alignment with feminism. And while mixing politics and music might elicit more than a few yawns, many of the reviews and features written about female musicians who don't necessarily self-identify as feminists or infuse their lyrics with overt political content reduce their subjects to several tried and true stereotypes: martyr, saint, goddess, or bad girl. Alternately, artists like Chrissie Hynde and PJ Harvey are often identified as feminists by the media (regardless of their protests), simply because they are female and, on occasion, outspoken. And many bands that evolved out of the riot grrrl movement are still branded as such more than a decade later; some all-female bands who were never riot grrrls but made music around the same time, like the Lunachicks and 7 Year Bitch, have suffered endless pigeon-holing as riot grrrl bands.

The "women in music" category shouldn't even exist anymore—perhaps it shouldn't have been created in the first place. Unfortunately, for both mainstream culture and indie rock, we still need it. A set of ovaries doesn't mean you can't rock any less; we all know that, and some women—particularly those social visionaries who emerged from '70s punk communities—never had to be convinced. And while many of us feel that "women in music" has been thoroughly dissected by anyone with access to the Internet or a laptop over the last ten years, frankly, things haven't changed enough to diminish the necessity for books like this one.

The mainstream music industry has churned out a one-dimensional, oppressive, and, let's face it, boring parade of female musicians over the years. Yet despite this, amazing women have found their voice in popular music, inspiring audiences and future artists. Early blues women like Bessie Smith, Ma Rainey, and Billie Holiday not only moved audiences at the time but continue to inspire music fans and musicians alike—women like Mia Zapata of the Gits emulated their style. The to-this-day-underappreciated Wanda Jackson performed her brand of feminist rockabilly in the '50s and '60s, gyrating her hips in mock imitation of Elvis Presley and singing songs like "My Big Iron Skillet," in which she protects herself from her lover by wielding the traditionally feminine kitchen item.[6] It's only been about thirty years since Janis Joplin swaggered like a sailor, and fourteen years since Ani DiFranco released her eponymous, unapologetic, angry first folk album on her own Righteous Babe Records. During punk's cultural revolution of the '70s, "women in music" usually meant disco queens or soft-pop divas. So while the mainstream music industry has continued to churn out culturally acceptable versions of femininity along predefined lines—from the Chiffons to Britney Spears—the underground, in all its forms, has always offered something to counter it.

The punk and indie culture of the '70s and '80s has become so ingrained in American popular culture that Cleveland's Rock and Roll Hall of Fame annually inducts more and more musicians who grew in status from subculture figures to cultural icons. Next to Elvis and the Beatles sit underground music's own royalty: David Bowie, the Velvet Underground, the Ramones, the Talking Heads, the Clash, Elvis Costello, and the Police. Sadly, among the underground kings sit only two queens: Maureen Tucker, the drummer for the Velvet Underground, and Tina Weymouth, bassist for the Talking Heads. (Patti Smith has been consistently cut from the inductee list.) None of these women hold the same artistic cachet as Joe Strummer, Lou Reed, or David Byrne. The absence of women in this paean to rock music is as noticeable as an unsettling silence can be on the perpetually bustling streets of New York City.

This limited recognition doesn't only happen in Cleveland. When asked to comment in Michael Azerrad's *Our Band Could Be Your Life* on the lack of women populating D.C. bands of the late '70s and early '80s, Ian MacKaye, essentially one of the founders of the testosterone-heavy D.C. hardcore scene, is quoted as saying, "There's a certain kind of aggressiveness that leads the boys to pick up the instruments."[7] I gave him the benefit of the doubt, initially. Maybe the quote was taken out of context, or was true to the D.C. scene specifically, which did become increasingly aggressive and male as hardcore took off. MacKaye, after all, became a staunch supporter of women's presence in the late '80s and early '90s, when Bikini Kill shared bills with his band Fugazi, who evoked the tragedy of rape in their song "Suggestion." Women did populate D.C.'s stages, but as a result of the hyperaggressiveness of later hardcore, most were relegated to behind-the-scenes work like photography, 'zine-making, and political action. That said, there were a smattering of female bands (like the all-girl hardcore band Chalk Circle) and band members who remain footnotes to the larger, male-dominated scene. Azerrad spoke with Chalk

Circle cofounder Sharon Cheslow about the D.C. scene's lack of women. Cheslow's reply: "The angry young boy thing was very romanticized. Angry young girls were a threat."[8] Contrary to MacKaye's assertion, women needed to express aggression, too, but were relegated to the sidelines, either by individual self-censorship, the lack of other successful female musicians to act as role models, or the scene's own culture of female exclusion.

When I spoke with Ari-Up of the all-female U.K. band the Slits, she spoke of feeling as if the Slits' work and influence exists "in exile." When U.K. punk's visionaries are rattled off by journalists, the Clash, the Sex Pistols, and the Damned always take top billing, with an occasional mention of the Slits and the X-Ray Spex. In general terms, the punk and indie world is littered with females who have not only withstood punk's intolerance toward women, but who have twisted societal notions of femininity in knots. Even in punk, a culture hell-bent on making people uncomfortable by its behavior and appearance, the very presence of women onstage frequently caused discomfort in the scene itself.

A widely accepted notion of indie culture has always been its advocacy of leftist, progressive, and radical politics in all forms, and its rejection of the capitalist monotony of popular culture. However attracted we might be to these progressive ideals, we're also products of a larger society and dispensing with the dominant culture's values is not easy. Our wardrobes are potent examples of this paradoxical counterculture phenomenon. While there are certainly those who refuse to wear the uniform, the subgenres that grew out of the initial rise of punk culture have indoctrinated their own styles and looks: Some punks still wear liberty spikes and Mohawks; goth kids still go out in whiteface; indie rock owns a rumpled thrift-store look and champions the nerd aesthetic; rockabilly and psychobilly circles mix bondage gear and '50s vintage; hardcore circles accept crewcuts, baggy shorts, and T-shirts. And while preaching the value of individuality, we are often guilty of donning, as well as expecting from our peers, the uniform of the underground.

While some members reject notions of being "cool" and the mainstream consumer culture, there is still the process of acceptance or suspicion within the subculture, based on a style aesthetic that did not seem to exist in punk's early days. The Ramones wore leather jackets and sneakers and had long hair. Debbie Harry wore dresses and a layer of makeup fit for a drag queen. While Siouxsie Sioux played with bondage gear and *A Clockwork Orange*-style droog makeup, the members of the Slits refused to comb their hair. Exene Cervenka mixed vamp with vintage; Television donned ragged T-shirts and embraced a minimalist style. All of these artists formed their own aesthetics, both visually and musically, within the same community—one which initially championed the individual over uniformity. The demonizing of those who don't toe the fashion line within a subculture once made up of those demonized by the larger culture is ironic, and a strong indication that mainstream values of consumerism have taken hold.

What, then, if we extend this pervasive single-mindedness to sexual stereotyping? What is the culture at large promoting in its images of womanhood, even today? Regardless of the expansive women's sections in chain bookstores and the growth of women's studies in colleges nationwide, we still live in a male-dominated culture. Regardless of the offerings of leftist indie culture and easy dissemination of dissent via the Internet, we still live in the era of the boy: magazines like *Maxim, Stuff,* and *FHM,* Comedy Central's *The Man Show,* the *Girls Gone Wild* video series, and male rage acts like Limp Bizkit and Eminem, to name just a few, belie how the culture really feels about women's social progress.

While many principles of feminism have come to be accepted by popular culture, there are also many reminders in the media that women continue to bear the brunt of beauty complexes, stereotypical assumptions about what constitutes women's cultural taste, and the burden of strict codes of acceptable behavior. The message is that women can only be so transgressive. Radical behavior is still a threat. This is even true in the supposedly avant-garde world of punk and indie rock, which has consistently sidestepped feminism while espousing other aspects of lefty politics, like environmental activism, anarchism, or veganism. Once women, even in this scene, go "too far" or get "too angry," as they did during the heady riotgrrrl days, the subculture tends to shun them.

This gender discrimination reduces real revolutions by women in punk and indie rock to a faint echo, co-opted and stripped down by a pop culture that consumes what limited progress it can swallow and spits back the rest. This watered-down version of the strong female might make the "real deals" all the more potent, but it also continues to limit their visibility and, subsequently, the inspiration such women can provide. While all-dyke punk band Tribe 8 identify themselves as "castrating" "dildo-swingers" and retain mainstream invisibility, Madonna and Britney make front-page news for a five-second, hopelessly staged liplock. Chart-topper Alanis Morissette was defined as "angry" (though not obviously threatening) for her revenge song "You Oughta Know," while Lydia Lunch's garbled shrieks and growls go unheard. Avril Lavigne, a popular, twiggy recording-industry version of pop "punk," sings traditional teenage-girl love songs about skater boys, while Kathleen Hanna's lyrics question the motives of Lavigne's beloved. In a larger culture that never fails to compulsively promote the least harmful, most sexualized versions of the angry female, true subversion is once again retreating underground, leaving the real pioneers—who paved the way for MTV's girl-on-girl kiss or a woman publicly castigating her ex-lover—with the fewest accolades.

Politics were more commonplace than pining about love during punk's heyday in the '70s. The Raincoats assumed an openly assertive feminist stance, and Crass member Eve Libertine accused Christ of "cuntfear" in the scathing rant on Christianity "Reality Asylum." The group also stenciled political messages all over Britain, one of which was "Stuff Your Sexist Shit."[9] Legend has it that Poly Styrene of London's X-Ray Spex was so intense, she scared the wits out of Sex Pistols singer Johnny Rotten (née John Lydon), arguably the embodiment of British punk anger.[10]

The glory of 1977 wouldn't last forever, though, and as Azerrad succinctly remarked in discussing the downfall of hardcore, "By '83, the idiots were taking over."[11] As punk was discovered (and predictably watered down) by popular culture, female musicians faced the same scrutiny in circles where they should have found support. In the American working and middle class where punk thrived in the late '70s and early '80s, many suburban boys coming out of the metal scene may have been shocked by the confrontational stance of a woman like Wendy O. Williams, the chainsaw-wielding lead singer of the Plasmatics. Some boys, for all of their rebellious attitudes, still had very limited images of womanhood.

You would think that men involved in punk at the time, with socially progressive stances on fronts like veganism, the straightedge lifestyle, or rejection of the oppressive structures of corporate corruption, would have been as evolved in their treatment of women, but history, lyrics, personal experiences, mosh-pit politics, and the women within these pages tell us differently. Sonic Youth member Kim Gordon's 1987 tour diary for the *Village Voice Rock and Roll Quarterly* contains the following account: "The fan boy picked up this broken drumstick that had flown onto the floor and threw it back. It speared into my forehead. At first I thought it had bounced off of Thurston's guitar. Shocked, I didn't know whether to cry or keep playing, but then I just felt incredibly angry. It took a long time to resolve that incident, 'cause it really made me feel sick, violated, like walking to the dressing room after a set, having some guy say 'Nice show,' then getting my ass pinched as I walk away."[12] In the same account, Gordon also documents having firecrackers flung at her and having her "ass bit" when the band played in Switzerland.[13]

Even after firm groundwork had been laid to shatter long-standing stereotypes of women in the music scene as either groupies or just plain out of their element, the beat went on. Tribe 8 vocalist Lynn Breedlove contends that when the band formed in the early '90s, they were the only dyke punk band in San Francisco, where at the time, she recalls, a "lesbian renaissance" was under way. The Gits' drummer Steve Moriarty noted the male-centricity of the seemingly progressive Seattle record label Sub Pop, which became the bastion of the grunge sound that possessed '90s culture: "Most of those Sub Pop bands were really male-oriented," Moriarty said. "They were sort of the boy bands that always had a male lead singer, and Sub Pop had very, very few female-led bands, and very few bands that really recalled punk music." Even before grunge hit it big and introduced the mosh pit to a new generation of blindly aggressive fans, Courtney Love took a dive into the audience at a Hole show, and was subsequently assaulted by the men who caught her. Apparently, the indie parade of angry, strong, and independent women hadn't changed many male fans' attitudes toward female musicians, even toward someone as tough as Courtney Love.

The title of this book was inspired by a Sonic Youth song of the same name. Besides a nod to Kim Gordon for acting as a remote mentor to me as I discovered myself, "Cinderella" invokes the fairy tale's disenfranchised main character, foiled by her circumstances at every turn, and sneaking out to the ball that ultimately leads to her emancipation. The difference between the Cinderella stories documented here and that of the fairy-tale version lie in who holds the glass slipper. The mythic Cinderella's escape lies in a perfectly fitted shoe held by a prince, while these real-life Cinderellas spun their magic out of thin air.

The women profiled in *Cinderella's Big Score* have experienced varying levels of success, notoriety, and obscurity, from the legendary Patti Smith to the largely ignored Poison Ivy and the women of Crass to sex-positive Peaches and the dyke trio the Butchies, who are still gaining musical ground. This is in no way meant to serve as a comprehensive work on the history of women in punk and indie rock; instead I profiled those women to whom I *wanted* to pay tribute—whether for the potency of their transgressions of indie culture and the culture at large or for their subversion of traditional feminine roles in music, or simply because I'm a fan. What these women have in common is that they are all pioneers, Medeas, cowgirls, artists.

A comprehensive history of women in indie rock would be virtually impossible. Women's contributions to this scene have been vast, not only as musicians, but as 'zine editors, sound engineers, managers, producers, record distributors, public relations managers, record label owners, artists, poets, activists, and fans. Their contributions and passions run deep.

And, of course, the ideas put forth in this book in no way speak for an umbrella indie culture. That would be impossible, as there are many, many mutations of this once-small community. Scenes exist with their own regional influence, are the voices of their members, and evolve on their own terms all while being affected, like every social phenomenon, by larger cultural forces. This being said, the examples provided here are meant to serve as just that— examples of how indie culture has contradicted itself throughout the years, and how these women have stood as examples of the subversion within it. Nothing written here should be taken as a sweeping assumption about every local scene, every record label, or every mosh pit. No one book could ever cover every corner of this culture.

⁂

These women demonstrate that it is not the ovaries that make it so miraculous that they can strum a guitar just like the boys; it's the power of their subversion and its impact on both indie and mainstream culture that are significant. The recording industry is constantly cashing in on the women-in-music card and classifying female musicians as feminists for the mere ownership of a guitar—and the media dutifully follows. MTV's website bizarrely likened blockbuster Barbie doll Christina Aguilera's performance on a recent album to that of an anticapitalist Poly Styrene. Aside from both performers hitting a few of the same high notes, this is a wildly inaccurate comparison and a strong indication that for the media, ovaries are still the easiest link from one female musician to another.

Expectations of women have consistently been more structured and confined than those of men; we have always been expected to walk a thinner line for our gender. *That's* why this book is about women in rock, and why every artist profiled in these pages possesses a set of ovaries. As our culture detours down a dangerous road of increasing conservatism—from the George W. Bush administration's agenda to the squelching of antiwar and antigovernment sentiments—subversion in all forms becomes more precious. As censorship on both the individual and governmental levels becomes more severely skewed to make the right more comfortable, it becomes increasingly important to note individuals and movements that have embraced rebellion and self-expression in the face of intolerance and orthodoxy.

In *Backlash: The Undeclared War Against Women*, Susan Faludi notes that through trend journalism, what suddenly turns a given idea into fact is the mere repetition of it.[14] With the many examples of women in the music industry today, critics mistakenly opine that our victory has been won, and use the number of high-profile female musicians, regardless of how irrelevant or mundane their stances are, as proof positive that women have leveled the playing field and shattered the glass ceiling. Repetition does not mean that gender bias in mainstream music and indie circles has disappeared. As long as sort-of-angry-but-still-camera-and-fashion-friendly women like Gwen Stefani receive mainstream accolades for being "different," there will always be room for one more story about intelligent, questioning, truly subversive, sometimes feminist, angry, hard-working, creative individuals transgressing cultural boundaries.

Works that honor transgressive artists are as vital as transgressive art itself, if only to inspire others. And indie rock is very good at inspiration, helping to launch careers where there was no hope of one before: The Runaways inspired the Germs' Darby Crash to form one of the first L.A. punk bands, and the general musical havoc wreaked by the Sex Pistols was a watershed for countless subversive U.K. bands like the Clash, X-Ray Spex, and Siouxsie and the Banshees. If just for the example of what a strong-willed human with an idea can do to subvert a world within a world, writing a book celebrating women in this scene is still worth it.

I wrote this book to remind myself that artistic bravery still exists in an increasingly apathetic larger world; that honest, self-made avenues of expression separate from the intrusion of big business still exist. In part, I wanted to honor the women who have made me feel less isolated and a little less insane in a world so focused on commerce and physical perfection. Mostly, I just love these ladies for their music and their individualism, for their unflagging ability to scream for me and explain what I can't always vocalize. I hope I've done them justice.

Part I

AMERICA IN THE 1970S

Introduction

I AM WOMAN, HEAR ME WHISPER

THE BIRTH OF PUNK ROCK AS A MOVEMENT HAS CHANGED THE face of music forever. It has created a thriving network of independent businesses and fostered artists who operate outside of the mainstream recording, publishing, magazine, and, hell, even fashion industries. Punk and indie rock have allowed disaffected artists and fans to communicate with each other, building far-reaching, self-created communities formed by mutual inspiration, admiration, and disgust with bloated mainstream culture. The nebulous "underground" has grown into a self-sustaining society built on self-expression and the rejection of the overmanufactured pop culture fantasy continually force-fed to us. The entire indie-music world continues to flourish on the two most important principles of early punk, ideals that are ultimately more important to punk than narrowly categorizing the music by its stepped-up speed and bloodied screams: 1) individuality is paramount, and 2) *anyone* can make great art.

Mainstream American culture in the 1970s hardly reflected these punk ideals, nor did the popular music reflect the political landscape of the country. The number one song on *Billboard*'s charts in January 1970 was "Raindrops Keep Falling on My Head," a Burt Bacharach song performed by B.J. Thomas. At the time, the country was embroiled in the Vietnam War, civil rights as well as the women's and gay rights movements were being bitterly contested, American cities were experiencing severe urban decay, and the Manson Family murders had only months before been in the headlines. And B.J. Thomas sang "Raindrops Keep Falling on My Head."[1]

In "Raindrops," the narrator happily shrugs his shoulders when assaulted by "bad" weather. Of course, the inane optimism of the song was part of the reason for its success (as was it being on the soundtrack of the popular movie *Butch Cassidy and the Sundance Kid*). The song's prominence on the charts tells us something of the desire for mass cultural escapism, as well as a wholesome aesthetic that had usurped the tired, commodified hippie culture.

The popularity of songs like this and many others helped spur the birth of punk. Revulsion at the success of one-dimensional music and its hesitancy to deal with pressing issues of poverty and urban decay created the perfect climate for artistic backlash. Like much of the decade's popular culture, almost all of the '70s soft rock singer-songwriter catalog feels repressed—as if the sexuality, power, and humanity that make music such a potent cultural force has been squeezed out, or maybe just cleverly hidden under all those breathy high notes and whispering drums.

In the book *Precious and Few* by Don and Jeff Breithaupt, soft rock is aptly and mockingly referred to as "Cauc[asian] Rock," a play on the term "cock rock."[2] Most rock critics passionately derided the soft rock behemoth, and none more passionately than Lester Bangs. As he artfully wrote in the rock 'zine *Who Put the Bomp*: "[I]f I hear one more Jesus-walking-the-boys-and-girls-down-a-Carolina-path-while-the-dilemma-of-existence-crashes-like-a-slab-of-hod-on-J.T.'s-shoulders song, I will drop everything . . . and hop the first Greyhound to Carolina for the signal [*sic*] satisfaction of breaking off a bottle of Ripple . . . and twisting it into James Taylor's guts until he expires in a spasm of adenoidal poesy."[3]

It's not shocking today that James Taylor might irritate someone to violent fantasy; but at the time it was. Bangs' rage toward the status quo in music sprung from the fact that he *knew* better music—like the chaotic Stooges—existed. And yet what he and others like him heard emanating from major labels and across airwaves was a chipper B.J. Thomas.

While "Raindrops Keep Falling on My Head" was irritating in its polite refusal to engage in any real political commentary or reflection, it was emblematic of the blinders worn by the record industry. The boundaries broken by, and subsequent immense popularity of, the Rolling Stones, Bob Dylan, the Beatles, Jimi Hendrix, the Doors, and countless other popular (male) acts during the '60s were not taken into consideration by a recording industry so afraid of risk.[4] Instead it relied on a few sure-fire platinum sellers for its income.[5] Rather than continuing on the trajectory rock had created during the '60s, soft rock acts like Carole King, Debbie Boone, and the Carpenters took the place of revolutionary rock performers and politically minded folksingers. In *We Got the Neutron Bomb*, music journalist Harvey Kubernik comments on the state of music in Los Angeles: "By '71, the Elektra/Asylum Records singer-songwriter type music was all this town was offering. . . . [T]hey . . . were very locked into the traditional Brill Building verse/chorus/verse style. . . .When [Jim] Morrison died, I said to [Ray] Manzarek [keyboardist for the Doors], 'Well, maybe Jim wasn't supposed to see all this singer-songwriter shit take over his label.'"[6]

The early '70s saw a parade of singer-songwriters, popular folk musicians, and soft rockers hell-bent on mellowing the American pop playlist. James Taylor, Carole King, Simon and Garfunkel, America, Jim Croce, Carly Simon, Don McLean, Maureen McGovern, Neil Diamond, and Dawn all had number one hits between 1970 and the end of 1972. Although singer-songwriters and other thriving soft rock and folk acts did occasionally produce material steeped in politics, or music that explored the darker side of life and the culture at large (e.g., Joni Mitchell and Bob Dylan), most soft rock lacked variety and visceral passion. Typical formulaic singer-songwriter/soft rock material consisted, more often than not, of gently played acoustic guitar and piano, violins here and there, and a lithe voice that often faded to breathlessness for accentuation. Vocally, most female folksingers opted for (or were urged toward) an asexual, feathery lightness, while lyrics expressed love and longing, veiled in overly simplistic, innocent imagery to make their rather banal and placid points.

In contrast to the confrontational style of Jim Morrison and the Doors, the Carpenters, a duo composed of a happy-go-lucky keyboardist-song-writer and a quiet drummer with a soft, sweet voice, were signed to A&M in 1969.[7] The Carpenters proved to be the perfect conservative antidote for the selections offered on *Morrison Hotel*, released in 1970, the same year the Carpenters had their first hit, "(They Long to Be) Close to You." While women like Janis Joplin wielded an ever-present bottle of liquor and had an arrest record for "vulgar" language, Karen Carpenter was demure and quiet, dressed modestly in polyester that often matched her brother's outfit.[8] In *She's A Rebel*, author Gillian Gaar notes that the Carpenters were so serene and nonthreatening as compared to the previous decade's rock icons, they garnered the rare, open affection of Richard Nixon.[9] The popularity of the duo was demonstrated through nineteen painfully pristine Top 40 singles throughout the decade.

In "(They Long to Be) Close to You," actually a cover, Carpenter invokes imaginary birds as a replacement for physical lust. The opening line suggests a teenage naiveté at feeling desire for the first time. The narrator never expresses her desire to actually touch her would-be suitor, only to be near him (or her). Carly Simon's 1972 number one hit, "You're So Vain," albeit peppier than other soft rock hits, admonishes a self-absorbed lover. With sexual conquistador Mick Jagger on backing vocals, Simon's admonishment is tempered, as if to avoid isolating male listeners. Jagger's stamp of approval serves to soften the blow of the sassy subject's realization about her lover, and, through his infamously macho reputation, implies a reluctance to let Simon put her autonomous stamp on a work that might otherwise serve as a mark of liberation. While "You're So Vain" is thankfully lacking in self-loathing and could even be viewed as female victory in popular music, Simon's bite is allayed thanks in large part to the song's harmless musical accompaniment.

With feminism on the rise, Helen Reddy had a show-tune-type hit in late 1972 with "I Am Woman," which remained in the Top 10 for eight weeks. The song came up against a lot of industry resistance and mainstream criticism, and was a big victory for the feminist movement, but the song itself was fairly run-of-the-mill Top 40 pop. Although "I Am Woman" contained fairly radical lyrics, it was performed with the sassy energy of the wisecracking, zany Broadway musical character who gets all the good lines but ends the show without a lover. In other words, the song never really strayed far from "These Boots Are Made for Walkin'" or other women's pop songs of the era. Like much of the emerging feminist movement and nearly the entire soft rock catalog, "I Am Woman" appealed to middle-class white women and more mainstream cultural sensibilities.

—————————

While "cauc rock" dominated much of the airwaves, mainstream hard rock morphed into a genre that had more to do with commodity than art. Lavish stage shows in large arenas, high ticket prices, and gobs of concert memorabilia came to epitomize '70s hard rock. Led Zeppelin, the Who, the Rolling Stones, and progressive rock bands like Yes favored masturbatory solos, dramatic light shows, and enormous venues over intimacy or spare sets. A line had been drawn for hard rock fans: On one side stood godlike musicians, and on the other stood humble and adoring fans who might privately fumble through renditions of "Stairway to Heaven" in their bedrooms but certainly didn't have the option of taking to the stage themselves.

With gigantic tours came even more adoring women and a thriving groupie culture. As the Doors, the Beatles, Elvis Presley, and countless others had done before, "cock" rockers like Robert Plant and Gene Simmons became notorious for the gaggle of teenage girls they could bed on any given night. Male rock stars during this period seemed to measure their musical worth not only in how many seats they could sell, but in the lengths to which they could coerce decadent sexual favors from their female fans.

Cock rock's reputation for drumming up a willing harem perpetuated the music scene's division of labor. Women were expected to play the adoring fan or willing sex toy, either way a testing ground for male rock star power. Picking up a guitar themselves in the hard rock arena was unimagined; men were the active participants in rock life. Without any onstage role models, is it any wonder women didn't wrestle for the mic? While women could certainly appreciate the music and its power, the connection was weakest at the point where music should have the deepest effect—the point of inspiration. Cock rock made it clear to most women that being *near* the rock star was as good as it gets.

The birth of punk in America was a direct reaction not only to the banal soft rock sensations but also a response to this hyped and highly commodified hard rock scene and the insipid heavy rotation of the soft rock catalog on radio. Rather than appearing to Joey Ramone in a glue-sniffing-induced moment of enlightenment, punk had been brewing quietly since the '60s. Fuzzy garage bands like the Seeds played quick, angry two-minute songs, and the Velvet Underground melded '60s garage sounds with a flood of noise and feedback, telling stories of drug abuse and isolation. In the late '60s, the MC5 took the garage band sound to a harder, noisy extreme, with more of an emphasis on loud guitars and relatively unbridled screaming matched with a radical political stance. But it was Detroit's Stooges who took the thrashing garage sound to its limit. As the Ramones would years later, the Stooges promoted a delinquent image that liberated rock from the grip of its decaying royalty. While the Beatles declared themselves more popular than Jesus and Led Zeppelin preened and pranced around the stage, the Stooges played "I Wanna Be Your Dog." A seething, wiry Iggy Pop yanked the audience in an entirely different direction than did the ruling rock demigods of the day. Beyond the crumbling Motor City economy that influenced both the MC5 and the Stooges, Jim Morrison inspired Iggy to incite his audience rather than dominate it. He eagerly went a step further than Morrison to provoke reaction, mutilating himself onstage and forcing audience participation by jumping on fans, screaming and cursing, rolling around in broken glass, spitting, or, most famously, carving into his chest with a piece of glass. The invisible barrier between performer and audience had been broken down.

The New York Dolls started playing downtown Manhattan in 1970. Dressed in women's clothing and high heels and draped with scarves, the Dolls stripped the rock and roll sound back down to its original verse-chorus-verse structure, and placed depravity and fun over technical prowess—establishing, like the Stooges and the MC5, that rock was any-one's property. "I don't know where the glitter thing came from," lead singer David Johansen once said. "We were just very ecological about clothes. It was just about taking old clothes and wearing them again. I think they called it glitter rock because some of the kids who used to come to see us put glitter in their hair or on their faces. The press figured it was glitter rock—the term itself came from some writer, but it was just classical rock and roll."[10] There was the other side of this ethos of submission to the audience—one that had less to do with squelching egos in a rush of shorter songs and more to do with submitting to the feminine.

A late-'60s folkie named David Bowie dropped his floppy-hatted gen-teel appearance and performed as Ziggy Stardust, a space-age superstar per-sona who nudged the English glam craze into America. The space theme and the drama of glam played a big role in inspiring young kids who knew about Bowie to follow a different cultural road, one where platform shoes and makeup feminized the male rock star. The kind of hero worship afforded to glam was actually what groups like the Stooges managed to avoid. Glam's drama and theatrics, however femme, encouraged its fans to *emulate* the unattainable, manufactured celebrity of David Bowie, Roxy Music, or T. Rex's Marc Bolan. Los Angeles dove into the campy space age, too, with local bands like Silverhead and Zolar X, who claimed to be from outer space and talked in a made-up language. Ohio was also home to a local movement of underground '6os bands like the Choir and early-to-mid-'7os acts like Cleveland's the Electric Eels, Rocket from the Tombs, Akron's Devo, and the Bizarros. Underground music, particularly in Cleveland, predated nihilist acts like Pere Ubu.

There was an underground—whether glam, punk, or otherwise—brewing in the United States, but still mostly centered in Los Angeles and New York. There's no single band that inspired the birth of American punk; instead, there were small pockets of people littered all over the country who felt they were finally being spoken to and for when they heard the Velvet Underground, the Stooges, or the New York Dolls.

While some define punk purely by a song's sound, the music that sprung up simultaneously and spontaneously all over the country in the early '7os signified an artistic liberation from a suffocating culture where boredom or isolation induced a dramatic musical explosion.

A writhing, raw young poet named Patti Smith infused her music with a strong undercurrent of female emotion repressed from the mainstream. All the passive sexuality, genteel affection, and stifling confines for women in the mainstream rock arena made Smith's brand of rebellion and vision even more potent and revolutionary. She strove for a gender-neutral self-expression—the female predator invisible in cock rock. Laying her own improvised version of the usually hypermasculine beat poetry over garage rock, she wrote words for "the common man," often focusing on humanity and the world as a whole, not on saccharine themes of love. Sometimes, she sounded as if she were speaking in tongues, conjuring all of the voiceless women in mainstream music, hitting notes that were lower and more desperate than the softness that came to stand for popular music in the '7os. Smith was herself without compromise.

When mainstream female musicians of the day were afforded a sex drive, it was decorative and usually passive and demure. Linda Ronstadt, who had twelve Top 40 hits from 1970 to 1978, sang a lot of covers straight—"(Love Is Like a) Heat Wave," "That'll Be the Day," "Tracks of My Tears," "It's So Easy")—which automatically limited her self-expression (and it should be noted that while Smith also performed a number of covers, it was what Ronstadt *didn't* do with them that limited their interest and impact). For the cover of *Silk Purse*, Ronstadt sat in a pig stall, posing like the age-old male fantasy of the sexy farmer's daughter. The cover prompted Lester Bangs to write in *Creem*, "Oh Linda, sweet Linda, if you couldn't sing a lick those lips would still carry you a lot farther than oh, say, Chi Coltrane. Unfortunately, this may have been your finest hour."[11] Bangs' tongue-in-cheek criticism certainly mocked the approach the record industry took to selling traditionally attractive women. Other women, like Olivia Newton-John, followed the same route, exuding a less-than-subtle mix of blatant sexuality and girl-next-door sweetness. Even the swaggering, nontraditional Janis Joplin vowed to try harder to love her partner, so as not to lose him, in "Try (Just a Little Bit Harder)." Joplin's lyrical content had wider range than what the soft-rock females championed, in songs like "Me and Bobby McGee" (written by Kris Kristofferson), "Mercedes Benz," and "Down on Me," but many of her love songs still positioned the devil-may-care songstress in a position of submission or wanting, as in "Try (Just a Little Bit Harder)." Patti Smith, on the other hand, placed the narrator as the dominant force—the lover who will desire, seduce, mesmerize, and pin down rather than "try (just a little bit harder)," or allow love or lust to go unrequited. Smith consistently took the role of muse-maker, embraced male heroes like Bob Dylan and Arthur Rimbaud, and brought the raw human emotions bubbling underneath the polished surface of hollow love songs to the fore of her music.

In 1974, members of the newly formed, guitar-driven Television approached CBGB, a club on the Bowery, and convinced owner Hilly Kristal to allow them to play. Kristal remembered, "Since at that time we weren't open on Sunday, I decided to give Television a try out, about three and a half weeks hence, on a Sunday. The admission was one dollar. It was not an impressive debut—at least, not in my opinion. There were only a few paid customers and not too many more friends. They not only didn't pay admission, but didn't have any money for drinks."[12] While the Sex Pistols later gussied up nihilism in stylized clothing, Television embodied minimalism, singing songs like "Blank Generation" (which was never officially recorded by the band, but written for it by Richard Hell), a rumored precursor to "Pretty Vacant" by the Pistols. The band returned to CBGB's stage with the Ramones in tow, and the club started booking other local bands. In December 1975, the first issue of *Punk*, a local 'zine covering New York's new music movement, labeled what was happening at CBGB as "punk." The same term had been used almost a decade earlier to describe '60s underground garage rock.

Although Patti Smith has consistently maintained that she can't be confined to punk, she certainly set a precedent for the influx of women to come. Since she ended up on Arista, a major label, her work was easy to find and was, for a lot of music fans, their first introduction to the new sounds coming out of New York. By the mid-'70s, Smith was practically covered monthly in magazines like *Creem*. The Avengers' Penelope Houston recalls her introduction to the new sound through Smith: "I remember hearing Patti Smith's *Horses* when it came out, and that really blew me away."[13]

With bands like the Patti Smith Group, the Ramones, and Television touring the States and Europe, no individual punk scene was created in a vacuum. While each region developed its own sounds and symbols of the underground, touring bands informed and, along with a proliferation of rock magazines, inspired other artists and outcasts to try creating music for themselves. K Records cofounder and Beat Happening member Calvin Johnson explained his experience in the film *Songs for Cassavetes*: "When I was eleven or twelve years old, in '72, '73, [I] started listening to music like rock and roll music, and getting interested in rock and roll. And as I got into, like, high-school era, I'd hear the people who were into rock and roll—they were like musicians, and their language didn't make sense to me, because I was interested in music, but I was interested in music 'cause it felt good, or it worked in a way that made your mind think about things, but they seemed to have this point of view that they'd say things like, 'Well, that song is only three chords! Anyone could play that!' . . . And I just thought, like, 'Well, so what if it's easy? It's what I want to hear.' So then punk rock came along and said, 'Yeah, that's right. You don't need to be a great musician to do it. In fact, there's no right way to do it. There's just, there's just doin' it.'"[14]

Of the touring bands at the time, the Ramones were probably the group to which new converts could most easily relate. Their lyrics blurred the Morrison mojo and stifled the pretentious, presumptuous, aggressive sexuality channeled through the likes of Mick Jagger and Robert Plant. Instead of burying J.R.R. Tolkien references in their lyrics or portraying themselves as pagan fertility gods offering themselves to the female fans, the Ramones rejoiced in the mundane. "Now I Wanna Sniff Some Glue," "Beat on the Brat," and "Blitzkreig Bop," with their accessible lyrics and fairly ego-less stance, returned rock to its audience.

While the Ramones, Television, Blondie, Talking Heads, and the Patti Smith Group were playing CBGB and signing major label contracts, the Los Angeles glam headquarters of Rodney Binghenheimer's English Disco was both an early promoter of David Bowie[15] and, before its eventual demise, a meeting place for punk teenagers like Belinda Carlisle and Jane Wiedlin (both of the Go-Go's).[16] The L.A. glam scene also attracted Suzi Quatro fanatic Joan Jett and David Bowie wannabe Cherie Currie, two members of the all-girl band the Runaways.

Assembled and orchestrated by English Disco scenester Kim Fowley, the Runaways were a courageous and often-overlooked band. With only Patti Smith and a few early '70s girl-rock groups like Fanny or Deadly Nightshade as role models, these five teenage girls performed rock songs from a girl's perspective.[17] In 1975 the Runaways combined a sexually charged act with tough-girl personas leavened by humor. Their simplified lyrics reflected their experience as teenagers; their image and sound was rawer and more honest than those of most other female acts of the time. As Gary Stewart said of the band in *We Got the Neutron Bomb*: "[E]ven the stuff that didn't work was done as a reaction to the empty spectacle that rock had become. They don't have a legacy like the Ramones in terms of great songs or records and people acknowledging them as an influence, but they made more of a difference at the time than they'll ever get credit for. They came along when they were needed."[18]

"The Motels, the Dogs, and the Pop! had put on a series of shows called 'Radio Free Hollywood' [in 1976] and they were kind of pop bands," former Germs manager Nicole Panter says. "This was before [West Coast] punk, but it was the first real 'do it yourself' thing."[19] Comprising of a few fledgling groups that booked and promoted their own shows, the alliance also named "Radio Free Hollywood" was the beginning of a self-sustaining scene in Los Angeles. Rodney Bingenheimer went from running the English Disco to promoting punk on Los Angeles' KROQ radio station in August 1976.[20] Punk might not have been powerful enough to overthrow disco that bicentennial year, but in San Francisco and Los Angeles, the DIY ethic was contagious. By 1977, West Coast bands like the Screamers, the Weirdos, the Dils, and the infamous Germs had formed, and both cities housed scenes that were much more organic, spontaneous, and youthful than New York's. On the East Coast the promise of recording contracts that was palpable in the wake of deals with New York bands like the Ramones, Blondie, the Patti Smith Group, and Talking Heads was probably attracting groups who prioritized a contract over chaos.

Major label contracts inevitably filtered out some homegrown quality, but the underappreciated West Coast acts were able to retain a grittier and less polished sound than their New York peers. The music was urgent and homespun, the vocals delivered with more punch, staccato, and speed. West Coast music was thick with fuzzy static and echoes, with a dose of surf guitar thrown in every once in a while, as befitting the locale. Punk attracted young fans on both coasts, but Hollywood's population, so haunted by young, disaffected kids, added to the scene's spontaneity, drama, and unabashed energy. Even today, nothing from the period seems calculated. Pleasant Gehman, a fixture in the L.A. punk scene, wrote, "'Do It Yourself' became a key phrase. Everybody involved in the scene was young, naive, and enthusiastic enough not to worry about whether or not what they were doing could actually be pulled off."[21]

In the early days, erasing the rules of rock meant erasing those stifling roles for women, too. The Avengers, one of San Francisco's first punk bands, was led by Penelope Houston. She recounts: "I felt that things were pretty egalitarian, and I felt like the scene was so small that just being a punk was enough to join you in with a bunch of people, and you were accepted, and the idea that there were boy punks and girl punks or male punks and female punks or something was not really something anybody thought about. If you had gone to the point of becoming a punk, and basically being an outcast from the whole mainstream, then you were in, you know?"[22]

Nicole Panter agrees: "Yeah, it was very egalitarian. It wasn't like—'Ooh, look, women,' or 'Oh god, women.' In fact, I knew stronger women in general during that scene than I've ever met in my life."[23] Of course, these weren't the only women on the American stage; among others, there were the San Francisco–based Nuns, led by Jennifer Miro; Los

Angeles' Alice Bag, of the Bags; Annie Golden of Brooklyn's Shirts; and in 1978, an early version of the Go-Go's, with Belinda Carlisle, Jane Wiedlin (then Jane Drano), Margot Olaverra, Charlotte Caffey, and Elissa Bello (who was replaced by permanent drummer Gina Schock soon after the band formed).

Most fans and band members from those chaotic days deny punk's sexism, but latent prejudice occasionally bobs to the surface in punk's oral histories. In *Please Kill Me*, scenester Eileen Polk paints the following portrait: "Johnny [Thunders], Richard [Hell], and Dee Dee [Ramone] all had that tortured 'I need to be saved by a woman' look. And all the women fell for it. They'd start out buying them drinks, and then they'd buy them dope . . . [a]nd then they'd get dumped and then they'd go on to the next guy."[24]

Ivan Julian, guitarist for Richard Hell and the Voidoids, says, "Basically Richard had a lot of girls around because he used them to get high, you know? They would get him high and have sex with him. And when those two things weren't happening, then I guess he thought the girls were annoying."[25] For some girlfriends of band members, their usefulness was in remaining on the sidelines, as well. Jena Cardwell, then-girlfriend of Germs guitarist Pat Smear, recalls her status at Germs rehearsals: "We'd be totally ignored, sitting there like lap dogs, just waiting, until it was time to go buy some beer or drive them somewhere."[26] These instances not only point to latent sexism within punk, but also to how women's own perception of their place in rock and roll wasn't always easy to overturn.

In *We Got the Neutron Bomb*, L.A. singer Hal Negro comments on punk beauty: "One thing about punk rock, it wasn't the best look for some girls. The girls that we started out with were pretty homely types."[27] Apparently, for some the "no-rules" ethic of punk only covered half of the spectrum. Further proof of the foothold standard images of beauty had are clear in original Go-Go's member Margot Olaverra's account of their 1980 London tour. Margot refers to the "Go-Go's diet" manager Ginger Canzoneri put the girls on, which consisted of tiny weekly stipends, and offered incentive bonuses for losing weight. Olaverra contends in *We Got the Neutron Bomb* that the Go-Go's diet made "borderline anorexics" out of the girls, and led some members, like Jane Wiedlin, to use crystal meth to induce weight loss.[28] Though this type of "incentive plan" may sound like a major label marketing scheme, this particular tour occurred prior to their IRS record deal in 1981.

Nevertheless, punk let women show their angry, wild sides. And, in most cases, punk allowed women to be *themselves*—rare still in the corporate music world. Punk also made room for women to express sexuality freely—something the mainstream feminism of the day was hesitant to embrace, lest it be confused with traditional and sexist gender roles. While feminism struggled with the sexism of mainstream America, bands like the Germs had a female manager, a rotating number of female members, and a permanent bassist in Lorna Doom. Joan Jett produced the Germs' *(GI)*, and Patti Smith led New Yorkers to the future of rock. The real challenge for punk women in the '70s was getting the mainstream to take them seriously, as artists and as women who bucked conventional standards of beauty and lifestyle.

Against the drab, earthy aesthetic of mainstream '70s life, punk made manifest a palpable anger at the denial of individuality and rebellion and at the mainsteam's avoidance of contemporary social issues. Set against a backdrop of the overt sexualization of artists like Linda Ronstadt and Olivia Newton-John, or the good-girl image of musicians like Karen Carpenter and Marie Osmond, punk women received, within the music world (and outside of it), the grudging respect other women sought. Within punk circles roundly ignored by the larger spheres of national politics and mainstream music, the Avengers and the Nuns opened the Sex Pistols' legendary final show at San Francisco's Winterland in January 1978; Exene Cervenka wrote her haunting lyrics for X; Poison Ivy of the Cramps played (and continues to play) effortless and amazing rockabilly guitar; and Wendy O. Williams of the Plasmatics stripped down to little more than strategically placed pieces of electrical tape for live performances, and shot machine gun blanks at rapt audiences. By creating a new, visionary culture built on individuality, with a healthy dose of chaos thrown in, punks both female and male were living as if the revolution had already arrived.

Chapter 1

BABELOGUE

Patti Smith

"THESE THINGS WERE ON MY MIND: THE COURSE OF THE ARTIST, the course of freedom redefined, the re-creation of space, the emergence of new voices," wrote Patti Smith about her experience in early 1970s New York.[1] Smith has since been defined as the godmother of punk, a visionary, a conjurer, and the woman whom nearly everyone interviewed for this book mentioned at some point. But Patti Smith can't be reduced to something as simple as the "godmother of punk," for her vision captured downtown New York before punk trampled CBGB's beer-covered floorboards. In combining poetic mantras with garage rock, Smith didn't create punk, but she was able to connect with its fans. "I've always considered myself a 'worker,'" she said in a 1996 interview. "I always thought that if there were a band of people who were proud to be called 'punk' or felt they initiated it, then they should be allowed to have their slot. I don't feel like I'm particularly deserving of the punk rock label, since that was a movement that came after what my group did. But a song like 'Rock n Roll Nigger' addressed people who were outside society, and if I ever addressed anyone in particular, I was addressing people who were so miscast and misplaced that no one ever even gave them a label."[2]

Her first single, "Piss Factory," in 1974 depicted Smith's earlier life as a factory worker in New Jersey. She stripped her songs of the folky sound that had come to define "political" music of the late '60s and early '70s—music that, despite the angry lyrics, was performed in such a way as to merely jostle the listener, like a soft shove instead of a full-on punch. Smith, as a musician and as a woman, introduced something entirely new. "Piss Factory" featured her spitting spoken word over piano and guitar, the lyrics blistering with the anger of firsthand experience. "Piss Factory" painted the factory as a place from which a woman, a worker, had no escape. In Smith's rendition of factory life the assembly line worker was a hero(ine) for tolerating it and for finding her own respite, but never a martyr to it. Smith's worker resists the suffering, the heat, the weakness she feels, and transcends it to preserve her inner self.

But the poem, the single, the song, all came long after the fact. In 1967, Smith defected from the piss factory and working-class Jersey, where she had briefly attended Glassboro State Teachers College until she was kicked out for being pregnant. Smith gave the baby up for adoption, packed up her unflagging adoration for the Rolling Stones, Bob Dylan, and Arthur Rimbaud, and dragged herself to New York City with aspirations of becoming a painter. After living for a short time in Brooklyn before a jaunt to Europe (where she tried street performing), Smith eventually moved into the Chelsea Hotel in 1969 with visionary and as yet undiscovered photographer Robert Mapplethorpe. The two began milling around the entrance to Max's Kansas City, where they camped on the curb when they couldn't make it past the front door. Leee Childers, one-time manager of the Heartbreakers, said, "I admired Patti's guts to sit there and say, 'This is where I want to go, and if they don't let me, I'm just going to sit out front.' It was a very punk attitude way before there was a punk attitude."[3] Eventually, Smith and Mapplethorpe did make it past the front door, and became a part of the early '70s Max's scene. Gerard Malanga, a poet who hung out with the Warhol crowd, set Smith up with a reading at the Poetry Project at St. Mark's Church in February 1971. She teamed with rock critic, record store clerk, and guitarist Lenny Kaye for the performance. Kaye provided musical backing for her poetic rants. Of that event, Smith recalled, "I remember that night vividly. . . . There was a full moon. Because I was reading a lot of [Jean] Genet at the time, I dedicated my performance to crime. . . . I had a lot of energy then, a lot of irreverent bravado. . . . It was really exciting. One of the great nights of my life. If you heard a tape of it, it might not seem so exciting, but the actual air of the night was really electric and joyous."[4] She continued collaborating with Kaye and pianist Richard Sohl over the next few years, giving freeform music and poetry performances at key venues like Max's, Le Jardin, and the Mercer Arts Center.

Soon after her Poetry Project reading, Patti published *Seventh Heaven*, and her reputation as a poet soon took off. Richard Hell once said, "Patti would just reel this stuff off and it was so hot and she was so sharp, but she was so sweet and vulnerable at the same time. She was the real thing, there was no mistaking it."[5] It was also around this time that Smith cowrote and performed the play *Cowboy Mouth* with Sam Shepard.

Smith created her own unique vision of beat poetry, commonly perceived as a male art form, and made it her own. She often wrote about women from a more masculine perspective, either by making women her muse or by speaking to them with admiration in her work. Her strong vocal intonations seemed an exaggerated, spoken-word version of Bob Dylan's songs. She stressed or slowed down words, climbing an octave in the midst of a syllable. The result combined qualities of mysticism, romanticism, and the overtly sexual, all with distinctly accessible, everyday language. Her fusing of literature with rock and roll revealed Smith's desire to assert herself as an artist in the vein of the male writers and musicians she respected. Her artistic androgyny, which few female musicians had dared to express before her, wound all the way down to her clothing, which often included a tie or a baggy T-shirt—her lithe body and shaggy hair serving as an homage to Rolling Stones guitarist Keith Richards.

Unlike Led Zeppelin's groupies, Smith wanted to *be* her male idols as much as she longed to be around them. And, unlike other women who fawned over male musicians, she internalized and emulated the things she liked about them, creating her own statements, forging a new musical woman. She existed as an artist in a new space somewhere between male and female, using both typical and atypical symbols of both genders, like characteristic notions of female hero worship and simultaneous male sexual aggression, to conjure her own unique voice. Smith's stance against a society (and a music industry) that was split down the middle for acceptable "male" and "female" behavior, and then divided again between the progression of women in the working world and those who had more arcane notions of what women could or couldn't be, was truly revolutionary. In an interview for *Melody Maker*, Smith expounded on her seeming genderlessness: "The thing is, being a woman is irrelevant so far as the artist in me goes. When I'm working and dipping as far as I can into my subliminal, I get to a point when race and gender and all that stuff no longer exists. When an artist is creating you feel let out of your cell. You want to devour everything and sometimes you don't even feel human."[6]

Smith's indie releases would end with the "Hey Joe"/"Piss Factory" single, released on Mapplethorpe and Kaye's Mer label in 1974. In early 1975, what was then the Patti Smith Group—Kaye, Jay Dee Daugherty, and Ivan Kral—opened for Television at CBGB. According to CBGB owner Hilly Kristal, the reception was tremendous enough for the club to give them an indefinite four-nights-a-week residency: "The band was great, Patti was great; every show was special. Their audiences, because of their notoriety, were composed of writers, artists, musicians, and other celebrities (all fans). It was a most unusual crowd ranging from punks to professors. The audience reflected *her*."[7] Clive Davis, head of Arista Records at the time, was in the audience during what became a seven-week residency for the band, and quickly signed them to his label. During this period, Smith also lent her mystical tirades to the music rags *Creem*, *Rolling Stone*, and *Crawdaddy*, producing stream-of-consciousness pieces that were more fan worship than criticism, a polar opposite of the more common academic style of rock journalism popularized by *Rolling Stone* in the '70s.

Perhaps the best example of Smith's reinvention of gender is her rendition of Van Morrison's "Gloria," which appeared on her landmark first release for Arista, *Horses*. "Gloria," as written by Morrison, is pretty standard male-fantasy fare: Man sees and desires woman; woman seduces man, who surrenders before learning her name. Smith's version keeps the song's original pronoun, "she," a hang-up certain female pop singers still can't get over. As she describes, "Gloria" was her way of proving that rock and roll was not merely a pursuit divided by gender; that a good song was good no matter who was performing it. "'Gloria' gave me the opportunity to acknowledge and disclaim our musical and spiritual heritage. It personifies for me, within its adolescent conceit, what I hold sacred as an artist: the right to create, without apology, from a stance beyond gender or social definition, but not beyond the responsibility to create something of worth."[8]

This kind of artistic androgyny not only aided in bridging rock's gender gap, but encouraged women, many because of their introduction to Smith's work, to create music of their own. Her early success and groundbreaking artistic stature among those who went on to lead the New York scene to infamy—especially Richard Hell and Joey Ramone—set a precedent for relative gender equality in early punk.

One of Smith's signature onstage traits was her sheer physical abandon. She had mastered the ability to become transfixed, firmly planted in a kind of simulated musical hypnosis. Thrashing, flailing, and twisting herself around during instrumentals meant she never had to stop speaking; it became the physical continuance of her improvised linguistic tirades. Patrick Goldstein depicted such madness perfectly in *Creem*: "Patti slinks in and out of the shifting spotlight, whirling like a dervish, blindly diving into a fetal 'Hunchback of Notre Dame' crouch; frugging, jump-roping, arching her back like an alley-cat in heat, assaulting Lenny with jungle fervor; first knocking him down, than luring him erect, feigning a leap into the aroused mass of spectators; dangling then suddenly recoiling an extended foot towards the crowd's clammy outstretched hands as if charming a snake. . . . This is no mere performance."[9]

The follow-up to *Horses*, *Radio Ethiopia*, was released in 1976, and the Patti Smith Group went on tour opening for Bob Seger. In Tampa, on the last night of their tour, Smith accidentally twirled herself right off the stage and fractured her spine. "I really look at that accident as a product of, y' know, their, their lack of community," she told NPR in 1996.[10] According to Smith, the fall was in part due to Seger's road crew ignoring her requests for better lighting and more stage space. She took the next year off to recuperate. "It was in this period that the punk movement came to the forefront," Patti wrote. "It seemed to me that rock and roll was back on the streets, in the hands of the people. I trained, we regrouped, and we joined them. And our bywords we gleaned from the scriptures, 'Fight the good fight.'"[11]

Smith and her band returned with the aptly titled *Easter*, which hinted at her physical and spiritual resurrection. As lasting an impact as Smith continues to have on the underground scene and particularly on punk, her gender duality and improvised literary style have barely made a ripple on the surface of popular music. Given how mainstream radio has treated music made by underdogs (and by outcast women), is it an accident that "Because the Night"—a song cowritten by Bruce Springsteen—garnered the most airplay? The album also featured the classic "Rock n Roll Nigger," where Smith's allegiance to the outcast remains fierce. The song celebrates the alienation of Smith and her alignment with those most typically viewed as socially undesirable.

The song goes on to name Jesus, Jackson Pollock, and grandmothers as "niggers," too; her aim was to redefine the word as having weight for all outcasts and socially denigrated figures, much like Yoko Ono and John Lennon attempted to do in their song "Woman Is the Nigger of the World."

Before retiring to raise her children with MC5 guitarist Fred "Sonic" Smith in 1980, the Patti Smith Group released one more album, *Wave*. Their last show took place in Florence, Italy, in 1979, in front of seventy thousand fans. Smith's next work wouldn't surface until 1988's *Dream of Life* album. Cowritten and coproduced with her husband, *Dream of Life* was her first album without Lenny Kaye, although Jay Dee Daugherty and Richard Sohl both appeared. *Dream of Life* was far tamer than her albums with the Patti Smith Group and featured "People Have the Power," which later became the anthem for Ralph Nader's 2000 presidential campaign. After a period of terrible personal loss that saw the deaths of her brother Todd, her husband Fred, Robert Mapplethorpe, and Richard Sohl, Smith released the 1996 album *Gone Again*, featuring Television's Tom Verlaine and coproduced by Kaye. *Gone Again* met with critical raves, and Smith experienced a resurgence of interest in her work. The album *Peace and Noise* followed in 1997; 2000 saw the release of *Gung Ho*; and in 2004 she issued *Trampin'*.

Although she had performed a few sporadic shows and readings between her retreat in the 1990s and the release of *Gone Again* in 1996, Smith officially returned to the stage again following the 1996 release of *Gone Again*. Her long gray hair whipped and whirled, framing her like that of a diminutive Medusa. Smith's songs still throbbed with possibility and encouragement, and burned with an optimism and youthfulness unmatched by younger bands. Patti Smith is living proof that rebellion, individuality, and truthfulness have nothing to do with age, and everything to do with love and bravery. Viva la people, viva la Patti.

Chapter 2

QUEENS OF NOISE

The Runaways

"A DEFINING MOMENT FOR ANY TEEN MISFIT IS FINDING OTHERS like yourself, even if the only thing you share is the feeling of not belonging anywhere else," Joan Jett was quoted as saying in *We Got the Neutron Bomb.*[1] The misfit teen girl has few peers, and this was especially the case thirty years ago when the Runaways formed.

Just teenage girls themselves, the Runaways started a band and played their own original music at a time when few grown women were doing the same in the rock arena. They were an epiphany to young, female music fans and to boy rock fans too, who finally had the example of bona fide bad girls to unlock their fan-boy hearts. Does it matter if they were more spectacle than substance? The Runaways' legacy hasn't changed the world. But when no other delinquent girls doubled as rock stars, their legacy is that they existed at all.

Culturally, it's been easy to write off the Runaways. After all, they were masterminded to some degree by manager Kim Fowley, an older, successful record producer with a rather questionable reputation who liked to hang out at Rodney's in Los Angeles. Whether an all-girl band was Fowley's brainchild or that of guitarist Joan Jett is famously and hotly disputed. This much is true: Fowley met Runaways lyricist Kari Krome at Alice Cooper's birthday party in 1975, where the two discussed Krome's interest in writing lyrics. Krome put Fowley in contact with Joan Larkin (Jett), a friend who had taught herself to play Suzi Quatro songs on guitar.[2,3] Soon after, Fowley met drummer Sandy West in the Rainbow Bar and Grill parking lot, and with Micki Steele (later the Bangles' bassist), the trio of Jett, West, and Steele recorded a demo in August 1975. The Runaways gave a few early performances at the Whisky A Go-Go on Sunset Strip. Later that year, at Sugar Shack, L.A.'s teen glam hangout, Jett and Fowley approached singer Cherie Currie, who eagerly agreed to audition. Lead guitarist Lita Ford and bassist Jackie Fox, who replaced Steele, also auditioned for their parts.[4,5,6] A contract with Mercury Records and the Runaways' first national tour followed in 1976. Their raw, loud first album, *The Runaways*, which included the classic teen-girl anthem "Cherry Bomb," was released the same year.

Currie took the stage as a nymphet, wearing heels and lingerie, while Jett and Ford put on a good cock rock show that reflected the band's heavy rock and glam influences. "Girls just have their balls a little higher, that's all," Jett assured *New Musical Express* (NME).[7] The Runaways sang about their experiences as fifteen- and sixteen-year-old "bad girls," which meant they didn't stray very far from sex, drinking, drugs, breaking up, and being tough. At least their songs weren't filled with regret or purity. "I mean, the whole thing is, we're not really trying to make a point out of anything," Currie said at the time. "It's just what comes out of frustrations." West chimed in, "We're putting our lives into music."[8] The girls indulged in choreographed routines onstage that included a mock beating of Currie, at the end of which fake blood poured from her mouth.

The Runaways may be the only example of a prepunk, 1970s all-female rock band that produced stereotypical female fan behavior in a front row of screaming boys. Currie documented the Runaways' rise in her 1989 autobiography *Neon Angel*: "In the darkness Joan [Jett] leads us all on stage, and when the spotlights come up, I am in another world. Dozens of guys fight security in front of the stage, just to get closer to us. They hold up our record album covers and posters and signs. They shout our names. They reach out their hands towards us."[9] In an interview, Fox recounted an incident in Liverpool in which male fans tried to rush the stage.[10] Male worship of female musicians was hardly a tradition in rock and roll, and prior to punk, indie, and the rise of Madonna in the '80s, it was a rather uncommon phenomenon. Male bands were meant to be marketed for the irrational behavior of *female* fans—not only because these screaming devotees buy records, but because female fans, particularly teenagers, were indiscriminately seen as swooning suckers for rock musicians, unconditionally loving of their male idols irrespective of musical substance. As Lori Twersky noted in an article reprinted from the '80s rock 'zine *Bitch*, the sweeping generalizations and careless waving away of female fans by critics (and by the recording industry, who shamelessly markets schlock to this age group) is the sexist notion that when properly obsessed, teenage girls will engulf any young, available musicians and dote truckloads of innocent, romantic affection on them.[11]

The Runaways slightly, briefly tipped the sexist scales as the band that sent young men into the swaying, crushed, and desperate front rows of fandom, making young girls' adoration seem perhaps more symptomatic of their age than their gender.

The band toured through most of 1976 and 1977, leaving a lot of press coverage in their wake. Fans were happy to watch B-movie, girl-gang delinquency become a rock chorus, but the media was far from kind. In a 1998 interview, Jett commented on the reactions the girls suffered in the press: "First, people just tried to get around it by saying, 'Oh, wow, isn't that cute? Girls playing rock and roll!,' and when we said, 'Yeah, right, this isn't a phase; it's what we want to do with our lives,' it became, 'Oh! You must be a bunch of sluts. You dykes, you whores.'"[12] A review of their 1977 *Queens of Noise* album opened with "These bitches suck." Talk about a hook. *Creem* writer Rick Johnson went on to say: "Despite what the West Coast Blow Job Coordinator might say, they're not any good, they're not so bad they're good, they're not *anything*. Their only hope for crawling out of the mung heap is making those sperms wag their tails and their collective slurp appeal is enough to make your entire body feel like morning mouth."[13]

The criticism they received was certainly disproportionately harsh for young girls fumbling their way through the sexist rock business, but the Runaways' fun with double-entendres didn't help to silence critics, either. The hit "Cherry Bomb" promoted the '70s new rock female as part sexually assertive, part terrorist guerrilla, but its play on words like "cherry" reinforced the Runaways' jailbait stereotype. Lyrics like those in "Cherry Bomb," which expressed young female desire in a decidedly dominant way, also played on the adult male fantasy of being seduced by underage girls. "Don't

Abuse Me" admonished people who latched on to the girls' celebrity, and in Jett's "My Buddy and Me," the girls depicted themselves as a rebellious girl gang opposing societal norms.

The girls' defenses against Fowley, though, were allegedly weak. Reports vary on the level of damage his verbal abuse inflicted, but Jett, Currie, Krome, and Ford have all said that Fowley berated them by calling them "dog meat."[14] Micki Steele, who went permanently AWOL soon after her recruitment, asserted that Fowley repeatedly hit on her.[15] Ford initially left the band after just three days, citing her discomfort with him as the reason for her speedy departure.[16] In addition to the confusion of the group's appearance as alternately tough and simply sexual, Fowley's tight grip on the Runaways' image eroded their strong stance as a band, making their teenage sexual aggression seem more a product of Fowley's marketing imagination than a natural expression of the girls' libidos.

The Runaways themselves, though, displayed an unwillingness to dive into their roles as pinups. Currie told *Creem* reporter Patrick Goldstein, "This isn't a tits and ass show." Jett added, "Shit, I don't even have any tits or ass."[17] West commented, "I'm not a feminist, but I still didn't like the group being called 'sex kittens' or 'teenage jailbait' by Kim."[18] The diverging accounts of what happened behind the scenes and the girls' open resistance to their sexuality taking precedence over their music reveal the obstacles the Runaways were too young to effectively battle during their career. With these kinds of pressures, it's no wonder Fox and Currie both quit in 1977. Vicki Blue replaced Fox and Jett took over lead vocals.

The Runaways toured relentlessly and released four albums between 1976 and 1979. After power struggles with Fowley, the departures of Fox and Currie, and disputes over whether the band should indulge in punk or metal, they officially split in 1979. Fowley, however, made an ill-fated attempt to drum up a new set of girls in 1985.[19]

These self-proclaimed queens of noise inspired the legendary Germs and launched the careers of Lita Ford and Joan Jett. Jett created the Blackheart Records label and released a 1980 solo album on it. "I Love Rock 'n' Roll" hit number one in 1982 and eight Top 40 hits followed. Ford became the only female heavy metal guitarist to be taken seriously during the '80s, landing two Top 40 hits between 1988 and 1989. After leaving the Runaways in late 1977, Cherie Currie appeared in the film *Foxes* and released her memoir, *Neon Angel: The Cherie Currie Story*, in 1989. Jackie Fox is now a lawyer, and Sandy West sporadically performs and records. In 2001, Vicki Blue (now Tischler-Blue) completed *Edgeplay*, a film that explores the effects the rock and roll lifestyle had on the members of the Runaways. (Currie and Jett did not participate in the film.)

The Runaways may not have been lyrical geniuses, or musical virtuosos, but they were more than the "blow job queens" caricatured by the press. Five outsider girls abandoned the technical demands of cock rock, yet managed to retain its bravado and honestly and powerfully expressed teen lust and anger.

Chapter 3

THE GIRL IN THE BAND

Tina Weymouth

DENIM PANTSUITS? CLEAN, COLLARED SHIRTS? FRESHLY SHAMPOOED
hair? If everyone at CBGB was hell-bent on pure artistic expression, how
did normalcy go over? The Talking Heads, based in New York City, were
among the first new wave bands to play the venerable club. Rather than
flagrantly dismissing their middle-class, suburban appearance, the band
appeared to be embracing it. In the midst of so much outright derision of
the average American's existence by other musicians and CBGB regu-
lars, the Talking Heads seemed to embody this experience in their
appearance and their lyrics. Songwriter and lead singer David Byrne told
Nick Kent of *New Musical Express*, "I just thought that lyrics could be
used to strip down conversations, just normal day-to-day conversations
and dialogues, and strip away all the phoney embellishments and posturing right down to essentials so that they would actually say something
directly, without having to throw in all the 'Oh yeah, baby' or 'Hey,
bitch, I'm comin' to get ya right now.'"[1]

Drummer Chris Frantz and bassist Tina Weymouth both grew up in
military families, and Weymouth's family bounced from California, where

she was born, to bases all over America and Europe. She dabbled in music in her teen years, but never considered it a serious pursuit. Weymouth played with a D.C.-based handbell group when she was twelve and, as a fan of folk music, taught herself to play guitar at fourteen. "I became the captain of the cheerleaders, but it didn't make me any happier," she once said. "I still always felt really left out and different."[2]

Frantz, Weymouth, and Byrne all attended Rhode Island School of Design (RISD) before moving to New York together and creating the Talking Heads. Byrne had played with two bands, Revelation and Bizadi, before forming the Artistics with Frantz at RISD in 1973. Like so many girls of her age and era, Weymouth became an avid fan of her friends' music without embarking on her own project. She told *Guitar Player* magazine in 1984, "I was at every [Artistics] performance and every rehearsal. It was very, very loud. You couldn't stand closer than fifty feet because it was so loud and abusive."[3] Songs like "Psycho Killer" came straight from the Artistics' catalog, but in contrast to the abusive Artistics, the Talking Heads employed forceful throbs and rhythmic stabs of sound, accompanied by Byrne's hiccupping vocals. His energy was stretched tightly, like a rubber band, and was audible in his taut voice. There seemed to be an unidentified shock possessing his face and his body flailed like a "twitching marionette."[4] He came off as a man about to explode from coloring so compulsively within the lines. This controlled rage is perfectly conveyed in "Psycho Killer," where a heavy, foreboding bass line supports Byrne's staccato bursts of accentuation. "In the early days," Weymouth said, "I was trying to pay attention to both rhythm and melody as a means to tie together the drums and David's extremely bright, no mid-range guitar and vocals."[5]

Weymouth, who was self-taught, was offered the position of bassist after Byrne and Frantz couldn't find anyone who satisfied them. "We wanted someone who wasn't stylistically formed yet or obsessed with technical virtuosity. Plus we thought it was modern to have a female in the group who wasn't featuring her voice or her breasts," Frantz explained to *Rolling Stone*.[6] In contradiction to Frantz's rationale, writer Gillian Gaar reported that Byrne once confided his concern about adding Weymouth to the lineup to *Melody Maker*'s Caroline Coon. "Rock and roll is thought of as a male music," he stated. "I wasn't sure how it would be received."[7]

In early 1975, the trio played its first show at CBGB, opening for the Ramones. A recording contract with independent label Sire Records followed soon after. According to Gaar, Byrne put Weymouth through another audition once they were signed.[8] This second audition may reveal more about Byrne's worry that Weymouth, as a woman, could "handle" her role than about how she'd be received by audiences and critics. She succeeded, though, creating rhythm that, according to *New Musical Express*, was a "solid, hypnotic, repetitive line that support[ed] the rest of [the band]."[9]

Their ability to so authentically appear normal made the Talking Heads all the spookier. They stood out in both image and sound from the New York scene's trademark depravity. Their first album, *Talking Heads: 77*, saw the addition of the Modern Lovers keyboardist Jerry Harrison to the band, and included the songs "Psycho Killer" and "Don't Worry About the Government." The Talking Heads' seemingly apolitical stance wasn't always welcome; the latter song was met with a bitter hailstorm of boos on a European tour with the Ramones. Even if they didn't share the angrier strains of punk, the Talking Heads were kindred spirits. "I think we shared the idea that a lot of the music around us wasn't speaking to us," Byrne contended, "and we had to make something simple that did speak to ourselves and to our friends. And if that meant you could do it with three chords and with the limited abilities that you had, that you didn't have to be a virtuoso to do that, you could find a way to use the tools you had at hand."[10]

The band released *More Songs About Buildings and Food* in 1978, *Fear of Music* in 1979, and *Remain in Light* in 1980. After releasing four albums with the Talking Heads, Frantz and Weymouth formed a side project, the Tom Tom Club, which signed to Island Records in 1981. The Tom Tom Club featured Weymouth as lead vocalist and full collaborator with Frantz. "The spark was that Jerry and David decided in 1981 they were going to do solo projects," Frantz said cheekily in 2003. "But we also had a meeting with our accountant. He informed us that we had about two thousand dollars in the bank. So we thought, 'Hmm. Jerry and David are doing solo albums, we need some cash, what are we going to do?'"[11] The Tom Tom Club attributed part of the decision to make an album to Byrne and Harrison's encouragement,[12] but the Talking Heads appeared to have had internal tensions around the same time. It's alleged that Weymouth secretly sought a new singer for the Talking Heads, and asked Adrian Belew, a guitarist for David Bowie and Frank Zappa, to replace Byrne.[13]

The Tom Tom Club was more traditionally melodic, heavy on rhythm, and infinitely more synth-pop-sounding than the careening Talking Heads.

Their single "Genius of Love" has been sampled dozens of times and still gets frequent club play today. Weymouth's melodic vocals sound doubled, even tripled. They were harmonized with the help of her sisters Lani and Laura, and lay ethereally over a hypnotic synthesizer hook. The sisters even toured with the Talking Heads in 1982 and performed "Genius of Love" in the band's 1984 film *Stop Making Sense*. With a successful first album under their belts, Weymouth and Frantz resumed recording with the Talking Heads, who then released the albums that would further cement their career in mainstream music. *Speaking in Tongues* (1983) featured "Burning Down the House," and 1985's *Little Creatures* offered "Once in a Lifetime" and "Road to Nowhere." After 1988's less-than-stellar *Naked* and Byrne's announcement in a 1991 interview that the band was breaking up, the Talking Heads officially disbanded in 1994.

In an interview with *Rolling Stone*, Weymouth commented on how the Talking Heads' middle-of-the-road image was received: "We feel emotional about our songs. . . . But maybe other people just want us to explode. I think sometimes we almost do spin out of control—I feel like I'm driving a car very fast on a mountainous road. But some things are just too . . . embarrassing to do onstage."[14] For girls who saw a glimmer of hope in the example of punk's women but were too self-conscious to take Patti Smith's path of expression, Weymouth was the "normal" girl who successfully carried the band's off-kilter, stripped-down funk rhythms. She was proof for those outside of the bohemian New York set that a regular girl could teach herself to play. And she inspired those women who were not interested in singing lead vocals, the more typical path for a woman in rock. Weymouth's muted dress and short hair added to her low-key persona. The Talking Heads' style, which was generally bereft of overt or dramatic emotion (with the exception of Byrne), allowed Weymouth to transcend a sexual persona so commonly expected of female performers in the '70s, while her subdued presence made it seem possible to be a fully integrated, unaltered female in a band.

The band's conscious separation from emotion in their songs can also be viewed as repression, the very thing early punk railed against. Being embarrassed by impulsive behavior is exactly what punk intended to dispense with. As Legs McNeil described in *Please Kill Me*, punk was about acting on impulses as if the world were on the verge of collapse: "Punk wasn't about decay, it was about the apocalypse. Punk was about annihilation. Nothing worked, so let's get right to Armageddon."[15] Punk stood in opposition to the eroding optimism of the radical ideas of the 1960s; the Talking Heads represented the individual just before he or she exploded into pure impulse. Weymouth seemed to exist in the middle of the band's onstage tension without diving directly into it.

After the Talking Heads' split in 1994, the Tom Tom Club continued producing albums—they've now released five studio and one live—and continue to perform. Frantz and Weymouth also performed with Jerry Harrison as the Heads during the 1990s. The pair also witnessed the Happy Mondays' infamous implosion while coproducing the band's last album, *Yes, Please*, in 1992. In 2002, Weymouth and the Velvet Underground's Maureen Tucker became the only women of the early underground to be inducted into the Rock and Roll Hall of Fame. The powerful clarity of her bass lines is reflected in the advice she shared in *Bass Player*: "The point is to move people, not bore them with meaningless technical prowess."[16]

Chapter 4

GIRL GERMS

Lorna Doom and Nicole Panter

IN THE LINER NOTES TO *WE'RE DESPERATE,* A COMPILATION OF
Los Angeles punk dating from 1976 to 1979, Pleasant Gehman wrote of the city:

> The suburbs were crawling with kids who were bored, kids who
> were feeling rebellious and stilted in their white-bread environments,
> kids who wanted more than a backyard swimming pool, braces, the Bee
> Gees, and Peter Frampton, who had Saturday Night Fever every day of
> the week but weren't into disco.
>
> Meantime, in the cheapo, crumbling apartment buildings on the
> palm-lined side streets in the foothills and flats of Hollywood, there
> was another breed. These kids were slightly older, in their early to mid-
> twenties, mostly; some were art students or art-school dropouts, some
> were aspiring musicians and actors, and some were plain old druggie/
> degenerates. But they all had one thing in common: They were noncon-
> formists who loved rock and roll and were, consciously or uncon-
> sciously, seeking an alternative lifestyle.[1]

The Germs fell into the first category; they were restless suburbanites
who managed to compress every inch of superfluous art out of punk. From

their first impromptu performance, the band's full force assault of chaotic noise and screaming delivered at machine-gun pace ultimately pulled the L.A. scene toward the double-time hardcore sound that would eventually hijack Orange County in 1979. Germs guitarist Pat Smear explained: "With the Germs, we went out of our way to say and do most people would never say or do—it was a reaction to our disappointment in other rock stars. . . . It was like, 'We're gonna fucking start a band, and we're gonna change our names, and we're gonna fucking be this thing—we're gonna really be like that 24-7, and we're not going to fake it! And we're gonna be the most this, or that, or whatever; and we're not gonna puss out! Whatever it is we're gonna be, we're gonna be the most—if we're gonna be punk, then we're gonna out-punk the Sex Pistols! If we're gonna be the worst band ever, then we're gonna be the fucking *worst* band ever!'"[2]

In 1976, Pat Smear (née Georg Ruthenberg) and Darby Crash (Jan Paul Beahm) took a break from their high school routine of worshipping David Bowie and forming religious cults with classmates to try and catch a glimpse of Queen singer Freddie Mercury at the Beverly Hilton. They ended up meeting two Thousand Oaks high school students named Belinda Carlisle and Terri Ryan. "Terri Ryan and I met in art class at Newport Park High School," said Carlisle. "She introduced me to a lot of music like Iggy and the Stooges, New York Dolls, and Roxy Music. We were into the same things—England, for one—and we started going to clubs around sixteen or seventeen. I'd pick her up, and we'd go to the Rainbow. We were, like, the local freaks in school. I went from being a cheerleader, fitting in, to being a total freak."[3]

The four decided to form a band and, after some initial name changes, the Germs were born. The group had originally settled on the brilliant Sophistifuck and the Revlon Spam Queens. But, as Crash told the punk 'zine *Slash*, their name changed to the Germs when they couldn't afford the cost of printing such a long name on their T-shirts.[4] Smear claims, though, that the name meant to insinuate "the germ of an idea."[5] Beahm initially changed his name to Bobby Pyn before settling on Darby Crash. Ruthenberg became Pat Smear, and bassist Ryan adopted the name Lorna Doom. Shortly after the Germs' formation Carlisle contracted mononucleosis and was replaced on drums by Donna Rhia (née Becky Barton). Following Rhia's departure, a rotating cast of characters filled the drum seat, including Nickey Beat, X's D.J. Bonebrake, Cliff Hanger, Don Bolles, and Rob Henley.

The Germs began promoting themselves by postering Los Angeles and wearing Germs T-shirts, long before they had written any songs. The quartet, with Rhia drumming, played its first show opening for the Weirdos at the Orpheum in 1977. It was more sloppy disaster than performance, with the band members faking their way through songs in between smearing themselves with melted licorice and dipping the mics in peanut butter. But what might have looked, felt, and sounded like a disaster turned out to be a triumph: They had out-punked L.A. The Germs managed to create total chaos in the ten minutes they performed before getting booted from the stage.

At the time, L.A. band the Screamers had replaced requisite punk guitars with synthesizers, an entirely new sound for the era. The Weirdos, a guitar-driven band responsible for the punk classic "We Got the Neutron Bomb," took their cue from the raw English punk sound rather than the more arty style coming out of New York. Both bands, though, were a bit older, and the Screamers, in particular, were steeped in a performance-art tradition. The Germs were the first really *young* L.A. band since the Runaways (who were, not surprisingly, a major source of inspiration for the Germs). The band released their first 7", "Forming," on their friend Chris Ashford's What? Records in 1977.

After leaving home at sixteen for Los Angeles, Nicole Panter recalls:

> In '76 I moved up to Marin County for a year. . . . [A]t some point, I met some other people, these really wild girls who lived in Marin County in a cabin in the woods. . . . [W]e would hitchhike into the city because there was a once weekly show at Mabuhay Gardens. Like once a week the punks took it over, this was '76, it was kind of the proto-punks, [there was] this girl named Mary Monday, who might have been a transvestite or something. I have these vague memories of these shows I saw there. It was like transvestite cabaret or something, kind of prepunk. . . . [W]hen I was living in Marin, there was a *Village Voice* cover story and it had [*Punk* magazine founders] Legs McNeil and John Holstrom sort of hanging out at a club in leather jackets and it said "All the Young Punks" in really big headlines, and that was the first time I knew that there was sort of a[n official] subculture for what I was involved in.[6]

Panter got involved in the Los Angeles scene through friends at L.A. punk 'zines *Back Door Man* and *Slash,* as well as through the bands the Motels, the Dogs, and the Pop!. She met Crash in late 1977 or early 1978 and quickly took on the role of the Germs' manager.

"I wanted to participate in something," Panter says. "Everybody was picking up a guitar, or writing poetry and reading it and I, because of the beatings, psychological and physical, that I had received as a kid—where I was told by my stepfather, 'You're stupid. You'll never amount to anything'— I didn't have the confidence that a lot of other people had that I could pick up an instrument or write something and read it out loud and survive having it be stupid."[7] Panter took on the typically male role of manager, rather than the more mainstream avenue women were afforded in the industry—as secretaries or public relations coordinators.

The Germs were intent on creating chaos, and keeping them focused was no easy task. "[T]here was a brat and authority-figure dynamic. They could be pretty bratty, but not seriously," Panter remembers.[8] She encouraged a resistant Crash to appear in *The Decline of Western Civilization*, Penelope Spheeris' account of L.A. punk, which probably contributed more to the Germs' renown than their modest recording catalog.

Doom, in the meantime, had bravely picked up the bass without knowing how to play. If punk was promoting the notion that a band could easily form in an audience, in a basement, or by anyone who loved music, then the Germs certainly embraced this notion wholeheartedly by bluffing their way through their entire first performance at the Weirdos show. The notion of women playing instruments, outside of the traditional female singer-songwriter-with-guitar role, was especially challenging; not only were you up against the popularly held notion that women "couldn't play"—particularly hard, nasty rock and roll—but, excluding a handful of musicians like Talking Heads bassist Tina Weymouth and Cramps guitarist Poison Ivy, women were still mostly singing and writing rather than playing bass or drums. The Germs, complete with a female bassist, were a band that broke ground for hardcore, a scene in which women generally played ancillary roles (with the notable exception of women like Black Flag bassist Kira Roessler).

The Germs released one full-length album, *(GI)*, on Slash Records in 1979. They had developed a more distinct sound, and the album is the best example of their full-force-ahead style. Since Joan Jett had been an enormous inspiration to Smear and Crash, she was employed to produce the album. According to Dez Cadena, one-time lead singer for Black Flag, a lot of people argued that someone else had played bass for Doom during the recording of *(GI)*, a myth Cadena dispelled numerous times.[9]

Within punk and indie rock circles, this criticism of female musicianship has occurred repeatedly, from critiques of the Adverts' bassist Gaye Advert and her ability, to comments made about Hole's *Live Through This* album, which many have speculated was really Kurt Cobain's work, not Courtney Love's. Many of the bands associated with riot grrrl, too, were disparaged for amateurish playing, even though they were often specifically placing politics over sound—a quintessentially punk ethos which seems to be forgotten more often when assessing female musicians. *(GI)* was viewed as relatively polished compared to the band's live shows; all of the Germs probably showed marked improvement by the time it was recorded. Drummer Don Bolles, who played on the album, called Doom the band's "secret weapon,"[10] and Cadena recognized *(GI)*'s bass lines as distinctly Doom's. In the context of the Germs' raw music, she wasn't a bad bass player and, as Bolles said, she held their sound together.

According to Panter, Doom was naturally very quiet, and rather than assuming Crash's messy, confrontational stance onstage, she stood still, hung in the background, and smiled her way through music that was inherently fast and mean. Instead of jumping on the bandwagon of punk stage dramatics, Doom was understated.

By 1980, the Germs were mired in disarray. Panter's displeasure with her managerial role had been evident since her lengthy interview in *Decline . . .* and she quit that year.[11] Doom hit her limit when Crash fired Bolles and replaced him with Rob Henley, who didn't know how to play.[12] She left the band in mid-1980, which lead to the Germs' eventual dissolution. Later that year, Crash assembled the short-lived Darby Crash Band (with Smear on guitar), and the Germs played a victorious reunion show on December 3, 1980, at the Starwood in L.A. Four days later, Crash overdosed on heroin and died.[13] Soon after Crash's death, Doom left the punk scene and fled to the East Coast. Smear released two solo albums in the late '80s and early '90s before receiving a phone call from Germs fan Kurt Cobain asking him to play guitar on Nirvana's 1993 *In Utero* tour and for their *MTV Unplugged* performance that same year. The gig led to a spot with Nirvana drummer Dave Grohl's next project, the Foo Fighters, and Smear played on 1997's *The Colour and the Shape*. Original Germs drummer Belinda Carlisle went on to sing with the Go-Go's, who had five Top 40 hits during the '80s. She embarked on a solo career after the band's breakup in 1985; her six solo albums were run-of-the-mill pop, less catchy than the Go-Go's, and a far cry from her early punk days. Nicole Panter wrote for and performed on HBO's *Pee-Wee's Playhouse*, created a book of short stories called *Mr. Right On and Other*

Stories, and contributed to various magazines and journals. She now teaches creative writing courses at the California Institute for the Arts.

While the initial circle of Los Angeles punk was relatively small, Panter, Doom, and the Germs, as well as their peers in X, the Screamers, and the Weirdos, helped propel a host of Southern Californian bands, including Black Flag (which paved the way for U.S. hardcore), the Circle Jerks, and Social Distortion. Lorna Doom and Nicole Panter's contributions to the Germs stand as pivotal to the band's legacy, and that of the seminal Los Angeles scene.

Chapter 5

WOMAN OVERBOARD

Debbie Harry

"ROCK AND ROLL," SAID BLONDIE FRONTWOMAN DEBBIE HARRY in 1976, "is a really masculine business, and I think it's time that girls did something in it."[1] No one infused more "girl" into CBGB's new rock scene than Harry. Then again, if "sexy" in the 1970s meant a dash of the "jiggle factor" popularized by Aaron Spelling's *Charlie's Angels*, she wasn't doing that, either. The difference between Debbie Harry and typical sex kittens of the *Angels* variety is as vast as the gap between the bawdy, sassy Mae West and the wounded, helpless Marilyn Monroe. As a band, Blondie gave a nod to 1960s Brill Building pop, which was wrapped up in the old-school tradition of singing other people's songs (and feelings) for a living. Far from emulating the sighing girl-group singers of this tradition, Harry taunted fans with her looks and growled at the adoring men that littered the audiences. While the contemporary mainstream female singer-songwriters of the day hid their feelings behind veiled metaphors, Harry sang self-assuredly. The snarl in her smile was made palpable in her forceful shouts, and men were clearly dispensable in her frequently contemptuous lyrics.

Blondie's presence in the CBGB/Max's Kansas City's scene proves that sounds other than punk grew out of the same community of bands. It was only later that labels like "punk" separated the Ramones from Blondie, but in the '70s, when fewer boundaries or distinct sub-genres existed, straight-forward punk outfits and Blondie's own punk pop were able to draw the same crowd and share the same stage, as well as influence each other. "We're a rock and roll band, not a punk band," Harry told one reporter, "and when you take away all the 'isms' and the 'osophies' that's what it all comes down to—the basic rock and roll elements."[2]

Born in 1945, Deborah Harry escaped her suburban New Jersey home and came to New York City in 1965, later joining a Capitol Records venture called the Wind in the Willows as a backup singer. The group dissolved in 1968, and she worked a host of different jobs, including a stint as a Playboy Bunny. "I wanted the money. It was a goal and something I always had held in front of me in my younger life. When you're younger, you have idyllic dreams of things to do, I did it, and it's not so good. It's pretty disgusting work."[3] By the early '70s she had fallen in with New York's downtown crowd and joined the girl-fronted Stilettos, which included other future members of Blondie. "We used to play CBGB's on a Saturday night to twenty-five people with Television. You'd trickle onstage and trickle offstage. We were the house band for six months," Blondie guitarist Chris Stein told *Creem*. "And how we got into CBGB's, one of the girls in the Stilettos was screwing one of the guys in Television at the time," he added.[4] When Harry defected from the Stilettos, she took most of the band with her and, with Stein, formed Blondie. After a few personnel changes, the 1976 version of the band, with Stein on guitar, Clement Burke on drums, Jimmy Destri on keyboards, and bassist Gary Valentine, emerged to record their first single, "X Offender."

Blondie gained renown by playing CBGB, surging full throttle into one quick and energetic song after another. In updating the sound of the sugar-coated assembly-line pop singles of the '60s, Blondie were inspired by an entirely different set of influences than other CBGB favorites like the Ramones or the Patti Smith Group. Singles like "X Offender" offered escape from the aesthetic severity of a band like Television. But Harry put her own twist on the songs, guaranteeing the band's contributions would not be written off as pure pop. For the scathing "Rip Her to Shreds," Harry once wore a wedding dress, and tore it off onstage. She recalled, "I ripped the dress off and I said, 'This is the only dress my mother ever wanted me to wear, 'cause we never agreed on clothes,' and nobody laughed."[5]

Their break from the New York sound was infectious enough to land them a deal with the Private Stock label in 1976, and the band released *Blondie*. After one album, they opted to sign with Chrysalis. As producer/guitarist Jon Tiven recalled in Blondie's *Platinum Collection* liner notes, "I remember well the Blondie gig at the Village Gate when the entire upper echelon of Chrysalis Records turned up to cement the deal, while the rest of the New York bands just looked at each other and said 'Why not us?' The rise to the top of the charts wasn't exactly instantaneous, either, as there was still a tremendous amount of resistance to any band from *that city* getting on the radio."[6]

Mainstream radio in the U.S. finally caught up to Blondie when they released "Heart of Glass" from the *Parallel Lines* album in 1979, and the band managed to land seven more Top 40 singles. (In England the band got plenty of radio play and had many chart hits already.) A string of albums followed *Parallel Lines* before Blondie broke up in 1982. Harry then released a few solo albums and sang with the Jazz Passengers in the '90s. She appropriately appeared in John Waters' paean to the '60s, *Hairspray*, as well as landing supporting roles in a few other films in the '80s and '90s. Blondie re-formed in 1998, and subsequently released *Blondie Live, No Exit*, and *The Curse of Blondie*.

Outside of making enchantingly singable pop, Harry was utterly charming as the clowning beauty, a multidimensional figure rarely seen among the tired images of smoldering, serious, beautiful frontwomen. Behind the almost sickly sweet "In the Flesh," there was defiance in her strong voice, a lingering nasty streak lurking in songs like "Kung Fu Girls," and her always sharp, ever-present wit. Unfortunately, Chrysalis' marketing of Harry created the allusion of an icy enigma that belied the warm and spontaneous persona she presented at CBGB. Blondie's sarcastic edges were further dulled down with ad copy like "Wouldn't you like to rip her to shreds?" Another Chrysalis ad teased, "Worth every inch," emblazoned above a picture of Harry outfitted in a leopard-print catsuit. Songs like "One Way or Another" conveyed a certain sexual aggression, and Harry was definitely enjoying her sexual power. "Ms. Harry is disarmingly frank about the sexist role she plays," Brian Harrigan reported in *Melody Maker*. " 'It's a cheap trick,' she says, and then swivels her chair to look at the poster of herself pinned to the wall above her head. [*The poster was one of her wearing a see-through black blouse.*] 'This,' she adds, with some measure of disgust, 'is not my idea of a poster. I didn't know anything about it until I saw it, and it certainly wasn't my idea.' . . . 'Record companies exercise their powers in all kinds of ways,' Burke hints darkly."[7]

The rock media didn't help the situation, either, with headlines like the one from *New Musical Express*, "Sex Kitten Sharpens Claws, Headline Writer Blunts Brain,"[8] or an article from the same magazine on Blondie that was cheerfully referred to as "Male Chauvinist Pigs' Corner."[9] Other winners included: "Return of the Teen Nymphette,"[10] "Blondie Cometh: The Sensuous Pout from CBGB,"[11] and "Blondie Bombshell."[12] Since Harry couldn't easily fit the temptress slot unless she was stripped of her sarcasm, the industry simply shrugged its shoulders and deleted it. "It is very annoying," Harry said of the compulsion to feature her without other members of the band. "After a certain point, we were sort of getting into it and I was getting most of the attention, until we were hip to what the name of the game was. It was weird and frightening and annoying and insulting, and sometimes it was good but now it's gotten to the point where we're taking it and using it to our advantage."[13]

Debbie Harry has never been properly credited for her behind-the-scenes contributions to the band. While she was serving as Blondie's enigmatic lead singer, the sheer strength of her voice was ignored as often as was her songwriting prowess. Unlike the girl groups Blondie referenced, Harry wasn't just trotted out to sing what her male bandmates had laid down. She cowrote many of Blondie's classics, like "X Offender," "Rip Her to Shreds," "Heart of Glass," "One Way or Another," "Dreaming," "Union City Blue," "Call Me," and "Rapture," among a slew of others. Of the eight singles that hit the Top 40, Harry cowrote seven. She could slip seamlessly from pining, lovelorn ballads one minute to experimenting with rap, in the popular "Rapture," the next. By combining the packaged girl-group personas of the '60s with her assertive stance, Harry created a much more interesting and complex female image for pop music.

Even though she achieved iconic status in the pop world, Debbie Harry still suffers from the "dumb blond" stereotype. When the new underground talks about '70s female influences, she is rarely held up as the strong, angry, and inspiring example of female creativity she most certainly was.

Chapter 6

THE WORLD'S A MESS; IT'S IN MY KISS

Exene Cervenka

IT'S NO SURPRISE THAT X'S FAMOUS FIREBRAND STARTED AS A poet, stumbling upon music the same way she tripped over John Doe at a poetry workshop in Venice, California, in 1977. Reports of what happened next vary, but the most common story is that the two began sharing their poetry while Doe, a bassist and vocalist, was forming a band with rockabilly guitarist Billy Zoom. Soon after, X was born and, along with the Screamers, the Weirdos, and the infamous Germs, quickly became a signature band of the emerging L.A. punk scene. Like the Germs, X was also featured in Penelope Spheeris' *The Decline of Western Civilization*, where they were placed at the climax of the chaos Spheeris conveyed in her cult classic.

X connected the roots of American rock and roll in Zoom's rockabilly guitar style (he once played with rockabilly icon Gene Vincent) with punk in drummer D.J. Bonebrake's driving beat. Unlike the Cramps' mix of rockabilly and punk that became a celebration of the antiquated and the futuristic, X's songs painted the darkness of American life, the desperation produced by a faltering economy that had seized many American cities in the 1970s. Their mix of country, rockabilly, and punk, along with Cervenka and Doe's haunting lyrics, set them apart from the other bands on the L.A. punk scene. With droning vocals and rockabilly riffs that bobbed up above the punk rhythm, their music told stories of the true Hollywood Boulevard, though every X song still related to the larger world. Even the single "Los Angeles" is a wistful, writhing goodbye, comprehensible to anyone isolated or driven to madness by his or her surroundings.

Born Christine Cervenka in Chicago, Illinois, in 1956 and raised in Tallahassee, Florida, Exene hopped the first ride to Los Angeles she was offered in 1976. She met Doe in 1977 and he asked to use her poem "I'm Coming Over," in his new band.[1] Much to Zoom's dismay, Cervenka wanted to sing her own words rather than turn them over to Doe. "I admit it," Zoom has said. "I was originally horrified that John was bringing his girl-friend into the band."[2] Cervenka ended up providing the perfect comple-ment to Doe's voice, conveying the sadness of their lyrics, often sounding like a weeping woman against Doe's unfazed steadiness.

X played their first show at their own house party and began gigging around Los Angeles soon after. They were among those who flocked to the Masque, an underground, illegal basement club opened by Brendan Mullen in 1977.[3] The Masque hosted shows and threw debauched parties, becoming a communal playing, meeting, drinking, and drugging space for the solidi-fying punk scene. "The audience at the Masque was just like us," Doe recalled, "and there was no division between the bands who played there and the people who went to see them."[4]

X quickly became known as one of the signature bands of L.A. punk and released their first album, aptly named *Los Angeles*, on Slash Records in 1980. The album, still hailed as a classic, contains the title track, as well as the grotesque "Johnny Hit and Run Paulene" and a cover of the Doors' "Soul Kitchen." In 1981, the band released the equally powerful *Wild Gift*, and in 1982 joined the majors (Elektra) for the release of *Under the Big Black Sun*. Doe and Cervenka were married in 1983 after the release of *More Fun in the New World*. The band broke up a few years later (as did their marriage) but in the early '90s Doe and Cervenka resurrected X (with the original lineup) and released five more albums. Although their last original release was *Hey Zeus!* in 1993 (the live *Unclogged* followed in 1995), the past couple of years have seen the occasional X tour. Cervenka has published three books *(Adulterers*

Anonymous, Virtual Unreality, and *A Beer on Every Page)* and written commentary for Kenneth Jarecke's collection of war photojournalism, *Just Another War.* She has also released the solo albums *Old Wives' Tales, Running Scared, Surface to Air Serpents,* and a spoken-word EP. In the mid-'90s, she formed a punk band called Auntie Christ and released one album, *Life Could Be a Dream.* Her current project is the Original Sinners, with whom she released an album in 2002.

Exene Cervenka exudes pure power. This sense of assuredness emanates from a stark emotional purity and her ability to fully, bravely expose herself without posturing. She hits high notes without compromise and her voice conveys a raw severity and nakedness, once prompting John Doe to extol: "She had poems that were obviously songs, plus she was cut from classic lead singer cloth. She was such a badass! I pretended to be, but Exene was the real thing. She had the ax to grind, the sadness of her mother's death, and the unusual wiring that made it possible for her to throw a drink in somebody's face and still be right. She totally delivered as a lead singer."[5]

The duality of emotion that emerged from Doe and Cervenka's collaborative writing worked perfectly with the themes and execution of their songs. Doe's smooth, unwavering vocals came across as the veneer that hides our humanity, particularly surrounding the culture and myth of Hollywood. Cervenka's voice acted as the foil to the songs' surface perfection—the dark interiors residing beneath the melodies in songs like "Sex and Dying in High Society." The calm and chaotic blended into bloody fairy tales: under smooth surf guitar, the simultaneous joy and mourning of Leadbelly's "Dancing with Tears in My Eyes" (from *Under the Big Black Sun),* the jumpy, catchy "We're Desperate" *(Los Angeles),* the wistfulness of "The Night Our Love Passed Out on the Couch" *(Wild Gift),* or the vocal drawls laid over rapid-fire rhythms in "Johnny Hit and Run Paulene." Furthermore, X's nontraditional duets represented the relative gender equality of the community from which they came, never devolving into the sentimentality that marked much of mainstream male and female duos of the time. X's songs were often about love's disintegration, whether permanent or temporary. "Johnny Hit and Run Paulene," a song about a rapist named Johnny stalking anonymous women referred to as "Paulenes," portrayed rape as a human tragedy rather than a gendered one by employing both Cervenka and Doe's voices.

Cervenka's literary power comes from simple imagery that's hardly predictable. Her lyrics don't employ abstract phrases that require hours of headsplitting interpretation. "Most of my songs are written about love, which is not to say they're not political," she explained in 1990. "The people I am closest to are not misled by society's mores, except in love. It is fascinating that people can overthrow all parts of society except love relationships. An otherwise completely liberated woman can go years and years in a destructive relationship."[6] While popular lyrical representations of women in love usually revealed breast-beating, flowery faithfulness, or a sense of the world terminally falling part, Cervenka described an immediacy of feeling without overindulging in it. Her love songs seem to encourage commiseration instead of merely depicting heartbreak. With wistful and simple sadness, they give the impression of the slurred story of a drunk as the bar shuts down around her—a woman and her story, lonely and unfinished. Whether her intention or not, the breadth of her work proves that female singer-songwriters had a lot more to say about love than had typically been allowed prior to punk.

In 1982, she collaborated with Lydia Lunch on a book of poetry entitled *Adulterers Anonymous*. Each woman's work was showcased separately, with lines added by the other writer. Although Lunch and Cervenka have entirely different literary styles—Lunch is often consumed with images of physical decay that represent spiritual rot while Cervenka's desolation is expressed, as it was with X, through ordinary objects and moments internalized—the book reads like a lovelorn wail, a bleak look at abandoned lives being rebuilt. While the two women appear very different on the surface, the way their visions intersected in their collaborative poetry erased the disparity and created a new literary voice—one that was hardly typical in the supermodel-riddled '80s, which enforced a "smile and look pretty" standard for women. Lydia Lunch comments, "We didn't edit or change what the other wrote, [we] simply supplemented, carrying on the thought. Exene and I complement each other's narratives, using a call and response technique. We have very different ways to expresses our frustrations, but our moral imperative is very similar. Tell the truth about the injustices which we feel run rampant over the individual. Give voice to those less articulate. Play town crier. Scream into the void."[7] Besides countering the exploited image of submissive womanhood and the fiction of cattiness and competition between women, the most palpable aspect of their collaboration is the breadth of their work and experience as artists and as women, which spans decades. Lunch and

Cervenka later collaborated on a spoken-word album entitled *Rude Hieroglyphics*, released in 1995.

Cervenka's image also ran counter to the natural, earthy 1970s woman. While thrift store dresses, boots, piles of jewelry, and dark eyeliner may have been popularized by Madonna in 1985, it was arguably first donned by Cervenka in the mid-'70s. In the '70s punk 'zine *Search and Destroy*, Cervenka highlighted the way in which her punk aesthetic stunned the Hollywood landscape:

> Well, if you go outside with hair like this and this lipstick on; if you were wearing a polyester pantsuit you would cause a disruption in this town. That's what people don't realize about Los Angeles. People in New York and London, like the people who reviewed our record in London, say, "What do *they* have to be desperate about?" [Referring to X's "We're Desperate"] . . . Every time I leave the house everyone makes fun of me, gives me a hard time—people on the bus, all these kids going to school, all these people in Beverly Hills. And they stop me on the street and they go, "Oh my God!" and then they just look at each other and walk on like I wasn't even a human being that had *feelings,* and usually I cause a scene by telling them off![8]

Of her life as an artist she has said, "I look at being an artist that way, as some sort of contribution. I feel there's a virtuous aspect to what I do. I hope that doesn't sound too pretentious, but I feel like that's a lost thing in our culture. I feel good that I can add a little of that here and there."[9] With her moody mixture of intelligence and sensitivity and her comfort with being at odds with the world, Exene Cervenka has done more than a little good in her nearly thirty years of artistic contributions.

Chapter 7

MARRIED TO MYSELF

Penelope Houston

THE SAN FRANCISCO–BASED AVENGERS INADVERTENTLY HOLD A
legendary place in punk's history as one of the two bands, along with
the Nuns, to open the Sex Pistols' final show at the Winterland on
January 14, 1978. Purportedly one of the first bands of the Bay Area
punk scene, preceded only by the Nuns and Crime, the Avengers also
opened for the Go-Go's and X, among others, in their short-lived two-
year career.[1] While Patti Smith and Exene Cervenka are usually the
first women to pop up on what amounts to a short list of 1970s punk
inspirations (and even they are sometimes still overlooked), Penelope
Houston was a true enigma as the lead singer of this groundbreaking
West Coast band.

Houston grew up entrenched in music (her mother has a Stanford
doctorate in the field), but didn't think seriously about joining a band
until she went to San Francisco's Art Institute for printmaking and drawing. "[W]hen I lived in Seattle . . . I went out and saw friends that were
starting really strange bands," she says. "The Tupperwares, who later

turned into the Screamers, were friends of mine. When I moved to San Francisco to go to art school, I immediately fell in with people that were in bands and people that were photographing bands and just the whole sort of punk aesthetic. . . . I was kinda lucky because the Avengers were my first band and I kinda jumped right into that, but it seemed pretty natural to me."[2]

Maybe luck was on the Avengers' side—Houston practically tripped over the opportunity to become their lead singer in 1977. "I had some friends at the Art Institute that were starting a band. One day I was in their warehouse, and they had a PA set up. I had never sung through a microphone before. They were gone for the day, so I had six or seven hours to sing along with records. I found it so powerful to have this PA. They came back, and I said, 'Well, you've got your lead singer right here!'"[3]

With Danny Furious on drums, Greg Ingraham on guitar, and Jonathan Postal on bass (who was replaced by Jimmy Wisley in mid-1977), the Avengers started out playing covers. "We did 'Pissing in a River' by Patti Smith," says Houston, "Lou Reed's 'Hit Me with a Flower [sic],' and a few other songs. I remember I went to L.A. and visited my friends who had turned into the Screamers. I realized at that point that we had to be original, we had to write our own songs, and we came back and we wrote all our own songs."[4] The band collaborated on most of their music while Houston penned the majority of the lyrics. The Avengers tried their new songs out on an audience for the first time at San Francisco's premier punk venue, Mabuhay Gardens. Houston recounts: "We'd written, I don't know, maybe seven songs that week, so I was thinking, 'How am I gonna remember all these songs?' Somebody had made the copies of set lists wrong, so the guitar player was playing a different song—maybe it was like, the second song in—than the bass player and the drummer. I just was standing there thinking, 'I can't remember how this song goes! It sounds so weird.' Then I thought, 'Oh, I'm never going to be able to perform. I'm freaking out here.' And then everyone stopped playing after a half a minute, and we were all looking at each other like, 'What are you playing?' 'Well, what are you playing?' And then we figured out that they were playing two different songs. I kind of took a deep breath and said, 'Okay, I guess I can do this.' But it was pretty terrifying the first time."[5]

The Avengers built a fast following and, in less than a year, were booked to open for the Pistols the night Johnny Rotten immortalized the question, "Ever get the feeling you've been cheated?" and stormed offstage and out of the band. Beyond marking the demise of the Sex Pistols, the Winterland show has also been pegged as a turning point for punk—from an enthusiastic, youthful underground community to one with a potential for corporate co-opting, as evidenced by promoter Bill Graham's interest in producing a punk show that simulated the formula of the stadium concerts punk hoped to avoid. "People were throwing a lot of stuff onstage," Houston recalls. "I remember when the Pistols were up there, someone threw a camera onstage. I mean, the stage was basically littered with stuff. . . . We felt out of our element, you know? We were used to playing the Mabuhay, and it being totally packed, and people being crazy, but in a certain way we recognized, and this was a gigantic rock show. People who came there to see the Pistols, a lot of them had never seen a punk band, and they wanted to see some kind of freak show, a punk rock zoo and stuff. It was a little bit on the frightening side."[6]

For much of her career with the Avengers, Houston's hair was cropped in a blond buzzcut and her face free of makeup, allowing audiences to easily mistake her for a boy at first glance. In her androgynous play and in photos depicting an intently blank stare, Houston openly challenged her viewers to recast their image of a woman.

But her shouts and screams of desperation remain her lasting mark. The Avengers trounced the quiet political demands of folk by invoking anarchy and by removing gender (and any niceties, for that matter) from the decade's larger political dialogue. The Avengers rejected Western values like capitalism and the country's penchant for violence in "American in Me" and "Open Your Eyes," and soulless work in "White Nigger." Their song "Uh-Oh" is a denunciation of marriage. In "We Are the One," the song for which they're best known, the Avengers explored the potential of the punk generation to change the world.

Having released only one three-song 7" in 1977, and no formal album, the Avengers broke up in June 1979. As Houston explains: "We were on our second guitar player and it was sort of changing. We were musically changing our direction, and I'm not sure everyone was happy about it. . . . It just felt like we'd hit this glass ceiling, and we couldn't get any further. At that point, we just had one 7" out, a three-song 7", and we'd done a bunch of different recordings, and they hadn't come out. We had a deal for another record that was supposed to come out, which actually wasn't released 'til two months after we broke up. . . . [S]omehow, if we'd gotten signed and been able to put out an album, and been able to go on and do more songwriting, it probably would have helped us. . . . We needed to try to move on creatively, and didn't have a way to do that."[7]

The Avengers' songs have been included on a few punk compilation albums, as well as recently reissued compilations like *The Avengers*, originally released by CD Presents in 1983, and Lookout!'s 1999 *Died for Your Sins*.

After the band split, Houston left San Francisco and moved, for a short time, to Los Angeles, and then to England to work with the Buzzcocks' Howard Devoto. It was during that time that she began to appreciate the way outcast artists like Tom Waits and the Violent Femmes were infusing sarcasm, anger, humor, and honesty into more acoustic-sounding, yet still offbeat, music. Inspired by tamer music that retained the underground's sharpened edges and alternative views, Houston began to write her own music in the same acoustic style. She has since evolved into a prolific acoustic singer-songwriter, a road not necessarily appreciated by most punks. The underground scene gave way to its more oppressively dogmatic tendencies during the '80s, as Houston illustrated in an interview with writer Richie Unterberger: "I did an interview with *Maximumrocknroll* [a radio show and 'zine, each augmenting the other], and on the air they accused me of selling out. I just thought that was outrageous because, obviously, if I wanted to sell out, I'd re-form the Avengers and go touring around. . . . I sold out, I got nothing. No, I never sold out. I still have my punk attitude."[8] Since leaving the Avengers, she's released eleven solo albums and three collaborative ones.

Greil Marcus once hailed the band for finding their distinct voice, spare of pretense. He likened the Avengers' unique aesthetic to a new way of speaking when he wrote, "They had learned a language, where nearly everything that went into a song was broken down and made up again from as close to nothing as anyone could get, and for a long moment it seemed as if this new language could say everything—or anything worth saying. Try to speak another language, and you may find you can't talk at all."[9] With Penelope Houston at the helm, the Avengers helped usher punk into the Bay Area with a straight-ahead sound and their very own language of social transformation.

Chapter 8

BIKINI GIRLS WITH GRETSCH GUITARS

Poison Ivy

THE GARISH, SPELLBINDING CRAMPS SEEM TO HAVE BEEN LARGELY forgotten as part of the 1970s New York City subculture. Despite the fact that their involvement in this scene is often overlooked and that they are frequently left out of music compilations, rock history books, and magazine articles documenting the history of underground music, the Cramps did coin the punk offshoot "psychobilly," which has been their lasting legacy. "People still continue to write books about that scene without including us, like it never happened," Cramps vocalist Lux Interior has remarked.[1] Guitarist and cocreator Poison Ivy once said: "We were always able to get good gigs at all the best punk clubs, we'd sell out multiple nights, and kids loved us, so we're not complaining, but the rock writers hated us, and we were written off as some kind of clown act. . . . Media-wise, it was like we didn't even exist in New York, yet we'd sell out everywhere we went just by word of mouth."[2]

The Cramps first played live at an audition night at Max's Kansas City in 1976 and were immediately booked for Saturday night gigs, propelling the understated and slightly rarefied New York scene into dimensions beyond experimental variations on garage rock and more in line with the underground's direct pop descendants, the Ramones and Blondie. They melded punk rhythms with rockabilly twang and surf music, and steeped the result in Interior and Ivy's personal fetishes.

The Cramps mixed a '50s horror/sci-fi B-movie and comic book aesthetic with certain cultural relics of the poor South. Their logo was taken from the original *Tales from the Crypt* comic book. And while the new punk ethos wholeheartedly rejected American pop culture, Interior and Ivy cherished its trinkets and castoffs. The Cramps also added bizarre, left-of-center sexual play to their creepier, less-serious paeans to Americana. New York City's scene was renowned for its pared-down aesthetic, which may have contributed to the Cramps' diminished role there being virtually forgotten. Given the bands that were already defining New York's trademark look at the time—Television, the Talking Heads—critics might not have known what to do with the Cramps when they arrived.

The band's visionaries—guitarist Poison Ivy (née Kirsty Wallace) and singer Lux Interior (Erick Purkhiser)—met in Ivy's hometown of Sacramento, California, where she was embarking on another treasured-yet-outdated American pastime—hitchhiking. Their strangest decision to date was moving to Interior's native Akron, Ohio, where the duo tried to get a band going for two years. "At the time, the only way you could find rockabilly was on the original 45s; there weren't any reissues of it," explained Ivy. "We were finding some incredible records around the Akron area because a lot of people from the South had moved up North to work in the factories and had dumped their records. So we were hearing all this stuff and at the same time, there were contemporary bands we liked. We loved the New York Dolls and the Stooges, so we were excited by that. We had boring jobs, we were taking speed, and with the combination of those things, we ended up going to New York."[3]

After moving to New York City in 1974, they met Bryan Gregory, who became the Cramps' other guitarist. "Bryan wanted to play guitar, and I wanted to play guitar, so we both played guitar," Ivy said. "We didn't want more than four people in the band, that part we knew. And the kind of music we play is so rhythmic; we couldn't see why a bass was essential."[4] Bryan's sister Pam "Balam" Gregory played drums before Miriam Linna, who was eventually replaced by Nick Knox. "We came to New York thinking, because of this single picture [of CBGB]," Interior remembered, "that everyone walked around looking like the New York Dolls. And of course nobody did . . . it was all jeans and boring."[5]

The band descended upon Los Angeles in 1978, where they opened for the Runaways. A warm reception on the West Coast urged them to leave New York. They moved to Hollywood that same year, where they found a more vibrant punk scene with a more colorful aesthetic, a place where the Cramps seemed to fit. IRS Records founder Miles Copeland recalled, "People definitely took to them here. Walking down the street in the hot Los Angeles sunshine with Lux and Ivy and Bryan Gregory in their vinyl suits was something else. People looked at them like they were from another planet."[6] A deal followed from IRS Records, and their first album, *Songs the Lord Taught Us,* produced by Alex Chilton, was released in 1980. The Cramps would later have legal trouble with IRS, and subsequently encountered a number of problems with other labels as well. They have come to value self-sufficiency and independence and have reissued much of their old material on their own Vengeance Records label.

The Cramps not only merge two outcast genres—rockabilly and punk—they also fuse modern sexual freedom with a '50s retro look. Interior wears vinyl catsuits and prowls the stage like an S&M hustler; Ivy grinds suggestively while conjuring rockabilly riffs equal to anything laid down in Memphis' historic Sun Studio. Their richly colored album covers offer Halloween versions of '50s pinup girls, and the songs are bawdy to the bone: "Journey to the Center of a Girl," "Bend Over, I'll Drive," "Can Your Pussy Do the Dog?"; a 1983 album is called *Smell of Female.* The Cramps celebrate sexuality by treating it with a cagey, campy sense of humor, and still manage to retain its dark underbelly.

Interior's androgyny—his high heels and makeup—shift the lead singer's sexuality to a gray area where both genders share the power. Ivy exaggerates her sexuality, wearing tight-fitting latex and vinyl, high heels, and cartoon vamp makeup while engaging in the typically male pursuits of songwriting and playing lead guitar. "That's the rawest they'll ever see," she said of being onstage. "I feel superhuman up there. There've been times when I've been real sick and as soon as I step out there . . . nothing."[7]

Her effortless guitar playing took the old rockabilly scene so polarized by gender and updated it with rock's emerging female face. In this way, Ivy channeled her female rockabilly ancestor Wanda Jackson, who maintained a distinctly traditional '50s appearance while singing from a strong female perspective—a woman who might fight, drink, and stay out late, defying her husband, in songs like "Hot Dog! That Made Him Mad." Jackson was at the behest of the men who wrote many of her songs, though. Ivy, on the other hand, was Interior's coconspirator since the Cramps' inception and even produced the 1990 album *Stay Sick!* herself. She is not the only woman to make contributions to the band, however. The Cramps have featured female musicians sporadically throughout their history, including early drummer Miriam Linna and bassist Candy Del Mar.

In an interview with *Guitar Player*, Ivy talked about her experience with rock's sexism: "[I]f I am recognized or credited, people will say I play as tough as a guy. In a way that's insulting, because for one thing, I play different. It's got nothing to do with guys. No guy taught me how to play. I taught myself. And you'd be surprised how much you can learn yourself, just listening to a lot of records and watching people play and hanging out with a lot of players, rather than having someone show you his clichéd way of playing. Try something original. And I'm sure there's even something about being a girl that has an original flair to it, and women should try to allow that to come out in their playing. And that can be something pretty scary, too. People expect us to be timid, and it can be the other way around."[8]

Remarkably, the Cramps are still together today, and retain their very distinct aesthetic sensibility. Most importantly, as Ivy has said, "We get taken lightly because there's humor in our music, yet humor is rebellion to me."[9] Humor is something that has too easily been forgotten as an essential part of earlier generations of punk rock. Luckily, we still have Poison Ivy and the Cramps to remind us.

Part II

BRITAIN IN THE 1970S

Introduction

NO ONE'S LITTLE GIRLS

You offer independence, but demand I toe the line.
You say you give me freedom, but you hang on to the key,
Well, don't you think, perhaps, the decision's up to me?
So tell me if I'm dreaming if I want to live,
And I'll tell you you're just scheming to make me give
More than I want to, more than I can;
You don't want a person, you just want woman.
—CRASS, "DRY WEATHER"[1]

PUNK HAD DELIVERED ON ITS PROMISE THAT ANYONE COULD make great art. Mainstream music stuck to its own equal-opportunity credo: that anyone, especially artists who made the most money, could produce vapid hit after hit. Mainstream music in Britain and the United States didn't vary much during the 1970s—Led Zeppelin and the Rolling Stones held an equally bloated stature in both nations; ABBA and the Osmonds charmed audiences internationally, as well. While B.J. Thomas' "Raindrops Keep Falling on My Head" topped the U.S. charts in January 1970, Rolf Harris garnered the number one spot for the same month in Britain with "Two Little Boys." Although Britain was as blind to its social problems as the U.S. was, "Two Little Boys" was a more appropriate reflection of world issues than the American chart topper.

"Two Little Boys" is the story of friends who grow from playing "soldiers" as children into adults fighting a war. The song heralds the brotherhood of soldiers and the loyalty of the boys' friendship; one saves the other from death on the battlefield. The song's popularity might have stemmed from criticism of the British government's tacit support of the American involvement in Vietnam, or from the fact that it offered palatable sentimentality and avoided thorny criticisms of the home government. While the themes of the song were more relevant to the times than the sunny "Raindrops," musically, it falls into the light end of folk and soft rock. "Two Little Boys" was actually sung as a children's song (Harris was a star presenter on children's television at the time); Harris thumped the wood of his guitar for percussion, and occasionally let his voice fade away for emphasis.

As for the rest of the chart, there were fewer women making appearances on the U.K.'s Top 20 than there were on its American counterpart. The women who did make it were more varied than the middle-of-the-road crooners in the States, though. While New York's Blondie hit the U.K. Top 20 eight times during the '70s, only "Heart of Glass" hit the Top 20 in the States that decade. Seventies artists like ABBA, Blondie, and Olivia Newton-John, who produced some of the U.K.'s most successful singles of all time, don't even appear on America's list of best-selling singles artists (the two lists do share Diana Ross and Donna Summer). Female singer-songwriters do not appear as frequently in the early '70s in the U.K. as they do in the U.S., although the popularity of acts like ABBA and Olivia Newton-John proved the timidity of the British charts.

ABBA, more joyous and less staid than the Carpenters, were a squeaky clean Swedish quartet composed of two men and two women, whose wardrobe resembled four separate parts of a larger jigsaw puzzle, muting the members' individuality. Although far catchier than the Carpenters', ABBA's songs expressed the same pop levity as those of the Osmonds or chart rival Olivia Newton-John. Singers Agnetha Faltskog and Anni-Frid Lyngstad harmonized so succinctly, their voices sounded duplicated. The female chorus competed with a nonthreatening mass of strings, guitars, drums, and other accompaniments. The lyrics—mostly concerned with love and love's loss—never reached the epiphany the music promises, and the drama of ABBA now sounds as dated as their all-white, flared and feathered outfits. Nonetheless, the quartet enjoyed great success on the British charts, landing thirteen songs in the Top 20 between October 1975 and the end of 1979.

Olivia Newton-John was another pervasive presence on U.K. charts in the '70s. Reminiscent of stateside soft rock women like Linda Ronstadt, Newton-John belted many of her songs, lending them more of a torch song or rock ballad feel. As usual with the music of popular female crooners of the day, Newton-John's hits in the U.K. generally covered well-trodden territory: "Hopelessly Devoted to You," "If Not for You," "Little More Love," and "Long Live Love."

Other women who clambered their way into the Top 20 arrived via disco, like Tina Charles with "Dance Little Lady Dance," "Dr. Love," and "I Love to Love (But My Baby Loves to Dance)." Like Newton-John's compulsion for love songs, Charles' route was a fairly predictable route for disco queens, and her music wasn't far from traditional female pop fare. American soul singers Candi Staton ("Young Hearts Run Free") and Freda Payne ("Band of Gold," "Bring the Boys Home") both hit the charts in Britain, as did longtime British television and cabaret favorite Shirley Bassey. A few adult-oriented artists from the States, like Judy Collins and Dionne Warwick, made an appearance from time to time, too.

Socially and culturally, Britain was primed for the shakeup punk sought. Beyond the country's social problems and its dull pop culture, glam had been on the rise since David Bowie's Ziggy Stardust days in the late '60s and early '70s. Where glam had been more of an underground phenomenon in the United States, it was clearly a pop enterprise in the U.K. Both Bowie and Gary Glitter had nine Top 20 hits by 1974, and T. Rex landed in the Top 20 thirteen times in the same period. American singer and bassist Suzi Quatro had four Top 20 hits in the U.K. between 1971 and 1974 and only one in the States, in 1979. Quatro's main claim to fame this side of the Atlantic was as rocker Leather Tuscadero on the hit show *Happy Days*—and, of course, as an inspiration for her female rock descendants.

Despite the uneven chart treatment, Suzi Quatro was influential for both female U.K. and U.S. rockers. She played bass and had a brash image that was unusual for high-profile women in pop music. Her music, however, should continue to be filed under "bubblegum," for professional songwriters fed her the lyrics to songs like her U.K. hit "Can the Can." As always, singing professionally written songs inhibited individual control over her image and her message. Nonetheless, Joan Jett referenced Quatro as the inspiration for her own female rock swagger, as did the Talking Heads' Tina Weymouth and the Fastbacks' Kim Warnick.[2] Despite her bubblegum material, Quatro still provided an alternative for female musicians in the '70s, and when set among the plethora of singer-songwriters and disco divas, she was a refreshing change from the women who shared the rock landscape with her.

Quatro, suffering the same fate as Jett's first band, the Runaways, was presented as a female novelty more than a serious talent. In *Popular Music and Society*, Frank Oglesbee documents Suzi Quatro's automatically sexualized image by citing a *Creem* review that described her as "a beauty, a sex monster, a humping wild-eyed witch from Detroit without using gimmicks like boobs, knockers, etc."[3] In both the American and British press, Quatro's, and later Jett's, more confrontational style was retargeted to suit the imagination of young boys. Mark Perry of *Sniffin' Glue*, arguably the first punk fanzine in London, reviewed the Runaways' classic "Cherry Bomb" in the 'zine's premier issue: "It's tight driving punk rock all the way, there's loads of lovely groans and sighs from the girls ([a]ll under eighteen, by the way) which should move a few punks—all the way to the toilet."[4]

Quatro never politicized her career, choosing to present herself as a rocker first and, at times, according to Oglesbee, insisting that rock should never be intellectualized.[5] She rejected the sex symbol status put upon her by the press, most dramatically by posing for a centerfold in a 1974 issue of *Penthouse*—completely clothed from head to toe. In this way, she preceded X-Ray Spex's Poly Styrene, who declared that she would shave her head if she ever became a sex symbol, a threat she later made good on.[6]

These musicians' open defiance of the sexual roles routinely slated for women in music not only highlights the necessity to actively resist objectification in ways that allowed for no misinterpretation by the press, it also underlines that actions like these would have most likely cost mainstream crooners like Newton-John and Ronstadt their careers. Yet as these actions prove, control could be had in the world of punk. As Pretenders leader and early punker Chrissie Hynde has been quoted, "It's not screw me—it's screw *you*!"[7]

―――――――――

While mainstream music might have looked similar on both sides of the Atlantic, punk in Britain was quite different than its American, or at least New York, counterpart. New York punk has always been viewed as art-driven, whereas the Los Angeles scene was decidedly more a chip off the ol' London vitriol. *Punk* writer Mary Harron describes the difference between New York and London in *England's Dreaming*: "[E]verything had been more proficient in New York. There was a sense of chaos [in London], and New York was not about chaos. . . . American Punk had no politics at that stage."[8]

The two countries' underground music scenes were not entirely segregated from one another, though. It's widely alleged that Malcolm McLaren, manager of the Sex Pistols and co-owner of Sex, the shop in London that largely defined the punk "look" for the mainstream (although early U.K. punks mostly assembled their own clothes and styles), found inspiration for the Pistols in the New York Dolls and Television in the early to mid-'70s. McLaren had, however, been exploring confrontational, rock-and-roll-inspired clothing with his partner Vivienne Westwood since they opened their King's Road shop, originally called Let It Rock, in 1972.[9] Simultaneously, pub rock—rhythm-and-blues-based rock and roll that, like the New York Dolls, separated itself from massive instrumentals and lengthy songs—was popular all over London. The 101ers, Joe Strummer's band prior to the Clash, was a pub rock band, as were the (proudly sexist) Stranglers, who were often misaligned with the core of British punk bands. Additionally, the New York Dolls (whom McLaren attempted to manage toward the end of their career) and Iggy and the Stooges toured London in the early to mid-'70s. The English papers regularly covered New York's scene as glam rock was reported on and followed in the States. As Siouxsie Sioux explained, "Punk wasn't a calculated movement. It was a complete fluke, initiated in a post glitter world where Bowie had retired and started to look like a golfer, and a load of us were looking for something new. Clubs and gigs were the only source of new music for us, though we were starting to hear new stuff from America, things like the Ramones, Jonathan Richman, Patti Smith, Television, and Richard Hell. Gradually a hardcore group of fifteen or twenty of us would see each other out all the time. It was simply luck that we met up and connected."[10]

In a way, the Sex Pistols were a fluke, too. Childhood friends Paul Cook and Steve Jones had been attempting to put a band together since the early '70s, and Jones approached McLaren for help with an early assemblage of the group, eventually adding John Lydon (who became Johnny Rotten) to the lineup in 1975. In a scene filled with pub rock bands like the 101ers and Eddie and the Hot Rods, the Sex Pistols played their first show on November 6,

1975, at St. Martin's Art College. At their first club gig at the Marquee Club on February 12, 1976, an impulsive, friendly tussle between John Lydon and a Sex shop employee launched the band's infamous reputation for violence. Early Pistols shows inspired the Clash's Joe Strummer and the Buzzcocks' Howard Devoto, as well as garnering the band a following that included the likes of Steve Severin, Siouxsie Sioux, and Billy Idol (then Bill Broad), who gained notoriety in the English papers as the "Bromley Contingent," after Severin and Broad's hometown.

The general signifier of British punk's rise was the 100 Club Punk Festival in September 1976, a two-day event that featured the Sex Pistols, the Clash, Subway Sect, the debut of Siouxsie and the Banshees, the Damned, Chris Spedding and the Vibrators, the Stinky Toys (a French band with a female lead singer), and the Buzzcocks.[11] Less than a month after the 100 Club event, EMI signed the Sex Pistols, and punk's rejection of British traditions, particularly the Pistols' antics, quickly became the focus of the British press. Besides the usual coverage of punk's offenses—general shock journalism on punk dress or outbreaks of violence during shows—the Sex Pistols' "Anarchy in the U.K." single met resistance at the printing plant, where workers refused to package it.[12] It seemed that any punk misstep made the papers and, subsequently, offended mainstream British sensibilities. Slits singer Ari-Up remembers,

> There was a mixture of extreme exuberance, such a way of feeling free, just a lift of the shoulders, the heavy weight that we carried, it was totally gone, especially when we were walking—not by ourselves— whenever we walked with a crowd of our people. It was a constant celebration without the champagne. . . . It was just us in our world, and no one could touch us, no one could do anything, we're here to change things, and it's going to happen whether we want it or not, it's just a written destiny, almost, it's a divine intervention. And we just knew this was it, we started something. . . . I'm not just talking about the Slits, I'm talking about fans, people, friends, guys, women, and men—we all shared that same type of feeling. That was one side of the coin. Now the other [side] of the coin, it was the extreme opposite. . . . It was people attacking us physically, it was people trying to violently put us out of our—not misery, but our happiness.[13]

Punk's nihilism was prominent in London, and no one publicly harbored as much piss and vinegar as Johnny Rotten. The Sex Pistols' revulsion is most potent in "No Feelings," where Rotten relates his apathy toward religion, unfaithful girls, and his disdain for the general population. The only person immune to the hatred in the song is Rotten himself. Punk both rejected participation in mainstream culture and gave voice to the frustrations of working-class youth and art students alike. U.K. punk was rooted in a more overt political conversation than was American punk, and understandably so: While America's turbulent Vietnam politics had given the country a political hangover (and leftist politics were deeply tied in with the reviled hippie generation), London was struggling with a widening class gap that informed both the feminist and punk movements.

Cheap labor was seemingly in abundance all over England in the early '70s. The Labour Party came into power in 1974 with Prime Minister Harold Wilson, followed by James Callaghan. Labour had come to prominence in the early twentieth century with the hope of obtaining working-class Members of Parliament (MPs) by creating a party with socialist ideals that could garner the powerful support of trade unions.[14] Ironically and sadly, by 1977 Great Britain, under the Labour government, had 1.6 million unemployed people[15] This social and economic disaster infused punk's political conscience in bands like the Clash and Crass—directly influencing its young fans, many of whom had been rendered listless by the country's vast unemployment problem.

While the feminist movement in the United States had been started by radicals disillusioned by their marginalization in the New Left, but then embraced by middle-class women whose issues took center stage, British feminism rose from the labor strikes within the working classes and later gained the support of women on the upper rungs of British society. The '70s saw Parliament passing acts to protect victims of domestic violence and rape, along with the Equal Pay Act in 1970 and the growth of battered women's shelters.[16] British activist and author Erin Pizzey spearheaded the creation of battered women's shelters in both the U.K. and U.S. when she opened the very first shelter in England in November 1971.[17] Pizzey also wrote a groundbreaking U.K. tract on the subject, entitled *Scream Quietly or the Neighbors Will Hear*.[18] The most widespread feminist activity of the decade, however, occurred with underpaid working-class women striking for pay improvements. Labor issues were paramount in both the feminist movement and the punk explosion; a string of national strikes throughout the 70s, indicated the severe toll unemployment took on the British population, and demonstrated the scale on which these problems plagued the disintegrating British empire.

Of course, unemployment was not the only motivation for joining the growing underground; some, like the future members of Siouxsie and the Banshees, bonded over a sense of alienation and a desire to dress and act the way they wanted. Banshees cofounder Steven Severin once declared, "We didn't have any manifesto other than that we were willfully perverse and anti-everything."[19]

As in the U.S., most punk women in the U.K. were living as if "the woman question" had been resolved, and the conversation more often turned to the effects of consumerism and media imagery that reinforced archaic notions of womanhood. While the tenets of feminism certainly moved beyond political rhetoric and into their lives and work, female punks tended to concentrate more on subversions of sexuality, as in Siouxsie Sioux's bondage and fantasy gear, or in the deposing of capitalism and consumerism as evidenced by the lyrical themes of X-Ray Spex and the Slits.

Some were artists, others were just isolated; some were angry, and others bored. To reduce the catalyst for the emergence of U.K. punk to anger at the missteps of the Labour government or as a simple "bollocks!" to the Queen is misguided: As in America, outsiders needed something more than force-fed living-room culture, or coma-inducing guitar solos. As Crass member Penny Rimbaud wrote in his autobiography, "The Pistols were incidental; it could have been anyone. The bands were secondary to an attitude, an attitude born on the streets rather than manufactured in Tin Pan Alley. Music couldn't sound like punk, it either was or it wasn't. Punk was a statement of authenticity that couldn't be adopted as the flavor of the month."[20]

While bands like the Clash sang of the working man or soldier and did it well, women were often cast in their songs as yet another pressure on the already oppressed man. While rallying for social rebellion, the Clash were rather traditional in their treatment of gender roles. In *The Sex Revolts*, Simon Reynolds and Joy Press note the boys' club created by the unifying rally cry of the Clash, whose militaristic ideas about revolution embodied punk's more political side. The authors point out that the Clash's catalog is noticeably bereft of female subjects and voices.[21] This charge isn't entirely true; yet the Clash dealt heavily with working-class plight, and women were mostly portrayed as drains on working stiffs' bank accounts. Songs like "Death or Glory" and "The Magnificent Seven" lamented the financial strain of having a girlfriend. In their cover of Vince Taylor's "Brand New Cadillac," a heartless lover drives away forever, leaving her man behind for a better material life. While the Clash didn't write "Brand New Cadillac," its theme reinforced the Clash's general lyrical attitude toward women. The band mostly sidestepped the issue of sexism, with the notable exception of their song "Red Angel Dragnet," which mentions the danger women face walking alone. They consistently spoke out against racism and classism, though, and specifically incorporated reggae into their riffs. In life, however, they did make an effort to promote female bands, by teaching members of the Slits how to play and booking them in opening slots at their gigs. In 1977, the Slits accompanied the Clash on the White Riot tour.

As in more mainstream music the idea of women being "in the way" of men's development as artists definitely existed in the U.S. and U.K. punk scenes. In "No Feelings," Sex Pistols vocalist Johnny Rotten has no use for women's availability and romantic presence, proudly stating that if a girl came around looking for him, he'd beat her. Perhaps the most infamous affront to women within the "inner sanctum" of the punk brotherhood lies in the example of Nancy Spungen.

Spungen was the longtime girlfriend of Sid Vicious, and was allegedly killed by him in 1978. She is widely held responsible for causing Vicious' downfall by introducing him to drugs. In *England's Dreaming*, Leee Childers, the Heartbreakers manager who was in London at the same time as Spungen, confided the following: "If the Heartbreakers brought heroin to England, then Nancy brought it to Sid."[22] Later on in the same account, Childers reiterated, "Almost immediately I heard that she had found Sid and hooked up with him. A cold chill ran down my spine when I heard, and from that day on, Sid was no longer the person I knew."[23] In *Please Kill Me*, Malcolm McLaren brutally recounted his impression of Spungen: "When Nancy Spungen came into my shop it was as if Dr. Strangelove had sent us this dreaded disease specifically to England, and specifically to my store. . . . I was ready to fucking fumigate the place. I said to the band, 'This doesn't bode well, guys. This is a bad omen.' . . . But I tried in every single way possible either to get her run over, poisoned, kidnapped, or shipped back to New York."[24]

In the same way that Casey Cola is intimated in Darby Crash's downfall in Los Angeles when she overdosed with him, and Courtney Love is suspected of masterminding Kurt Cobain's death, Spungen took the fall for

Vicious' heroin addiction. The Sex Pistols saw Spungen as an interference—a longtime issue in the male rock arena, and one not assuaged by the progressive ethos of punk, nor by the growing population of women accepted as serious musicians and partners in social rejection. As much as punk rejected the norms of mainstream British society, true gender equality remained a thorn in its side.

Mark Perry, the *Sniffin' Glue* editor who once rejected a sexist ad for the Damned, stated in the previously cited Runaways review, "I've always hated girl bands, singers, etc. Rock 'n' roll's for blokes and I hope it stays that way. Girls are good for one thing and for one thing only—going shopping for glue."[25] Although Perry cites the Runaways as an exception, and never includes this disdain for women entering the blokes' inner circle in later reviews of Patti Smith, he follows up his opinion of them with a mention of the Runaways' power to banish punks to private masturbation sessions. In the 'zine's fourth issue, Perry reinforces punks' toughness by saying, "Punks are not girls."[26]

Many women involved in the '70s punk scene shied away from the feminist label and the punk label, too, in favor of their more individualistic and complex vision. Most of the original underground wanted nothing to do with movements, but as it became more popular, punk's ethos of thinking for oneself quickly devolved into a lot of shallow imitations and rigid fashion rules. Bands like Crass, the Slits, and others knew that the deep political problems of Britain didn't end when every girl from twelve on up was safety-pinned to her heart's content.

Crass and Poison Girls both engaged in creating directly feminist art as a part of a larger anarchist agenda. Crass' album *Penis Envy* might be the first beginning-to-end overtly feminist punk album, written and sung almost entirely by Eve Libertine and Joy de Vivre. Crass incorporated feminism as part of their vision of a complete overhaul of society, one free from all forms of exploitation, torture, war, and capitalism. Poison Girls were led by Vi Subversa, a droll, heavyset woman who proved the new underground could give voice to a woman in her forties who'd left housewifery behind. Poison Girls bitingly depicted how love and work kept women down, in songs like "Old Tart" and "Lovers, Are They Worth It."

Rather than measuring female musicians for their sex appeal, punk audiences found value in women who infused the stage with women's experience, like Subversa. Residual sexism, however, was still alive and well. The Adverts experienced this firsthand when they released their first single in 1977, "One Chord Wonders," on Stiff Records, an indie label that was the first to sign a

British punk band when they signed the Damned in September 1976. For the Adverts' single, Stiff chose a large picture of Gaye Advert (née Atlas), the band's bassist and only female member, as the sole representative for the cover. Advert member T.V. Smith told Jon Savage, "It suddenly hit home—we've got a good-looking girl in the group and that's what's going to happen. . . . It cheapened it for all of us."[27] Gaye also sustained harsh criticism for a supposed lack of musical talent throughout the Adverts' relatively short career. In an even brasher move, Stiff tried to submit an ad for the Damned's album in *Sniffin' Glue* that featured a naked woman's body with Gaye Advert's face superimposed on top.[28]

It was punk's nihilist philosophies that shocked parents and middle-class suburbanites the most; its most notorious symbol, coming a mere thirty-plus years after World War II, was the swastika. Prevalent in London, Los Angeles, and New York, the swastika was punk's way of rejecting the former (and governing) generation's values. As Berlin, an early friend of Siouxsie Sioux, succinctly put it, "What's the worst thing you can do to your parents who'd fought and died in the war? Really fuck them off."[29] However it was intended, embracing the swastika sat uncomfortably next to, and probably diluted, the fiercely wielded rejection of fascism. The use of the swastika and the latent sexism within punk created isolation within its own borders. Rejection of the mainstream values of Londoners was crucial to punk's potency, and the swastika was a potent symbol of that rejection. Embracing shock value had been an important aspect of McLaren and Westwood's thriving Sex shop; the store even sold T-shirts bearing a hood worn by a rapist who terrorized Cambridge University in 1975.[30]

The differences between American and U.K. punk hardly stopped at the British mixture of rock and politics. Although rock music in Britain was hard to find outside of late-night television programming like *The Old Grey Whistle Test* (which actually highlighted a lot of underground music but was later a frequent victim of punk criticism), there were several print outlets promoting rock and underground music. In *England's Dreaming,* Jon Savage documents the centrality of the media in the dissemination of music information in Britain. *New Musical Express, Sounds,* and *Melody Maker* were produced for music devotees in London but read nationally and, since they were committed to weekly music coverage, they were usually in a scramble for content. As punk solidified as an independent genre it got constant coverage to fill page space.[31] The media in America was decentralized and didn't rely on weekly national music papers. Regional music was covered by local papers like the *Village Voice*, the *L.A. Weekly*, or *NY Rock*, which rarely reached outside of their immediate communities and into the suburbs and outlying areas. Thus the punk movement reached American mainstream culture far slower than the way it crashed into Britain's mainstream discourse.

Prior to the rise of punk, the music industry in London was producing as dull a catalog as the mainstream American industry. Savage notes that K-Tel compilations of hit singles of the decade "account[ed] for 30 percent of all record sales" by 1976 in Britain.[32] The only television music programming other than the late-night *Whistle Test* was BBC's *Top of the Pops*, which began airing in 1964 and had a documented seventeen million viewers by the late '60s.[33] Paul Fryer contends in the journal *Popular Music and Society* that *Top of the Pops* followed a by-the-book programming formula, stripping acts of their individuality and subjecting them to the whims of the show's producers.[34] Fryer reports that *Pops* even banned audience dancing during the '70s in order to maintain its "family" environment.[35]

Top of the Pops was extremely popular and influential, and promoted only those acts that had already hit the charts. While the show kept its subversion light, it managed, with its "nonthreatening" environment, to bring the underground acts that had hit the charts into Britain's living rooms. Blondie, the Ramones, the Buzzcocks, and the Sex Pistols all appeared on the program, introducing the general public to the new underground in a way that American shows like *American Bandstand* or *Solid Gold* never did.

But as popular consumption made punk more chart-friendly, it suppressed the complexities the movement initially strove to embrace, and allowed anger to devolve into entertaining stage posturing. Subversive acts appeared on a set familiar to British viewing audiences since 1964, thus stripping them of the community which made the subculture such a threat to British culture and nearly guaranteeing a certain level of decorum deemed suitable for television. As in America, Britain's *Top of the Pops*, as well as the media's sensationalized accounts of punk's antisocial indulgences in their most extreme forms (like violence at Sex Pistols shows and the use of swastikas in fashion), along with the press' infatuation with calling punkers the "'wreckers of civilization,'"[36] as the *Daily Mail* tagged Siouxsie Sioux and others—all colluded to both demonize and dilute punk's message.

And, while punk was more easily disseminated to the masses in Britain by the centralized media, let's not forget that English punk was far more visually compelling than New York's version. There was simply more to react to and so it got more attention. U.K. punk maintained a higher energy level and conveyed a more concrete "Fuck you!," which made it more attractive to some, and more repulsive to others. The turbulent lives of the bands and scene members were constant tabloid fodder and rendered impotent a larger message of true revolution.

Due in part to the press' sensationalism, television gave punk airtime, and so a few punk artists held Top 20 chart positions. In America, the most commercially successful act to come out of CBGB, Blondie, didn't hit number one until 1979 with "Heart of Glass," followed in 1980 by "Call Me"—both songs, it could be argued, were actually pure pop. The Ramones and Television failed to hit the Top 40 at all, while the Patti Smith Group hit number thirteen in 1978 with "Because the Night" (cowritten by Bruce Springsteen). The Talking Heads' "Take Me to the River" made it to number twenty-six in 1978 and the band didn't have another hit until 1983 with "Burning Down the House." In contrast, the Sex Pistols hit number four on the U.K. charts in June 1977 with "God Save the Queen" and remained in the Top 20 for six weeks; "Pretty Vacant" hit number ten in July 1977 and stuck around for five weeks; "Holidays in the Sun" appeared in the number fifteen slot in November 1977 and stayed on the charts for five weeks. The Clash signed to CBS for £100,000 in 1977,[37] with their album climbing to number twelve on the U.K. album charts; the Jam hit number twenty; and the Damned debuted in the thirties. The Adverts' "Gary Gilmore's Eyes" hit the Top 20 in August 1977. Of course, bands that really expanded and stretched the sonic landscape of the underground, like the Slits, Poison Girls, or Subway Sect, didn't make the charts at all. Nor were they on major labels until the Slits were signed in 1979, as all of the aforementioned were.

As far as television appearances went, in addition to *Top of the Pops* and *The Old Grey Whistle Test*, the mass media coverage of punk included: the Sex Pistols on BBC1 on November 12, 1976;[38] a documentary on punk that aired regionally in the Thames region on the *London Weekend Show*;[39] and perhaps the most infamous (and entertaining) of all punk's television coverage, the December 1, 1976 *Today* show appearance by the Sex Pistols with Bill Grundy, which made the papers when Pistols entourage member Siouxsie Sioux flirted with a rowdy Grundy, and Pistols guitarist Steve Jones spewed a Tourette's-like stream of obscenities, calling Grundy a "dirty fucker" and a "dirty bastard."[40]

While all this hype might have recruited some new converts, it also bred contempt. Although more widely disseminated in England, punk was still a major threat to mainstream British life, more vilified by the day as more and more youth latched on to the shallower aspects of punk culture represented in the media, and the interest in random violence and vapid fashion prevailed. Slits singer Ari-Up recalls:

> You could really feel a witch hunt thing. I was actually stabbed in the middle of the road, in daylight. Me and [fellow Slits member] Palmolive were walking, and I had this huge dirty-old-man, big coat I was wearing—it was cold. [I was] so lucky I was wearing that with several layers, because some guy—a disco, John Travolta guy—was just like, 'Here's a slit for you!' Maybe he knew who the Slits were, but he just attacked me from the back before I could know what happened to me. I didn't even really feel the pain. . . . And I looked, and I saw my coat slit from the top right to the bottom. . . . I'm lucky it only cut my ass—the knife caught it, but I didn't feel it, the knife stabbing. . . . It never really hurt me, until after it was burning a little, but it wasn't enough to really say it was a disaster. But it really stuck in my mind, like, look at how the press [was] always trying to say that punks were the violent people. . . . [P]eople were scared of us, and cops were on us, too, that we were the violent ones. But it was the other people around us that were violent.[41]

While in retrospect it might seem that in 1977 punk was dominating the charts and taking the world (or at least England) by storm, it had more of an influence on the U.K. charts than it ever did in America. Popular acts like ABBA, Rod Stewart, Kenny Rogers, Elvis Presley, and Wings chugged along as if punk hadn't even whispered, let alone stood up and screamed.

Many of these '70s punk luminaries—bands like the Clash, the Damned, Siouxsie and the Banshees, Crass, the Raincoats, and Essential Logic (as well as Poison Girls)—and their postpunk offshoots thrived well into the '80s. Punk's simultaneous volatility and popularity in Britain pointed to its potential as a cultural force. The '80s saw bands like the Clash selling out major arenas worldwide, their videos being aired on a fledgling MTV. Punk, with a much larger and more fractious audience, would become an international household word.

Chapter 9

VOODOO DOLLY

Siouxsie Sioux

ELECTRONIC DRUMS AND SWOOPING STRINGS, MELODIES, keyboards, and samples don't necessarily scream "punk," but for Siouxsie and the Banshees, it's their signature sound that developed out of untrained noise. The Banshees' music seems prettier today partly because they have been doing it for so long and partly because, in company with the dissonant sounds of Joy Division and Echo and the Bunnymen, they inadvertently transformed atmospheric, sonic discomfort into a new aesthetic. The Banshees never intended to be punk (in fact, they reviled the label altogether), nor did they aim to be branded as "goth." In the States Siouxsie Sioux will probably be remembered longer for this goth image (however unwanted) than for the way she romped around 1970s London trailing the Sex Pistols with a young Billy Idol in tow. And while she was making music in the late '70s, it wasn't released in the United States until 1980.[1]

For all the group's fans' swooning sadness and dark romanticism, the Banshees' songs tend to focus more on the violence and horror that lurks just beneath the surface of normal-looking situations. Take "Kiss Them for Me," one of their most well-known U.S. singles: Under the fray of sweet guitar riffs and a swirling dance beat, Sioux tells the story of Jayne Mansfield's imagined last words before dying in a violent car wreck.[2] The cover of the band's 1986 album, *Tinderbox*—a framed picture of a pink and maroon rural sprawl, heavy with lush clouds—is soothing upon first glance. Examine the bottom of the picture, though, and you'll find the fierce, taut cone of a tornado snaking up into the sky behind a lonely farmhouse.

This duality has always informed the band's music and image. Beneath their campy decadence the Banshees were intent to disturb. Sioux's iconic look served the same end—the beautiful, Kabuki-like mask of makeup that frames cold, stark, unblinking eyes, is all antiglamour. Sioux wore vinyl fishnets and flaunted a hyper-real feminine sexuality that lay somewhere between Cleopatra's and a *Clockwork Orange* droog's—mixing sex with darkness. Women like Poly Styrene and Lora Logic embraced the asexually bizarre; punks like Sioux and Ari-Up flung their sensuality about, eliciting simultaneous attraction and repulsion, while many in the larger culture viewed (and still do view) punk women as "ugly" for rejecting contemporary beauty standards. Of the record industry's take on this new sexualized female rocker, Sioux recently mused, "I'm sure they just hoped we would go away. If you were a female then, you were supposed to be the male idea of what a female in a band should be like . . . like Joan Jett and the Runaways."[3] Sioux once said her fetish clothing functioned "to show that erogenous zones are overrated . . . and that tits are no big deal."[4] As noted in the Banshees' biography, the Cure's Robert Smith's own iconic look was modeled after Sioux's.[5] "I love getting into imagery," she said in 2004. "I'm still very seduced by all of that. . . . I don't really want to see a rehearsal room vibe up on stage. I would rather sit at home with my records and my candles than see this rehearsal room onstage. I do like to see someone create something visually."[6]

Born Susan Dallion in 1958, Siouxsie Sioux spent most of her childhood as a loner. She found David Bowie, circa 1972, fascinating: "[Bowie's image] was definitely the man/woman of the future and, although nothing was ever said, you understood it instinctively just by the imagery and the sounds that he used. It was about tearing down the old traditions and clichés. It was a brave new world, a springboard to accentuate your own individuality."[7] She soon became involved in the London club scene, where her sister was a dancer, and met Banshee bassist Steve Severin at a Roxy Music concert in

1975.[8] The pair were oddities in their respective suburban neighborhoods, and started attending Sex Pistols shows around London with other newfound friends, including Bill Broad (later Billy Idol). The rabid press quickly named the youthful debauchers "the Bromley Contingent."

The Banshees first appeared in September 1976 at the legendary two-day 100 Club Punk Festival with a pre-Pistol Sid Vicious on drums and Marco Perroni on guitar (later to join Adam and the Ants). The 100 Club Punk Festival is often noted as the sign that punk had taken off in London, but Severin recalled the scene differently: "[T]he whole thing was based around thirty people going to see the Sex Pistols at the 100 Club, and I'd know twenty-nine of them."[9] Their performance at the festival is still considered disastrous by the press and by the Banshees themselves. They ended up playing a savage, twenty-minute rendition of "The Lord's Prayer." "At least I knew the words to that," Sioux recalled, "and I wanted to do something beastly around religion, trash a holy cow."[10] The set might have been a sonic disaster, but victory was gained by other means. "Boom splat, boom splat, that's how Sid went," Sioux told Jon Savage in *England's Dreaming*. "It captured the spirit of how to do things: it was a shambles but something much more memorable than doing something we rehearsed."[11]

A few weeks before the notorious festival, Sioux made the news at Islington's Screen on the Green, a movie theater that hosted a Buzzcocks/Sex Pistols show. In the September 11, 1976, issue of *New Musical Express*, a photo of Sex Pistols Johnny Rotten and Steve Jones appears at the bottom right of the page, but it's Sioux's photo at the top and center, probably placed there in hopes of drawing the voyeuristic reader's attention. Charles Shaar Murray called her a "chick in S&M drag with *tits out*."[12] For the Green show Sioux had squeezed into a vinyl teddy, with cutouts for her breasts and stomach. The Banshees weren't even a band yet and they were already making the papers, as Severin explains: "Me and Siouxsie harassed Malcolm to let us support the Sex Pistols at the Screen on the Green even though we weren't a band at all," he told *The Guardian Unlimited*. "We did a five-minute rehearsal at the Clash's studio, plugged in with Sid Vicious on drums, and split up afterwards. It took us five months to do another one."[13]

And while the Sex Pistols shocked Britain with their seething hatred for the government and the royal family, Sioux elicited immediate gasps from mainstream Britain with her unabashed nudity—nudity that functioned more as a statement against sexual repression and modesty than as solely a tool of attraction. Interestingly, Murray doesn't dwell on the fact that there was also a swastika strapped to Sioux's arm during the show, a curious oversight given that his article's theme was punk's grand "fuck you" to the general establishment, musical and otherwise.

Sioux elicited a similar reaction from TV host Bill Grundy, when the Sex Pistols were hastily booked to replace the band Queen as guests on the *Today* show in December 1976. She and her cohorts were brought in to frame the Pistols. "McLaren had always had this idea that the band would have an entourage made up of the biggest freaks he could find, with Warhol's Factory as the model, and so we all went on TV," explained Severin.[14] The dimwitted, ill-prepared Grundy was drawn in by Sioux's play on sexuality and femininity but obviously missed the intended irony. In his eyes, she was either a stripper or spank-happy dominatrix. He contributed to the notoriety of both Sioux and the Sex Pistols when he egged them on to "say something outrageous"[15] on live television. Grundy openly flirted with Sioux, which, along with the Pistols' solicited invective, garnered a flood of attention from the mainstream English press.

After the infamous *Today* show aired, the Banshees (Sioux, and Severin adding a drummer and a guitarist to the lineup) started gigging around London. By 1978, the Banshees' roster consisted of Severin on bass, John McKay on guitar, and Kenny Morris on drums. (The Slits drummer Budgie would later permanently replace Morris, and the Cure's Robert Smith would serve as an on-again, off-again guitarist throughout the early '80s, followed by a string of others.)

The band released its first album, *The Scream*, on Polydor in late 1978. "Right from the start, we wanted to be timeless," commented Severin. "None of the songs were about current affairs. That was deliberate, as I saw that as the downfall of a lot of so-called 'punk' bands."[16] A string of sixteen albums and numerous chart hits followed, until the Banshees announced their official split in 1996.

Sioux has admitted to wrangling with men in the industry throughout her lengthy successful career: "I think men feel they have to say they're pro-woman, and I wonder deep down how many men actually think that. I can speak for one. I know Budgie [now Sioux's husband] is totally trustworthy and open as a person. . . . In all the years, with all the men that I've worked with, they've all had a problem. Nearly all of our managers found it awkward to talk to me, just couldn't talk to me."[17]

Although Sioux was a kindred spirit and visionary in the broiling, nonconformist air of British punk, she and the Banshees were intent on creating their own sound, on setting themselves apart, and on expanding the scope of their imagination. Punk might have continued churning out similar-sounding bands that followed in their forerunners' wake, if not for the Banshees and others like them who incorporated abstract sounds, horrific screams—created both by vocals and guitars—and tribal rhythms that helped expand the punk repertoire. Sioux's vocals were clear and haunting—at times deep and almost monotone, and at other times lilting. The Banshees' music mirrors the similar complexity of Sioux's hard, oppositional stance melded with her more mystical side. Ethereal sounds, like echoing strings, deceive the listener to the darkness that can lurk in the story of a song. Songs like "Peek-A-Boo," from the 1988 album *Peep Show*, may seem like merely dark dance music; however, the verses' lyrics hold more than the song's rather simple refrain. While the first verse describes an obedient female lover, ostensibly a sex worker who's acting both submissive and dominant depending on her partner or voyeur, the second verse returns the power to the supposedly denigrated woman, displaying the contempt with which she views her patrons; the whole song becomes a portrait of the emotionally turbulent life of a sex worker.

By the 1980s, many female voices in the underground were muffled. And while the mainstream continued to offer the typical pop-song fare, Sioux was producing music outside the realms allowable for pop stars, displaying and expressing oppressed, oft-misunderstood characters in a violent or compassionate light. The Creatures, a project started by Budgie and Sioux in 1983, is more ancient, mystic, and tribal. While the Banshees sound angrily ethereal and spooky, the Creatures, who have released six albums to date, employ a collage of percussion in their spare sound.

Sioux's enduring feminine sentiment appears in the Creatures' "Standing There," included on the 1989 album *Boomerang*, where she energetically rebukes strange, catcalling men. As with the Banshees' music, the Creatures' off-kilter sound collages are juxtaposed with lyrics that bite. Sioux and Budgie continue to record as the Creatures, but the Banshees disbanded in 1996. However, 2003 saw them reunite for what they called the Seven Year Itch tour.

Sioux's oeuvre of simultaneous lush sounds and stark imagery reflects the same complexity that fashioned an entirely new female icon. Britain's new wave allowed for all of the characteristics that normally polarize pop culture's female images. Drama, imagination, and homemade glamour were finally integrated with overt sarcasm, anger, sex, and humor, rather than appearing as singular traits of one-dimensional women. As one of the most recognizable faces of Britain's new wave pioneers, Sioux's emotional and aesthetic multiplicity stood as a very public reminder that anger and impulse weren't singularly male.

Chapter 10

NUMBER ONE ENEMY

The Slits

"THE SLITS—THAT'S THE THING WITH US, WE'RE LIKE ONE OF
them old blues people," singer Ari-Up says. "You know them old people that
are found in New Orleans in a little hut, in a little shack, with their little
guitar and their little banjo? And they're like, 'Yeah! We started the blues!'
And they never got paid shit, nothing, for starting the whole thing, you
know? That . . . reminds me of the Slits. Of course, we were totally put in
exile, we were totally sabotaged, we were totally hated, most of our reviews
were of outrage, and just, 'Ew! These girls look disgusting and they can't play
music, they can't do anything!'"[1]

Thus was the fate of the first recorded all-girl punk band from London.
The Slits were in on the dirty ground floor: bassist Tessa Pollitt came from the
Castrators, and guitarist Viv Albertine was in Flowers of Romance with Sid
Vicious and Keith Levene, later of Public Image Ltd. Ari-Up's mother, Nora,
was friends with Joe Strummer and dated the Pistols' Steve Jones; drummer
Palmolive lived with Strummer for two years, and discovered punk with him.
(Two other members, Kate Korus and Suzi Gutsy, both left to join other bands
very early on in the Slits' life.) Palmolive says, "I liked the in-your-face, and I

liked that it was crazy, and it was just different. . . . You know when you get tired of something and you just look for something else, and you go, 'Sure, why not?' I didn't take it extremely seriously, but [with] a 'Yeah, why not?' kind of attitude. And I liked the idea of dressing up. I liked the idea of being onstage."[2]

Palmolive had been planning to start an all-girl band, so she approached the fourteen-year-old Ari-Up at a gig in 1976. Neither Ari-Up nor Palmolive can remember if the band performing that fateful night was the Patti Smith Group or the Clash. Ari-Up recalls:

> The thing that stuck out to me more . . . than the gig itself was the audience. I was fascinated with how people looked. . . . The one who stuck out to me most of all was Palmolive, because she had a pig dangling from her ear—a fake one, not a real one. Well, it could be real, 'cause Viv had real Tampax hanging from her dress. So anyway, Palmolive sort of just approached me. . . . 'Cause I was still in my schoolgirl outfit, I had this long dress, long hair, and [was] really, really sort of tame looking—I was like, "How the fuck does she see through me, [know] that I'm a totally wild beast, just waiting to explode? How can she see that?" She saw it because, I think, she was just not watching the external stuff of the punk uniform, safety pin and all that shit. She was . . . very spontaneous and fiery. . . . And her main concern was, could I skip school, was I still in school, more than if I was gonna be the wrong image or hippie or whatnot.[3]

Palmolive recalled, "I found Ari and she was very crazy and I loved it, you know. She was just a brat, and I thought, 'Oh, that's great.'"[4] Albertine, however, was a different story. "Yeah, those two, they decided they were gonna have a girl band," says Ari-Up of Korus and Palmolive, "so they went to Viv with it, and she absolutely refused. She's like, 'Uh, girl? Been tried before. Gimmick, I'm not joining no gimmick, blah blah blah.' [She had a] very hostile reaction."[5, 6]

After a series of chaotic rehearsals, the girls played their first show opening for the Clash in 1977. "I remember throwing the sticks at Ari, screaming at her," Palmolive laughs. "I remember very clear[ly] my drums sliding all over the stage. I didn't know I had to hold them down. I never knew, because usually, you know, you practice at home, you put [down] a block of cement or something. But we weren't that technical. I mean, you have to consider, we had only been playing for two or three weeks, practicing at home, so you can imagine how it sounded."[7]

Things weren't much easier on Pollitt, who said, "I remember at one point onstage, me and Palmolive looked at each other in amazement as if to say, 'What the fuck are you doing?' We were all playing a different song from each other! But we got away with so much, and the audience didn't care. The energy was what mattered. We were playing from the heart. Literally. With spirit."[8]

Shortly, Albertine was after them to join the band. "The whole thing evolved into a really full, proper unit when Viv joined," Ari-Up explains. "Finally, she made up her mind. She saw us at the first show, and that was it—she chased our asses, she was stalking us, and just said . . . there can be no Slits without her, and she made sure of that. She was at every call, all day, all night; she would make sure we'd see her until we said yes. She was easy to say yes to, eventually, 'cause she looked just the part, and she sounded just the part."[9]

There are only two official recordings of the Slits' early punk years, from approximately 1977 to 1979. By their 1979 debut, *Cut*, they had found funk and dub beats, a style they continued on 1981's *Return of the Giant Slits*, before breaking up. A compilation, *Retrospective*, was put out by Rough Trade and Y Records in 1980, and a great cross-section of songs can be found on their *Peel Sessions* album, released in 1989.

For the Slits, and for Ari-Up in particular, having a female perspective is very different from the feminist label with which they're often associated. "It was more a personal thing," she says, "and being just naturally rebellious, without being told how to be rebellious, and being naturally unconditioned, trying to be unconditioned, without really forcing it. . . . We just wanted to be females without being what females were supposed to be. We just wanted to be us."[10]

Footage of the early Slits gigs reveals girls who crashed into each other and bounced all over the stage, wearing wide, almost feral, grins on their faces. Ari-Up would issue a curdling scream, splitting tightly wound London wide open. The girls never took themselves too seriously and, as a result, took musical risks that later in their career infused dub reggae in with harsh punk choruses, which elicits either extreme discomfort or avid praise.

When the Slits are recalled in print, they're usually described as feminist, with a reflexive nod to the band's name mentioned first. Original member Kate Korus thought up the name, but had not initially intended the double-entendre. "We were just thinking of an aggressive name, a short, spiky name,"

Ari-Up recalls. "So Slits to me was more like, Slits! Slitting up, slitting the knife, you know? But then, 'cause we were women, we realized there was a double edge to it, but we didn't play on it as much as people just took it as that, with a bit of a dirty mind. . . . But we weren't thinking of it like, 'Let's, yeah, let's have Slits 'cause it's pussy.' . . . Right away, we couldn't never get radio air for that, 'cause the name itself was like, 'Oh! Slits! How dare you,' you know? 'How vulgar.'"[11]

"Typical Girls" is almost always declared the Slits' feminist anthem. "It's to go against that typical image of what was constantly said to us on every magazine, on TV, every day in society," Ari-Up says.

> How we should do [everything], what we should wear, what kinda hair, what kinda clothes, what kind of relationship towards men, what attitude towards eating. I remember when my mother even used to tell me how to hold my cup, delicately, with the pinky and the ring finger up in the air, and how to be towards men, all the games that you're supposed to play, how you're supposed to eat, how you're supposed to walk . . . how you're supposed to talk . . . every day thrown in your face, and that's what "Typical Girls" was about. . . . We were very humorous, and it was very offensive to people to get a mixture of aggressiveness, to have the right and to demand to be ourselves, so don't step on us for that, 'cause we will bite off your head for it, but at the same time, to be humorous and witty and just joking about everything, and that was so offensive to people at the time, a lot of people.[12]

The Slits evolved quite a bit between 1977 and 1981. Moving from impulsive, roughly played guitar to a concentration on more rhythmic structures that reveal their affinity for reggae and dub, the Slits went from being pure punk agitators to exploring tribal sounds. Listening to the Slits today—after years of exposure to the Clash, dancehall, hip-hop, and the static, abrupt stops and starts of generations of scratching DJs—can be deceiving. This collage of rhythms, which once seemed messy, may now be more palatable to listeners.

When Ari-Up, Palmolive, Pollitt, and Albertine recorded, toured, and generally wreaked havoc, there weren't as many categories for music (or for girls, for that matter). The Slits were less focused on timing than many punk bands. Their percussion was spontaneously slowed down and sped up, causing some critics to scoff. Once Palmolive left the band and joined the Raincoats, drummer Budgie (later of the Banshees) sat in, followed by the Pop Group's

Bruce Smith: "Palmolive just sped up and slowed down and then it would sort of grind to a complete halt, you know, kind of fall apart and get back up again," Smith says. "But it was utterly unique and, as a result, you had to sort of pay attention. And if you were just there for the sort of rock and roll and the beer, then you weren't going to like it."[13] Most of that rhythm came from Palmolive's limited contact with rock and roll. "When I faced the drums," she explains, "I had a kind of virgin mind about it. . . . I didn't like the sound of the high hat so much, so I didn't use it. So when it came, it developed without me. It's not like I programmed it or I envisioned it or anything. . . . [I]t just came out like that, more, kind of a tribal . . . something. . . . It's like when you give a little kid a crayon and say, 'Okay, go make a picture.' In some way it can have a good thing about it that a sophisticated thing wouldn't have."[14]

The Slits careened through rhythms with a kind of attention deficit disorder—slowing for a bit and then kicking back in for either the chorus or the verse. In the liner notes to the *Cut* CD reissue, Albertine comments, "We consciously thought about getting girl rhythms into music and concluded that female rhythms were probably not as steady, structured, or as contained as male rhythms."[15] Ari-Up adds, "There's a very systematic pattern to boys' music—it's very, like, A, B, C, and this is where it goes, straightforward. But when you hear girls' stuff, it's like an ocean of emotion, it comes in waves. . . . It goes through these different moods . . . like the tide coming in and out, and so there's no ABC rules, there's no uniformed rules. If you even listen to girl bands now, the way they even touch the guitar, they experiment. . . . So I don't want to sound like I'm trying to categorize us being emotional and the boys are the logical. I just mean that in musical approach, they are ruled by rules more than we are."[16]

By the time the Slits were honing their punky reggae on *Cut*, Albertine noted, "people were so impressed by the album that they assumed [producer] Dennis [Bovell] played all the instruments. But the only track he played on was 'New Town.'"[17] This kind of backhanded compliment underpins the notion that only a man could "clean it up" as well as the Slits had by the time of *Cut*'s release. After all, Smith comments, it's the job of the producer to help organize ideas: "That's what you're hired to do when you're producing someone who's young and not particularly experienced," he says. "That's your job, is to try and [say], 'Okay, what you want to do is this.' . . . And then to try and bring that along and introduce someone to what it means to make a record, because it's a totally different experience than just going out there and blasting for half an hour or so. Records are . . . a completely different thing, and you have no idea of that when you're nineteen, eighteen years old, or whatever they were. . . . They worked very hard, and I know that they did, but I don't think for a moment that how that record sounded was not how they wanted it to sound—not one bit. I'm absolutely convinced that they were extremely happy about that. That really, they were striving for that all along. They just didn't know how to do it."[18]

Although their punk brothers were supportive, the girls still had to deal with the larger culture's rejection of anything outside of traditional standards of beauty for women. "That really got them upset," explains Ari-Up, "because walking on the street, they didn't know how we sounded. I mean, it was just the way we looked, [that] was just enough to get them crazy. And ugly, oh! . . . It was just like, 'How can girls do that? How dare they,' you know? 'How ugly, how disgusting!' It was really wild. And the guys got it too, but then [with] the girls, like, women, it was just too much."[19]

The Slits were one of the acts on the famed White Riot tour of 1977, along with Subway Sect, the Jam, and the Clash. "[I]t was a boys' club thing," Ari-Up says of the tour, "where it was allowed for the boys to wreck the hotels, to be totally insane, doing whatever the fuck they liked, and that was okay with the bus driver. But we, who even didn't carry on half . . . [as] outrageously as the boys, the bus driver had to be bribed to let us on. Yeah, they had to pay money just to let us on the bus sometimes. He refused to drive us."[20]

With that same driver at the wheel, filmmaker Don Letts stripped as the bus bounced down the highway. "He pulled down his pants and showed his ass out the window to everybody. Because that was a funny thing to us, the shock reaction—not that it was just that, but because there was so much racism still going on back then, and to see a black ass out the window, you know, it's really showing, 'Fuck you all! This is the new generation coming up!' And it was still more acceptable. He wasn't thrown out by the bus driver, but the Slits were."[21]

Ari-Up also sang with the New Age Steppers, a dub collaboration of postpunk artists, who released their first album in 1980. These days, she's performing with a new band called Ari-Up and the True Warriors, tramping between New York and Jamaica, and designing her own clothes.

Palmolive is now a born-again Christian, and lives with her husband and children in Massachusetts, where she does video editing and teaches. Albertine, it's last heard, was a producer for the BBC, and Pollitt lives in West London.

As ABBA crammed their cherubic charm down Europe's collective throat, while the Clash and the Sex Pistols knotted their rhythms around "male" notions of speed, hooks, and verse-chorus-verse, the Slits tore punk's tempo down. More than anything, the girls reinvented punk to suit themselves. Hardly "Typical Girls" and all the better for it, the Slits often take a back seat to their groundbreaking male compatriots. "Number One Enemy," indeed—and sorely overdue for a revival.

Chapter 11

THE DAY THE GIRLS TURNED DAY-GLO

Lora Logic and Poly Styrene

There was so much junk then. The idea was to send it all up.
Screaming about it, saying: "Look, this is what you have done to me,
turned me into a piece of Styrofoam, I am your product. And this is
what you have created: Do you like her?"[1]

—POLY STYRENE

THE BEST OF BRITISH PUNK WAS INTENT ON DULLING THE SHEEN
of mainstream British society, revealing the ugly and the angry underbelly of
a population struggling under a fading empire and a limp economy. While the
Sex Pistols and the Clash both championed a raw candor about the state of
Britain in their individual ways, X-Ray Spex employed and embraced cultural
kitsch as a means to the same end. They were loud and angry, but X-Ray Spex
were also colorful, like a garish umbrella traveling down a bleak and foggy
road in London's East End. While other bands embraced an assault of the
senses, X-Ray Spex seemed to come from left field. And as 1977's punk yielded
to its own brand of fashion and compulsive consumption, X-Ray Spex spoke
of the downfalls of materialism and the excessive plasticity of popular culture.
Exemplifying their capitalist critique are trademark songs found on X-Ray

Spex's 1978 LP, *Germ Free Adolescents*: "The Day the World Turned Day-Glo," "I Am a Cliché," and their most enduring classic, "Oh Bondage, Up Yours!" (which was not on the original LP, but was added to the 1993 reissue).

As a teenager, Poly Styrene (née Marion Elliot) ran a small clothing stand in London's Beaufort Market. According to *England's Dreaming*, she would design new items made from old leftover stock. "[I]t was meant to be an extreme version of tack," she said of her designs.[2] She was soon drawn to the honest ugliness of punk, and submitted an ad to the weekly *Melody Maker*, looking for "Young punx who want to stick it together."[3] The ad attracted a teenaged, artistic rebel from Wembley named Susan Whitby. Susan had been playing saxophone for three years, honing her own sound and listening to David Bowie and Roxy Music. "I started [playing sax] when I was thirteen years old," Whitby (who soon changed her name to Lora Logic) says. "I chose the sax because my parents wanted me to learn an instrument at school. I was bored with the usual piano, violin, guitar lessons which I had already tried. I was not very inspired by the way those instruments were taught at school. I saw the sax could more easily cross over into pop music."[4]

Elliot's ad in *Melody Maker* led to band auditions. "They just appeared," said Elliot of the other future members of X-Ray Spex.[5] After changing her name, Logic showed up at the Spex audition. According to Logic, X-Ray Spex's manager was interested in signing men on for the project, but saw the potential of having a female on sax instead.[6] Logic's sax proved to be a huge contribution to the band's sound; she offered blissful saxophone yelps in response to Styrene's screaming condemnations.

Logic recalls a near-instant musical camaraderie and immediately felt drawn to Styrene. "We just seemed to click, like we'd known each other before. I thought [Poly] was wonderful, bubbly, creative, and completely alternative. We were both wearing the same sort of granny clothes, too."[7] When the media celebrated the twenty-fifth anniversary of punk, Styrene told *The Guardian Unlimited*, "Straightaway I was in the papers because it was different enough to be interesting—I wasn't like Carly Simon, I had short hair and braces on my teeth. I used to wear an army helmet with goggles, plus a pair of stilettos and Day-Glo socks that didn't match."[8] Styrene's Day-Glo socks and stilettos would become the wardrobe fare of many new wave women during the '80s.

X-Ray Spex started performing in 1977, and their first gig was at punk home base the Roxy. Logic comments: "[I]t was pretty wacky—there was hardly room on the stage for the band. I remember the boy with a glowing electric light bulb in his ear, the safety pins, pogoing up to the ceiling, boys bashing heads with each other 'til they bled. I was a wee bit scared. But we all liked the freedom of expression and individuality like we'd never experienced before, and which, to my knowledge, had never occurred in the music scene before. I think everyone was conscious of the historical significance."[9] She recalls "stand[ing] quite still amongst all the chaos," much as her sax acted as a musical adhesive to Styrene's from-the-gut wailing.

Unlike their female contemporaries in the Slits and the Adverts, X-Ray Spex didn't come under the same kind of critical fire for making "bad" music, or not "playing well." Their sound and their melodies were tighter than most bands', and they had a distinct, energetic pop edge that might have made the Spex slightly more accessible than grittier acts. They are considered one of the best of 1977's British punk alumni, a band that offered a bizarre and garish vision of the world—from their sci-fi-inspired name to their polyester visions of greed and decay. In *Spin* magazine's coverage of punk's twenty-fifth anniversary, *Germ Free Adolescents* is named one of the "fifty most essential" punk albums of all time, beaten only by records from the Ramones, Wire, X, and the Clash.[10]

Styrene and Logic were not playing with contemporary notions and markers of female sexuality in the same ways as were contemporaries Siouxsie Sioux and legendary British scenester Jordan, though. "It was refreshing to not have to conform to the traditional posturing of women in bands that you see all the time. Poly and I came across as naturally asexual—two people who came onstage carrying Day-Glo plastic shopping baskets and plastic rats," Logic remembers.[11] Styrene was even quoted as saying, "I would shave me 'ead tomorrow if I became a sex symbol!"[12] Which she did—at Johnny Rotten's apartment prior to a concert at Victoria Park. As Mark Paytress recounts on the liner notes for the 2002 compilation *The Anthology*, Jah Wobble, Rotten's longtime friend and bassist for his postpunk venture, Public Image Ltd., once described Styrene as a "strange girl who often talked of hallucinating. She freaked John out."[13] So few women were threatening enough to effectively scare men out of preconceived visions of the restrictive gender roles that were invariably carried over into the 1970s; it is funny to imagine Rotten, so frightening to the press himself, terrified by a nineteen-year-old girl with braces.

X-Ray Spex, and particularly Poly Styrene, are often seen as having been a directly feminist force in British punk, especially their popular, "Oh Bondage, Up Yours!" The song is introduced by Styrene, with her usual snide glee, bucking the notion of girls' obedience before bursting into song.[14] This line aside, the feminism of X-Ray Spex more generally stems more from Styrene and Logic's insistence upon individuality and originality in a scene already falling prey to repetitive interpretations by the mainstream media and fans alike. Where U.K. punk is known mostly for humorless rage, Styrene and Logic were joyfully angry, liberated by the freedom punk afforded them. And amid all the jubilant chaos, they were able to provide a solid, relevant social commentary.

The feminist label placed upon female musicians is still a journalistic reflex, especially with punk. Patti Smith and Chrissie Hynde are often represented as feminists, even though both have stated an artistic agenda over a personal or political one on numerous occasions. In the same way, Styrene's "Bondage" is frequently interpreted to mean liberation from female bondage, as opposed to her reference to freedom from capitalist bondage. Logic says,

> I think Marion felt that everyone was in a type of bondage—restricted, crushed, and alienated by modern materialistic society. The goal of our society is sense gratification—that is the only prize on offer. But one can never satisfy the senses; it is an impossible goal. I know she saw, and still sees, modern civilization as divisive and cruel to the spirit of both men and women. No societal conventions were going to hold her back, least of all the role normally assigned to women. When she sat down to write her lyrics, I doubt she thought to herself, "Now, let me see how I can forward the feminist agenda." But being a strong girl with things to say, I am sure she naturally gave other girls the confidence to express themselves, too, whereas before they may not have had such a vocal "girl-next-door" type of role model. [15]

While Styrene shaped the world as she saw it in her lyrics, Logic was sculpting her own freeform saxophone sounds. She often produced staccato wails that faded quickly, like those of a sax player whizzing by in a car—a sound not often heard in punk, particularly from an instrument so strongly associated with jazz.

According to Lora, after returning from a Russian vacation with her parents in late 1977, she called to find out about the band's next rehearsal. "'Didn't you know? We've got a new saxophonist.' He copied all my sax parts and I was out of the band. There had been some reviews saying that the sax sound *was* X-Ray-Spex, and the manager told me [Poly] felt threatened by another female presence attracting attention. I think Marion is an enormously talented person, but not the easiest person to stay close to, or work with."[16] Earlier, drummer Rich Tea was asked to leave the band for refusing to cut his hair—one of the trademark ways in which punks symbolically separated themselves from the idealism of the 1960s hippie era. (It's also symbolic of the way punk strayed from its ethic of individualism and toward more uniform behavior.)

After leaving the Spex, Logic attended art school before assembling her own project, Essential Logic. "I had no intention of going back to music. I was quite disillusioned by the hurtful experience I'd had with Marion. However, a chap called Geoff Mann kept approaching me to record a single. He had his own label, Cells. I said I didn't have a band so he told me to put one together. Eventually I succumbed, and rang Rich Tea."[17]

Essential Logic, although underrated in comparison to the Spex, did allow Logic to stand apart as sax player, songwriter, and singer, to much critical success. Essential Logic's music is haunting and danceable at the same time. X-Ray Spex's trademark undercurrent of sliding sax shifts form in Essential Logic, as Logic wails against stop-start postpunk beats. Her exit from the Spex might have been less than harmonious, but Essential Logic became the perfect vehicle for her to express her own personality.

Greil Marcus once wrote of Essential Logic, "[T]he woman in the lead is so unusual, so full of nerve and good ideas, that she can make most everything else on or off the radio seem cowardly and complacent, a failure of brains or will or both, the result of compromises likely not evident even to those who've made them."[18] Essential Logic produced three albums between 1979 and 1982 and two LPs in 2001 and 2002; they continue to release music online.

After a mystical breakdown/vision in 1978, twenty-one year old Poly Styrene decided to quit punk in favor of a spiritual path, and eventually joined a Hare Krishna sect, as Lora Logic had also done when she was eighteen. As Logic recounts: "I had a close school friend who had given up her rock and roll life, and moved into a temple on Soho street. I saw an amazing change in her for the better, and so I also started visiting the temple. I was very attracted by their motto, 'Simple living, high thinking.' Getting up early and chanting the Hare Krishna mantra helped me give up drinking, smoking, and drugs— things I had wanted to give up before, but could never find the inner strength to leave behind."[19] Logic collaborated with Styrene again in 1995 for a new X-Ray Spex release, *Conscious Consumer*, and later participated in a short-lived "reunion," sans Styrene. "It was put together with another singer and I played with them for a tour, but you can't really have it without Poly."[20]

In 2002, Castle released X-Ray Spex's *Anthology*, which includes all of *Germ Free Adolescents*, as well as live tracks, demos, and a few '90s releases. Logic now lives in India with her husband and children, and Styrene is a Hare Krishna priestess living in London with her husband. One album may seem like a blip on the radar against the heftier discographies of other punk bands, but X-Ray Spex, particularly Styrene and Logic, infused the scene with their own punk-fueled, antimaterialist vision, and made quite a mark— no small feat in a country that saw the blossoming of countless distinctive bands during that period.

Against the increasing societal impulse that responds to marketing and consumption over the support of honest art, their message transcends British politics in the '70s. Their energetic anticapitalist message grows more potent as our collective need for consumption swells to a frightening high. Twenty-five years later, Styrene's shrieking still sounds more than nostalgic; Logic's sax conjures even more bliss and power against the dearth of new sounds in today's punk. Sadly, what may have seemed like paranoia about the world's marketplace and its effect on modern life in 1977 has become a reality in 2004. Take the assault on society's abundance of useless information from their song "Plastic Bag," in which Styrene highlights the madness of advertising and the drain it has on culture. She describes her mind as a retainer for the urge toward consumption, and portrays herself as confused, eating a meal of Kleenex and using Weetabix as tissue. In all of their work, the Spex were able to foresee not only the future of music, but the end result of the consumerism Styrene so reviles. Both their music and their message remain timely and foreboding.

Chapter 12

SHAVED WOMEN, COLLABORATE!

Joy de Vivre and Eve Libertine

AFTER THE CLASH, THE SEX PISTOLS, THE BUZZCOCKS, AND THE Jam had been signed and antiheroism became iconoclastic; once punk had warped into faddish fashion and imitation over individuality, by 1978, Crass, along with the bands they played with—Poison Girls, Flux of Pink Indians, Dirt, and others—stood as the true conscience of Johnny Rotten's cry for "Anarchy in the U.K." The political venom they spit was out of concern for the human race; the populist, anarchist collective reminded the safety-pinned masses of punk's original message—mostly lost in the mire of media misrepresentation and fan behavior—"There is no authority but yourself."

Crass was a collective of artists living communally in a farmhouse in Essex, growing their own vegetables, and releasing their own records and those of other bands on the Crass label. They produced art and films, staged protests and acts of artistic and political insurrection, and reinvigorated the waning antiwar movement in Britain. Crass cofounder, drummer, songwriter, and commune founder Penny Rimbaud quipped in the preface to Crass' book of lyrics, *Love Songs*, that the Sex Pistols "were just about as radical as a good old British rail sandwich: plenty of plastic wrap and no content."[1] Or, as their song "Punk Is Dead," on their first album, *The Feeding of the 5000*, declares:

> Movements are systems and systems kill.
> Movements are expressions of the public will.
> Punk became a movement 'cause we all felt lost,
> But the leaders sold out and now we all pay the cost . . . .
>
> Well, I'm tired of looking through shit stained glass,
> Tired of staring up a superstar's arse.
> I've got an arse and crap and a name,
> I'm just waiting for my fifteen minutes of fame.[2]

Crass' motivations went far deeper than the mere criticism of punk as a movement, yet they still stand as an urgent reminder for revisionists that the "leaders" of the first generation of punk in the U.K. were only as revolutionary as they were reactionary to the mainstream. The political punk that Crass embodied envisioned an anarchy beyond what had become a mere expletive directed at the Queen. Their brand of revolution was in direct response to the mindless devotion and hollow incantations into which punk had quickly dissolved.

This peace/punk/anarchist/artist collective started when Rimbaud's rundown farmhouse was christened a commune in 1968. He met his first commune cohort, Gee Vaucher, in art school; she would create the signature Crass visual art—grand collages that set middle-class, apple-pie images against a backdrop of war and destruction. Steve Ignorant—whose searing Cockney voice places the band at the crux of punk and London's desperate working class—began collaborating with Rimbaud in 1977. They were soon joined by the other members of the collective: guitarist Phil Free, bassist Pete Wright, N.A. Palmer on rhythm guitar, and eventually, haunting vocalists Eve Libertine and Joy de Vivre. According to Rimbaud's autobiography, *Shibboleth*, the band's original name, Stormtrooper, eventually changed to Crass at Ignorant's suggestion. He was inspired by a line in David Bowie's "Ziggy Stardust."[3]

Libertine recalls, "Before I joined the band, I always went along to the gigs and was always moved by the raw energy. In the early days Crass quite often emptied venues, leaving me about the only person in the audience. Following a one-off series of gigs in New York, I began to feel there was a rather one-dimensional quality to what was then an all-male outfit—the onstage politics lacked a feminist angle, a problem that was easily solved by Joy and myself joining the band."[4]

"I went [to Dial House, the Crass commune] as a gawky, stuttering fifteen-year-old," de Vivre recalls. "[I]t was close to where I lived and anyone with a question mark in their head and rebellion stirring in their heart heard about the place and ventured across the fields to find it. Gee and Penny had created a sort of haven out of the crooked, rambling cottage, which, although dark and pokey, seemed full of light and space. The look of the place was so different to what I'd known—there was no obvious furniture, no TV, and, probably to the surprise of local youth, no drugs—which suited me. I was a bit of a misfit among my peers. I felt utterly drawn to the place but at the same time, strangely intimidated. I just kept going, watching, listening, helping in the garden. I remember being either mute or ramblingly incoherent as I tried to understand and be understood."[5]

Very few punk bands at the time included feminism under a general banner of political philosophy without being interpreted as singularly feminist. Furthermore, few bands that included men were seeing feminism in the light in which Rimbaud and Ignorant were, albeit at Libertine's urging. She explains, "[W]hen *Penis Envy* was released, to avoid the inevitable stereotyping that would have occurred, Rimbaud and Ignorant represented it on radio to emphasize that the feminism that it promoted was an issue that involved both women and men."[6] To Crass, feminism was wrapped up in the complete undoing of societal structures and culturally created boundaries that they envisioned. As de Vivre says, "The most obviously feminist lyrics did come from the women, but the feminist element was as deeply rooted in our spectrum of ideas as pacifism was—we were none of us more or less inclined toward these philosophies."[7] Sexism was one of countless issues Crass were concerned with, and they should not be viewed solely as a feminist band. De Vivre later contends, "It is not easy to isolate feminist activities of the band, they're so tied in with the wider philosophy about compassion, respect, pacifism. We sprayed neat stenciled messages onto sexist advertisements . . . we were just as likely to do the same to ads that limited and oppressed men."[8]

Like their engagement in all art forms—from visual to aural to guerrilla street actions like graffiti—Crass attacked with antiwar messages; reminders of Hiroshima and the threat of nuclear war; critiques of the tyranny of capitalism, religion, classism, imperialism, sexism, racism, and

Thatcherism, among many other complex systems of oppressive Western culture. They were working to infuse empty punk and listless radicalism with ideals enlivened by top-to-bottom revolution. This well-rounded, attack-from-all-sides philosophy extended and informed their stage shows, as well. "Crass' live performances were extremely tight, one song flowing into another," de Vivre describes. "TV sets as backdrop, showing images of horror, beauty, banality, accentuating the lyrics and the sounds. Huge banners frame the stage, starkly spray-painted with symbols and statements. Mick Duffield's films preceded each performance."[9]

Crass presented issues, but had enough respect for its listening audience to allow them to make their own informed decisions. In a 1983 interview for *Maximumrocknroll*, the band (who conducted interviews as a collective and left individual names out of their responses) said, "[T]his refusal of ours to hand out crutches has been one of the major sources of attack on us—that we have always given the questions, not the answers. The answers are the crutches, and everyone has their own individual answer. . . . All we can do is ask the questions, and destroy the answers from any answer that develops."[10]

Pointing out the ways in which sexism traps men and women, punks and nonpunks, and society and the government was incorporated into Crass' overall philosophy, and took the form of activism, performance, and songwriting. Even before the 1981 release of *Penis Envy*, an album that dealt specifically with sexism and featured lead vocals by Libertine and de Vivre exclusively, feminism was prevalent in Crass' work. On the 1978 album *The Feeding of the 5000*, a song written by de Vivre entitled "Women" was included. She recalls, "I didn't think of becoming involved with performances until I wrote 'Women' in the winter [of 1977] and very nervously but with determination, got up on stage and yelled the poem through a drowning, surging mayhem of feedback, pounding, chaotic chords, and erratic, rackety drumming." De Vivre's lyrics did much of what the women's movement didn't do at the time, and what the riot grrrl phenomenon would lay claim to in the 1990s: She wrote from a nonacademic perspective, making feminism every woman, every radical, and every punk's issue:

Fuck is women's money.
We pay with our bodies.
There is no purity in motherhood,
No beauty,

Just bribery.
It's all the fucking same.
We are all slaves to our sexual histories.[12]

The opening track on the same album, "Reality Asylum," is an intense rant against Christianity, specifically the symbolism of the crucifixion. Libertine's voice quakes with anger and is set against a droning, discordant organ and far-off operatic wailing. Venomous words spit from her mouth, her emotions unraveling as she accuses Christ and the Church of, among many other offenses, "cuntfear."[13] The rant clearly crosses gender—as it is an excerpt from Rimbaud's book *Christ's Reality Asylum*, and as Christianity has, of course, greatly impacted men as well as women. Libertine's voice is particularly effective and moving in rejecting the Christian guilt complex, conveying the suffering of humanity, and listing the failures of the church, especially when considering the church's long history of brutally oppressing women. When Crass first pressed *The Feeding of the 5000*, "Reality Asylum" was replaced by a minute of silence entitled "The Sound of Free Speech" because every pressing plant they approached refused to print the album, largely due to the song's controversial lyrics and the album's artwork. (The Southern Records reissue does include the track.)

Penis Envy allowed Crass free rein to address feminism, and as Rimbaud wrote in *Shibboleth*, "Our sexual politics, although forcefully expressed in all our past albums, have largely been ignored. So, with nothing but the slightest whisper of male voices, Eve Libertine and Joy de Vivre fronted an assault that introduced our primarily male audience to a whole range of fresh ideas."[14] When asked if punk fans balked at the album made from a feminist point of view, Libertine responds, "Overall, the reaction was positive, although there were a few punks who objected to a record with 'just girls on it.' Surprisingly, the press seemed to like the album, but that was completely undermined by their saying at the same time that the women in the band 'were attractive enough to be taken seriously.' Since that time, it is clear from the feedback that I have received over the years that the album has had a hugely positive effect on women, and also men, from all over the world."[15]

"The Crass women's album didn't come out of the blue," de Vivre says, "but it was still a lot different from what other women were doing in punk. The stupid stuff about 'ugly women' had been used already by the dimwit music press . . . except that in our case the journalist who was hooked on the idea conceded that the women in Crass weren't ugly . . . actually quite attractive . . . very sad, very insulting. And that such ideas still hold sway is laughable and horrible."[16]

For *Penis Envy*'s final track, de Vivre and Phil Free wrote a horribly sentimental, sickeningly sweet satirical love song entitled "Our Wedding." Read by de Vivre over what Rimbaud described as "a backing track of silky strings,"[17] the lyrics read:

> All I am I give to you,
> you honor me, I'll honor you.
> Reaching for each other, come what may,
> We'll forsake all other love.
> Just we the two, one flesh one blood,
> In the eyes of God.
> I am yours to have and hold,
> I'm giving you my life
> Never look at anyone but me,
> Never look at anyone, I must be all you see,
> Listen to those wedding bells,
> Say goodbye to other girls.
> I'll never be untrue, my love,
> Don't be untrue to me . . .[18]

Palmer, posing as a record rep, offered the song to the teen romance magazine *Loving*. The magazine bought the song and printed it on a bridal-white flexi-disk, which it distributed in copies of the magazine. The album version of "Our Wedding" was aptly described by de Vivre as having featured "bells descending into miserable washes of sound at the finish," while the flexi-disk version was given to *Loving* without its distorted ending.[19] The magazine suffered great embarrassment when Crass' very public deception was revealed.

Legal troubles hounded Crass from the start. The same larger culture that had subsequently leapt upon punk as a movement after shallowly sensationalizing it began hindering Crass' ability to have their message widely heard. Libertine explains:

> [The single "Reality Asylum" from *The Feeding of the 5000*] led to us being investigated by the police "Vice Squad" who threatened us with prosecution under archaic blasphemy laws. Eventually, the case was dropped. We were given a strict warning "not to do it again," which was of course, to us, like a red rag to a bull. From then on, rather than

attacking us directly, the authorities adopted the policy of harassing those with whom we dealt, making it increasingly difficult to organize gigs or find shops that were prepared to sell our records. It was obvious to us that this policy was one that enabled the authorities to limit our activities without creating the media coverage that would have resulted from more direct attacks.

We were under constant surveillance by MI5 (the British Secret Service), who made little pretence of their interest. We were featured on numerous government files and were the subject of several investigations by government agencies. We were banned by the BBC (almost certainly on MI5's insistence). When *Penis Envy* entered the national charts at number 16, the next week, when sales had rocketed, it didn't even appear in the Top 100.[20]

Crass famously created a tape meant to be a phone conversation between Ronald Reagan and Margaret Thatcher, in which Thatcher takes responsibility for the deadly loss of an enemy ship during the Falkland Islands War and Reagan threatens to nuke Europe. After much speculation about it being an act on the part of the KGB, a newspaper approached Crass about the "Thatchergate" tapes, and the band tumbled into a vortex of media attention.

Not long after the infamous Thatchergate and another obscenity charge, Crass disbanded in 1984, as they had vowed to do from the start. By this time, Free said, the band was taking itself as seriously as everyone else was. "After seven years on the road, we had become the very thing we were attacking," reads *Best Before*'s liner notes. "We had found a platform for our ideas, but somewhere along the line had lost our insight. Where once we had been generous and outgoing, we had now become cynical and inward. Our activities had always been colored with lightness and humor, now we saw that we had been drawn toward darkness and an ill-conceived militancy."[21]

The band and, eventually, the members of the commune, began to go their separate ways, but Rimbaud and Libertine's work would sporadically surface over the years. "At the beginning [of 2003]," Libertine says, "Penny, Gee, and myself created the Crass Agenda, working with jazz musicians, filmmakers, and dancers in regular performances of Penny's new writings. We have a monthly show at one of London's leading jazz venues."[22] De Vivre hasn't performed since leaving Crass, but says, "I've been working on writing and illustrating children's stories, recovering my desire to paint. I write poetry but I haven't performed except for once at an antiwar event in November 2002. . . . My life is not as overtly political as it once was, but I try to be conscious of what I am creating in everything I do . . . even working in a bookshop. My creativity doesn't always reflect the political, but if it isn't political, I hope it's celebratory, a reaction to the gift of life."[23]

That is the continuing beauty of Crass and, in effect, what Crass was: "a reaction to the gift of life." By fostering individuality, anarchy, and peace—concepts that remain threatening to established culture and the conformity on which so much power tenuously rests—Crass has not received the mainstream recognition afforded less troublesome bands like the Sex Pistols. But Crass and its legacy are a lasting reminder of the optimism, spirit, and potential of the 1970s punk movement and best refute the claim that punk is violent or ignorant—and that it was always a male concern. In the end, Crass erased gender altogether. Their own words embody their best lesson: "You're the only you."[24]

Chapter 13

SHOUTING OUT LOUD

The Raincoats

ARRHYTHMIC, CHAOTIC POLITICAL COMMENTARY EMERGED from and swirled around three girls with no formal training—violinist Vicky Aspinall, guitarist/vocalist Ana da Silva, and bassist/vocalist Gina Birch, along with an ever-changing percussion section. These three broke from punk's delivery-by-assault method, incorporating world music instruments and sounds, a pounding bass drum, and tribal percussion. The Raincoats were more punk in ideology than what straightforward punk had become by 1979. Their sound seemed to emerge from thin air and their rumpled clothing and knotty hair was a departure from what had become the standard punk girl uniform—the vinyl, pierced, cat-eyed creations. The Raincoats embodied the punk creed of independent thinking, reinvention, and resistance.

By 1979, the enviable shock that belonged to the Sex Pistols and the quaking passion of the Clash had become de rigeur in London. And these two bands had become the standard bearers of rebellion. The sound, too, had become familiar; the bands so famous it seemed the time had come for the underground to reinvent itself again. The Raincoats were not the only band, nor the only women, who defected from punk for the more political and avant-garde world now classified as "postpunk": Among others, Essential Logic, Liliput, Kleenex, the Delta 5, and the Au Pairs all shuffled away from punk in favor of experimentalism. Each new project usurped the space punk had cleared incorporating more obscure lyrics, many of them based in feminism and leftist politics; broken rhythms, often inspired by dub and reggae; and unsteady vocal sounds, all in the lawless scope of the young underground.

Gina Birch and Ana da Silva became friends while attending art school in London in the mid-'70s. Da Silva grew up in Madeira, Portugal, and moved to London to attend Hornsey Art College in 1974. As a child, she took piano lessons, and she bought her first guitar as a teenager.[1] Da Silva was immediately taken with the freedom of expression she found in her new home. "I just felt so excited to see all these people dressed in different things," she recalls. "I went to a couple of gigs and things like that. I just thought that was the place to be because people could just be something different from everybody else and nobody even bothered looking."[2] The most contact Birch, who had moved to the city from Nottingham, had with making her own music up until then was strumming along to Joan Baez and Bob Dylan. "I remember when I came to London," Birch said, "I had about four albums with me. I had a Prince Buster album, I had *Sgt. Pepper*, and I had a Melanie album, I think the first one. And I had Toots and the Maytals' *Funky Kingston*."[3]

Following a few early attempts at collaboration, Palmolive, who had grown unhappy with the Slits, joined the lineup on drums. "Something in me was very dissatisfied," Palmolive explains. "Plus, [we had] the regular tensions of having four very strong personalities [in the Slits]. You know, but there were specific things that were happening, and I took a stand, and so that didn't compute too good. . . . Personality-wise, we [the Slits] just didn't get on."[4] As it had with the Slits, Palmolive's tribal, off-kilter style contributed heavily to the Raincoats' ever-changing sound. Shirley O'Loughlin became the trio's manager. The group slapped a notice looking for a violinist up on a record store wall, and found Vicky Aspinall, who generally played in an extremely high pitch, as if she'd wound the instrument's strings too tightly.

In their performances, Birch remembered, the group made a distinct decision to toss out the theatricality so many other bands had adopted. "[W]e really learned in public," she said in 1996, "and we were never really into a kind of idea of show business. And we were quite shy, really. Groups like the Slits, Ari-Up, and Palmolive, they really liked to show off. I really like that, I'm not saying it's a bad thing. But we were never like that. . . . [I]t was like watching a process, which the audience kind of felt they were privileged to kind of spy in on."[5] But the Raincoats' vision wasn't always as plain to their audiences. "The whole experience was empowering, but many people didn't know what to make of us," Birch once explained. "We were a strange, unexplained presence. We didn't fit in and as a result, we were sometimes looked down upon."[6]

Rough Trade released their first album, *The Raincoats*, in 1980 followed by *Odyshape* in 1981, the 12" EP *Animal Rhapsody* in 1983, and *Moving* in 1984. Feeling estranged from punk and seeking spirituality, Palmolive left soon after their first album was completed. She was replaced by Ingrid Weiss, and subsequent Raincoats albums feature various drummers. Palmolive says, "I thought it was the people, and then after six months with [the Raincoats], I realized it wasn't the personalities. There was something in punk that was very dead, really. And the whole music business was very corrupt—I didn't want anything to do with it. So, after six months, I decided to leave the Raincoats and leave the whole scene."[7] She later explained one of the moments when it became clear to her that the subculture was isolating for her: "I remember [leaving] a gig one time. I decided to go with earplugs to the gigs—you still could hear because it was so loud. But it [was] like I got a high out of being a little detached. . . . You see everything in perspective somehow; it sends you somewhere else. So I was in this kind of mode, like just looking around. I put [in] my earplugs, and I saw the kids coming out of a gig that I had played, and they looked so wasted. They all drank or whatever. . . . You know, I really felt I had a responsibility, that I gave them that, I helped that."[8]

Four years after Palmolive's departure Reach Out International Records released *The Kitchen Tapes*, capturing a particularly joyful performance at the Kitchen in New York City. By 1983, the Raincoats had a straight world beat sound, with strong wailing vocals, and left-field clicking and chirping instruments that crept in around violins and bass drums. They seemed to stuff any kind of sound that excited them into their songs. The result was a cacophony of noise sounding like the band inhabited a Celtic rainforest populated with Amazon women.

Birch cited their painstakingly democratic process as part of the drain that led to the group's split in 1984. This same "democratic process" might also explain the concentration of different noises they incorporated, as well. Afterward Birch played briefly with the experimental Red Krayola, but none of the Raincoats completely invested themselves in another music project again, aside from da Silva, who scored some films. Public interest in the Raincoats waned until Kurt Cobain began invoking their name as an influence. While in London, Cobain tracked da Silva down at the antique store where she worked, looking for a copy of the first Raincoats album. In the liner notes for *Incesticide*, Cobain wrote: "A few weeks later I received a vinyl copy of that wonderfully classic scripture with a personalized dust sleeve covered with Xeroxed lyrics, pictures, and all the members' signatures. There was also a touching letter from Ana. It made me happier than playing in front of thousands of people each night, rock-god idolization from fans, music industry plankton kissing my ass, and the million dollars I made last year. It was one of the few really important things that I've been blessed with since becoming an untouchable boy genius."[9]

In 1993, Cobain and his wife, Courtney Love, convinced the label their bands were both signed to, Geffen, to reissue *The Raincoats* and *Odyshape* (for which Sonic Youth's Kim Gordon, also on DGC, wrote the liner notes), as well as a new Raincoats record, *Looking in the Shadows*, that arrived in 1996. Cobain's connection with da Silva led the Raincoats to re-form and open for Nirvana on their European tour. (The American leg of the tour was cut short by Cobain's suicide in 1994.) Sonic Youth's Steve Shelley, who joined the Raincoats as their tour drummer, released the *Extended Play* EP on his Smells Like Records label in 1994. Birch dove into directing videos during the Raincoats' renaissance, and later formed the Hangovers, who released the 1998 album *Slow Dirty Tears* on Kill Rock Stars. Even in their '90s reincarnation the Raincoats retained their trademark authenticity onstage, prompting the *Boston Phoenix* to write, "We'd become used to punk's disdain for the very notion of rock stars. What took place on stage that night went deeper. Forgotten lyrics, muffled notes, and all, the show confirmed that sometimes the most energizing and exhilarating and shocking thing performers can do is to speak as themselves, and that such honesty is a means for making the most immediate connection with an audience."[10]

Besides stepping away from the stale orchestration of choreographed performances, the Raincoats and other previously mentioned postpunk artists aimed to separate themselves from traditional rhythms, but not merely for the sake of experimentation. "The basic theme in rock and roll is what goes on between men and women," they told Greil Marcus in 1980. "Rock and roll is based on black music. And it's based *in* the exclusion of women and the ghettoization of blacks. Which is why we want to put a little distance between what we do and the rock and roll tradition."[11] The result is a clash of sounds, instruments, and effects.

"When we started, we didn't say, 'Let's form a feminist band,'" da Silva told *Billboard*. "But by merely starting a band and defying stereotypes, we became one. I'd rather have us considered on musical terms, as well, however."[12] The Raincoats were a distinctly female band, though. Early on, they recorded a rousing cover of the Kinks' "Lola," desegregating the content men and women were expected to stick to in pop music and creating stark, spare instrumentation in comparison to the smooth acoustic guitar that accompanies the original. While often overtly feminist, the Raincoats' material was still deeply personal. Avoiding breast-beating dogma, the mournful "Only Loved at Night" sympathetically depicts a woman who is only suited for secret lovers. The intimation is that she's too unattractive for men or women to want to commit to; the song's narrator laments that lovers won't look at her face, and won't be seen with her in daylight. The more overtly feminist "No One's Little Girl" is a violin-led chant, followed by a sing-along chorus for the fiercely independent, which rejects marriage and encourages female autonomy.

In reimagining underground music, the Raincoats inspired the likes of Kurt Cobain and Kim Gordon, leaving an indelible mark on indie rock.

Part III

THE 1980S

Introduction

CRUEL, CRUEL DECADE

NINETEEN EIGHTY SAW THE ASCENSION OF RONALD REAGAN TO
the presidency, and a legion of Bible-thumpers suddenly empowered by his
rise. Also on the rise was a feminist movement that had not only inspired
thousands of housewives back into the office, but spawned new female conservative figureheads to counter its revolutionary message. Phyllis Schlafly,
who started the Eagle Forum in 1972, came to national prominence in the
'80s. The organization and its leader championed a pro-American, anti-
Equal Rights Amendment (ERA) Christian mission.[1] Concerned Women
for America (CWA), formed by Beverly LaHaye in 1978 in direct response
to the ERA, toed the religious right's party line.[2,3] By the time Reagan took
office and began name-checking such conservative women's organizations,
as well as attending their functions, the religious right's women were armed
and empowered to take on the increasingly complacent left.

The proliferation of religious and politically conservative fervor did not
bode well for feminism. As Susan Faludi argues in *Backlash: The Undeclared
War Against Women*, Reagan's trickle-down theory, while having proven
impotent in economics, did effectively disseminate the cultural and social

agenda of the New Right to the population at large. Advertising and mainstream magazines like *Good Housekeeping* attempted to reel in career women by pushing for a return to the home and hearth, something they attractively dubbed as "nesting"[4]; fashion trends featured new, restrictive lines—replete with frills, stilettos, miniskirts, and "body-squeezing garments that reduced the waist by three inches"[5]—that marked a return to traditional femininity.[6] The media began positioning the "biological clock" as a threat to single women, as did the now-infamous *Newsweek* article that mistakenly averaged a forty-year-old single woman's probability of finding a husband as less likely than the possibility of being killed by terrorists.[7] The stories and studies bolstered the nesting trend, reported on the specter of unfulfilling careers, and launched a widespread, widely reported fear in mainstream female culture of spinsterhood and barren wombs.[8]

Neoconservative thinking was hardly limited to the nation's outlook on feminism, and the music and arts arenas were not immune to Reagan's Cold War, pro-family politics. Bruce Springsteen's brutal portrait of a working-class veteran's suffering, "Born in the U.S.A," ironically, became the nation's adopted patriotic anthem and was usurped as the pro-war Reagan administration's rallying reference point.[9] *Rolling Stone* reported that after a column written by conservative George Will praised Springsteen for his patriotism, Reagan stated while campaigning in New Jersey: "America's future . . . rests in the message of hope in songs of a man so many young Americans admire: New Jersey's Bruce Springsteen."[10]

And more injuriously for the First Amendment, by September of 1985, the Parents' Music Resource Center (PMRC) had presented its case to Congress, arguing that the content of much of rock music was corrupting America's youth. The PMRC was headed up by Tipper Gore and included evangelist Jim Baker's wife, Susan.[11] The Senate hearing resulted in some amusing video clips of a squirming Tipper reading explicit lyrics, as well as long debates on censorship in the public and in the media. The row was temporarily resolved when the Recording Industry Association of America (RIAA) agreed to sticker "offensive" albums with parental advisory warnings. (The impact of rap on 1990s white suburban youth would soon springboard this debate back into the public arena after 2 Live Crew released the album in 1989 *As Nasty as They Wanna Be,* and Ice-T's band Body Count released "Cop Killer" in 1992. Body Count was Ice-T's rock outfit, but the song brought his main genre, rap, under fire.) In 1989, ultraconservative North Carolina senator

Jesse Helms served as a figurehead for the right's crusade against the National Endowment for the Arts, incited by the NEA-funded Cincinnati exhibit of Robert Mapplethorpe's homoerotic photography.[12]

By the early '80s, the recording industry was suffering financially, too. Music sales, at 5.1 billion in 1978, fell to 4.6 billion by 1982, attributed in large part to the growth of competing forms of entertainment, like cable TV and video games, as well as blank cassette tapes, which allowed people to circumvent record purchases by copying albums illegally.[13] Between January 1, 1980, and the birth of MTV on August 1, 1981,[14] light rock artists like Rupert Holmes ("Escape [The Piña Colada Song]"), Captain and Tennille, Olivia Newton-John, Christopher Cross, Barbra Streisand, Kenny Rogers, REO Speedwagon, Hall and Oates, and Air Supply all had number one hits. Thankfully, these adult contemporary artists were occasionally tempered on the charts by the likes of Blondie and Joan Jett.

Cable upstart MTV went on the air in the late summer of 1981 and inadvertently ushered in a host of marginal bands from England, giving them instant exposure in the States. In order to increase the content "diversity" on a network that sidestepped black artists until the nonthreatening and video-ready Michael Jackson proved his popularity in 1983, MTV turned to a host of lesser-known international acts that produced mostly keyboard- and electronics-heavy music to widen the station's video rotation.[15] Overseas acts like the Police, Duran Duran, U2, Adam and the Ants, Culture Club, Men at Work, the Pretenders, Billy Idol, INXS, Eurythmics, and Erasure all enjoyed stateside success during the '80s thanks in large part to MTV exposure. Other acts, like the Cure, Depeche Mode, the Smiths, Echo and the Bunnymen, and Siouxsie and the Banshees, began to inform the lives of teenagers who dug a bit more deeply in their local record shop bins.

Additionally, in 1977 the American record industry tempered the media hubbub punk had caused by recategorizing bands that demonstrated a punk aesthetic as "new wave" in the hopes of garnering a wider audience for the subversive genre.[16] In the Top 40, the moniker stuck to a new and very broad genre of bands whose songs consisted of electronic drumbeats, usually British or Australian accents, and sparer, more melodic guitars and keyboards than those of standard American pop.

By the early '80s, and probably largely due to MTV's need for content, the musical gender gap had narrowed a bit. Pat Benatar and punk scenesters Joan Jett, Blondie, and the Go-Go's had Top 40 hits, with both Blondie and

Jett hitting number one. The Pretenders broke into the Top 40 with "Brass in Pocket"; Eurythmics singer Annie Lennox mixed soulful vocals with a tougher, butch look that included a crewcut and suit. Eurythmics had a number one single in 1983 with "Sweet Dreams (Are Made of This)."[17] Pure pop acts Irene Cara, Toni Basil, Starship, and Bonnie Tyler all held number one positions during the decade, as did '70s hard rock vets Heart. All-girl pop acts Bananarama and the Bangles also garnered number one spots. After the cross-genre megasuccess of Jackson's *Thriller*, the relatively monochromatic MTV "braved" the cultural climate and opened their format up to the comeback efforts of Tina Turner and Aretha Franklin, as well as R&B newcomer Whitney Houston, choreographer-cum-singer Paula Abdul, and a grown-up Janet Jackson, all of whom climbed to number one during the decade. And popular artist Prince promoted dexterous drummer Shelia E., sexual protégés Vanity 6, backup singers Wendy and Lisa, and Apollonia (his costar in the embarrassing yet oddly classic film *Purple Rain*).

Although the new network was populated with vastly different images of women—from a brazen, guitar-wielding Joan Jett to the homespun innocence of Whitney Houston's toothy smile—political commentary and serious confrontation were still missing from the bevy of female musical offerings. As popular culture began toeing the conservative line, record companies, MTV, and, judging from the popular female acts listed above, American music fans shied away from anything deemed too controversial.

For every female-fronted band and solo artist, there were dozens of male-fronted rock bands whose videos used women as decorations. Mötley Crüe's video for "Girls, Girls, Girls" could have also doubled as a Frederick's of Hollywood fashion show—which was nothing compared to Duran Duran's "Girls on Film" video, which in its unedited version showed full frontal nudity. The J. Geils Band decorated its "Centerfold" video with teddy-clad "schoolgirls," and ZZ Top awarded a homely shoe salesman with a librarian in racy clothes after a run-in with the ZZ Top girls in "Legs." The hip-shaking, gum-chewing ZZ Top girls became fixtures in a trail of the band's videos, looking utterly bored as a continual breeze blew through their Aquanetted hair. Robert Palmer sang "Addicted to Love" in front of lines of nearly identical women; Van Halen paraded models buried under frumpy clothing in "Hot for Teacher." In "1999," even Prince's backup singers, Wendy and Lisa, displayed a thinly veiled homoeroticism during their closeups. With the exception of "Hot for Teacher" and "Girls on Film," all of these songs reached the Top 20. "Addicted to Love" and "Centerfold" both reached number one.

Although the relative diversity of female musicians offered throughout the '80s was a welcome change over the folk- and diva-only banquet the previous decade had served, the women decorating male videos were fairly stereotypical. Rock has always served as a harbinger of contemporary sexual and social boundaries, but this type of hollow hedonism merely reflected the social confines of beauty for women in rock—submissive, white, thin, and existing mainly for men's physical satisfaction. Such images presented to preteen suburban girls with a limited number of cultural offerings fostered the view that female sexual potential was only relevant when viewed through the eyes of men. As Naomi Wolf described it in *The Beauty Myth*, "MTV sets the beauty index for young women today. . . . For young men, 'beauty' is defined as that which never says no, and that which is not really human."[18] It is not sexual imagery that's been a hindrance to women in rock (or anywhere else in the culture)—it's the lack of options for what's deemed "sexy" that damages women's view of their sexuality. This same dearth of options in popular music has kept less-feminine, outsider women on the fringes of rock history.

Thus was the state of music videos in the '80s—with the one now-obvious exception of Madonna. Alluring millions of fans worldwide, Madonna became a target for the right and the left during the '80s. Madonna initially appealed to the popular culture on a number of levels: Young women wanted to emulate her, young men wanted to ravish her, and most mainstream journalists delighted in a "new craze" on which to dedicate plenty of ink and endless commentary on her "trashy" clothes and "pre-feminist sexuality."[19] She was utterly capable of bucking MTV's dull rotation of monotonous women by clocking in a few early and memorable moments: a bare bellybutton, visible lace bras, and a love of provocative dramatics—typified by her performance on the MTV Video Music Awards, where she rolled around in a wedding dress while singing "Like a Virgin."

Madonna and Cyndi Lauper suffered endless comparisons during the mid-'80s, and both received an enormous amount of mainstream attention, something that was denied women like Exene Cervenka—who was "quirky"(to use a popular term in journalism for any artistic women off-kilter from the national standard), too, and yet wrote serious, pained rock music and shouted and moaned onstage. Furthermore, the mainstream women's movement largely ignored the '80s travails of women like Cervenka, Lydia Lunch, and Kim Gordon, while naming Lauper one of *Ms.* magazine's "Women of the Year" in 1985.[20] The differences between Madonna and Lauper, in the mainstream music world's eyes, were clear, though. In Jay Cocks' *Time* magazine article comparing the two, Cocks describes Lauper as "dippy," "brassy," and her outfits as what "gypsies might wear if they had proms."[21] He also praises her immense voice, but goes on to say that "Madonna has the look" and a "phone-for-sex" voice; her body and image are "a dream off the back of a locker door."[22] Whether you love or hate Madonna, her seemingly endless versatility and compulsive button-pushing has held both women and men spellbound.

The fact that both Cyndi Lauper and Madonna brought something innovative to the gender-related pop music table is indisputable, as is the relative notion of them being "strong women." Yet, for all of their supposed subversion, Lauper's image was depoliticized in the mainstream press. Although journalists referred to her as a feminist, her threatening political stance faded into lesser descriptions that likened her to the animated, ultra femme Betty Boop.[23] She did make decidedly feminist statements, as Gillian Gaar notes in *She's a Rebel*, "citing the church, the family, and the government as 'the three biggest oppressors of women that will ever come along.'"[24] Although "Girls Just Wanna Have Fun" was described by both *Ms.* and Cocks as a "feminist" anthem,[25] her biggest political statement musically, "She Bop," offered a synth-heavy sound and flippant attitude toward masturbation by men *and* women. The song's meaning was consequently rarely brought up in the press. Had they grasped the song's theme, suburban American parents may not have looked on as approvingly as their pajama-clad daughters bounced around to it at slumber parties.

Career longevity and cultural impact aside, the underlying difference between the two women who most memorably embodied the decade's pop culture vision of female individuality was that while Madonna was sexualized, Lauper remained impish—as if the passionate, lovable oddball she purported to be could never be truly sexual. While Madonna was sexually threatening to some, more for the assertion of her sexuality than for her clothing (although her bare belly and lace stockings became quick cultural markers of women gaining control of their sexuality), Lauper was more *visu-*

ally threatening to others. A tongue-in-cheek comment made in *Time*'s coverage of Madonna's first tour in 1985 reported teenage girls' quick embrace of Madonna's look: "[I]f you wanna be like Cyndi, you have to dye your hair orange and fuchsia, and your parents freak."[26]

However pearl-clutching her image may have been to a Reagan-steeped Middle America, Madonna had co-opted and popularized a punk subculture that had been questioning and subsequently rejecting everything since its official beginnings in 1976—particularly notions of acceptable fashion. Thrift store clothing, shaved heads, dramatic makeup, fishnets, and combat boots—these all became the earmarks of a developing statement on confrontation and individuality in fashion. Madonna and Lauper brought the look to the mainstream as part of a more pop-friendly and, arguably, emptier musical package. Along with her "new" image, Madonna brought a trunk full of trite lyrics on the long-standing tradition of pop music, love: "Burning Up," "Borderline," and later, "Crazy for You," "True Blue," and "Cherish," among a host of others. When she wasn't singing about love in her earlier works, she was singing about partying or dancing: "Everybody," "Holiday," and "Into the Groove" embody this best. In contrast to the banal lyrics Madonna offered against a backdrop of subversive imagery, punk music usually addressed the issue of love to revile it. According to Jon Savage in *England's Dreaming*, "Singing about love only reinforced pop's 'private' status in society: Punk was public, determinedly *in* the world."[27]

It's widely accepted by many, from Madonna's biggest fan to her worst critic, that she liberally appropriates aspects of gay, black, and Hispanic subcultures. What hasn't been noted in cultural criticism or the press at large is that Madonna also appropriated a punk sense of style in her supposedly new "transgressive" fashion sense. Her rise to fame as a "visionary" lay in the repetitive, collective, and popular notion that she burst out of thin air when, in fact, a trail of rock history is revealed in her wake. Madonna effectively harvested what she wanted out of other subcultures, and ended up, in fashion terms alone, a more sexualized, less antagonistic version of these subculture counterparts. As *Time* magazine described, she influenced the wardrobes of young girls as a passing phase, not as a commitment to a more marginal life. Madonna, while eliciting an onslaught of cultural critique and the horror of the religious right, ultimately offered a bubblegum sound and a sexual availability that separated her from the anger and confrontation of her punk contemporaries, and spared the girls who emulated her style from the inevitable social exclusion punk—or even Lauper's orange hair—threatened.

While Madonna and Lauper were the mainstream "rebels" du jour, Plasmatics frontwoman Wendy O. Williams was trotted out as a reminder of the horrors that lurked in the world of punk rock for women. Williams made countless television appearances, mostly without reference to the music she was performing—focusing instead on her theatrical stunts, which ranged from chain-sawing a guitar in half to driving a school bus through a pile of televisions. The meaning behind it was secondary to the scare-tactic journalism Williams' Mohawk and electrical tape "bras" elicited. Punk was a constant source of fright for parents in the '80s, fostered in part by organizations like Back in Control Training, a California group that held a 1985 "Sound and Fury" conference aimed at reversing the apparent "brainwashing" teens received from punk and heavy metal.[28]

The mainstream recording industry continued to ignore many smaller bands and gobble up a few critically acclaimed indie bands like X (who, even with a major label contract, didn't receive widespread popular acclaim). Meanwhile punk morphed into something much more exclusionary in the outlying areas of Los Angeles, like Orange County. Due in no small part to slanted media exposure that labeled punk rock as violent extremism, the art form fell victim to its own overexposure. The harsher, faster, more homogenized, and more aggressive sounds of hardcore became popular with kids who had limited first-wave access, suburban upbringings, and their own axes to grind. Hardcore honed its aggression from punk, but narrowed its nihilism and impulsive self-expression to the individual release of anger onto more personal targets than punk's broader social agenda had. While X was reveling in Americana, both with rockabilly-inspired punk and with references to companies like Coca-Cola and Motorola in their song "We're Desperate,"[29] Black Flag songs like "Revenge" were more emotionally confrontational and more cathartic, in a sense, than X's intimate and articulate storytelling. Hardcore developed a more rigid and mob-mentality fan base than that of the first wave of punk.

Hailing from Hermosa Beach, California, Black Flag inadvertently started it all when guitarist Greg Ginn wanted a scene closer to home, one that was organic to his neighborhood.[30] Ginn started Black Flag and the pioneering SST Records, and Hermosa Beach had its own contentious scene, separate from that of the Hollywood punks. Black Flag defined the sound of what became known as hardcore—deep, driving bass lines and a rhythm that went a step beyond punk in both speed and aggression. If punk was performed impulsively from the gut, hardcore was wrenched unwillingly from the bowels. Thundering, deeply felt vocals mixed with bass-heavy speed created a haunting and inescapable assault on the senses, stronger even than most of what punk had produced thus far. For the genre's aesthetics and place of origin—dissatisfied youth living in the shadow of an urban scene—it developed an acutely violent streak. And, once aggression became commonplace, the new scene didn't foster equal gender involvement.

Black Flag's original lead singer, Keith Morris, recalls, "When the hardcore thing really took off, it became more of a macho, testosterone-overdrive thing, the stage diving and the slam pits. Most girls didn't want to have anything to do with it."[31] Brendan Mullen stated that "[f]emale attendance plummeted."[32] Avengers vocalist Penelope Houston comments, "[A]t that point, girls were basically excluded from hardcore, probably to everybody's satisfaction, because most girls are not into million-mile-an-hour testosterone-driven dumb punk. Yeah, it did seem like after the Avengers broke up, there was a point in '81, maybe '80 to '82, where there were a lot of hardcore bands, where the whole audience would be guys and they'd all be stage diving, and they'd all be doing the pits and everything, and behaving very much like apes."[33]

Meanwhile, the wave of punk females and women making indie music in the '80s—women like Joan Jett, Kim Gordon, and Lydia Lunch, not to mention mid-1980s Black Flag bassist Kira Roessler—had certainly circumvented any societal notion that women should be seen and not heard. The female presence that was generally lacking in hardcore more likely had more to do with the unfortunate intolerance that festered within the scene than with willingness on the part of women to participate. Anything outside of that which fit the narrow strictures the members of the scene themselves imposed—including physical aesthetics, mosh pit behavior, and the general intolerance promoted by some of the bands—was unacceptable and drove many away from hardcore.[34]

Much has been made of the misunderstood lyrics that became such a burden to hardcore's legacy. As Michael Azerrad notes in *Our Band Could Be Your Life*, songs that intelligently commented on racial polarity in America could be misinterpreted as racist.[35] Anthems like Black Flag's "White

Minority" and Minor Threat's "Guilty of Being White" added to hardcore's bad reputation, and were easy points of contention for critics, drawing angry and aggressive fans who might have had more interest in white power than in free expression.

If hardcore was attracting a crowd that was misinterpreting commentaries on race, it was undoubtedly causing the same kinds of misinterpretations surrounding sexual politics. Taken out of context, "Jealous Again," from Black Flag's 1980 EP by the same name, alienates women when the protagonist stops himself from physically lashing out at his girlfriend. He opts out of violence not because it's wrong, but to avoid a confrontation with the police. The song also reinforces the stereotype of female lovers as stifling and suffocating. Although fans and critics (myself included) defend songs like these as simply painting a negative portrait of an all too common American male mindset rather than serving as an actual expression of the band's beliefs, it is easy to imagine this subtlety being lost on many. It does seem that this form of "social critique" might wear thin. And how effective is it, really, if many fans miss the point?

Hardcore wasn't the only arena in which songs like "Jealous Again" cropped up. Lee Ving, lead singer of the underground L.A. band Fear, consistently called his audience "faggots" during shows. He defends it in *The Decline of Western Civilization* by saying it was used to incite the audience by calling them something they were afraid of.[36] While his point is valid, the bile with which he utters the epithet makes one wonder if using it to elucidate the homophobia in the audience is really just an excuse to use the word, especially given the decidedly macho anger displayed by much of Fear's audience.

Big Black maintained the same stance of pushing the "no rules" boundaries within the underground community. Their catalog offers songs about the mutilation of women and uses racist, ethnic, and homophobic slurs generously, all under the guise of button-pushing and challenging indie rock's political status quo. Big Black founder Steve Albini defends his work in Azerrad's book, stating that more than speech has to change in the name of open-mindedness: "I have less respect for the man who bullies his girlfriend and calls her 'Ms.' . . . than a guy who treats women reasonably and respectfully and calls them 'Yo! Bitch!' The substance is what matters."[37] Certainly, Albini is correct that actions speak louder than words, yet without the constant presence of the other speaking for her- or himself, to balance things out, the popularity of so many lyrics in this vein is troubling.

For instance, Big Black's "Fish Fry" expresses a desire to beat, have sex with, and dump the body of a lover. Fear's "Fresh Flesh" depicts someone who longs to kill a lover with sex, and "Precious Thing," also by Big Black, portrays a lover who can only admire his partner when she's physically dominated. Are these songs meant to reinforce misogyny or critique it? The answer isn't clear-cut. Surely, artists aren't responsible for the misinterpretation of their lyrics, but the songs don't necessarily work without a voice to counter it. It's safe to say that more than one woman has felt alienated by them.

Regardless of whether or not these lyrics and attitudes contributed to the scarcity of creative women and other marginalized groups during the '80s, easily misinterpreted satire wasn't the only face of underground rock during the decade. If Ronald Reagan did nothing else for the left during his White House tenure, he thankfully fed the fire of many an antiestablishment band. While the record industry slept through the early '80s, the indie rock scene, along with its countercultural compatriot, the separate, burgeoning rap scene, became a national movement in earnest. What had originated in small circles in New York and Los Angeles organically spread via word of mouth and by way of homegrown 'zines to Boston, D.C., Minneapolis, Austin, San Francisco, and eventually nearly every urban center, as well as many suburbs, throughout the country.

However, many of the major label bands that introduced the new sound to college students had relatively little female input. The higher-profile bastions of college rock, the many amalgamations of music that grew out of punk, and the bands that the recording industry had dubbed "college rock"—groups like R.E.M., U2, Hüsker Dü, the Replacements, Meat Puppets, Mudhoney, the Clash, Fishbone, Minutemen, the Dead Milkmen, Violent Femmes, and later Fugazi, Jane's Addiction, and the Red Hot Chili Peppers—were all-male acts. At the same time, bands that received less mainstream recognition, like Black Flag, the Cramps, Beat Happening, Sonic Youth, the Sugarcubes, Fastbacks, and the Pixies, among others, offered mixed lineups; and all-female bands, like Frightwig, the Pandoras, and D.C.'s Chalk Circle and Fire Party, inspired the women who'd later usurp the boys' club in the 1990s. The general public, however, rarely saw underground rock's female face.

Although indie rock leaned to the political left of the country, its members were still products of the national mindset, and sexism was still an obstacle for women in the scene. Tribe 8's Lynn Breedlove contends that although there have always been scenes and subgenres that foster leftist political values, "[sexism in punk]'s always been the case. . . . I heard in the early '80s and stuff that shit would always happen. People would be drunk, they'd be high. Sexism has always been there in the punk scene, I mean, in any scene. It's just pervasive. Which was a shock to me because I was like, 'Oh, punk is like, you know, not what propaganda says it is. It's nonracist, nonhomophobic, nonmisogynistic.' Bullshit! It's got all those elements in it."[38]

In *Rock She Wrote*, Team Dresch founder Donna Dresch wrote about her hesitancy to start playing guitar: "I kept *thinking* I could do it. But, I would get so mad that this boy would tell me that I couldn't."[39] A member of the all-female Frightwig told *Maximumrocknroll*, "I got hit in the face in Denver. Because they were saying, 'Show us your tits, play faster,' and I told them to get up and strip but that snowballed into, 'You all have small penises!' . . . They were taking their dicks out, these so-called punk rock skinheads. When it comes to anarchy, they can't handle it. Women on stage freaked them out."[40]

Scene violence, particularly in the now-factionalized circles of hardcore and punk, was a problem in a lot of places in the '80s. *Maximumrocknroll's* lengthy letter pages published missives that documented various cities' troubles with skinheads, most commonly, New York and San Francisco. *MRR* even opened an ongoing roundtable discussion in 1984 to mend bridges between battling factions of punk fans.[41] As open-minded as *MRR* was to the overall problem of scene violence, it didn't address sexism with the same sense of urgency.

Despite the persistence of sexism in such a transgressive subculture, the indie scene had certainly come farther than the '80s mainstream had. And with an influx of new fans and music, the '80s also saw the aforementioned subgenres develop, sometimes by region, and sometimes by the aesthetics or ethics of individual bands. Bands like the Dead Kennedys, MDC, and Fugazi (later in the decade) in the U.S., and Crass, Conflict, and Rudimentary Peni in the U.K. promoted overt, radical political agendas, while bands from places with indie rock scenes like Athens, Georgia; Olympia, Washington; and Minneapolis, Minnesota handled politics on more subtle levels than did traditional leftist punk. Most of the bands that made it over state lines weren't bubbling over with women, either. And while in retrospect the numbers might seem minimal, the acceptance of female performers was more widespread, allowing for more variety and less typically feminine posturing than in the mainstream—slowly making way for women who were smarter and more substantive than Madonna, more overtly political and abrasive than Cyndi Lauper, and who developed an aesthetic that lay outside of mainstream culture's restrictive beauty codes.

Chapter 14

CONSPIRACY OF WOMEN

Lydia Lunch

AS AN ARTISTIC MOVEMENT PUNK ENCOURAGED REJECTION, AND it also catalyzed rejection of itself. The new wave spurned "no wave," a short-lived, dissonant noise movement that sought to puncture the punk sound by eliminating all similarities to rock and roll rhythm structures. Combining droning ambient noise with spurts of sound, no wave reflected, however inadvertently, the sounds of the frenetic urban landscape from which it was born. "For the most part, no wave dealt with interpersonal revelations concerning anger, frustration, insanity, discomfort," Lydia Lunch explains. "Punk was more political. No wave had a short life span, as any movement with so few structural rules, by its very nature, morphs quickly."[1] Jim Sclavunos, bassist for Teenage Jesus and the Jerks, drummer for Beirut Slump and 8 Eyed Spy, and an early Sonic Youth drummer, told Alec Foege in *Confusion Is Next: The Sonic Youth Story*, "We all pretty much held punk in contempt. . . . For its self-satisfaction, for its self-indulgence, and various nostalgic trends. It just seemed like a very easy scene for a bunch of losers. And we were determined to be bigger losers, I guess."[2]

Another antipunk and no wave creator was Lydia Koch, a sixteen-year-old

121

runaway from Rochester, New York, who was dubbed Lydia Lunch when she began stealing food for hungry friends. She says,

> I picked up *Last Exit to Brooklyn* [by Hubert Selby Jr.] at twelve or thirteen, and believe it to be what opened my eyes to a true literary underground. Reading Genet and Henry Miller led to the Stooges, the Velvet Underground, and the New York Dolls, who inspired me, at fifteen, to run away from home, hit the Greyhound station, and head to New York City. I bummed around for a couple of weeks, went back upstate, lied about my age, got work in a hotel, saved up for a couple of months, and hit the city again.
>
> By the time I got to New York, I felt that most of the music that had inspired me was in itself too traditional. I wanted to create something that sounded unlike anything else. Catching Suicide at Max's Kansas City and Mars at CBGB's helped define the direction I wanted to go in. I met James Chance, who was already playing psychotic jazz at loft parties. He took me in as I was about to be ousted from a hippie crash pad in Chelsea. I found a broken five-string guitar and started writing the songs for Teenage Jesus.[3]

Rather than competing in the vicious grab for crucial spots on CBGB's or Max's lineups, no wavers like Teenage Jesus and the Jerks, Suicide, James Chance and the Contortions (Chance was also a member of the Jerks), Mars, and DNA played alternative spaces, effectively divorcing themselves from the rapidly expanding punk crowd.

The Jerks removed any rhythm and blues left in punk, pounding faster thudding rhythms underneath dragging bursts of guitar noise, with Lunch's top-of-the-lungs vocal delivery sounding as if she were shouting from the top of a cliff and playing to an audience fifty feet below. The rough, raw desperation so clearly evoked by her voice burgeoned during her tenure with both the Jerks and Beirut Slump, with whom she played guitar at the same time. Beirut Slump offered brutal noise—a bass drum and guitars that sounded like '70s horror movie strings played backward.

Lunch's career as a self-expressionist, a self-identified "hideous, screaming bitch,"[4] is littered with scads of one-off collaborations. She was a member of the renowned '80s project 8 Eyed Spy, which employed more traditional rhythms—played chaotically, of course. The group successfully combined saxophone sounds and surf guitar with Lunch's screaming vocals, gliding above the instrumentation. An abbreviated list of her other artistic mutations include collaborators as diverse as the Birthday Party's Rowland S. Howard, Einstürzende Neubauten, Michael Gira of the Swans, Henry Rollins, Nick Cave, Kim Gordon, and Foetus' Jim Thirlwell. She has made films with Richard Kern, and poetry collaborations with Exene Cervenka, and produced a library of solo work, spoken word, and books like *Paradoxia: A Predator's Diary*. In what would unknowingly become her most high-profile project, she collaborated with Sonic Youth on the single "Death Valley '69," a song that depicts the Manson Family murders. "When two elements combine or combust, a third entity arises, which would not exist separately," she says of her extensive collaborations. "It allows both parties a new freedom to express themselves in a way that they might not have considered previously."[5]

Lunch formed her own record and publishing company, Widowspeak, in the mid-'80s allowing her to freely distribute her multimedia assaults. "I'm very successful," she once remarked, "in the sense that a lot of people who create on a similar level of intensity and diversity don't have the opportunity to find a vehicle for release of their material. I've been stubborn and tenacious enough to ensure that everything I've done has been documented on record, film, or some kind of release. That's where the success comes in—I'm more interested in documenting these periods of emotional instability than making sure everyone gets a copy."[6]

Widowspeak's initial release was the cassette *The Uncensored Lydia Lunch*, her first recorded foray into traditionally defined spoken word. By the time the cassette was released, though, Lunch had already developed her confrontational, distinctly literary, and always accessible style of writing, which has been compared to the work of such luminaries as Jean Genet and Henry Miller. She screams her prose, and then suddenly dives into an unexpected whisper. Her delivery is always in an intimate tone that can make her work uncomfortable, especially as she deals in conversational taboos—self-revelation, abuse, profanity, unrelenting female anger, and forthright desire.

The myriad ways in which Lunch intrepidly expresses herself and educates her audiences are impressive; she never settles on one mode of expression for long without trying it from another angle, through another medium. She has never identified herself as only a musician; music has worked as a backdrop for the words she writes, speaks, screams, rattles, and rants. What has been unflagging throughout her career, and is perhaps more significant than the breadth of her work, is the level of intimacy she is willing to allow;

the brutal, confrontational, powerful way she asserts herself, all while appearing somehow vulnerable and naked. Lunch has described herself as a "confrontationalist," once commenting, "[M]y job is to confront apathy and confront all the forces that tend to batter each of us down with all kinds of oppression, even self-oppression. I consider that the main job of the art that I do—to rattle the cage, to wake people up, wake myself up, confront all that would conspire to keep us down."[7]

What Lydia Lunch reveals in her work is more provocative than the noisy hard rock of a band like Hole, who similarly revealed full-force emotional purging in their lyrics. There's nothing masking the brutality and stalwart honesty in Lunch's work; her voice and her words take center stage, rather than being mired in noise that often overpowers. With innards laid bare and with nothing to hide, Lunch's rants reveal a very personal oppression, avoiding traditional allegories for suffering. Watching or listening to her perform spoken word is to have her sitting on your shoulder, shouting in your ear. It's the brutal truth of the human experience, whether it addresses habitual patterns of self-abuse, relationships, sexuality, or violence. Lunch comments on this kind of expression:

> When, as a young girl, I wanted to break free from a protectionary emotional deadness, I had to rebuild my emotional landscape. In order to do so, I sought extremes of sensation. I need to be throttled. I feed on intensity because it's part of my makeup. My body of work has concerned the schism where a mutual exchange of energy becomes convoluted, misinterpreted, unbalanced. It's difficult to find people to engage with, who won't be frightened or damaged by my passion, or my desires. I never wanted to threaten a partner I was involved with, but often their fear of me, of my potential, of my needs, forced them to overreact in a way that was both destructive to themselves, and harmful to me. They found it difficult to reconcile how someone who loves them, who they loved, could demand such extremes of passion. Within the intersection of violence, sensuality, and intellect, I glut on the possibility to investigate the trigger pulses that drive someone smart enough to know better almost over the edge. It is at that excruciating brink [that] I sup on the intermingling of overstimulated energies, which is the root of my obsessions.[8]

In an interview for the online magazine *Scrawl*, she described what she sees as the goal of her work: "I just want to express myself in a way that's most therapeutic to me and to other people that feel the same frustrations, and that want to go deep enough to try and find healing at the other side of the fucking gaping wound. Which is our psyche, which is our soul, you know? That's what's important to me. And I am reaching out to the most wounded. And it is like a social duty to reach out to those that have been most traumatized. To those that are so sensitive that maybe they've become hardened. That they then turned numb and that they want to get to the other side of it. . . . And it is like a specific brand of psychotherapy. As opposed to general psychiatry or general psychology or counseling. And I do view my work as a social duty. As far as my spoken and written work, I *do* view it as a social duty, and I'm not a politician, so therefore, it's not for everyone. And I don't want to convert people."[9]

Through Widowspeak, Lunch released *Hysterie*, a compilation of her earlier work with Teenage Jesus and the Jerks, 8 Eyed Spy, Beirut Slump, and other collaborations. A compelling example of her spoken word is available on *Crimes Against Nature*, a collection of performances recorded between 1984 and 1992. Accompanied by liner notes that outline the way disenfranchisement encourages so-called "offensive" art, her lyrical venom and literary nakedness are in top form. "Conspiracy of Women" points to what men have done with power—war and oppression—and urges women to pick up their guns. In it she describes her own militia: "My language is not silence. My song is the scream."[10]

As women in '80s pop music benefited from feminism while carefully maintaining traditional forms of female desire, Lunch produced work like "Daddy Dearest," a letter to her father that starts off politely conversational and then builds to a painstakingly detailed account of the sexual abuse she suffered at his hands. The work culminates in a rapid-fire tirade against him. While she is constantly documenting victimization, she is also providing liberation from persecution, submission, and silence.

Lunch was astoundingly prolific at a time when feminism was subject to the religious right's growing army of conservative women, and artistic freedom was being tested nationwide. She has contributed her own unique, sometimes frightening, always honest self-expression, while avoiding self-censorship at every turn, often in the face of the rather limited agenda of mainstream feminism. It can be argued that she has widened the foundations on which feminism was built by celebrating that which was labeled as pornography—the category under which her films with Richard Kern are routinely grouped.

"To me, I always like the term 'humanist,' which I think I am," she once mused. "I'm pro-sex, pro-pornography, pro-NRA. That divides me from a lot of the so-called feminists who I've readily debated, as well as other forms of censors. We need more equality across the board. I think feminism certainly is not an outdated idea. I consider myself a 'femi-nazi' (a term which I use to my advantage) because in a lot of 'conspiracy of women' speeches, I'm making a sarcastic proposal. It's not completely eliminating half the population, but finding a planet where women could be by themselves just to see if it would make any fucking difference. Not, of course, painting all men with the same fucking broad stroke. Realizing that my target is men in positions of power which the average man, sadly, completely lacks. My target is always the politicians, the fathers, the forefathers, the fuckers, the corporate soldiers."[11]

Chapter 15

STUNT PRIESTESS

Wendy O. Williams

PICTURE A WOMAN COVERED IN NOTHING BUT SHAVING CREAM,
wielding a chainsaw or a machine gun; or a leather-bustier-clad woman driving a school bus toward a wall of televisions in the desert; or a Mohawk-sporting girl jumping from an exploding car. With a resumé like Wendy O. Williams', Madonna revealing her precious bellybutton on MTV seems to recast the "Material Girl" as merely another video decoration. Williams was sexy without being submissive to her audience, exuding a genuine rebelliousness, while Madonna's insurgency, as shocking as some found it, was (and remains) inarguably choreographed. Most importantly, Williams' vision paved the way for other women like her—that is, if there *are* any women like her.

Like many a restless girl before her, sixteen-year-old Wendy Orleans Williams left her hometown suburb of Rochester, New York, to see the world. When she answered an ad for a Times Square audition in 1977, Wendy met Rod Swenson, who became not only her partner but the cofounder and manager of the Plasmatics. Swenson recalls, "Wendy had the most extraordinary energy of anybody that I think that I've ever met. Mostly before I met her, people always had trouble keeping up with me. People thought I was one of the most extreme people they'd ever met. Whatever I was, she was more by orders of magnitude, and that's partly how she just fired me."[1]

Musicians Richie Stotts, Chosei Funahara, and Stu Deutsch were recruited to round out the rest of the Plasmatics' lineup. A bit later, Wes Beech was brought in on guitar, as well. Swenson had previously worked on videos for the Ramones, shooting some of their earliest footage, and had some offers to manage bands. "Wendy, it turns out, was looking to be in a rock and roll band. It just seemed to all come together, and then we made an intentional decision to go for it. The Plasmatics, then, was a conceptual thing that was built around her and went through about seventeen different musicians over the course of ten years. Then some product was put out with her own name separately, as a solo product."[2]

The Plasmatics quickly started releasing records on their own label, Vice Squad, because, not surprisingly, record labels were reticent to take on such an act. They eventually signed with Stiff in England and, by 1983, had inked a deal with Capitol Records and released *Coup d' Etat*. Two metal-influenced solo albums, *WOW* and *Kommander of Kaos*, followed, the former garnering a Grammy nomination in 1985. Williams even recorded a rap album in 1988 under the name Ultrafly and the Home Town Girls. It was, however, her last recorded effort.

The Plasmatics played distinctly heavy metal riffs at punk speed, sometimes dissolving into lengthy, noisy guitar solos; they were undoubtedly the precursor to underground bands that melded the two styles in the late '80s. With a direct, guttural delivery that skirted typical affectations of female singers, Williams would scream her guts out in speedy early songs like "Butcher Baby" and "Monkey Suit." She mixed her thrashing with a good can-can kick and shimmied her nearly bare chest at loyal audiences.

The Plasmatics were known mostly for their destructive pyrotechnic stage shows, which, for all the dramatic spectacle, transformed metal's über-machismo arena—not only by homespun theatrics but by the addition of a thrashing, chainsaw-wielding woman who danced and writhed in her underwear. As the venues they played expanded to accommodate their fans, so did their flair for the spectacular: Dry ice snaked from behind the drum kit and song breaks were lit by well-timed spotlights. The guitarists were accompanied by the sound from Wendy's ever-ready sledgehammer, which she wielded to decimate radios and televisions during the course of the show.

She's often credited with being one of the first women in America to sport a Mohawk. As with the whole punk movement, these kinds of "firsts" are difficult to document, but she was certainly the first woman to appear on network television with one. Swenson explains, "You have to understand what it was like for Wendy, who was the first woman ever on American television—the first person that most people ever saw—with a Mohawk haircut. [She] went from having this more stereotypical 'good look,' and all of a sudden, did this to her hair, [and] how radical that was for people. . . . [Our audience] all had kind of Beatles haircuts. . . . The Mohawk haircut was something that she wanted to do from quite early on, but she thought it would be more striking if she got people used to her the other way and then cut it off. And so that's what she did."[3]

At the Palladium in 1979, the band drove a car out onstage and blew it up, which became emblematic of the Plasmatics. The number of stage props used and the destruction the band would commonly wreak led to accusations that the Plasmatics were doing it all for the publicity, and there was certainly a method behind Williams' madness. She was intent on seeing women perceived differently in rock and roll. "One of the things that she didn't like in particular," recalls Swenson, "[was] the way women were placed in ordinary male rock bands or say, later on, in videos, as kind of coffee tables or disposable accoutrements or window dressing for men's sexuality. Yet what she was herself was somebody who was extremely sexual, she was an exhibitionist . . . but she also felt that women were afraid to express their sexuality on the one hand; and on the other hand, that women were often typecast simply as accoutrements to men's image."[4]

Beyond revealing the strong, physical, and confrontational side of her gender, Williams was commenting on America's materialism. She explained in a television interview: "With the Plasmatics, I have the opportunity to do what I love, which is smash these things and show that they are just things. People in our society, I think, place too much value on material things. That you go to work and you save your money so you can buy these material things. Don't get me wrong—I love them, but I hate them, too. That's why I love to smash them. I mean, nothing turns me on more to . . . blow up a car and to see the hood fly fifty feet up in the air. . . . I like seeing TV sets sitting on top of ladders, and being smashed and falling on the floor. I like the sound that it makes, I like the way it looks. . . . I like getting my lungs filled with smoke, and I like feeling exhausted from getting a sledgehammer and smashing [a TV] until it's a pile of debris. It gets my blood going."[5]

With mantra-like fervor, she stressed that the meaning behind the Plasmatics' stage show was simple: The swirling dust from a television was an example of how to express aggression and anger without hurting anyone. More importantly, Williams was using the platform of sensationalist media coverage, which reporters were only too happy to shower on her as they relished her shock factor, to criticize mainstream culture.

The Plasmatics wrangled a healthy amount of mainstream attention, in no small part due to brash performances on Tom Snyder's *Tomorrow* (their exploding car blew a hole in the studio ceiling) and *Solid Gold*, an all-sequins-and-smiles Top 40 network variety show. The band also appeared on *Second City TV* with John Candy, and Williams appeared on an early, regionally televised *Sally Jesse Raphael*. While punk purists may have balked at the amount of television exposure the Plasmatics were receiving in the '80s, Williams continued to spend her airtime promoting the self-expression and equality she so firmly believed in. When one reporter asked her why she would get upset when men noticed her body before her face, intimating that Williams was "asking for it," she responded, "Well, I like people to take me as a whole person. I like to be accepted as the whole person, the whole being. You know, like, I mean, I'm against chauvinism. Chauvinism can be male chauvinism, female chauvinism. To me, a pig is a pig. It's high time people realize that women do have minds of their own, and that the female body is not dirty."[6]

The kinds of messages that Williams and all of the Plasmatics were sending to middle-class America met with predictable, and sometimes violent, resistance. In 1981, the Milwaukee vice squad cuffed her for simulating masturbation with a mic stand and a sledgehammer. She wasn't just arrested, she was sexually assaulted and beaten: "He [a vice squad officer] was standing at that point, and he was saying, 'Shut up you filthy cunt.' And he kicked me in the face. I was screaming because I was in so much pain. I was screaming because I thought I was going to die. I thought they were killing me. He continued to say 'Shut up,' and kicked me again, twice in the face, cutting my eye and breaking my nose. Then he jumped on top of me. He had his knee on my back and his arm on my neck. His hands were on my throat. He was choking me, rubbing my face into the ice."[7]

For most people Williams was an enigma—compelling far beyond the antics of the band. Her most public and most consistent rebellions were physical ones: a body covered in shaving cream, muscular arms that could destroy TVs and stereos. And with her extensive stunt work, she took physical risks rarely performed by women. Even against the backdrop of women who flooded punk's early years with wit, anger, and boundless energy, Williams' ability to shock seemed to be teetering at the very edge. "All my life," she recalled, "any history on me, is that I've never been one to walk the middle of the road. I've always been an extremist, and I've always been way over the edge—I'm a fanatic. I mean, you know, like, I'm not encouraging everybody to be a fanatic, too, but what I have found that works for me is rock and roll."[8]

Besides sawing countless guitars in half, she drove a school bus through a mound of television sets for a Plasmatics video and skydived naked for a *Playboy* centerfold shoot—the only way she would agree to pose for them. For a solo single entitled "It's My Life," Williams bounced behind the wheel of a convertible racing through the desert at 75 miles an hour. With the car still in motion, she climbed a rope ladder dangling from a helicopter flying above her, hanging in mid air as the helicopter flew away. On a pier in New York, with thousands of witnesses, she drove a car into a stage loaded with equipment and jumped from the car just as it hit the stage. Both the car and the stage exploded. Swenson remembers, "People [were] running around, as she was on the ground for a few minutes afterwards, and saying, 'Are you all right? Are you all right?' She kind of props herself up and says to them, 'Am I all right? I feel fucking great.'"[9]

"In 1988 we decided to go on a hiatus, but basically, [we] knew that that was going to be it," Swenson says. "It took a long time, but because she got involved in other things, animal rehabilitating and other things, at some point, she felt that she wasn't doing enough to respond to the world and that she was complicit. . . . And she felt that when she wasn't out there in this strong way, challenging in this very intense way, doing these things that other people . . . even if they thought that they were right, wouldn't have the courage to do. Without that kind of chemistry, I think, ultimately she came to feel that she was, in a way, participating in something that she didn't want to participate in anymore."[10]

In April 1998, after almost ten years of working as an animal rehabilitator and leading a relatively quiet life, Williams went into the woods near her Connecticut home and shot herself. "The animal rehabilitating was something that she did while she was buying time in a way," Swenson explains. "Doing something in a local way that was very positive, saving lives of these small animals that were mostly being threatened by the expanding human colonialist—whatever you want to call it. But that wasn't enough to sustain her. In a certain way, her death was really a very conscious decision over a period of years."[11] In her ten years as a destroyer of all things rational (and electrical and expensive), as a fierce arbiter for freedom of expression, Wendy O. Williams managed to tattoo her laughing, burning vision of womanhood and her iconic stuntwoman legacy onto pop culture—and she hasn't been topped since.

Chapter 16

SONIC FORCE

Kim Gordon

SIMPLY PUT, KIM GORDON IS THE QUINTESSENTIAL INDIE ROCK woman. Beyond her songs, beyond her main gig as bassist, guitarist, cofounder, and singer for Sonic Youth, she's supported, promoted, and started dozens of other bands and projects, and has lent her voice, words, music, and vision to countless multimedia projects over the last twenty-plus years (as have her bandmates). As a result, her growth and development as an artist and as a woman has unfolded on the public stage.

During the 1980s, Gordon was one of the only women almost every girl in the indie underground could claim as a role model. Her presence onstage reflected, and still does reflect, someone infinitely comfortable with herself. Beyond the manufactured girl-rock image, she simmers with energy and a sexuality that never outwardly explodes, but is channeled through the hum of her guitar or the lilt of her sometimes joyful, sometimes growling vocals. Since Sonic Youth's inception, Gordon has consistently written songs that display facets of a complex femininity. As a result of her contributions to their provocative, intelligent, and dogma-free music, Sonic Youth became one of the only higher-profile bands of the '80s to consistently address women and gender, in writing or in song throughout their career.

Gordon has often pointed to her voyeuristic curiosity about the foreign and intangible elements of male behavior as what drove her to play bass for Sonic Youth initially. She wrote in a 1987 tour diary for the *Village Voice*, "In the middle of the stage where I stand as the bass player of Sonic Youth, the music comes at me from all directions. The most heightened state of being female is watching people watch you. . . . Loud dissonance and blurred melody create their own ambiguity—are we really that violent?—a context that allows me to be anonymous. For my purposes, being obsessed with boys playing guitars, being as ordinary as possible, being a girl bass player is ideal, because the swirl of Sonic Youth music makes me forget about being a girl. I like being in a weak position and making it strong."[1]

Creating music for years in a legendary band doesn't change the fact that Gordon still mainly identifies as a visual artist. Born in 1953 in Rochester, New York, she grew up in Los Angeles, California, and attended UCLA art school, experimenting with collage—an art form that would inform her musical work. "I think spatially in terms of dynamics," she told *Rockrgrl*, "light and dark or soft and loud, but if I were doing art I'd think the same way. That's just the way I work. I know Steve, Lee, and Thurston probably think about it differently than I do. Our music is really based on all four personalities."[2] Whether her bandmates approach songwriting in the same way or not, Thurston Moore and Lee Ranaldo have both commented on how integral Kim's visual sense is to the band's dynamics. Ranaldo told Michael Azerrad, "Her stuff is all very spare and minimal and yet it's very intricate. There's something about the way she thinks harmonically, rhythmically, that's really amazing to me."[3]

Gordon moved to New York City after finishing art school and soon began playing with two of her friends in the band they named CKM. The initials stood for the three women's first names, the other two being Christine Hahn and Miranda Stanton, and the short-lived CKM collaborated on a performance piece with artist Dan Graham. "There was one song," Gordon wrote in 1994, "called 'Cosmopolitan Girl,' based on this series of ads *Cosmopolitan* magazine did. I took the lyrics [*Cosmo's* ad copy] and made up a song from it!"[4] Through her friendship with Stanton she met Moore, who was playing with the Coachmen, and Ranaldo, who played in the Flucts and in dissonant composer Glenn Branca's orchestra. The drum set has housed numerous players, including Richard Edson, Jim Sclavunos, Bob Bert, and now permanent fixture Steve Shelley.

Gordon, along with guitarists, writers, and cofounders Ranaldo and Moore, first played together as the Arcadians at the Noise Festival, organized by Moore at a downtown New York art gallery. She later wrote, "The festival's name was a joke, inspired by the owner of Hurrah who said he was gonna close the club because all of the bands just sounded like a bunch of noise. Nobody even knew what a 'noise' band was."[5]

Soon after the Noise Festival, they changed the name of the band to Sonic Youth, a name Moore had been tossing around for a while, and the band began playing their wall-of-sound assaults at small venues around New York. While Moore and Ranaldo built a thick mass of dark feedback and droning, lengthy guitar skree, Gordon's bass line was a subtle anchor to Sonic Youth's more overt noise. Having joined the Arcadians as a guitarist and visual artist, Gordon was learning bass as she went, a characteristic that all the members of the band consistently attribute to Sonic Youth's full, haunting, and hypnotic sound.

If one thing has remained constant for the band, even with their forays into more traditional song structures, it's the constant hum, strum, and bang of guitar that reveals a dark underbelly. That's not to say that you can only appreciate Sonic Youth if you love dissonant noise. The layers of sound morph beautifully, beguilingly, into one another, making spontaneous, unassuming melodies underneath and around waves of noise. Moore once described Sonic Youth as "an anarchy band, and really into being loose, anything goes."[6] This anarchic mindset further shattered the boundaries of what DIY punk musicians could construe as music and, in the early days, the band was often noted for speaking in an entirely new language, albeit abrasive for some. "It was, 'What if we just played anything?'" Moore once explained. "It totally destroyed any preconceived idea of rock and roll as rhythm and blues–based music. It was totally liberating."[7] To explore the boundaries of sound, they also used alternate sources to produce new sounds, like drumsticks or screwdrivers impulsively stuck under guitar strings. In 1985, Ranaldo told the 'zine *Forced Exposure*, "You're frustrated during the rehearsal, the guitar's not being a good boy, so you pick something up and do something to it. It's not conscious at all."[8]

Sonic Youth blurred the lines of art and pop culture much as Patti Smith had done a few years earlier. Smith combined what our culture considers "high" art (literature) and "low" art (rock and roll), and Sonic Youth similarly stirred the artful aspects of less accessible experimental music with early '80s hardcore sounds, a bridge uniting listeners from both edges of the cultural spectrum. The band released their first five-song LP in 1982, followed by *Confusion Is Sex* and the live *Kill Yr Idols* EP in 1983 and *Sonic Death* in 1984. Nineteen eighty-five saw the release of *Bad Moon Rising*, the album that brought them acclaim outside of the avid inner circle of underground music fans, but only initially in the U.K. (It's also the album that culminates with the Lydia Lunch collaboration "Death Valley '69.")

Gordon's extensive lyrical contributions certainly can't be slotted into one category, but much of them animate Sonic Youth's work with meaningful portraits of female protagonists who do more than decorate the edges. Like Sonic Youth's musical fluidity, Gordon's characters are interchangeable; listeners of both genders can absorb female perspectives and portraits without feeling "alienated" by their subject matter, a common complaint about more obvious girl-issue rock. Her songwriting is diverse; some songs are direct indictments of behavior or straight narratives (often, from a first-person perspective), but the imagery—the lines sung to a nebulous "you"—is always malleable. Loneliness and desire are loosely wrapped around her simultaneously silky and unadorned vocal stylings to create, at times, urgency, longing, or viciousness in the simplest phrase.

Her voice, echoing and light on early works, invokes a ghostliness that further darkens the songs' intimated violence. On *Confusion is Sex*, "Protect Me You" traverses the inner need for protection of the (female) narrator, ostensibly throughout her life. The mood changes dramatically in the next track, a cover of The Stooges' "I Wanna Be Your Dog," featuring Gordon on shrieking lead vocals. Through the multiplicity of Gordon's performances, *Confusion Is Sex* presents complex female protagonists, from childlike on "Protect Me You" to the aggressor displayed on "Shaking Hell."[9]

Gordon's lyrical and musical scope is found on all Sonic Youth's work, from *Sister* to *EVOL* to 1988's acclaimed *Daydream Nation*—And in Sonic Youth's side project, Ciccone Youth, which paid homage to Madonna with covers of "Into the Groove(y)" and "Burning Up." Ciccone Youth embraced pop culture, something anathema to the underground of the '80s.

During the band's first decade, Gordon documented a lot of the aggression directed at her in her 1987 tour diary. While small presses like *Maximumrocknroll* bemoaned ambiguous scene violence brought on by the influx of skinheads in some regions, and while the late-'80s D.C. scene did its part to bear witness to the hovering silence of indie rock's women, Gordon and, to their credit, the *Village Voice* didn't ignore women's specific experiences with scene violence. Gordon confided the drumstick incident (documented in the introduction) in "Boys Are Smelly," as well as the story of a Swiss fan who continually bit her as she played, and an audience member who threw a handful of firecrackers in her face. Alec Foege documented a 1990 Roseland show where jumping male fans in the front row repeatedly knocked her mic into her teeth.[9] While most performers came face to face with projectiles and hostile fans (and still do), other members of Sonic Youth haven't publicly spoken of the same kind of repeated aggression Gordon faced.

In 1988, Gordon and Lydia Lunch collaborated on a side project named Harry Crews, an homage to the fiction writer of the same name. They only used titles of Crews' work, building songs around them. Lunch told Foege, "[Kim's] writing, like a lot of mine, is so abstract and so basic; she could be saying anything about anything. And in that sense, it's open to interpretation, which is beautiful."[10] Characteristic of Lunch's collaborations, Harry Crews lasted only a couple of years, resulting in one tour and one album, leaving both women to venture on to other projects. For Gordon, this meant producing Hole's 1991 debut, *Pretty on the Inside*, as well as serving as an A&R rep (along with bandmate Moore) for major label Geffen Records, to which Sonic Youth (and subsequently Hole and Nirvana) were signed. The guitar-driven dirge that reigns on *Pretty on the Inside* is surely what attracted Gordon to produce the album. However, Hole soon abandoned their characteristic sludge of guitars and abstract sounds, going for a more traditional structure on their next album.

Gordon also started Free Kitten with Pussy Galore's Julie Cafritz in 1992 and recorded two albums and an EP before employing the Boredoms' Yoshimi P-We on trumpet and drums and Pavement's Mark Ibold as bassist for the 1995 Kill Rock Stars release *Nice Ass*. With the addition of P-We and Ibold, Free Kitten created more electronic-sounding beats set off with loud guitars; Gordon's lyrics hark back to CKM—merging cosmetic advertising slogans with dance beats and looped guitar riffs on "Revlon Liberation Orchestra." The slogans, which in the commercial world work to induce our insecurity and thus our consumption, are hypnotically repeated over and over. The repetition of a phrase so many times reduces it to the ridiculous, and then the meaningless, liberating the listener from the stranglehold of advertising's exploitation.

By the time *Goo* and *Dirty* were released in the early '90s, Gordon's observations of the female experience were more straightforward, as were the song structures of these two albums. She examined white women's oft-sexual fascination with radicalism on the single "Kool Thing," where she asks guest vocalist Chuck D of Public Enemy if he and other radical men are willing to free subjugated women. While it was empowering to hear something like this rolled out over MTV's airwaves, there's a snicker hidden in there, too: Why still pin our hopes on rescue? Why shelter ourselves behind radical men? Why not drag ourselves out of the mire? *Goo* also features "Cinderella's Big Score," and "Tunic (Song for Karen);" the latter paints a portrait of a happier Karen Carpenter in the afterlife. *Dirty* made a significant turn toward the overtly political and included timely support for Anita Hill from Moore on "Youth Against Fascism." Gordon once again reverts to her collage impulse on "Swimsuit Issue," smirkingly dragging a list of supermodels' names over screeching guitar.[11]

By the time *Dirty* was released in 1992, Gordon was as established a bass player as any woman in the rock world, and chose to move from bass to primarily playing guitar. At the same time, Sonic Youth was firmly established as the forerunner of the "alternative nation"—a movement the mainstream record industry had finally awakened to. The band had developed their signature sound without falling into the trap of rehashing old material, and their sound is so original it has rarely been replicated by others. The well-established underground "cred" hasn't altered their ethics or outlook, though, and Sonic Youth continue to make exciting, innovative records that introduce the world to new sounds, both their own and those of their collaborations with emerging and established bands.

In the flood of Sonic Youth releases subsequent to *Dirty*—among them *Washing Machine; Experimental Jet Set, Trash and No Star; A Thousand Leaves; Murray Street;* and *Sonic Nurse*—Gordon's intrepid songwriting has remained constant and integral to the sound and scope of the band; she, Moore, Ranaldo, Shelley, and the relatively new addition, Jim O'Rourke, on guitar and bass continue to find fluid sounds and lyrics that are just as striking and fresh as Sonic Youth's earlier catalog. On *Jet Set*, Gordon wrote the song "Bone," about a young girl inescapably hardened by sex; *A Thousand Leaves* featured "Female Mechanic Now on Duty," which she once explained was a reaction to journalists' efforts to limit and categorize female musicians. *A Thousand Leaves* also offered "The Ineffable Me," where Gordon poetically displayed her resistance to confining definitions. The breadth of Kim Gordon's ever-evolving career certainly defies limitation. Ineffable, indeed; surpassed, never.

Chapter 17

FAST ENOUGH

Kim Warnick and Lulu Gargiulo

FOR TWENTY-THREE YEARS BASSIST KIM WARNICK, GUITARIST
Lulu Gargiulo, and songwriter/guitarist Kurt Bloch, along with a rotation
of fifteen drummers (with an eleven-year stint by Mike Musberger), played
hyperactive, saccharine punk pop laden with gloomy, soulful lyrics. Within
that time, an era that spanned and withstood so many musical mutations in
the indie world, Seattle's Fastbacks issued seventeen releases—a mix of EPs
and full-length albums on a host of independent labels, including PopLlama,
spinART, and Sub Pop.

Trends have come and gone, but the Fastbacks' pop punk and unassuming wisdom remained steadfast. While article after article expounds
on why the Fastbacks never "made it," in a sense, they've had one of the
most enduring careers a band could hope for. When asked by Seattle's
alternative weekly *The Stranger* to list her most memorable shows, Warnick
responded with a list any band would be proud of: "Opening for Joan Jett
at Wrex; opening for the Ramones in 1983 or '84 at the Eagles auditorium;
the shows in Japan with Seaweed and the Supersuckers in 1993; and all the
Pearl Jam dates in 1996, where we went as far as Istanbul and we finally

realized our ultimate rock and roll fantasy. Seeing the enormo-domes of the world *and* playing them was killer."[1]

"I knew Kim and Kurt from a very young age," comments Gargiulo, "and so I was sort of influenced by their influences. I definitely remember when I was probably fifteen, maybe sixteen years old, the first Ramones album came out, and just thinking how great that was, that it was so different than anything out there. It was so perfect, timing-wise, for my age. I mean, basically, it's just bubblegum music, but just in this whole new way of playing it that was just so meaningful to me even to this day. [It] just kind of feeds my soul, and that's basically what it did at that age, you know?"[2]

Gargiulo started playing guitar at nine years old. She recalls, "I was playing all those folkie kind of songs, and just playing open chords. Then once this whole punk thing came out, it was just like, 'Now *this* is music.' I didn't even know how to play that well once I started playing with the Fastbacks." The band began when Warnick and Gargiulo met Bloch through a friend in high school. By the time Gargiulo graduated, Warnick was playing bass with a band called the Radios, and Bloch was playing with his brother Al in the Cheaters. Gargiulo says, "The point when I decided, 'Okay, I'm going to play in a band—I'm going to do this myself' is [when] I went to this concert, and it was just the worst band. They weren't a punk band; they were just kind of a rock band. They were so bad that I told Kurt, 'These guys are so bad that I'm going to go start a band just to prove that I'm better than these guys.' So I got Kim and Kurt to sign up, you know, and [Kim] was already playing bass in another band. She'd thought, 'Okay, I'll do this too,' and Kurt said, 'I'll play drums,' and I decided to play guitar. We just started playing, and it was really bad. . . . I'll tell you, it was just horrible."[3] Aside from releasing a few singles and two EPs on the No Threes label between 1981 and 1984, the Fastbacks didn't release a full album until . . . *And His Orchestra* appeared on PopLlama in 1987.

There was only one club in Seattle, the Bird, where the Fastbacks were able to see punk bands, and there wasn't a thriving local scene when the band got together in 1979 either. When there were shows to see, there weren't many women onstage, aside from the Enemy, one of Seattle's first punk bands, which was led by a woman. "The only other band I can think of [that] I was sort of in awe of was Girlschool and, of course, Joan Jett. I mean, she knows how to rock—and the Pandoras,"[4] Gargiulo recalls.

Regardless of the dearth of local women from which to take cues,

Gargiulo and Warnick never really experienced any kind of peer sexism as female musicians. Gargiulo muses, "I think because I was such close friends with Kim and Kurt and we were like a team, like a family, I mean, Kurt didn't treat us any differently so I didn't really think of us as being any different. . . . I was just accepted as a musician, not as a woman, and I think that is unique in our situation."[5]

The sound that prevailed throughout most of the Fastbacks' career is angry, dreamy pop, sculpted around driving guitars. Warnick sings lead, harmonizing with Gargiulo, while Bloch has been the band's consistent, all-around songwriter. "In some ways, this makes the Fastbacks a classic girl group: Like the Ronettes, ABBA, and even the Cowboy Junkies, Warnick and Gargiulo mouth men's words," wrote Evelyn McDonnell in a 1993 *Rolling Stone* review of their album *Zücker*. McDonnell added, "However, they also play bass and guitar, respectively, in a democratic, DIY band, giving them more power than their predecessors."[6] While this general assessment is true—Warnick and Gargiulo were singing songs Bloch had written—they were also active musicians in the band. Either way, Gargiulo's not bothered by it: "I mean, I think Kurt is just an amazing songwriter, and I never felt frustrated wishing that I could write those words. . . . I was just so happy to be able to be in a band with somebody that could write such amazing songs."[7]

Like the Fastbacks' ability to overlay bubblegum punk with meaningful and emotional lyrics, Bloch's songwriting proves the interchangeability of gender in musical expression missing from the girl-group set; nothing about the Fastbacks sounds forced. Classic girl groups were basically assembled by behind-the-scenes Svengalis as a means for reaping rewards. Their lyrics often played on male fantasies of female feelings. Consider the following girl-group classics of the early '60s, and note the gender specificity of most of the songs' subjects: "Dedicated to the One I Love," "Big John" (The Shirelles); "Johnny Get Angry" (Joanie Sommers); "He's a Rebel," "Then He Kissed Me" (The Crystals); "He's So Fine," "One Fine Day," (The Chiffons); "I Will Follow Him" (Little Peggy March); "My Boyfriend's Back," (The Angels); "Be My Baby," (The Ronettes). All of these songs, written by men to be sung by women, are variations on themes of love, forgiveness, adoration, or just plain boy-craziness. Obviously, this phenomenon—of women simply repeating what men would like to hear them say—is most derisive to female singers when they are perpetuating female stereotypes. In contrast, the Fastbacks and their lyrical repertoire were in no danger of falling into this trap. Bloch's simply written lyrics are self-revelatory, evoking sensitivity and empathy without the grandstanding or sentimentality found in so much girl-group pop. The Fastbacks conveyed impulsive energy and honesty instead of more formulaic emotional fodder, which is one aspect that separates women's experiences in punk and indie, and particularly those of the Fastbacks, from the mainstream record industry. And also what makes those experiences in the scene so significant within the context of the larger culture; underground rock is one of the only artistic realms where women are given relative leeway for self-expression. Gargiulo and Warnick, like Kim Gordon and Kim Deal, are also unassuming onstage, the confident "Every Girl" musicians as opposed to the requisite sexual preening of mainstream female singers so prevalent in '80s mainstream pop.

Other than their catalog of great pop punk songs, the most charming thing about the Fastbacks is their unabashed love for their band and for punk rock. In response to why and how they lasted as long as they did, Bloch once responded, "The way I look at it, we're not under any pressure to do anything in particular. . . . We're not popular enough that anybody else is making their living because of our existence, so there's not a lot of outside pressure to keep doing stuff."[8]

In early 2002, Warnick announced she was leaving the Fastbacks for a band called Visqueen formed by Rachel Flotard and Ben Hooker. She told *The Stranger*, "The Fastbacks [have] done everything a band could possibly do for me. It's saved my life, it's taken me around the world, and I've gotten to sing those songs, which are some of my favorite ever written. But as much as those songs mean to me, I've just grown tired of having to be a singer in a band."[9] Visqueen has released two albums, one in 2003 entitled *King Me*, and 2004's *Sunset on Dateland*. Gargiulo hasn't been with a band since the Fastbacks called it quits. "Playing music, for me, even to this day . . . is being part of this small family which is your band, which is part of this bigger family of the music world, which is a very exciting world. Punk music in particular really does speak to me. . . . I miss that so much, you know?"[10] After twenty-five years, it's hard to figure out whose loyalty is stronger—that of their fans, or that of the Fastbacks to punk.

Chapter 18

NEW YEAR

Kim Deal

WHILE WOMEN'S ONSTAGE PRESENCE WAS MEAGER IN THE '80S, those who did play proved more than their ability: They proved they didn't have to compromise themselves to do so. Kim Deal's lack of compromise, in fact, is what made her all the bigger, louder, and more impressive with the Pixies, and beyond. The Pixies wouldn't have been one of the most influential (and certainly one of the most beloved) indie bands of the late '80s and early '90s without Deal's melodic bass lines and, depending on the song, cheerful shouts or hungry whispers. While the short list of '80s underground female alumnae range in image from emotionally blank to surreal to confrontational and intense, Kim Deal wasn't born of the bizarre, nor was she unshakably cool, or overtly angry. She was pure fun and, because of this, more accessible than many of her peers.

Breeders bassist Josephine Wiggs once told *Rolling Stone*, "When Sonic Youth came to London in '86, I was very struck by how cool Kim Gordon was. . . . Then the next thing was seeing Kim [Deal] play in the Pixies in '88. In a way they were self-effacing. They were just getting on with the job. At the same time, you could see that both of them had enormous charisma. But they weren't showing off. I was quite impressed with that. You knew that they knew that they were cool, but that was enough for them. They didn't have to shove it down anyone's throat. They didn't have to make a statement about it."[1] And that's precisely Deal's appeal: What she achieved was tangible and grounded. Her voice didn't, nor does it now, sound enraged or possessed. She sings clearly, albeit with plenty of force, pouncing about the stage, pounding her bass or guitar, and sporting that ever-present smile.

In 1986 college friends Joey Santiago and Charles Thompson IV (who went by Black Francis in the Pixies and, more recently, Frank Black) placed an ad in the *Boston Phoenix* looking for a bassist with an interest in "Hüsker Dü and Peter, Paul and Mary."[2] Deal, then married and credited on the first two Pixies albums as Mrs. John Murphy, was the only person who showed up for the audition. (Deal divorced Murphy in 1988.) "She wasn't just cool and enthusiastic," Black told *Total Guitar*, "she was perfect, because we wanted a female bassist who could sing harmonies."[3] Deal also suggested David Lovering as a drummer. The new band sent their demo to Britain's 4AD Records, and released *Come on Pilgrim* in October 1987, which made it to number one on the U.K. indie charts.

The Pixies played driving, hard-edged rock, made alternately more punk by Francis' bloodcurdling screams and more by with Deal's softer vocals and Santiago's surf-sounding guitar. Even the loudest Pixies songs are melodic and easy to sing to, if you can decipher Francis' psychobabble. Their songs were infectious and loud, tumbling with spunk from the first note to the last. The band quickly became the favorite of thousands of indie fans, releasing four more albums before breaking up in 1993. They reunited in 2004 and embarked on a tour that would take them through North America and Europe.

Prior to joining the Pixies, Deal and her twin sister Kelley had played together as the Breeders when they were teenagers in Dayton, Ohio. Deal told *The Guardian Unlimited*, "One acoustic guitar, two girls singing. And they loved it, these bikers in the audience; they had tears in their eyes. We played Hank Williams' songs, Everly Brothers, blues songs, a few originals. It was really good."[4] While the Pixies suffered some internal strife, one thing was clear: Deal's contributions were diminishing as her years with the Pixies wore on. "I've been singing less and less in the Pixies. Just oohing and aahing. Charles is the lead singer. Not only that, he sings every fucking one!"[5] Black commented in 2004, "It just became a grouchy thing. More than anything, it was just people being unhappy in their personal lives."[6] In 1989, Deal was asked to leave the band. Prior to her departure from the Pixies, Deal and Tanya Donelly of the Throwing Muses, who were also on 4AD, embarked on a new project, also named the Breeders, in 1989. With Josephine Wiggs on bass, Britt Walford on drums, and Deal on guitar and vocals, they released an LP entitled *Pod* in 1990; the majority of the songs were written by Deal. As the Pixies disintegrated, she asked Kelley to join the Breeders in 1992, to augment the departure of Donelly, who left to form Belly after the Breeders' *Safari* EP came out. Kelley played lead guitar, and Jim MacPherson replaced Walford on drums for their 1993 album, *Last Splash*.

Although the Pixies consistently blew critics and indie fans away, they never really broke mainstream ground, aside from their slowed-down version of "Wave of Mutilation," which appeared on the soundtrack for the film *Pump Up the Volume*. Of course, the pop music industry had usurped scads of underground bands by the time the Breeders' *Last Splash* came out. Nevertheless the album gained major mainstream attention, especially the song "Cannonball." The Pixies' influence on the Breeders was, in some ways, obvious: They mixed distorted vocals with acoustic guitar, meshing country, surf, and indie rock elements into a distinct sound. The Breeders had mellower moments, however, and worked more within a groove, maintaining the cool Deal contributed to the Pixies without employing the vocal highs and lows, the alternate wailing and whispering, and the calm and chaos for which the Pixies are so well-known.

When the Breeders went on hiatus in 1995 (due to sister Kelley's drug bust), Deal learned to play the drums and wrote and produced an album for a new side project called the Amps. Of the Amps she told *Spin*, "The vocals were cranked, more emphasis on the lyrics, so you don't need a full, working band to play them. . . . Plus, I like the idea of being a total asshole and playing all the instruments. Kelley went around calling me the Artist Formerly Known as Kim."[7] Kelley reemerged with the Kelley Deal 6000 album *Go to the Sugar Altar* before the Breeders returned in 2002 with a tour to promote their new album, *Title TK*.

Riding the wave of female performers that sprang up in the mid-'90s, the Breeders achieved the rare combination of mainstream popularity with music that reflected a rare level of complexity, sensitivity, and fun. They could be sweet and sensitive one minute in the soft, strumming introduction to "Do You Love Me Now?," and crass the next in "I Just Wanna Get Along." While most indie women who had signed to major labels were subsequently reduced to preexisting marketing categories—bands like Hole and L7 were the "angry" bands; Mazzy Star, Björk, and Sinead O'Connor offered etherealness—all-male bands like Nirvana and Soundgarden were free to run the gamut of deep emotion and rock star irresponsibility. Somehow, so were the Breeders.

The '80s were another story; popular culture's more superficial landscape made it harder for women who didn't fit the mold of the female performer with a face full of makeup and precarious stiletto heels, which is where Kim Gordon and Kim Deal departed in image from most of their contemporaries. Thanks to London's foray into bondage and war paint in the '70s, the punk "look" had been clearly established by the '80s. As the indie fan base grew, and different kinds of music attracted wider audiences, indie rock and hardcore toned the "look" down a notch to T-shirts and jeans, partly in opposition to the images of aspirational wealth and beauty the mainstream offered. In fact, the entire mainstream music industry decorated its female stars like Christmas trees, with all the lace, sequins, hairspray, and accoutrements they could find.

In comparison Kim Deal seemed so "normal." As she told *Spin* in 1995, "I know I come off lookin' like a fuckin' haggy housewife, compared to all these other women in rock, and that's fine with me, man. So I don't wanna wash my hair, fuck you, this is how I look."[8] While MTV paraded submissive and sexually available video mavens through every cable-ready living room in 1987, Deal defied this singular image. That year rock and roll fans were otherwise assaulted with the likes of teen bubble gummers like Debbie Gibson and Tiffany, and saw releases by Bananarama, Heart, Gloria Estefan and Miami Sound Machine, Janet Jackson, and the Bangles. Aside from the Bangles and Heart, all of these performers were singers above all else, while Deal was actively contributing to the writing and arranging of her bands' music, working outside of the traditional female role of lead singer. Against the loud, long notes Heart's Ann Wilson belted with heavy doses of drama, the Casio keyboard beats of more dance-oriented artists like Lisa Lisa and Cult Jam or Exposé, and the layered harmonies of the Bangles that stayed within a key or two throughout their entire career, Deal sang with clear simplicity that very often grounded the screeching antics of Black Francis.

In the thriving 1980s indie underground, Deal stands as a female icon for her talent and her transgressions both creatively and personally. Nineteen eighty-seven saw an incredible swell of influential signature releases: R.E.M.'s *Document*, Big Black's *Songs About Fucking*, Hüsker Dü's *Warehouse: Songs and Stories*, the Replacements' *Pleased to Meet Me*, Dinosaur Jr.'s *You're Living All Over Me*, and U2's first crossover album, *The Joshua Tree.* These albums don't just point to the vibrancy and genius of the underground in the mid- to late '80s; this all-male roster stands as a testament to just how refreshing it was to see a woman like Kim Deal claim a spot on the stage.

Part IV

THE 1990S

Introduction

TRUEPUNKROCK-SOULCRUSADERS

You don't make all the rules, yeah!
I know what I'm gonna fuckin' do
Me and my girlfriends gonna push on through
We are gonna stomp on you, yeah!
You're dumb, I'm not
You're fucked, I'm not.
—BIKINI KILL, "THIS IS NOT A TEST"

WITH A BUSH AS PRESIDENT, WOMEN ARE NEVER SAFE. WHEN the Oval Office was occupied by George Bush Senior, the Gulf War and the threat (once again) of the Supreme Court overturning *Roe v. Wade* loomed without popular female voices of dissent to counter the conservative agenda. The ominous beginning of the decade did nothing to ease American women's malaise. The indie underground, however, helped fuel a pro-feminist, pro-woman backlash that would indelibly alter the scene's face and voice.

As if in response to the Parents' Music Resource Center's dogged attempts to brand and vilify subversive content in rock and rap music through its "Parental Advisory" sticker campaign, the top of the singles charts at the start of the decade was rarely controversial. As for women on the charts, the early 1990s had witnessed the recording industry's leap back into a maze of light pop and dance singles, neglecting the strides women like Pat Benatar, Joan Jett, and Debbie Harry had made.

The female acts that hit number one during the late '80s and early '90s were strictly pop or R&B acts, and expressed little if any political or subversive content. Some notable exceptions were Madonna's 1989 video for "Like

151

a Prayer," replete with depictions of burning crosses and interracial relationships, images that were still discomforting to mainstream America. Her video for "Express Yourself" offered plenty of crotch-grabbing, while "Justify My Love" was banned from daytime MTV airplay for its portrayal of sadomasochism and lesbian erotica. While Madonna's subversions were more palatable than underground offerings at the time, they still sent shivers down the mainstream's spine, as typified by her loss of a large Pepsi endorsement in the wake of the "Like a Prayer" controversy. Aside from the general public's introduction to the atypical and minimalist Sinead O'Connor in the 1990 video for her number one hit "Nothing Compares 2 U" and the bolder feminist messages of Salt-N-Pepa and TLC, neither of whom hit the top spot, the charts' top positions were held from 1989 through 1994 by mostly mundane songstresses like Whitney Houston, Mariah Carey, Janet Jackson, and Paula Abdul.

Paula Abdul had six number one hits between 1989 and 1991 alone; Whitney Houston held the top spot three times between 1990 and 1992, with a sprinkling of Top 10 hits in between. Janet Jackson reached number one five times between 1989 and 1994, and Mariah Carey, eight times from 1990 to 1994. All four touted carefully crafted, nonthreatening, and glamorous images, and were only extreme in their use of sequins and hairspray. Their hits were often garden variety love songs: Among Carey's most successful of this period were "Vision of Love" and "Dreamlover," while Houston's "I Will Always Love You" remained at number one for fourteen weeks. Abdul's most successful single was not the danceable, peppy "Straight Up," but the ballad "Rush, Rush," and Jackson's "That's the Way Love Goes" remained in the top spot for eight weeks in 1993.

None of these new pop divas carried an instrument with her, either. These performers were mostly vehicles of studio songwriting—a strategy often employed by the music industry to control and contrive what emotional face their audiences would see and to generate hit after formulaic hit. And, as usual, the result is a kind of synthetic and utterly nonthreatening package of female emotions—a grieving, forgiving, willing-to-love-again devotion. Predominantly written by men and performed by women, these time-tested song models of the passive female and active male are represented most often in the love song format, complete with trite and saccharine-sweet lyrics.

The early '90s also saw a bevy of ballads by men like Bryan Adams,

Color Me Badd, and Boyz II Men, although these songs shifted in and out of the top spots around hits performed by the aforementioned divas. While the male acts offered songs that displayed an active seduction and objectification, the divas were decidedly passive and submissive. In his hit "Cream," Prince ticked off a few sexual demands, while Whitney Houston sang that she'll indulge in anything her lover wants in "I'm Your Baby Tonight." After Mariah Carey's cover of the Jackson 5's loyalty anthem "I'll Be There," Sir Mix-A-Lot took the top spot with his paean to large women, "Baby Got Back." Abdul's tender ballad "Rush, Rush," was knocked out of the top spot by EMF's "Unbelievable," an admonishment of a lover for poor treatment of the male narrator. "Rush, Rush" also battled for number one with Color Me Badd's carnal "I Wanna Sex You Up." The dialogue acted like a call and response of stereotypical male and female sexuality; the male's rampantly heterosexual mating call, followed by the tirelessly loving, sexually restrained female's answer.

The emerging underground acts were the real indicators of Republican-induced female unease, though. By the early '90s, newly formed bands like Babes in Toyland, Hole, L7, the Lunachicks, and others stood as the antitheses to Whitney and friends. As the pop chart divas pined away, Jenny Toomey played with Geek and Tsunami and formed Arlington, Virginia's Simple Machines label; Tribe 8 geared up for the emergence of lesbian queercore on the West Coast. Positive Force, a D.C. political group with punk ties, curated a women's festival in 1989, while Olympia, Washington's progressive record label Kill Rock Stars wholeheartedly supported political punk, particularly when it was laced with feminism. Bands like Babes in Toyland were beginning to voice their objections to candy-coated romance, revealing women who were clearly not the providers of Houston's eternal and unconditional affection. While the pop charts continued to pump the love song narcotic, these underground acts hinted that the girl revolution to come was about self-preservation instead. Work by Babes in Toyland, the Lunachicks, and Hole hinged on expressing female anger, defiance, and instability, which pop music had habitually ignored.

Bands like L7 and Babes in Toyland used primal screams and guitars that ground out funeral dirges. They created songs that expressed the ugly and damaged part of the female soul—wounded by unhealthy love and abuse. The new crop of underground women revered the raw and angry female. "Lashes" by Babes in Toyland favors an ostensibly insane woman, saving bile for businessmen instead. And in Hole's "Babydoll," Courtney Love painted a portrait of the denigrated, struggling female—the end result of Whitney Houston's stalwart faithfulness.

Compared to the offering of the glammed-up chart artists, these songs connote a woman peeling off her made-up face to reveal a demon lurking beneath. The physical perfection expected of American women was ripped away, unveiling what lives beneath or, perhaps, what is created by these hollow expectations of womanhood: despair, isolation, and a desire for unadulterated revenge. Songs like "Babydoll" painted female flaws from a sympathetic point of view, rather than invoking the tired image, even prevalent in '80s indie and punk, of the unlovable, ugly, or worn girl.

By the time Hole and Babes in Toyland had formed, much absurdist indie and punk rock—bands like the Dickies, the Dead Milkmen, and the Butthole Surfers—had played out the idea of the ugly girl, with lyrics written mostly for laughs. The ugly girl provided comic relief. The Dickies penned "She's a Hunchback" (for *Stukas over Dickieland*), a love song for a deformed girl. "Cross-Eyed Tammy" appeared on the Dickies' *Second Coming*, and the Dead Milkmen sang an ode to their "Gorilla Girl" on *Big Lizard in My Backyard*. Written as jokes, the songs feature narrators who are painted as bizarre for loving disfigured women. In contrast, bands like Hole, Babes in Toyland, L7, and Lunachicks became *Carrie*'s prom night revenge for the hunchbacks, cross-eyed Tammys, and ugly girls, finally giving them voice.

And while the ugly girls were getting their due, the tide was turning against corporate rock, too. Beat Happening member Calvin Johnson and K Records cofounder Candice Pedersen held the International Pop Underground Convention in Olympia, Washington, in 1991; according to one promotional piece, it offered fifty bands in six days for the underground music community with "no lackeys to the corporate ogre allowed."[1] Pedersen told Michael Azerrad, "It was not about business; it was about really loving music."[2] The opening day of the conference was designated "Love Rock Revolution Girl Style Now," and featured, among others, Bratmobile, Heavens to Betsy, Bikini Kill, L7, the Spinanes, Mecca Normal, and 7 Year Bitch.[3,4] Slim Moon had assembled the first *Kill Rock Stars* compilation especially for the convention.

Many call this gathering a landmark event for indie rock—an opportunity for far-flung devotees to meet. For many, the IPU Convention solidified the ties between regional scenes, and also, the participation of women.

IPU's opening night also acted as a precursor to one of the most misunderstood punk phenomena, riot grrrl. The two hearts of the riot grrrl movement beat the strongest in the Northwest and D.C., two of the most active, influential scenes in the country. D.C.'s underground had gone through a myriad of changes by the late '80s. As had happened in other scenes where hardcore was prominent, audience aggression increased while female participation levels fell. Mark Andersen and Mark Jenkins noted in *Dance of Days*: "By mid-1981, the punks' 'letting go' had effectively barred women from both the dance floor and the stage. The dozen bands who played [D.C.'s] first massive Wilson Center show included only one woman, Toni Young, bassist of Red C. This was particularly striking since so many of the earlier local punk bands, including Urban Verbs, the Slickee Boys, the Nurses, Tru Fax and the Insaniacs, Tiny Desk Unit, DCeats, and the Shirkers had female members."[5]

Andersen and Jenkins go on to note that the 'zine *Critical List* referred to all-female hardcore band Chalk Circle's show as "bimbo nite."[6] As the authors document, the noticeable absence of women hadn't been resolved by 1986 and most were still relegated mainly to behind-the-scenes work, leading Beefeater singer Tomas Squip to dedicate a set to "all the girls in this town who want to make music."[7] While D.C. may not have produced a lot of female acts during this period, musicians with a political bent like Squip and Ian MacKaye of Minor Threat and Fugazi acknowledged the exclusion and oppression of punk and indie women. Fugazi wrote and recorded the song "Suggestion" to address sexual harassment and rape.[8] MacKaye also encouraged fans to make space on the floor where nonviolent dancing could occur—a request that was sometimes met with resistance by the growing audiences. Despite the support from local bands, though, women still weren't speaking for themselves.

Jenny Toomey remembers her own development and inspiration in D.C. during the late '80s:

> Besides having taken women's studies classes and reading brilliant feminists, what changed me were women getting in[to] D.C. bands, and the first example of that was Fire Party. It was really interesting; things that are just obvious now seemed like such revelations, like the

idea that clearly everybody was dating each other, right? And [Fire Party's lead singer, Amy Pickering] had dated a lot of boys who had been in rock bands. The fact of the matter was, when they broke up, or when things weren't going well in the relationship, he had carte blanche to tell his side of the story in the community, and nobody was ever surprised about who he was singing about. And what was neat was, when she got in a band, too, suddenly there was sort of a balanced critique of what was going on, as opposed to just his side of the story. They were totally great, and it was really inspiring, and instantly, I called my friend Derek, and said, 'Hey, you know, when you get home from school this summer, we're gonna be in a band.' And we did, immediately.'

On the West Coast, Seattle's Sub Pop label aspired to be the record industry's rock star machine model. Label cofounder Jonathan Poneman admitted as much in *Our Band Could Be Your Life*: "We're using a precedent set by Tamla-Motown and Stax, where you have this scene that is being born in a particular region and then you just have a machine you use to refine and perfect your product. You create a sensation, like Great Britain in 1962 through 1965."[10] At the end of the '80s, Sub Pop was known for promoting artists who fused metal and punk, and, as Poneman stated, for manufacturing celebrity around its roster. Meanwhile, Seattle's indie neighbor, K Records in Olympia, generated a softer and looser DIY aesthetic, producing pop that inspired riot grrrl. As so many bands in the culture had done before, Beat Happening and the K Records set reinforced the message that music-making was a timeless art of the people, and a task that could be undertaken by anyone.

Although the Seattle and Olympia music scenes in the '90s were distinct, they did inform each other. As Olympian and Bratmobile member Allison Wolfe noted, "In a lot of ways, you can't really separate it out," she explains. "Everybody kind of knew each other and were friends, so Nirvana is friends with Beat Happening, is friends with Bikini Kill, is friends with Bratmobile, is friends with Unwound, is friends with, you know, Seaweed. And we were all kind of friends, we were often all on the same team, going to the same shows and stuff like that, often playing shows together, but the way history looks back at it is like, 'Grunge was a totally male thing in Seattle and totally separate, and riot grrrl was totally girls in Olympia and totally separate,' but it wasn't really separate."[11]

And while bands like Seattle's Fastbacks had been producing music since 1979, the groups that eventually received copious amounts of world-wide attention were all male: Soundgarden, Mudhoney, Pearl Jam, and Nirvana. Even though men like Eddie Vedder and Kurt Cobain actively promoted feminism—Cobain aided in the Raincoats' revival and doggedly addressed the issue of rape, and his bandmate Krist Novoselic worked to raise money for Balkan rape victims; Vedder wrote a 1992 pro-choice piece for *Spin* and furiously marked his arm with the words "pro-choice" during a performance on MTV—they rarely influenced the minds of their mainstream male audience members with their feminist politics.

When Hole toured with Mudhoney in 1991 (just prior to the mainstream's "grunge" awakening), Courtney Love took a stage dive in London and was swallowed by the audience that caught her. According to Joe Ambrose in *Moshpit*, the audience "groped her, tore off her clothes, and shoved their fingers up her various orifices. When she finally got back onto the stage she was virtually naked and crying."[12] After the media's 1992 co-optation of grunge, Ambrose documents a now-infamous Nirvana show in Utah. Love watched from the wings as the band played "Rape Me," and noticed a female fan up front who had been engulfed by a group of men, who were "staring straight ahead . . . as they ripped her shirt, bra, panties . . . as they started mangling her breasts . . . hands on either side—her face was all screwed up in a scream—and the men were all glazed—*and staring straight ahead.* . . . [T]he girl was bloody and hysterical—her breasts and stomach looked as though she'd been clawed by jackals."[13] During a "Take Back the Night" march in Ithaca, New York—an annual event where survivors of assault march to symbolically "take back" areas that threaten their safety—marchers were heckled by a group of men, who hovered on their balcony and blasted Nirvana's "Rape Me." Once again, the ideals of indie music were left by the wayside in favor of misinterpretations of the scene's violence. These fans were obviously not in it for the politics; by this time, bigger shows and MTV's promotion of grunge and the "alternative" life-style invited an "in" crowd, alienating those who opted out of trends or fashion, or "fitting in."

In the early '90s in Olympia, Kathleen Hanna and Tammy Rae Carland, who produced the 'zine *I ♥ Amy Carter* and was later co-owner of Mr. Lady Records, were helping to run Reko Muse, an Olympia art gallery that showcased women's art. According to an interview in *Rockrgrl*, Hanna began noticing that the art shows skewed female and the rock bands who played the space to help pay the rent were almost all male: "I would come from the [women's] shelter where I had talked with fifty-year-old women who had been in incredible circumstances and survived them—gracefully. Then I'd go to the gallery and hear these lyrics that were like 'Oh baby' and 'My lady left me, she's such a bitch.'"[14] The experience helped Hanna to realize not only the need for an influx of the female perspective in the underground scene, but also the desire to make her own noise (which she did with Bikini Kill and later with Le Tigre). Hanna wasn't the only one inspired to rail against the sexism she had grown up with. Tobi Vail produced the 'zine *Jigsaw*, which often criticized punk for its male orientation and expressed her own feelings of isolation from the scene.

"[Tobi] wrote this great essay in the first *Jigsaw* fanzine she put out," Toomey recalls, "talking about the Yoko factor, and how when you're dating a boy who's in a band, there's inevitably a moment where he'll take you aside, and explain to you how Yoko Ono broke up the Beatles. And the idea of the discussion, whether it's even conscious or not, is not only to tell you that you're danger to his art, but that also, you're the opposite of his art. I think that's the most overt version of the Yoko factor, but I think the Yoko factor exists subtly, as well, where if you don't see any other artists that are women doing that work, it's hard to imagine that as a role that you'll ever be in."[15]

The collective exclusion Vail and Toomey expressed would be short-lived, though. Soon after *Jigsaw* appeared, Allison Wolfe and Molly Neuman produced their own 'zine, *Girl Germs*. With so many female indie rock fans and so few direct outlets for women's expression within the scene, it's doubtful that these were the only pockets of female resistance within indie culture, but Hanna, Vail, Neuman, and Wolfe are marked as the key figures who unleashed the riot grrrl fury. The women named the movement after an imagined "girl riot," and Hanna wrote a manifesto that outlined the basis of why riot grrrl was necessary. The movement itself resisted definition, so any girl could add, react, or use it in their own way and in their own communities. The basis of Hanna's manifesto, though, made riot grrrl a call to action for punk rock fans. In part, it said:

> BECAUSE we want and need to encourage and be encouraged in
> the face of all our own insecurities, in the face of beergutboyrock that

tells us we can't play our instruments, in the face of "authorities" who say our bands/'zines/etc are the worst in the U.S. and

BECAUSE we don't wanna assimilate to someone else's (boy) standards of what is and what isn't.

BECAUSE we are unwilling to falter under claims that we are reactionary "reverse sexists" AND NOT THE TRUEPUNKROCKSOUL CRUSADERS THAT WE KNOW we really are.[16]

Female punk rock fans took the new dialogue to heart. In a girl-heavy mosh pit during a Bikini Kill/Fugazi show, at a July 1992 benefit concert in D.C., the girls were squeezed up against the stage by eager Fugazi fans maneuvering for space. No doubt empowered by Bikini Kill's set, the girls formed a girls-only space in the middle of the pit. D.C. punk Erika Reinstein recounted the action in *Dance of Days*: "It was right in the middle of the 'pit,' and all these girls started joining it, and it became this really big circle. It was this really powerful thing where something that had been really violent and threatening for a lot of us became a safe space and we were protecting each other."[17]

Olympia's IPU Convention, the proliferation of girl 'zines, resistance like that displayed at the Bikini Kill/Fugazi show, and the rumblings of riot grrrl converged on the underground within a span of two years, in tandem with a cultural groundswell of new feminist thought.

By the end of the '80s, the mainstream media had taken feminism to task, with articles that outlined the movement's alleged betrayal of working women and promoted a cultural yearning for a return to the '50s. Feminist authors answered by documenting the culture's suppression of the movement. Future riot grrrls encountered their generation's mainstream feminist tracts in the early '90s: Susan Faludi's *Backlash* painstakingly documented '80s American culture and its subconscious attempts to oppress feminism, and Naomi Wolf's *The Beauty Myth* outlined ways in which beauty standards dominate and damage women. Both books were published in 1991 and circulated in women's studies classes and around young women's circles during this time. The books also opened the floodgates for a host of texts by young female authors who would become known as part of the "third wave" of the feminist movement.

Following the birth of the third wave, as if scripted to prove Faludi's central point in *Backlash*, came a threat to abortion rights in 1992. This threat galvanized a tremendous march on Washington, the March for Women's Lives, in April of that year. And shortly before the march, Anita Hill's accusations of harassment by Supreme Court nominee Clarence Thomas fired a national debate that brought feminism back to the political fore. As in the '70s when politics and art—in the form of punk and feminism—reached a boiling point, the '90s brought an artistic and political response to the long, heavy silence of the mainstream media regarding women's issues. And, as usual, the indie scene would prove vibrant and vocal, garnering the most media hype and the least serious attention to its goals.

Riot grrrl wasn't just a hip lifestyle option for young female music fans, but a necessary outlet for disaffected young women. The popularity of the riot grrrl phenomenon speaks to the amount of unwell young women who couldn't be diagnosed without it, like Betty Friedan's "problem that has no name." Feminism—and by virtue of its association—riot grrrl, both sought to define the more contemporary "problems that had no name" that haunted young women.

Regardless of the strides made by the "second wave" of feminism in the '70s, young women in the early '90s had still grown up with such pervasive problems as sexual and physical abuse, rape, eating disorders, female jealousy, homophobia, racism, and classism. And while more women in the middle class were part of the work force, a host of other challenges still confronted the emerging generation of young women just coming into adulthood.

Young women were eager to delve into the new world they were discovering and hungry for connections with other young women. With the help of, and exposure to, bands like Bratmobile and Bikini Kill, riot grrrl factions subsequently sprang up around the country. Thanks to the DIY punk ethic, any girl could form her own band, start her own 'zine, or light a fire in her community. Rather than being a movement based solely on the blind imitation of fashion, music, and political rhetoric, riot grrrl simply allowed a lot of young women to address issues previously disregarded in underground circles and in everyday life. As Allison Wolfe put it, riot grrrl meant to infuse punk with feminism, and feminism, so reflexively academic at the time, with punk rock's conversational tone.[18]

Riot grrrl aimed not only to support female self-expression through homemade art and music, but to encourage girls to explore the ways in which being an American woman can damage individual spirit, all while utilizing the inflammatory language and sounds of punk and personal, diary-form 'zines. It sought to begin a dialogue where girls could work through the patterns of jealousy our society encouraged between women, to come to a place where sharing work and experiences replaced *Cosmopolitan*'s ideas of female bonding through beauty and sex tips. Riot grrrl was whatever any angry girl wanted it to be.

To compensate for the years of being bumped, knocked, and relegated to the sidelines at shows, the members of the bands associated with riot grrrl aimed to provide for their female audience members the abandon so beloved by punk rock boys by insisting on girls-only sections at the front of their shows—an action that often caused riot grrrl's critics to balk at the notion of being relegated to the sidelines themselves. Although they weren't members of the riot grrrl movement, Tribe 8 experienced resistance at their shows when they wanted women at the front. Guitarist Leslie Mah says:

> When riot grrrl happened, and when we were playing shows at that time especially, [we were] like, "We want all the women in front. Boys in dresses are invited to come up front, too, but you guys have to behave." And there was some feeling from both boys and girls like, "Why is it so unfair? You're discriminating."
>
> And it's like, look, you can go to a show on the other 363 days a year and it's all boys up front, it's all boys in the pit, it's all boys on stage. Is anybody asking those boy bands, "Well, how do you think the girls feel when they come to your shows? Do you worry about them feeling alienated?" I've never ever heard anyone interviewing a boy band asking them that question, but we got asked that question almost every interview. "Well, are men welcome at your show? Are you being antimale?" If men had those feelings when they come to our show, those were their feelings. We're not responsible for them. Why aren't you asking boy bands the same questions? I think so many women who want to check something out feel alienated.[19]

For the legions of riot grrrls that rose during the early '90s, the press was less than welcoming to those who hungered for a galvanizing movement. Self-identified feminist and critic Jim DeRogatis, in *Milk It!*, his collection of musings on the '90s "alternative" music scene, comments: "[L]audable though their politics may have been, their brand of punk rock simply sucked moose cock."[20] *Entertainment Weekly*'s David Browne reported at the time that riot grrrls were "discovering punk rock," intimating that punk had fostered a solely male fan base (and an all-male music catalog) for almost twenty years.[21] *Rolling Stone* wrote that riot grrrl "apparently seeks to alienate," without commenting on whom, exactly, it was alienating.[22] *Newsweek* translated the dialogue of riot grrrl as "wildly mixed ideas from Madonna, *Sassy* magazine, and feminist critics like Susan Faludi and Naomi Wolf," when in actuality, Madonna and *Sassy* were hardly consistent with a movement inspired by homemade 'zines meant to fill the holes left behind by the mainstream media, and bands organized to contribute sexually charged and aggressive feminist music.[23] *Newsweek*'s profile of riot grrrl Jessica Hopper portrayed her as a "bundle of contradictions" because she could admire a boy *and* start a pro-choice group, reflecting the continuing misconception that feminists must be man-haters.[24]

In the same article, writers Farai Chideya and Melissa Rossi become the "bundle of contradictions" when they note that Courtney Love, who quite vocally separated herself from the movement, is described as wearing "vintage little-girl dresses that barely make it past her hips—all the better to sing songs about rape and exploitation."[25] This is just a repetition of the old misguided message that a victim of rape and abuse, by her dress or behavior, invites assault. The statement also dilutes the politics of riot grrrl by choosing to focus on the importance of dress and image over hard-line political stances. There were also countless female musicians who operated outside of riot grrrl (and were incorrectly identified as riot grrrls solely for being female and in rock bands), like Mia Zapata of the Gits and members of the Lunachicks, 7 Year Bitch, L7, Red Aunts, and Slant 6. Even Patti Smith, never a self-identified feminist and about twenty years too early, has been called the "original riot grrrl."

The media's misunderstanding and misrepresentation of riot grrrl and its aims inadvertently fostered solidarity among frustrated girls who declared a ban on the media, which, sadly, quickened the movement's decline. Wolfe explains the demise:

> A lot of times, journalists would never respect your wishes. You'd say you want a female photographer sent over and, of course, it wouldn't be; it would be some guy who's a complete ass, taking your photo and telling you what to do, and you'd say, "Well, only if you give us some copies of the photos." Of course, you'd never see copies of the photos.

You'd say, "Only if I can get a copy of the articles"; you'd never see copies of the articles. There was so much misinformation. Oftentimes the
angle was condescending, often pitting women against each other. I
mean, how many articles did you see where it was like, "Babes In
Toyland vs. Hole!" or "Kat vs. Courtney!" We're not the same, we don't
have to be the same, but we can all exist and be proud of each other,
and all make an impact on women in music, or just in music, or whatever you want.

So the media came in—and also, mass marketing—all of a sudden,
it got co-opted by the mainstream, our aesthetics or ideas, but watered
down, and kind of sold back at a higher price to the mass market. You
know, you'd go into Urban Outfitters and there'd be all these fake riot
grrrl bands playing over the loudspeaker, all these clothes that were just
like what we would wear. . . . This was never meant for the cheerleaders,
it was never meant for the mainstream, and it ended up just kind of
eating itself, or we ended up just abandoning it, because it became so
trendy, and it wasn't our fault.[26]

Riot grrrl was often criticized for failing to include race and class in its
dialogue, and it's true these diversity questions went unfulfilled. Yet if the
movement had been allowed to mature, perhaps it would have grown to
encompass such issues. Regardless, as a whole the underground has failed to
encompass issues of race on a larger level. It still remains a very white (and
straight) scene. With the exception of a few bands like Bad Brains, Fishbone,
Living Colour, and members of Skunk Anansie and Tribe 8, the underground's onstage figures were (and remain) mostly white. The mainstream
culture's rampant reinforcement of heterosexuality was constantly found
onstage, too. The occasional "faggot"-laced rant surely deterred punk queers
from taking the stage. For instance, the Adolescents proudly claimed apathy
for queers in "Creatures"; the Butthole Surfers refused gay advances in
"Butthole Surfer"; and the Dickies swore off girls in "Going Homo."

During the '80s, Axl Rose of heavy metal act Guns N' Roses promoted
homophobia, too, when he wore a T-shirt that read, "AIDS Kills Fags Dead,"
a play on the insect extermination spray Raid's logo and tag line. While the
brutish metal culture has stood at odds with punk for as long as the two have
existed, the immediate connection of gay culture with AIDS in both punk
and metal inadvertently brought the two scenes together on an issue and in
line with the underlying reflex in mainstream media. Of course, not all of
the underground responded to gay culture in the same way. Performance

artist Diamanda Galas has spent her career engaged in AIDS activism, and on at least one occasion, Fugazi's antirape song "Suggestion" was used to protest gay bashing, among other actions that supported gay culture. Many pockets of the underground have intrepidly engaged in positive political activism and inclusion—but not enough to break the glass ceiling for gays, still quite intact in the early '90s.

Surely, attitudes like these, satirical or otherwise, reinforced homophobic ideas of the members of their respective scenes and inevitably led to an absence of queers onstage. In reaction to the long absence and affronts to the culture that lived within the underground's walls, queercore arose in the '90s. It propelled expressive bands like Pansy Division, the Velvet Mafia, God Is My Co-Pilot, Fifth Column, Tribe 8, and Team Dresch, onto the stage and led to the creation of labels like Chainsaw, Candy-Ass, and Outpunk, giving queer culture its own avenue of punk expression, as well as infusing the often hetero-heavy scene with a more open integration of trans, bi, lesbian, and gay lifestyles within its ranks. Outpunk also released *There's a Dyke in the Pit*, an extended 7" featuring Lucy Stoners, Bikini Kill, Tribe 8, and 7 Year Bitch, a record benefiting domestic violence programs. The cover displayed two snarling dykes with Mohawks.

The deluge of criticism from those who balked at women-only pits and confessional aesthetics proved that not much had changed for women, within and outside of the music world, since the 1970s, when both punk and feminism sprouted in earnest. Riot grrrl might have been a phenomenon that reflected the specific needs of punk girls in the early '90s. Beyond the headache it gave DeRogatis and the like, the bands still had heart, energy, and anger, and once again gave women more equal standing. Moreover, many of the bands were precursors to later feminist outfits like Sleater-Kinney, a revamped Bratmobile, and Le Tigre. However unnecessary, noisy, or nagging '90s grrrl rock may seem to some, this much is true: Sonically, these women changed everything.

Chapter 19

LOOK RIGHT THROUGH ME

Mia Zapata

I don't need your social love I already feel misread enough
And what ails me is the fact that you smile
when you're walking on by
I don't need your social crap you wear it on your sleeve
as far as I can see
And what ails me is your pretentious stare
You never see the truth and when it hits me it gets a little heavy
And when it's laying over there it's fucking wide open and read.
—FROM "SOCIAL LOVE"[1]

A BAND LIKE THE GITS IS STILL A RARITY; LEAD SINGER AND songwriter Mia Zapata's lyrics are unadulterated, utterly personal confessions. A hybrid of blues, punk, and hard rock, the Gits melded Zapata's deep love of blueswomen like Bessie Smith and Billie Holiday with a raw rock sound that underscored the often brutal honesty of her lyrics. The band released *Frenching the Bully* on C/Z Records in 1992 and was just finishing *Enter: The Conquering Chicken* for the same label when Zapata was found dead, having been brutally murdered one night while walking home. It took ten years, but the Seattle police finally tracked Zapata's killer to Florida, and he was convicted and sentenced to thirty-six years in prison in 2004. With the help of the Gits' surviving members, both albums were reissued in 2003 on Broken Rekids, along with early recordings *Kings and Queens* and *Seafish Louisville*. Following Zapata's death bassist Matt Dresdner, drummer Steve Moriarty, and guitarist Joe Spleen (née Andy Kessler) played in a short-lived collaboration with Joan Jett called Evil Stig ("Gits Live" spelled backwards), and without Jett as the Dancing French Liberals of '48 in the mid- to late '90s. Filmmakers Kerri O'Kane and Jessy Bender are in the process of making a film, *The Gits*, celebrating the band and particularly Zapata.

The Gits met at Antioch College in Yellow Springs, Ohio, in the mid-1980s. Moriarty recalls his first impression of Mia: "We drank tequila all afternoon, two or three of us, and ended up hanging out, and from then on were friendly and then started the band. I instantly liked her; she was really open and really, really friendly and likable. You know [when] you just meet somebody that cuts to the chase? There's no small talk, there's no bullshit. They say, 'How are you doing?' and they *mean* it."[2] The four soon took over one of many abandoned buildings on campus, lined the walls with mattresses to soundproof it, and started playing together. Their sound encompassed the members' vast and varied musical backgrounds: Dresdner and Spleen were New York City hardcore fans; Zapata's tastes ranged from bluegrass and blues to '70s glam and punk, while Moriarty liked the Who, the Kinks, and mod.

"The music wasn't what we had in common, really," Moriarty asserts. "What we had in common was the bond and the friendship, the drinking and the temperament. If punk rock is three parts emotion, temperament, and rage and one part music, or three parts urgency and communication and one part music, then it's fine. We all had that sense of urgency; we were sort of all coming from the same place. The music just flowed out of that. We didn't even try to make music, it just sort of happened."[3] They originally called themselves the Sniveling Little Rat-Faced Gits (courtesy of a line in a Monty Python skit), but decided to shorten their name when it wouldn't fit on a cassette tape. The Gits developed a hardcore following at Antioch and, as fellow student Peter Sheehy declared in the liner notes for *Kings and Queens* (a tape originally made for their Antioch fans entitled *Private Lubs*), "In the Spring of 1989 it was difficult to walk across the campus without hearing the Gits blaring out of someone's dorm room window."[4]

Zapata, Dresdner, and Spleen all moved from Ohio to San Francisco in 1986, living and working at the Farm, a collective that taught inner-city youth about animals and was sustained by hosting punk and hardcore shows. The Gits continued playing, without Moriarty, who had stayed behind in Ohio. However, he did weigh in on their collective decision to move to Seattle. The four finally reunited when they all migrated to the Northwest in 1989 after San Francisco had become increasingly expensive, and the Mission began to fall victim to skinhead violence. "We chose Seattle," Moriarty remarks, "but we didn't really know about the music scene. We didn't move here because of the music scene. When we got here . . . Sub Pop was just taking off, and there were a lot, *a lot* of other types of bands here, too."[5]

The band, according to Moriarty, never really fit in with the swell of the underground in Seattle that tended to revolve around the Sub Pop set (although they shared an early Seattle show with Nirvana). The Gits wanted to retain the community they had created, sustained, and thrived on with their audiences, but Seattle in the late '80s had surprisingly few venues. They ended up mostly playing warehouse parties and basements, attracting a fringe fan base that lay outside of the majority of the underground. Moriarty explains:

> We really developed a hardcore following of misfits and dykes and radicals and homeless people and alcoholics. We really didn't have any pretense about being any different from the crowd, especially Mia. It was like, "I'm singing in this band, but I'm just expressing myself like you are right now. I'm singing the blues, and I'm singing for you, but I'm singing with you."
>
> We didn't do stage shows. The idea was to just to go up and pour your guts out. It was for people, it was about communication and expressing an emotion, and Mia did that better than anybody. I some- times quote her lyrics in just talking with people, because they're so profound. You could pick out anything and it's almost universal. It gets me through a lot of hard times, just thinking about things she wrote, and meditating on it. She'd say, "I tear my heart out and I throw it on the ground in front of you. I can't hide that I'm a social wreck" [from "While You're Twisting, I'm Still Breathing"].[6] That was who she was; it was like, "All I can do is be completely open and honest [with] you, and I know it's gonna hurt me, but that's the way I am," and that's how she sang. She just sort of poured it out, and that's the way we played.[7]

When Moriarty moved to Seattle in '89 he came with Valerie Agnew, who would later form 7 Year Bitch. In addition to Agnew, the four members of the Gits lived with another future 7 Year Bitch member, Selene Vigil, as well as members of the DC Beggars, in "The Rathouse." While the Gits rehearsed in the basement, Agnew and Vigil were supportive Gits fans and, inspired by Zapata, formed their band in 1991. "[They] shared the rehearsal space, and helped us out with gear," Moriarty remembers, "and a couple of years later, we [were] opening for them. . . . They all say that Mia was a big influence on them for wanting to be in a band at all, 'cause she encouraged them and inspired them, and they wanted to do it, too."[8] 7 Year Bitch released *¡Viva Zapata!* in 1994, the cover of which featured a painting of Zapata, ostensibly outfitted like her alleged distant relative, the Mexican revolutionary Emiliano Zapata.[9] The Rathouse also released *Bobbing for Pavement: Rathouse Compilation* on its own label in 1991, which was composed of unknown and previously unrecorded bands, in the hopes of encouraging other artists, particularly women, to make their own music.[10]

Zapata was a prolific songwriter and had a strong, sailing gravelly voice that seemed years older than she was. Like the Gits' avowed love of drinking, evident in many of their songs, she sang (and wrote) as if she couldn't hold it any longer, each line spilling forth like a late night, drunken confession. Her lyrics often conjure violent images that express her desperation, or love, as in "Beauty of the Rose": "Do me a favor/When I reach out my hand won't you please just cut it off/So I can make some sense of the situation taking me for all?"[11] While her lyrics remained personal—a blunt reflection of who she was—they were universal.

"She really lived true to herself," says Moriarty, "and was a living example of what social justice movements are about. If they're about alleviating poverty, she was probably one of the poorest people I've ever known. If [they're] about relating to the working class and the underclass of people in the world of all different races, creeds, and colors, she was somebody [who] did not discriminate for anything. You could be a really horrible person, and she would still accept you. I think that she lived true to a higher standard of political understanding than most people that are overtly [active] politically. She just didn't deal with all the bullshit and the rhetoric."[12]

Not all of Zapata's songs reflected emotion turned inward, though. In "Spear and Magic Helmet" Zapata intended to out a member of another band as a rapist. The song appeared on *Enter: The Conquering Chicken* and was later covered by Evil Stig:

'Cause I'm coming after you; you're nothing but a filthy scum
And now I'm out to ruin you and your reputation
Just because you sing in a band, you think I won't do it but
All I fuckin' see in you is one goddamn lame excuse.[13]

Zapata wasn't steeped in political dogma, though. "She wasn't an academic," Moriarty contends. "What she was was a really powerful, insightful, intuitive, amazing woman. And she was a tomboy, too, and she was bisexual, and she didn't care, and she just wanted to live her life the way she wanted to live it. She had a lot of problems, and she realized that a lot of people had a lot of problems, but she wasn't a separatist in any way. . . . She was just a person trying to live her life like anybody else. She was the salt of the earth."[14]

In a time when the divide between punk rock artists and their audiences was widening to match the gap perpetuated by mainstream success, the Gits clung to commonality and truth, in no small part due to the vision of Mia Zapata.

Chapter 20

COURAGE

Jenny Toomey

AMID COUNTLESS BANDS, PERFORMERS, AND THE TATTOOED AND pierced masses, the fiery Jenny Toomey continues to redefine what indie bravado really means. In the 1980s, like so many girls who rollicked in D.C.'s punk and rock spaces, she organized shows and political actions, lending a hand to the boys (and the smattering of girls) who screamed their guts out nightly. The result of Toomey's punk enlightenment was Geek, followed by Tsunami, and a record label, Simple Machines, which she shared first with Brad Sigal and then with Tsunami cohort Kristin Thomson. Toomey also played with the softer, more melodic Liquorice and Grenadine, as well as releasing a number of solo albums. By the time Toomey and Thomson called it quits with Simple Machines in 1998, it had grown into one of the most respected independent labels in the country. The pair also produced a how-to guide on launching independent record labels, and founded a Washington think tank called the Future of Music Coalition, which studies artists' rights with respect to the many implications of new music technology.

Toomey initially got involved in the mid-'80s D.C. punk scene while in high school, where fellow student punks included members of Bloody Mannequin Orchestra and political and skate punks, too. "What was kind of interesting back then," she explains, "and what I idealize about this time was that there were so few people that were involved in punk, that everybody was welcome. So, it didn't matter if you were super-hardcore, everybody hung out together. . . . There were a couple of very small venues, like the 9:30 Club, which had every kind of music at it. It was just as likely for the Bloody Mannequin Orchestra guys to go see [new wave act] 9353 as they would go see [D.C. punk band] Government Issue and things like that. Things weren't really factionalized. . . . So, you know, the gay bars also, the runaway bars, the goth/punk . . . it's all kind of mixed, 'cause anybody who's not just affirming whatever the regular social norms are finds the other. And they don't have the luxury of self-selecting, saying, 'Well, you know, you're punk but you're not straightedge, so you can't be my friend' kind of thing."[1]

The intimacy and openness of the scene allowed for a variety of bands to thrive, and the locale, the nation's capital, meant heavy political activism for those who were interested. Toomey hooked up with Positive Force, an activist collective that often collaborated with the punk community for benefits and protests, in her early years on the scene. "The activism was at least as important to me as being in a punk rock scene was," she says, "and that's actually what drew me to it. . . . When I first heard punk rock music, it wasn't the kind of music that really turned me on."[2] Although while growing up she performed as a singer with a professional choir, she didn't realize how natural it would be for her to join a band until she began discovering feminism at Georgetown University.

Much of the photography documenting the D.C. scene at the time, including the hardcore shows from which many women were alienated, was produced by women like Cynthia Connolly, who, with Sharon Cheslow (also a member of hardcore band Chalk Circle) and Leslie Clague, released the book *Banned in D.C.: Photos and Anecdotes from the D.C. Punk Underground.* Toomey and other women active in D.C. punk worked as booking agents and organized shows and benefits.

"I was at Georgetown and a combination of things happened," Toomey recalls. "I took some feminism classes and realized that it wasn't an accident that I wasn't in bands. 'Cause the fact of the matter is, there weren't any role models, there weren't any women who were in bands at the time."[3] In 1988, during her sophomore year of college, she launched a project named Geek, inspired by the tenacity of the girl bands before her, like all-female local act Fire Party, an anomaly at the time in D.C. "I sang in this choir, and I know how to sing," Toomey adds. "I mean, that was the underscoring of the fact that girls weren't in bands. You know, it was strange to me that having never helped somebody get a producer in the studio, or having never put together flyers, that I would somehow think that that was more my role than singing, when I had sung . . . professional[ly] . . . for three years."[4] Inspired by Fire Party and armed with a feminist framework, she wrote her first song for Geek, entitled "Herasure," which outlined how women's expression is obscured and oppressed through the use of men's language. "Very college-feminism-type revelations," she laughs.[5]

Geek toured nationally with Superchunk and Seaweed in 1990, the first tour for all three bands. The bands were green, the members were young, and they all helped arrange the tour, taking the democratic approach of rotating the headliner, depending on who booked the show. After meeting Toomey on tour that year, bassist Andrew Webster moved from Texas to D.C. and, with the addition of fellow activist Kristin Thomson, Tsunami was born. The two women had first met at a Positive Force rally in 1989, where Thomson watched as Toomey spoke to the assembled crowd. "I thought, who is that really cool girl that's so brave?" Thomson told the *Georgetown Voice*. "She was very comfortable talking up on stage. Her confidence was clear to me, even as a stranger."[6]

True to Toomey's inclination to cannonball headfirst into perilous waters, Tsunami were only together a month before playing their first show, a New Year's Eve party at Superchunk singer Mac McCaughan's house in North Carolina. By early 1991, after enlisting drummer John Pamer, the four brazenly agreed to support four Beat Happening shows (of which they made two, due to car trouble). With Toomey and Thomson handling vocals and guitars, Tsunami spent the early '90s touring and putting out singles, becoming an indie favorite. They remain one of the most musically respected bands to come out of D.C.

Inhabiting the world of jangling guitars characteristic of early '90s indie rock, Tsunami was wrought with intensity, squeezing adrenaline and driving rhythms into the fray. Toomey and Thomson belted the lyrics as if they were desperate to make their voices heard across an urban field. Tsunami's tightly wound music seduces, and their finely crafted lyrics (and decidedly female perspective) are often overlooked. On their 1993 debut, *Deep End*,

Tsunami's frustration with the facelessness of female muses is gracefully articulated in "In a Name," and "The Heart's Tremolo," from their second album by the same name, deftly portrays the deterioration of a relationship as a woman afraid of confrontation prepares to face a lover. After dropping a few singles in their touring wake, Tsunami followed their debut with three more full-lengths and intermittent singles.

During Tsunami's tenure, Toomey collaborated with Dan Littleton of Hated on a project initially called Liquorice, and worked with Unrest member and Teen Beat Records founder Marc Robinson in Grenadine—a crooning, loungey cocktail act that used heavy orchestration and production. "I liked that music more innately," says Toomey. "I love the Flamingos, you know? I covered the Flamingos, I covered Burt Bacharach. There's almost a hokey musical-theater quality to it at times, particularly on the second record. Marc Robinson was going through a very Tiny Tim period back then. I'm not kidding! This is what I mean about loving the freedom for the real freaks in the early punk rock scene. Marc Robinson truly loves all this weird stuff, and I think it made his art a lot more interesting. And he was a real beacon in that community."[7]

Tsunami's 1997 album, *A Brilliant Mistake*, reflects a similar production value (but not style) to Grenadine's; the album swells with a host of different sounds, as does Toomey's 2001 solo double album, *Antidote*. *Antidote* is full of looming country-tinged, often lovelorn songs with a distinctly feminist perspective, as in "Patsy Cline," which rattles a list of unbearable and paralyzing rules that act as woman-to-woman advice on keeping a controlling man.[8] Toomey told *Billboard*, "It is interesting to play music that's very personal as opposed to very political—not that I think there's a huge distinction. Relationships are as good a place as any to look at feminism."[9]

When Toomey first started her label, Simple Machines, in 1989, her partner was friend Brad Sigal. Soon after, however, Sigal split and Kristin Thomson willingly took the reins, and the two ran the label out of their house. "The original idea was to put out some Geek stuff," Toomey explains. "We did the Simple Machines series, which was six 7"s. And the idea was, by the time you'd put out the six 7"s, you'd know whether you wanted to really have a label. They were all compilations, and they were all packaged and tied around a theme, and very much like what Simple Machines ended up doing a lot of.

About three or four singles in, we got the opportunity to put out the Lungfish record and that's when we really became a real label. We incorporated, or got a business license, and created a partnership and began doing things legally, because it was such a great record, we didn't want to do anything wrong."[10]

Simple Machines ended up producing a lot more records than the intended Geek releases. All of Tsunami's work was put out on the label, as well as that of Scrawl and a host of other bands; the label had produced approximately seventy-five releases by 1998. Simple Machines also did the Working Holiday series of 7"s in 1993—one for each month of the year—and in 1994 released them as a full-length album. In an effort, in part, to bolster the indie underground as it waned following the post-Nirvana industry scramble, Thomson and Toomey wrote and published a book, *The Mechanics' Guide to Putting Out Records*, which sold hundreds of copies (and is now downloadable online). Following in the footsteps of all the punks who'd helped them succeed, Thomson and Toomey wanted to extend to others some of the support and education they had received from their peers in creating Simple Machines. Toomey elaborates:

> We were very lucky, and I can't ever give Dischord enough props, and Ian [MacKaye] and Jeff [Nelson] in particular. If Kristin and I ever had a question about anything, from how to send artwork to the folks who were going actually to make the sleeves, through to how to negotiate or deal with an artist who was unhappy with you, or what the proper price point was for selling a record, or any of these kinds of things, any time we had a problem—and still, to this day, if we ever do—we can always call them and they're always more than happy to help us. So, I think we had the luxury of not making mistakes that other labels had to, because we could watch other labels make mistakes in front of us. We're also worrywarts in some ways. As much as we have enthusiasm and we felt very fearless in some ways, putting out Dave Grohl's records, or asking Sonic Youth to give us a track, any of these kinds of things that we were able to do, we were just very careful business-wise.[11]

Simple Machines folded in 1998 while still in the black. Financial solvency aside, the label's goals were even more impressive. "We strove to: put out music we love and sell it for a fair price; make everything we did beautiful, interesting, and friendly; pass on skills and information (to avoid reinventing the wheel) . . . see personal pleasure and fun as a measure of success,"

Toomey and Thomson wrote.[12] Touring with Tsunami and working their requisite side jobs made juggling Simple Machines anything but easy, and the two women opted to close up shop rather than shortchange the label.

At the time that Simple Machines folded, the world of music was expanding beyond the independent *and* mainstream record biz. Deregulation by the FCC encouraged radio stations to consolidate, creating less on-air variety, and digital music formats changed the landscape of music distribution and production. Toomey rightly anticipated these unfolding conditions and formed the Future of Music Coalition (FMC) in 2000. "The original idea of Future of Music was that we would be the think tank," she explains, "and that's a glorified way of saying we would do the research, and we would do the convening, and we would do the translating. Everybody senses that radio's bad; what we would do is get the economists and the statisticians to document why radio had changed, and then we would translate that economic and statistical information into language that people and musicians might actually listen to, and the media, as well. Then we would convene the people who had those positions in public to actually move the debate to another level. That's the perfect measure of what we do."[13] FMC provides forums for musicians and industry leaders to voice their concerns face to face, as well as presenting information to Congress, as they did in 2002 with a report on radio consolidation.

Witnessing the breadth of Toomey's work, one wonders how she was able to enter each arena so bravely and freely. She muses:

> I think I was very lucky, because I bumped into good, supportive people at the right moments. I think a lot of it had to do with Positive Force, actually, the more I think about it—punk rockers mentoring punk rockers. If I wanted to put on an art festival in DuPont Circle but I wasn't old enough to sign the permit application for the D.C. government, somebody who was over twenty-one, who was also part of the same group, would go down with me and sign it for me. If I didn't know how to do sound but somebody had a contact, they would reach out for me. It was really a crash course in organizing, and also in collaborative organizing; the idea that everybody doesn't need to know everything, you just need to connect with people who know the things that you don't know, which I think has been incredibly helpful for us with things like Future of Music. 'Cause when we started, Kristin and I knew one thing: We knew the suspicion that artists and labels from the independent communities had around the technologies. And we also

knew that we had learned some little things that made us think that these technologies might disrupt the monopolies of distribution, manufacturing, and promotion that made it impossible for us to continue to run the record label. But that's all we knew.[14]

While she often says that her activism hinders her music-making, her ability to tackle new and divergent projects is an art in and of itself. Whatever the forum, Jenny Toomey is most certainly still making noise.

Chapter 21

PRETTY ON THE INSIDE

Hole

ONCE UPON A TIME, HOLE FRONTWOMAN COURTNEY LOVE WAS
as subversive a superstar as you could get. She was outspoken, sexy, dirty, and
intense. Her scarlet-smeared lips even dared to utter the f-word (feminism,
that is) in mainstream magazines and in the song "Jennifer's Body." Hole was
a noisy band, the music thick with imagery and writhing with restless anger
and scraping guitars that countered Love's gravelly screams. Once upon a
time, Hole's first album, *Pretty on the Inside*, was even outselling Nirvana's
debut, *Bleach*.[1]

When *Pretty on the Inside* was released by Caroline Records in 1991,
Hole was generating a sound steeped in metal and punk, cultivated by Love
and peers like Kat Bjelland (Babes in Toyland) and Jennifer Finch (L7), both
of whom had played with Love before in Sugar Baby Doll. (Love and
Bjelland also played together in an early version of Babes in Toyland.) The
ugly, the raw, the grime of women's lives was finally on full display in Hole's
repertoire. A label deal with Geffen didn't even change the topics Love was
covering in her songs. *Live Through This*, which was released in April 1994,
was replete with themes of abuse, isolation, and aggression, even if it was

musically more rock-radio-friendly than the first album. That same fateful month, Love became the object of first-class rock sexism—the kind inflicted on Yoko Ono for more than twenty years and on Nancy Spungen during her relationship with Sid Vicious—when her husband Kurt Cobain killed himself. Love was instantly, insidiously, to blame.

Born in San Francisco in 1965 and raised in Eugene, Oregon, Courtney Love was shuttled from home to home, and in and out of a number of reform schools. She learned about the new underground music at one of the many schools she attended. "An intern who was working for school credit came back from England and said, 'You should really be into this stuff, it's really you,'" Love told *Spin*. "And he gave me three records: Pretenders, Squeeze, and *Never Mind the Bollocks*. I decided then I was going to be a rock star."[2]

In an interview with Pamela Des Barres reprinted in *Rock She Wrote*, Love recounted, "Since I was a kid, show me any kind of male-oriented thing that can have a female protagonist and I'm there."[3] At sixteen, she moved to Portland and then, literally, all over the world earning money as a stripper.[4] Ironically, in the mid-'80s she auditioned for the role of Nancy Spungen in Alex Cox's *Sid and Nancy*, and landed instead the role of Gretchen, Nancy's friend in New York.

In 1989 Love met her Hole cohort guitarist Eric Erlandson (who was a Capitol Records employee at the time) after placing an ad in a Los Angeles paper. With Jill Emery on bass and Caroline Rue on drums (both of whom would leave by 1992), Hole became a full band.[5] The group released three singles before Caroline Records issued the Don Fleming and Kim Gordon–produced *Pretty on the Inside* in 1991. That same year Hole also released the "Teenage Whore" video, which displayed Courtney at her bedraggled-glam best. Hole's next album featured replacements Kristen Pfaff on bass and Patty Schemel on drums. Pfaff once said of becoming a bassist, "It was really intense work, just so that people would eventually accept me as a serious bass player. Because I realized right away that since I was a woman, I'd have to be better at what I did to be treated as an equal. Like, I'd have to take the music further. So I've worked my ass off." Schemel had a different experience. "I never felt like I had anything to prove," she said. "It was the general impulse to make music that drove me. I started playing drums when I was eleven and started playing in punk rock bands when I was like fifteen."[6]

Live Through This was released four days after Cobain's suicide. Pfaff died of a heroin overdose that same year and was replaced by Melissa Auf der Maur. In between *Live Through This* and Hole's final album, *Celebrity Skin*, Love returned to acting and eventually landed costarring roles in *Man on the Moon* and *The People vs. Larry Flynt*. Perhaps a byproduct of the public's fascination with her as a "widow," both roles placed her as the flaky, flighty (and in the case of *The People*, drug-addicted) wife of the films' protagonists. *Celebrity Skin* was produced by Smashing Pumpkins frontman Billy Corgan and released in 1998; Hole officially broke up soon after. Geffen then attempted to sue Hole for breach of contract, but Love won the countersuit. She has since released the wryly named *America's Sweetheart* on Virgin Records, and Melissa Auf der Maur has released her own solo album, *Auf der Maur*.

Whether you love Courtney or hate her, Hole was the highest-profile female-fronted band of the '90s to openly and directly sing about feminism. *Pretty on the Inside* contained self-revelatory character studies like "Teenage Whore" and "Pretty on the Inside," no doubt autobiographical accounts of Love's outcast childhood. *Live Through This*, on the other hand, is the angry, painful revenge of a woman who has existed on the margins. From the brutal dismemberment of "Jennifer's Body" to the stumbling, suffering beauty queen in "Miss World," and the question posed to a rapist (or perhaps to the audience members who molested her at a 1991 show with Mudhoney) in "Asking for It," Hole poetically and powerfully manifested and defended the denigrated girl.[7] "I Think That I Would Die" (cowritten by Kat Bjelland) contains a hearty invective directed at a woman who refuses to identify as a feminist. Hole also used pop, punk, and metal in equal doses, making *Live Through This* a thoroughly accessible rock album, even for Top 40 fans. Between *Live Through This* and *Celebrity Skin*, though, Hole's sound softened, and *Celebrity Skin* presented a band that had sunken deep into a reminiscence of '70s-flavored California rock, in album image and sound.

Even now, more than a decade after Cobain's death, nothing brings out unexpected, rusty sexist sentiment like a mention of Courtney Love. On tour in 1994 and 1995, Hole faced audience members jeering "You killed Kurt!"[8] The pop punk style and Nirvanaesque imagery (such as shared references to milk and blood) of *Live Through This* led to assumptions that Cobain had written the album for Love. Although she gained considerable fame after her marriage to Cobain, she was working as an actress and musician long before she met him, a fact her hordes of critics, and those who accuse her of killing her husband to promote her own career, tend to ignore. "We work so hard to get where we are," Love told Des Barres. "So when I hear people saying things like, 'Oh Courtney got that gig because of who she's married to,' it really pisses me off."[9] As Cobain wrote in the liner notes for *Incesticide*, "My wife challenges injustice and the reason her character has been so severely attacked is because she chooses not to function the way the white corporate man insists. His rules for women involve her being submissive, quiet, and non-challenging. When she doesn't follow his rules, the threatened man (who, incidentally, owns an army of devoted traitor women) gets scared. A big 'fuck you' to those of you who have the audacity to claim that I'm so naive and stupid that I would allow myself to be taken advantage of and manipulated."[10]

While Cobain was painted the willing martyr, the doomed artist, the quiet husband, Love, in the tradition of stereotypical rock wife, was, and is still, seen as manipulative, opportunistic, and ironfisted. It can't be coincidence, either, that the two women with whom critics take such issue, Yoko Ono and Courtney Love, are widows. Which leads one to wonder whether critics and journalists feel freer to verbally tear these women apart with their husbands unable to offer protection and refute the accusations.

In a shameless gouging of Love's eroding reputation, Nick Broomfield's 1998 film *Kurt and Courtney* explored the question of whether or not Love killed Cobain through the presentation of a collage of choppy interviews by those who knew Love personally and were critical of her, omitting anyone who might defend her character. The interviews and anecdotes make for a spurious, one-sided argument at best. The film's obvious bias prompted *Newsweek* to quip, "Maybe they should have called the film 'Courtney Hate.'"[11] Melissa Rossi wrote *Courtney Love: Queen of Noise*, a book rife with rumors of her personal life and details that fiercely denigrate Love, including long list of lovers, her habits in bed, and specific personal problems she had with Cobain.

Courtney Love is loud, contentious, brash, and impulsive. But is she really that frightening? The American public, including some fans of indie rock, continue to savage her, in part because she doesn't censor herself and in part because fans don't know what to do with a woman so outspoken, contradictory, and at times hostile. As Love herself once said, "All I have to do is lick my finger, stick it up in the air, and shit sticks to it."[12] Of course, her own public misconduct doesn't help, like her physical confrontation with Kathleen Hanna on the 1995 Lollapalooza tour. And her resistance to releasing a Nirvana box set in 2001 didn't make her too popular, either.

When asked in *Rolling Stone* if being a woman gave her an advantage when she started, she wryly replied, "Well, I wouldn't want to be the *other* thing."[13] When asked if she was averse to the "feminist" label, Love replied, "I'm a militant feminist. So I would respond positively to it. Because it's my definition."[14] On an Australian tour in the late '90s, Courtney gave a guitar to a girl in each audience, saying, "Play it loud and *don't* give it to your boyfriend."[15]

Moments like these can sometimes overshadow her more raucous, misguided ones and certainly render mute some of the more base assumptions made about rock's second most publicly loathed widow. The assumptions themselves, disappointing and tiresome, should have been put to rest by now. In the larger cultural scope, assuming a woman killed her husband for success, or could only make a good rock record if he made it for her, proves that even today when a woman stands in antithesis to the expectations placed upon her, it's feeding season.

Courtney Love's missteps, so devoured and overblown by gossip columns and news programs alike, only obscure the fact that a Hole album can pump adrenaline into every corner of a room, and that feminism can fit into fairly mainstream rock and roll. That much shouldn't be forgotten, at least.

Chapter 22

SMELL THE MAGIC

L7

L7 TRAMPLED THE TESTOSTERONE-INFUSED SOUNDS OF GRUNGE
and metal with their multivocal harmonizing, cynical snarling, and heavy, droning guitars. In some ways, L7's sound nestled nicely with the similarly heavy guitar sounds of grunge, which undoubtedly helped them land a major label deal with Slash/Warner and a main-stage slot on the 1994 Lollapalooza tour. In 1999, they even began their own label, Wax Tadpole, as part of the Bong Load Records enterprise. L7 look the "grunge" part too, wearing mostly jeans and T-shirts, their makeup smeared carelessly.

By mixing traditional aspects of tough rock-and-roll bravado with overtly feminist lyrics and actions, L7 have created their very own brand of "cock" rock, giving a nice twist to the traditionally male milieu. While they purposely sought to separate themselves from anything that made "a genre out of gender," as ex-bassist Jennifer Finch put it, they are overtly feminist in lyrics, and in life.[1] They were even named Feminists of the Year in 1992 by the Feminist Majority Foundation for starting Rock for Choice.

Suzi Gardner and Donita Sparks formed L7 in Los Angeles in 1985 while both were working at the *L.A. Weekly*. The two were joined by bassist Jennifer Finch after her short stint with Sugar Baby Doll, a collaboration with Babes in Toyland's Kat Bjelland and Hole's Courtney Love. L7 found a permanent drummer in Dee Plakas by 1988 and released their eponymous debut LP on Epitaph that same year. The band played a Seattle show in 1989 specifically hoping to land a deal with Sub Pop. "We put two of our friends, who happened to be on acid, in charge of the smoke machine," Sparks told *Entertainment Weekly*. Finch added, "All we could see was [Sub Pop cofounder] Bruce Pavitt's bald head walking for the door, waving his hands in front of his face."[2] The dry-ice mishap aside, Pavitt offered them a deal the next day, and L7 released the *Smell the Magic* EP in 1991. The merchandise that accompanied the album—posters and T-shirts alike—sported a woman sitting spread-eagled, with a man's face nearly swallowed by her legs. Puerile, perhaps, but worse had been served up by a litany of male rock and metal bands, from the Rolling Stones to Mötley Crüe.

It wasn't until the 1992 Slash release *Bricks Are Heavy*, produced by Butch Vig of Nirvana's *Nevermind* fame, containing the single "Pretend We're Dead," that the band wrangled national attention, though. *Hungry for Stink* followed on Slash/Reprise, as did *The Beauty Process: Triple Platinum*, after which Slash/Reprise dropped them and Finch left the band. In 1997, Nirvana bassist Krist Novoselic documented a tour he shared with L7 and released the short film entitled *L7: The Beauty Process*. Interspersed with live footage, Novoselic concentrated in his project on how the record business treats musicians. In 1999, after being dropped from Warner Brothers, the band decided to release their latest album, *Slap-Happy*, on their own Wax Tadpole label. Ex-Belly bassist Gail Greenwood replaced Jennifer Finch in 1996, but Greenwood then quit before the recording of *Slap-Happy*. Janis Tanaka, formerly of Exene Cervenka's band Auntie Christ, replaced her on bass.

L7's political activism came in many forms; besides adding some estrogen to hard rock, they founded the influential Rock for Choice in 1991, which promoted benefit tours aimed at raising money for abortion rights in conjunction with the Feminist Majority Foundation. "Fear was our motivation for starting Rock for Choice," Finch told *Rolling Stone*. "Just picking up the newspaper every day and reading about another piece of pro-choice legislation being put on the Republican chopping block was enough."[3] Following the first benefit, which boasted such luminaries as Hole, Nirvana, and Sister

Double Happiness and raised fifteen thousand dollars, L7 encouraged their friends to organize their own concerts.[4] Rock for Choice, still in operation, is now more than a decade old.

L7's activism didn't stop there. In 1999, L7 flew a banner over the heads of Warped Tour concertgoers that read: "Warped Needs More Beaver . . . Love, L7."[5] No matter how clipped, any kind of dialogue on gender is rare at an event like the Warped Tour, a corporate-sponsored showcase for bands walking the tightrope between underground culture and mainstream acceptance. The year L7 unfurled their "love letter" to the crowd the headlining acts included the all male-outfits Cypress Hill, Sevendust, Pennywise, Blink 182, Black Eyed Peas, Less Than Jake, Suicidal Tendencies, and Ice-T. (The Lunachicks played a side stage.) Gardner explained, "The motivation was making a kind of statement—not bagging on those tours—that some more women need to get off their asses and start making some heavier music. There's a shortage of women in the heavier side of rock and roll, and what we were basically saying was, what's the alternative?"[6]

L7's lyrics grew increasingly feminist and political as the band evolved. Their earlier records, *L7* and *Smell the Magic*, contain more party anthems than their later works, with the notable exception of the revenge fantasy "Ms. 45" on their self-titled release. By *Bricks Are Heavy*, though, L7 were politically inspired by a variety of issues. In that album's track "Everglade," the band glorifies their female protagonist when she confronts and castigates a drunken fan in the mosh pit.

In much the same manner as the D.C. all-girl midshow protest following a set by Bikini Kill, the subject in "Everglade" was attempting to hold her own in the often violent mosh pit atmosphere, which by its nature was more discriminatory and exclusionary to women, although certainly no picnic for most male fans, either.

In an interview conducted the year *Bricks Are Heavy* was released, Donita Sparks commented on the plight of some of their female fans in Europe: "I've noticed since we've been on this tour that it's all guys up front." Plakas went on to relay the story of a show they played with Nirvana, where she and Sparks jumped into the general melee at the front of the stage. "I got caught and this guy was pulling my hair. I felt like I was drowning in this big sea. I saw Donita's hand, she pulled me out and we both ran to the side of the stage. Fuck that. At our shows, I think to myself, 'If I wasn't in the band and I went to see us, I wouldn't go up front.'"[7]

In "Wargasm" on the same album, L7 take the image of gun-as-phallus a step further with a feminist portrayal of war as a national and sexual obsession. They even tapped Yoko Ono for samples of her signature screams on the track.

After sixteen years, L7 have released seven albums, the last being 1999's *Slap-Happy* on Wax Tadpole/Bong Load. While many bands of the early '90s faded into obscurity along with the mainstream's interest in grunge, L7 persisted, while continuing to wear their political agenda on their sleeves. Though their mainstream success was fleeting, they left a humble yet indelible feminine stamp on both hard rock and youth activism.

Chapter 23

BUTCH IN THE STREETS

Tribe 8

We have many penises. There's nothing wrong with them,
as long as they're detachable. And every penis is.
—LYNN BREEDLOVE[1]

IF YOU'RE A STRAIGHT BOY LOOKING TO GIVE A GOOD BLOW JOB, then Tribe 8's your band. Paper and pen is hardly the best means for describing the band's raucous dildos-to-the-wall queercore and confrontational stage shows, which beg for a surround-sound, volume-turned-way-up listen to convey how loud, incredibly infectious, and annoyingly smart they are. Tribe 8's onslaught of sound functions as a mirror, one that forces audiences to face their own homophobia, sexism, classism, racism, sexual repression, and, worst of all, humorlessness. Songs about castration, sex, and S&M avenge the girls left in Big Black's wake. And this mirror functions as a reflection as well—not just of funny, angry, and political musicians, but of the mostly disregarded punk dyke. Where lesbian desire has historically been packaged under the folk music umbrella in the form of love songs or softer protest anthems, or in the angrier punk folk of Phranc and Ani DiFranco, Tribe 8 gives audiences the liberating and unapologetic spectacle of true dyke punk rock.

Tribe 8's lead vocalist and resident provocateur Lynn Breedlove explains Tribe 8's political philosophy as "queer visibility, no assimilation, and love. Love for each other within the community and [to] show love to the rest of the community, to the world. It's like, look, we're funny, we're some dykes, we're out. See? Now you've seen one, a live one, and look . . . we rock, we're going to do stupid shit, and we're going to entertain you and you're going to like it. Now what?"[2]

Tribe 8 formed in San Francisco in 1990, during the era of MTV's cowardly censorship of Madonna's "Justify My Love." In the infamous video, Madonna trumped the queer community by creating a protagonist who experimented with both male and female lovers. Although Madonna kissed a woman in the video (which was quite provocative at the time), she never went so far as to strap on a dildo (as Breedlove does), which would have turned the video's heterosexual-male-fantasy element to ash and subsequently sent MTV packing. "Justify My Love" was racy spectacle as opposed to Tribe 8's more provocative, less voyeuristic call for queer visibility.

Leslie Mah, Tribe 8's guitarist, grew up in Colorado and loved punk. "I had an eight-track [of the] Sex Pistols' *Never Mind the Bollocks*. It was so exciting to me, 'cause I was like, 'God, this rocks harder than Aerosmith.' And there was a lot going on, but I was in Colorado, so we were somewhat isolated. It was kind of rare for the punk bands to make a stop over there, but a lot of the new wave bands started stopping in Denver." Mah had visited San Francisco in the early '80s and was so inspired by the women involved in the scene at the time, she and her girlfriend started their own band when they returned home. "It was pretty exciting," she says, "'cause Denver is such a weird place, and eventually—in the scene in Denver—me and my girlfriend would go to a show and we'd be the only girls there."[3]

Mah moved to San Francisco in 1988 because, she quips, she "heard there were some gays there."[4] Breedlove recalls, "Well, I call it the dyke renaissance of the '90s. Like there was one in the '20s in Paris—I think it [was] kind of like that, you know? Suddenly, everybody was doing art and performance and being queer and talking about class and race and gender and butch, femme, and perversion and whoa! Like [ex–Tribe 8 member] Flipper's café—her name is Silas Howard, but at the time she was Flipper—Red Dora's Bearded Lady Café. [She co-]owned it and did spoken-word events there all the time and [they] were packed, [there were] like fifty people in there, and we'd be there like sardines, and sweating. It was so great. People would be playing music and it was all rad and brilliant."[5]

Lynn Breedlove had been writing poetry since she was a child in suburban California. "I told [my parents] I wanted to be a poet when I grew up," she recalls. "I think I was twelve. I had loved Robert Frost in fifth grade, that snowy woods one. I was really impressed with that, and so I thought I wanted to be a poet and they were like, 'Oh, well, poets don't make any money. You'll get verbal skills once you get into law school.'"[6] She discovered punk rock through Black Flag in the early '80s, then went to college and ended up moving to San Francisco.

After Breedlove yelled out lyrics during an AA meeting in 1990, a friend asked her to play at her birthday party. "[We] charged over to the party and whipped out our five songs," she says. "Our pals were there, you know, twenty people, and they made us play the five songs over again and then Slade was there, who was our future drummer . . . and Leslie [was there], who wasn't in the band yet."[7]

"Lynnee and Flipper were playing at this party," says Mah, "and it was the first time—it was their first show and the first time they ever even really played and they were terrible, but they were just totally funny and their friends were all really excited. They were like, 'We really need a bass player, we really need a bass player,' and I had just gotten there. . . . I guess I went and just jammed with them and then I decided because everybody in the band were beginners that I should be a beginner, too, so I switched to guitar."[8] The rest of the lineup has changed over the years. Original member Flipper left in 2002; Slade Bellum, the drummer who joined in 1993, also left, as did bassist Lynn "Tantrum" Payne. Jen Savage entered on drums and Mama T on bass.

The band struggled with choosing a name until Breedlove's friend suggested the word "tribade," an ancient Greek and Latin word used (infrequently) to describe women who rub up against or penetrate other women (or men) during sex. The number "8" makes the name "kind of prehistoric and futuristic all at the same time," explains Breedlove.[9] When Tribe 8 started making a racket, lesbian (in)visibility wasn't being addressed in San Francisco's punk scene. According to Breedlove:

> San Francisco was full of out dykes with Mohawks, going nuts and moshing at punk shows. And there was occasionally a chick drummer like Killer in Typhoon, who later played in the Third Sex. She's like a big old butch and you're like, "Yeah, she's a dyke!" But no one was up

there singing about "I'm going to—blank—my chickie babe." You know, people were starving for it, and they were really happy [with Tribe 8] as a result of this big hole. I felt connected to my community. I felt loved. I was creating something I believed in and they were hearing it and going, "Yeah! Thank you. You're talking about shit that we need to hear onstage, because this is the stuff that we live every day." Nobody ever sings about that shit, and when people don't hear their lives are accepted in pop culture or in the media or anything, that's when they feel invisible and that's when they start blowing their brains out and vandalizing other people's property.[10]

The band released its first EP, *Pig Bitch,* on the Harp label in 1991, followed by the EP Allen's Mom in 1994 and *By the Time We Get to Colorado* on Outpunk in 1995. Their first full-length album, *Fist City,* chock full of political-, dyke-, and sex-positive rhetoric, was released on Jello Biafra's label, Alternative Tentacles, in 1995, as well. Alternative Tentacles has also released the subsequent Tribe 8 albums *Snarkism* and *Role Models for Amerika.*

Along with her band duties, Breedlove ran Lickety Split All-Girl Courier, an all-female bike messenger service which employed more than one hundred women. After taking a writing class with Kathy Acker in 1993, she embarked on her novel, *Godspeed,* the journey of a drug-addled transgender bike messenger, which was published by St. Martin's Press.[11] Leslie Mah has worked as a tattoo artist at the woman-owned and -operated Black and Blue Tattoo in San Francisco since 1996, and Silas Howard has recently cowritten and coproduced the film *By Hook or By Crook.*

The themes of Tribe 8's songs seem as packed with smirking, satisfying recriminations as the members' lives are with their various artistic pursuits. "Frat Pig" twists the notion of gang rape into feminist vigilantism, with the avenging perpetrators getting their due through an affirming, angry "play" of "gang castrate." By flipping the roles of traditional sexual violence, where the hunted (usually gay men, transgendered people, women, or children) become the hunters, Tribe 8 takes the notion of the rape confessional further, not just revealing and justifying victims' anger over sexual abuse or finding vindication in legal recourse, but reveling instead in their own form of "penile punishment." The phrase "gang castrate" situates the rapist as a resistant victim at the mercy of his former victims. And, if that isn't cathartic enough for survivors of sexual violence, the band regularly performs a dildo-castration stunt at their live shows. With the knife glinting in Lynn's hands, this performance upsets the traditional power balance and exposes the lurking male fear of castration to match the widespread threat of rape for women.

Tribe 8's enemies are not limited to rapists and frat pigs; on the album *Role Models for Amerika*, their targets include dismantling "Estrofemme"'s vapid, singular femme lesbian stereotype, as well as taking to task the punks that police the scene's sellouts in "Old Skool, New Skool."[12] *Fist City's* "Neanderthal Dyke" begs for a less theoretical, more liberated approach to lesbianism and feminism. While much of academia and the political left was embroiled in lengthy debates about politically correct language and behavior during the early '90s, Tribe 8 played songs like "Femme Bitch Top," "Barnyard Poontang" (both on *Fist City*), "Lezbophobia" (on the *By the Time We Get to Colorado* EP), and "Tranny Chaser" (on *Snarkism*).

The cover photo of *Role Models for Amerika* features an updated version of the Slits' image on *Cut*, with the band covered in paint rather than mud. Tribe 8's version depicts the unnatural urban jungle in fluorescent paint on a stark white backdrop rather than the Slits' original use of natural mud in an "unnatural" English backyard. The updated cover demands your attention, like the band itself; there's no way to ignore the five painted dykes in front of you. If the ladies' lyrics elicit simultaneous alarm, empowerment, and dis-comfort, their stage show reinforces the ever-present reversal of gender roles with fun displays of sadomasochism and oral sex. In Tracy Flannigan's excellent documentary on the band, *Rise Above*, the band cajoles a New York crowd to send up a straight boy willing to perform fellatio. After a few min-utes of harmless audience badgering, a man struggles up to the stage, is bound, and performs fellatio on Breedlove—but not after a heavy, uncom-fortable pause in the crowd.

While the band challenges the long years of heterosexism in the punk scene simply by irrefutably expressing their lesbianism, the band's fellatio stunt, like the mock castration, flip-flops the engrained gender power dynamic. Breedlove explained in *Rise Above*, "The blow job thing is all about being on your knees and you're in a submissive position. When you present an image to people constantly, that's going to rearrange their whole view of what reality is. That's the whole idea behind the capitalist media onslaught. But every time we do a show, and you see a guy on his knees, suckin' my dick, number one, he's on his knees, he's in a submissive position; number two, he's being penetrated; and number three, he's doing it voluntarily, to a woman."[13] Breedlove also contends that the mixture of a topless female and a strap-on displays the complexity of gender, complicating our collective reflex to slot gender into two preconceived boxes.[14]

Breedlove takes aim not only at patriarchy and white male privilege with her antics, but also at the ripe target of male rock stars. She revealed to Flannigan that her unapologetic swagger "[makes] fun of boys that play rock and roll, and it's all about, 'I'm a guy, and this is my dick, and I'm gonna go backstage and get a blow job, and I'm gonna sing songs to the girls about how bad they wanna do it, so when I get backstage there'll be fifteen babes lined up, wantin' to do it, and that's what rock and roll is all about. So, when I get up there and wag a rubber dick around, I'm making fun of that."[15]

Mah, on the other hand, is driven more by the live show than by the band's political motivations. As she explains, "I love to play live. That's why I do it. Honestly, I feel like putting a political message out there [is] important, but for me, I'm more of a visual person than someone who gets really caught up in information that's verbal. . . . A picture is worth a thousand words. For me, it's really physical and it's really spontaneous . . . whereas a political message is calculated and people deconstruct it and look for loopholes—it's not reality to me. It's very theoretical. There's theory and then there's life, and I feel the live show is more about life."[16]

Active since the early '90s, Tribe 8 no longer face the criticism they did early in their career. "Tribe 8 has almost become mainstream, kind of a household name in the gay world, so that's not so much an issue anymore," Breedlove says.[17] Early on, though, they struggled with more pervasive forms of censorship—of course, they also play more diverse venues than many other underground bands. "The punk ethic is really focused on playing all-ages shows and noncorporate shows," Mah explains, "but then it's like, well, if it's in some cool kid's basement or [it's] some really underground thing, it's going to be really hard for dykes to know about it, so then, yeah, we want to play a club. They'll hear about it, but then people under eighteen or twenty-one can't go. So you try and balance everything out."

During their first Michigan Women's Music Festival performance, they were greeted by a small group of protesters who believed that Tribe 8's message promoted violence against women and children, and that their performance had the potential to serve as a trigger for survivors of abuse. Mah describes the event: "Well, there has sort of been an ongoing, like, anti-S&M movement at the Michigan Women's Music Festival, and I'm not really sure what happened, but I think that they were having workshops and these were people who had never seen the band or knew anything about us but went on hearsay about what the band was about, and so they kind of focused on us, because the banners and everything that they made [said] that we promoted violence against women. They had banners that said, 'If you had been a victim of sexual abuse don't turn around now. Don't watch this band.' Then there was just this sign that said, 'Tribe 8 promotes violence against women and children.' I don't know what motivated people to focus on us in that way."[18]

In an interview with Todd Wiese, Breedlove said about the protests: "I promote violence against rapists, not women and children. So, we were all able to come to some kind of understanding that the 'peace love' thing was really great for women who need that and use that. And for us, anger and jumping around and screaming and yelling and wielding knives and rubber dicks is what helps us feel better. But we're all basically on the same track and that's the feminist track. So we had a couple of workshops where women were able to talk to each other about how different generations do the feminist trip."[19]

What most fans can agree on, whether straight, lesbian, bi, or trans, is that Tribe 8 is a courageous, provocative, and entertaining band who have been swaggering and strutting for over a decade. Here's to ten more years of dildo-swinging, gang-castrating fun.

Chapter 24

BABYSITTERS ON ACID

Lunachicks

"YOU HAVE TO LAUGH AT LIFE AND AT FUCKED-UP STUFF OR else you're going to lose your mind," contends Lunachick Theo Kogan.[1] Kogan's philosophy rings true throughout the catalog of the metal-punk Lunachicks. The band achieved a healthy balance of feminist lyrics and the ability to be, at times, as puerile and vulgar as their male contemporaries. Their loud, abrasive sound removed female self-expression of its earnestness with silly, depraved album covers like *Binge and Purge*, featuring the girls happily gorging themselves at a table covered with cake and mounds of other food. Flip over the CD and you find them covered in fake vomit. Equal parts teenage glamour and Halloween metal horror, the band created a female circus of noise, proving women could cover the same territory as their male peers—from the spectacle of bands like the Misfits in the late '70s and early '80s to the boozy chaos of a band like Murphy's Law (wholly without glamour or costume).

Lead singer Theo Kogan met bassist Squid (Sydney Silver) in junior high in Brooklyn, and Kogan eventually introduced Squid to guitarist Gina Volpe. The band consisting of Kogan, Silver, Volpe, second guitarist Sindi B, and original drummer Mike Fusaro was formed in 1988, when the girls were only sixteen. Kogan recalls, "I brought [Squid and Gina] together at a Herbie Hancock concert. . . . Yeah, I know, it's really sick."[2] Volpe adds, "Theo and Squid were friends with Sindi from their neighborhood in Brooklyn, and Sindi would come and hang out with us after school. . . . She didn't go to our school—she just came to corrupt the youth of our school."[3]

The decision to form the Lunachicks embodied the best of the '80s DIY spirit. Volpe recalls, "There [were] a lot of bands around, and that's what we did for fun. We would just go to shows and see bands. It's kind of what everybody did. And there were a lot of great bands and most of them were punk. Some were rock. . . . We'd just go from club to club and watch all these bands, and one day we had this realization that we ourselves could do that."[4]

Although their repertoire of musical influences that included women was limited, Kogan did have the examples of Siouxsie Sioux, Wendy O. Williams, and X-Ray Spex to encourage her. She doesn't remember much trepidation about being teenage girls in a band, either. "To us, [what] we always believed was, 'Well, we can do anything we want,'" she says.[5] And, of the decision to make the band an all-female one, Volpe explains, "We were already friends and we wanted to start a band together, so that just kind of happened naturally, that we were females. But once we realized that there were four of us, then we felt that we might as well keep it all female. We did have a male drummer [Kogan's boyfriend at the time], but that's only because we couldn't find a female drummer, and then we eventually did. We found Becky Wreck. And so that was a conscious decision, to get a female drummer and really become an all-female band."[6] After two albums, Becky Wreck was replaced by Chip English, who was then replaced by Helen Destroy in 1999.

At the group's third gig in 1990, Thurston Moore and Kim Gordon approached them about producing an album through the English label Blast First. Volpe says, "[Blast First] saw us as a novelty act, and we were. We were a bunch of young girls and we didn't know how to play for shit, and we were all eighteen and we were a total spectacle onstage. So they bought us amps and they put us in a studio to record, and then we went to England and we toured with Dinosaur Jr., opening up for them."[7] The resulting album was *Babysitters on Acid*.

The European tour went fairly well, although Kogan remembers the first night in England as a disaster. As she recalls, "We're opening for

Dinosaur Jr. and the very first show there were people throwing pint glasses at us from the back of the room, and it turned out to be a bunch of girls, we found out later. But it was very upsetting. I remember getting off the stage and I was crying. I think also 'cause I lost my voice that night or something, but people would throw shit all the time, and then it turned into freaks who would come up onstage and try to take their clothes off and stuff like that. I don't know if that's resistance, but you don't really want that."[8]

"There was always a mixed reaction," Volpe says of their audiences. "Most of the time, any women in the club would be totally psyched, totally psyched, and most of the time the men were, too, but there was always a mixed reaction. It was like, 'Yeah, they're great, they're women, it's great because they're hot,' or there would be guys who would be like, 'No, it's great because the music's great, and they're a lot of fun, and we get it.' So it was always kind of mixed between the bonehead reaction and just people who dug the music."[9] Their shows also served as respite for young outcasts. "What we found," adds Volpe, "which I really liked, was it seemed to be really young kids. Kind of the misfit kids, like any of the transgender kids or the boy who liked to wear makeup or all the misfit kids who didn't really feel like they fit in anywhere, found refuge at our shows. I always loved that."[10]

Unlike other female acts of their day—like the more obviously feminist Ani DiFranco and other folk singer-songwriters—the Lunachicks, while addressing womanhood in their songs, often portrayed it as sometimes jokingly repulsive. They occasionally reveled in demystifying the female anatomy. Their song "Plugg," for instance, on the 1992 album *Binge and Purge*, takes on the topic of menstruation and its accompanying discomforts. Songs that complain about the female condition are balanced by songs about sex and self-affirmation. The Lunachicks' most consistently feminist album, *Binge and Purge*, contains songs like its title track, which obviously deals with bulimia; the aforementioned "Plugg"; and "Superstrong," which, under a riding metal guitar riff, portrays the band as swaggering, street-smart girls schooled in self-defense. The 1995 release *Jerk of All Trades* includes a song about Barbie's aging complex ("Bitterness Barbie") and the pro-choice anthem "Fallopian Rhapsody."

"I think that, yeah, we were all feminists," Volpe says, "but whether or not everybody felt comfortable describing or identifying themselves with feminism was a different story, because everybody has their own idea of what feminism means. But what we were doing, I think, was just feminist in and of itself. You know, a lot of people have been taught to be so afraid of that word, so members of the band would be like, 'I'm not a feminist because that would imply that I'm a man-hating, castrating bitch-dyke and that's not what I am.' I'd be like, 'You don't have to be; look at what you're doing.' So we were, and a few of us were more vocal about it than others."[11]

The Lunachicks themselves reflect every female horror-movie stock character type: sexy, pretty, haunting, rebellious, sarcastic, and smart. But they are definitely not victims. Nor was it possible to pigeonhole them, and they hit a dead end when it came to garnering a major label contract. As the majors tried to promote new versions of womanhood that fell in line with grunge acts and the media's presentation of its aesthetic (L7 and Babes in Toyland had both landed industry contracts with Warner Brothers affiliates by 1992), the labels were at a loss regarding how to promote women who neither were a nicety, like the labels' torch-song acts, nor had the potential for sexual novelty or male fantasy, like, well, nearly every woman on mainstream radio. And while L7 and Babes in Toyland were accepted as "serious" musical acts, the more glammed-up and bizarre Lunachicks didn't fit neatly into any of these roles. Volpe explains: "A lot of labels wouldn't touch us because they didn't know how to market us, because they felt, '[They're] all female, so let's market them on their sexual appeal.' But we were so ridiculous. 'Well, we can't sell them as sex objects, really. They're pretty, but they're weird looking and they make fart noises, and it's just a little bit too complex for the mainstream to have pretty and [silly].' So a lot of labels wouldn't go near us, basically."[12]

She adds, "I think what happened was, there was a big feeding frenzy, and all the majors scooped up all these bands. We had pretty much been told this: L7 was kind of the litmus test for the industry and the fact that they didn't sell, like, five million records, you know, according to industry standards, that was a failure. . . . They said, 'We have L7, and they didn't sell enough records, so we're not going to sign any more female bands.'"[13]

While the Lunachicks didn't capitalize on the short-lived industry dip into the all-female rock talent pool, their mean, fun, comedic stage show changed a lot of minds. As Sindi B. once told *Alternative Press*, "The best thing about the Offspring tour was that two or three times, dads came up to me and said, 'I brought my daughter here to see you because this is how I want her to see women.'"[14]

The Lunachicks frequently toured and played with bands, like the

Offspring and Rancid, that generally drew more male (and more main-stream) fans than female ones. The ladies played the testosterone-fueled Vans Warped Tour in 2000, the same year L7 crashed the show with their "Beaver" banner. Volpe remembers, "A lot of women were like, 'We're so happy you're playing. We're so happy there're some women on this tour. It's great. Yeah! Thank you for playing.' For the most part, it was good. The crowd was good, and the audience was receptive, even if the kids were so young. . . . Even if the teenage boys would just stand there not knowing what to make of it, it was good to know at least they had been exposed to it. At least that we had a presence, whether they liked it or not, they got to see some women in other roles that they might not have known even existed."[15]

The Lunachicks released two more albums, *Pretty Ugly* (produced by Fat Mike of NOFX fame) and *Luxury Problems* on Go-Kart Records in the late '90s. The 2000 Warped Tour shows were their last official ones (the band claims to be on an indefinite hiatus). A 2002 CBGB reunion showcased a few members' new projects, and in 2004 they played with queercore outfit the Butchies the night before the March for Women's Lives in Washington, D.C. Theo Kogan has self-released an album entitled *Theo*, and has also modeled and acted in numerous films over the years. Gina Volpe, a painter, graphic designer, and illustrator as well as a musician, has had her work exhibited at the annual South by Southwest conference, as well as a few shows in New York. (Her illustrations appear on a few Lunachicks records, too.) She is now a lead singer and guitarist for the three-piece Bantam, who released their self-titled debut album on Volpe's Heavy Nose Records in 2002. Squid was last seen tattooing at FlyRite Tattoo in Brooklyn, playing with the band Team Squid, and appearing in films like Katrina Del Mar's *Gang Girls 2000* (which featured music by the Lunachicks). Chip English now drums with the punk band Suicide King, and Helen Destroy also played with New York City's Devil Kit. While they aren't generally recognized as a precursor to riot grrrl, in many ways the Lunachicks embodied its sentiment and gave female fans a fun, raunchy rock show of their own.

Chapter 25

50 FT QUEENIE

PJ Harvey

AS NIRVANA'S OUTSIDER SENSIBILITY AND DISSIDENT VOICE WAS introducing the mainstream to punk, and as bands like Bikini Kill infused the indie world with overt feminism, Polly Jean Harvey quietly armed minions of female archetypes and prototypes. She was that lone girl violently shaking the tree, her stories dropping like overripe fruit.

Harvey's first album, *Dry*, gave a hint of her innate musical skill, attracting a mixed audience to her work—both male and female, from "college rock" fans to members of the deeper, more dedicated underground. She also attracted the attention of serious music critics and, unlike the bands associated with riot grrrl, was never charged with creating what the media deemed "bad" music. While 'zine editors, journalists, and audiences argued about the position of revolutionary girl musicians, Harvey's brutal snapshots of female life and longing (like "Sheela-Na-Gig" and "Happy and Bleeding"), set against complicated garage-tinged guitar and hyperactive drums, were, curiously, above the fray.

Polly Jean Harvey grew up on a farm in Yeovil, England. A self-avowed tomboy, she was the daughter of a sculptor who promoted blues bands, and a quarryman, both of whom encouraged her creativity. As she told *Q* magazine, "As a child, I would always want to read out something that I'd written, or use marionette string puppets to act out plays. I'm talking from four or five years upwards . . . Performing is something that I've always loved and felt confident doing. I feel my confidence growing as I'm doing it. I'm not confident in a lot of other areas of my life, so I was naturally drawn towards this area where I felt very secure. I've always felt like I had something worth saying, or something worth performing in some way."[1]

She began playing the saxophone at the age of eleven and then bought her first guitar at eighteen, teaching herself Bob Dylan and Police songs. As a teenager in Yeovil, she spent her time watching local bands, eventually joining Automatic Dlamini with John Parish, and another group called Bologna in which she played saxophone.[2] At eighteen, Harvey moved to London to attend art school, but decided instead to form a trio with Robert Ellis on drums and Steve Vaughn on bass, named simply PJ Harvey. In 1991, they recorded their first singles for the Too Pure label and then released their first album, *Dry*, the following year on Island Records. After a tour in 1993 for their next album, *Rid of Me* (produced by Steve Albini), Ellis and Vaughn left the group. Harvey was left working with a rotation of well-honed musicians, including Tom Waits' guitarist Joe Gore, and, on keyboards, the seasoned Eric Drew Feldman, who had played with both Pere Ubu and Captain Beefheart.[3]

Harvey writes all of her lyrics and music and teaches them to shifting band members. Her 1995 album, *To Bring You My Love*, earned her a Grammy nomination, and to date, she has released seven albums, including a collaboration with John Parish entitled *Dance Hall at Louse Point*. Parish also coproduced *To Bring You My Love*. Harvey also released *4-Track Demos*, a compilation of 4-track versions of the songs from *Rid of Me* and unreleased tracks, and the demo version of Dry.

While she compulsively rejects classification by gender, her work is written from an extremely intimate place, telling stories of (mostly) women's aching and longing. "I only ever write as an individual," she once protested. "I'm not even aware of my gender most of the time when I'm writing."[4] While many female musicians of the early '90s were writing overt critiques of how they and women at large were affected by cultural forces, Harvey's work, both then and now, can be described as emotional snapshots—songs that reveal love or loss, isolation or lust, without honing in on gender, specifically. Her unsettling vocals are often a roller coaster ride from manic to sedate, underscoring the instability of her characters. Harvey delves deeply into the subjects and situations she creates, becoming almost possessed by them. As a storyteller she fully surrenders to her characters. As she told *NME* in 2000, "Every song has elements of fiction as well as elements of autobiographical content. They're not all autobiographical, there's a healthy amount of imagination that runs through them and I think you have to say that's pretty much every songwriter, really. . . . That's the role of an artist as I see it—to use your imagination to stimulate feelings in yourself and in other people that can spark off associations they can use in their own lives."[5]

Dry quickly seduced underground rock fans in 1992 and set a high standard for her forthcoming work. The characters on this first album ache with desperation, mental instability, and a deep desire for attention. The breakdown portrayed on *Dry* is the direct result of how the world treats (or rather, ignores) these lonely women. In "Sheela-Na-Gig" the song's subject is visually, physically splayed out; her need for someone to see her body's beauty and availability results in rejection. "Oh My Lover" reveals a saddened narrator trying to convince a lover she can tolerate another woman if he'll only stay with her. On first glance, songs with titles like "Dress" and "Hair" seem to evoke the obvious signs of femininity, while titles like "Plants and Rags" and "Water" evoke the traditional ties between women and the earth. One listen to the album, though, proves the songs' titles misleading, and paints the conventional characteristics of femininity, if they exist at all outside of the mind, as damaging and one-dimensional. Heavy with hypnotic guitar riffs and an utterly danceable rhythm, "Dress" tells the story of a woman eager to please a man with a dress he gave her, only to be rejected.

On her second full-length LP, *Rid of Me*, the desperate woman Harvey portrayed on *Dry* swings to the other extreme, from the pleading supplicant unraveled to a phoenix risen from the ashes. Her reborn woman sings hauntingly to a lover about her intrepid presence on the album's title song, while "50 Ft Queenie" raucously demands the sexual debasing of a gigolo at the mercy of an empowered female narrator.

On the *Trouser Press* website, writers Bill Wyman and David Antrobus note *Rid of Me*'s "ideological purity that pushes [it] to the edges of the impersonal on one side and the cartoony on the other," while they laud *Dry* and describe it as "a corrosive—yet somehow beautiful—portrayal of female trouble on a scale infrequently seen attached to musical forces so controlled."[6]

To Bring You My Love brought Harvey mainstream success, and the album combines electronic influences with a deeper, more abstract and ethereal sound than her earlier work displayed. Her 1998 album, *Is This Desire?*, began Harvey's turn from self-exposition to third-person narrative, showing desire in all its forms, from homebound or "spinster" women ("Joy" and "The Wind") to those enmeshed in loneliness, heartbreak, or love. Each song paints a particular, individual portrait, often using the subjects' names to tell their stories: Catherine ("The Wind," "Catherine"), Elise ("A Perfect Day Elise"), Angelene (eponymous), Leah ("My Beautiful Leah"), and Joy (eponymous). She once described her album *Stories from the City, Stories from the Sea* as "[t]he feeling of concrete or the feeling of sand that slips through your fingers and is gone. Time passing. All these different things. It's just highlighting a contrast of extremes that's in our lives daily."[7] Her 2004 release *Uh Huh Her* combines the starker, sparer musical elements of her earlier work while retaining her ability to embody the characters she creates. In total, her work is inspiring and wrenching, reveling in the evolution of a complete artist, from the manic and tortured individual to the empowered, mystic, dark lover, and finally to the storyteller astutely observing and translating the larger world.

While Harvey drops the breadcrumbs of a hundred untold stories, each album cover presents her physically inhabiting the world of her characters. Uninhibited by image, she whips her long, wet hair for the androgynous queenie on *Rid of Me*, and dons a glam red dress and matching makeup for the more polished *To Bring You My Love*. "In order to sing the songs correctly, I feel like I have to live them out in my face in some way," she explained.[8] In the same interview, she described her look for *To Bring You My Love*: "I actually find wearing makeup like that, sort of smeared around, as extremely beautiful. Maybe that's just my twisted sense of beauty. I'm always attracted to things which are a little bit too much, as you can hear in the music. Certain pieces of music that might seem unsavory or difficult for some people to listen to I might find very soothing."[9]

Regardless of the breadth of her characters and music, and the technical ability that allows Harvey to garner gender-blind acclaim, the journalistic reflex to lump her in with artists to which she has no ties other than her sex exists. Although she caustically shakes a finger at those who insist on a connection between Patti Smith and herself, the associations are made nonetheless, as well as several with the Pretenders' Chrissie Hynde. "I'm not even a big Patti Smith fan," she once declared. "It's very frustrating when people keep saying that. I'm almost paranoid now because I'm not allowed to sing the way I sing because it sounds like Patti Smith. I can't help it. And I would never try and parody [sic] anybody, let alone Patti Smith."[10]

And whether her exterior play on femininity reveals a "50Ft Queenie" or the degraded "Sheela-Na-Gig," some can't help but focus on her sexuality. *Slant* writer Ed Gonzalez refers to her as a "slithering creature of female-cum-hitherness [sic]" rather than a woman defining her own version of femininity.[11] *NME* captioned an article on Harvey after a moment in the interview when she jokingly castigated her inquisitor: "I'm just a raunchy sex queen. Is that what you want to hear?" *NME* answered with, "Yes, frankly."[12] Not that this kind of stereotyping affects PJ Harvey's ability to produce a constantly changing, intellectual, and emotional catalog of music. She liberates, inspires, disturbs, and astounds, making the "groundbreaking" work of female pop musicians look as breakable and empty as spun sugar. And when you're sitting in the depth and odd beauty of Harvey's world, it is.

Chapter 26

REJECT ALL AMERICAN

Bikini Kill

I'm so sorry if I'M ALIENATING SOME OF YOU
YOUR WHOLE FUCKING CULTURE ALIENATES ME
I cannot scream in pain from down here on my knees
I'm so sorry that I think!
White boy . . . Don't laugh . . . Don't cry . . . Just die!
—BIKINI KILL, "WHITE BOY"[1]

THE RIOT GRRRL INVASION DIDN'T END IN THE PIT—THE MUSIC
that drove them into it had to be reclaimed, too. Bikini Kill adopted the now traditional musical structure of punk and added wailing vocals that evoke a woman drowning, then bursting to the surface for a gasp of air. Bikini Kill members Kathleen Hanna, Tobi Vail, Kathi Wilcox, and Billy Karren witnessed the misogyny and oppression that had been allowed to fester in the underground by 1990, and confronted it head-on. Drummer and part-time vocalist Vail described her plight in an issue of *Jigsaw* this way: "I feel completely left out of the realm of everything that is so important to me. And I know that this is partly because punk rock is for and by boys mostly and partly because punk rock of this generation is coming of age in a time of mindless career-goal bands."[2]

203

True subversion must always face both resistance and contempt; and in Bikini Kill's case, they faced both around nearly every corner. The amount of negative attention the band suffered is testimony to just how provocative and confrontational feminism was, even for the '90s underground. *Punk Planet* editor Daniel Sinker wrote in *We Owe You Nothing*, "The vehemence fanzines large and small reserved for Riot Girl—and Bikini Kill in particular—was shocking. The punk 'zine editors' use of 'bitches,' 'cunts,' 'man-haters,' and 'dykes' was proof-positive that sexism was still strong in the punk scene."[3] Bikini Kill also grappled with heckling from male audience members who, consciously or not, were fighting to retain the power they enjoyed in the underground. Even Mark Andersen and Mark Jenkins, who remain supporters of the riot grrrl movement and the bands that spurred it on throughout their book *Dance of Days* wrote that Bikini Kill's performance during a March for Women's Lives benefit in 1992 "wasn't exactly music, but something potent and true."[4] The description is reminiscent of what the initial mainstream critics had written of punk circa 1976; the rules of what could be considered "music" that punk had supposedly ripped to shreds had resurfaced for these new, subversive female voices. Andersen and Jenkins also report that during a set in the U.K., Hanna's request for a girls' space in front of the stage elicited boos from the crowd; another incident at a show with British band Huggy Bear led *Melody Maker* to call Bikini Kill and riot grrrl "anti-men."[5] Once again, some fans weren't ready to relinquish power or recognize privilege. It should be noted, however, that a number of bands, particularly those from Olympia and D.C. (like Nation of Ulysses), as well as many audience members, did support riot grrrl aims and the larger cause of women's rights within the punk rock community.

The bands the media most associated with riot grrrl—Bratmobile, Bikini Kill, Huggy Bear, and Heavens to Betsy—were, in effect, starting from scratch: taking the scraps of '70s punk and all the later indie music they had digested and beginning anew. Bikini Kill, however, made the bold decision to appropriate the sounds that had come to signify classic male punk and use them to underscore a feminist agenda.

Kathleen Hanna grew up in Bethesda, Maryland, attending high school there and also in Portland, Oregon, where she became a self-described "band girlfriend," which in the '80s meant living vicariously through your boyfriends' bands. After moving to Olympia, Washington, to attend the Evergreen State College and prior to starting Bikini Kill, Hanna started the band Viva Knieval. At the time, Hanna was running Reko Muse, an art gallery in Olympia, with Tammy Rae Carland. Tobi Vail, who produced the *Jigsaw* 'zine, was playing with the Olympia-based band Go Team, whose lineup included Olympia/D.C. mainstay Lois Maffeo, Calvin Johnson, and Bikini Kill guitarist Billy Karren. Vail also played for a short time with Jenny Toomey in My New Boyfriend.[6, 7]

Jigsaw expressed Vail's own views and revelations on her outsider status within punk. "Until I was twenty my life was the mail," she told the *L.A. Weekly*.[8] Like many 'zine creators in the early '90s, Vail received most of her communication through *Jigsaw*, which Bratmobile drummer and cocreator of *Girl Germs* Molly Neuman, Allison Wolfe, and Hanna were all fans of. Kathi Wilcox and Vail had already been playing together at Evergreen when Hanna threw out the idea of starting their own band. In October 1990, they did just that. After enlisting Billy Karren (formerly of Eugene band Snakepit) on guitar, Bikini Kill went on tour in the summer of 1991, playing D.C. in June, where they felt they had a stronger effect on their audience than they had in Olympia. Feeling "politically isolated" in Olympia, Bikini Kill decided to pack up and move to D.C. that same year, though they would eventually move back to Olympia.[9]

Along with Neuman and Wolfe, Hanna and Vail, and D.C. punk Jen Smith and Bratmobile guitarist Erin Smith, developed *Riot Grrrl*: a moniker, a 'zine, and eventually, a consciousness-raising movement that would kick-start the grrrl whirlwind. Bikini Kill self-released a tape of their music in 1991, and put out two records in 1992, *Bikini Kill EP* (produced by Ian MacKaye) and a split 12" with Huggy Bear (produced by Nation of Ulysses guitarist Tim Green). The full-length *Pussy Whipped* followed in 1993, *The CD Version of the First Two Records* was released in 1992, and *Reject All American* came out in 1996. Aside from their first tape, all of their albums were put out on Slim Moon's Kill Rock Stars label. The "New Radio"/"Rebel Girl" single was produced by Joan Jett, and Hanna contributed to Jett's *Fetish* album in 1999 when she cowrote "Baby Blue."

The group toured nationally with bands like Nation of Ulysses, and internationally with Huggy Bear and Team Dresch, as well as sharing bills around the world with dozens of other bands before breaking up in 1998. Their "grrrl" reputation, which consistently preceded the band, and the heaps of media coverage identifying Bikini Kill as the "face" of riot grrrl weren't the only aspects of their career that put a strain on the band. Hanna once wrote, "It was also super schizo to play shows where guys threw stuff at us, called us cunts, and yelled 'take it off' during our set, and then the next night perform for throngs of amazing girls singing along to every lyric and cheering after every song."[10] Since their breakup, Tobi Vail has played with the Frumpies, which was formed in 1992 with Billy Karren, Kathi Wilcox, and Molly Neuman. Vail also works at Kill Rock Stars and maintains her web 'zine *Bumpidee*, as well as playing with other bands. Wilcox now plays with the Casual Dots, a project with Christina Billotte from D.C.'s all-girl Slant 6 and Steve Dore. Kathleen Hanna has played with Suture and the Fakes, released a solo album entitled *Julie Ruin*, and now performs with Le Tigre, all while doggedly, joyfully addressing and expounding on leftist politics.

The mainstream predictably pounced on Bikini Kill as eagerly as it ate away at riot grrrl. In a 1998 interview in *Punk Planet*, Hanna said, "I don't know many musicians and artists who have been treated as badly as me and some of my friends have. That's just a fact. I know it because I lived it. It can be really painful to have to face how fucked-up shit is and how scared people are."[11]

Reflecting on the misrepresentation to which Bikini Kill was subjected during the riot grrrl media melee, Vail decorated *The CD Version of the First Two Records* with the following statement: "I want to make it clear that we do not give a shit what people think of us. That is not what we object to in all of this. It is not about us being pissed off because of a bad review . . . It is about feeling like no matter what we say or do there continues to be this media created idea of 'Bikini Kill/riot girl' that has little or nothing to do with our own efforts . . ."[12] She went on to say, "We are not in any way 'leaders of' or authorities on the 'Riot Girl' movement. In fact, as individuals, we have each had different experiences with 'Riot Girl' and tho [*sic*] we totally respect those who still feel that label is important and meaningful to them, we have never used that term to describe ourselves *as a band*. As individuals, we respect and utilize and subscribe to a variety of different aesthetics, strategies and beliefs, both political and punk-wise, some of which are probably considered 'Riot Girl'. . ."[13]

As a consequence of becoming the focus of the riot grrrl circus, but also for their fiery, easy-to-grasp lyrics, Bikini Kill stand as the most recognized female punk band of the early '90s, and as the most potent threat to the male-dominant underground. The revolution Bikini Kill envisioned reflected a new brand of feminism; Kathleen Hanna often flashed the audience, sometimes pointing out her cellulite, scrawled the words "Bitch" or "Slut" on her stomach, and sang of sexual attraction to both girls and boys, allowing women, particularly feminists, to be at once angry and sexual. Thanks to Bikini Kill and other female punk bands of the time, the images of women shifted in underground music from misunderstood muses or heartless bitches to empowered, lovingly angry, educated protagonists.

Bikini Kill's anthem "Rebel Girl" worshipped at the altar of punk women—"Rebel girl, you are the queen of my world"—and followed up with "I think I wanna take you home, I wanna try on your clothes," turning not only the notion of the sexual aggressor from male to female, but replacing stereotypical female-female jealousy with physical and emotional attraction.[14] The attraction and love Bikini Kill expresses in "Rebel Girl" is for the swaggering outcast—the truly unique and sexually free woman: "They say she's a slut but I know she is my best friend."[15] "Rebel Girl" is the answer to the Dead Milkmen's "Punk Rock Girl," a love song where the protagonist falls in love and worships his punk rock partner. Eschewing the typical boy-for-girl fare, "Rebel Girl" is a tribute to and love song for another woman—for that risk-taking, questioning girl so often hated and misjudged.

Other work by the band spoke directly to sexual and physical abusers, liberating the victims' words from the pages of journals and 'zines. These turbulent lyrics stung with the pain of survival and physical oppression, as in "White Boy," excerpted earlier; or in the question asked in "Star Bellied Boy": "Why do I cry every time that I cum?"[16] During shows, the band often invited audience members onstage to share their own stories of surviving sexual abuse.

Other lyrics quiver with revenge fantasy, like these from "Suck My Left One":

> Daddy comes into her room at night
> He's got more than talking on his mind
> My sister pulls the covers down
> She reaches over, flicks on the light
> She says to him, SUCK MY LEFT ONE.[17]

Listening to their albums is like walking through a girl's messy bedroom, where black and white Xeroxed collages replace airbrushed posters of kittens or horses; where Cyndi Lauper is drowned out with bloodied screams backing a chorus of "Give Peace a Chance" (as in the song "Liar") and preening lip-sync is replaced by a prompt thrashing of a girl's imaginary guitar. Bikini Kill, along with X-Ray Spex and Crass, remain among the best examples of punk-rock political rage united with an optimistic longing for a better world. As a band they managed to mix academic theory with basic rhythms, emerging on the other side of the revolution grrrls imagined.

Chapter 27

SO MANY COWARDS AND SO LITTLE TIME

Bratmobile

IF NEITHER ACADEMIC FEMINIST DIALOGUE, MINDLESS POP, NOR serious political punk is what you're looking for, then Bratmobile, serving up pop escapism with a social conscience, just might be. Molly Neuman, Erin Smith, and Allison Wolfe's sharp feminist pop punk is smart and sassy. And while their use of spare drums, surf guitar, and schoolyard chanting can make uncovering the lyrics an archaeological dig, but once deciphered, they're well worth the work.

Wolfe and Neuman met while attending the University of Oregon in Eugene. While Wolfe turned Neuman on to bands like Beat Happening and the Melvins, Neuman introduced Wolfe to sociology classes and Public Enemy. "It really opened my eyes," Wolfe says, "and really got me thinking. And it was pretty easy to apply it to my own life and my own surroundings: 'Yeah, everything's fucked up!,' you know?"[1]

Inspired by the few Northwestern all-girl bands around in the late '80s and early '90s, like Calamity Jane and Viva Knieval, as well as by Northwestern musicians Tobi Vail, Lois Maffeo, and Beat Happening's Heather Lewis, and by the true DIY spirit of Calvin Johnson and Candice Pedersen's K

Records, Wolfe and Neuman were itching to make a contribution. "We were bored in Oregon, in Eugene," says Wolfe. "It was a real hippie town, and we were getting really politicized, but also really into this DIY thing, so we kinda started creating. 'Let's make our own fanzine!' We were very encouraged by people like Tobi [Vail] and Kathleen [Hanna] in Olympia, and we were like, 'Oh, let's do a band, let's do radio—we wanna have an all-girl radio show!' even though there was no such thing as college radio at the time there. We would start by having shows of other bands sometimes playing at our house, or helping to put on shows and things like that, but it wasn't really happening in Eugene, you know? So finally, we were just sort of like, 'Let's go to Olympia—we go up there every weekend, and we'll do stuff up there.'"[2]

Neuman and Wolfe were working on the feminist punk 'zine *Girl Germs,* which would come to be considered an arbiter of riot grrrl, along with their other 'zine *Riot Grrrl* and Tobi Vail's *Jigsaw.* To friends, they began talking up a band that didn't yet exist, Bratmobile, and in late 1990 Calvin Johnson kindly took them to task for it.

"I would write lyrics and things, and Molly was taking guitar lessons and kind of learning some chords, and I learned how to tune a guitar, but we didn't know much," Wolfe remembers. "And I remember Calvin Johnson from Olympia called down to us [in 1990] and said, 'Hey, I want you to come play this show'—and it was right after Bikini Kill started—'and it's gonna be you guys, Bikini Kill, and Some Velvet Sidewalk on Valentine's Day in Olympia.' And we were like, 'Oh! Huh? We're not really a band!' And he's like, 'But you always *say* that you're a band,' because we'd go up there and go to shows, go to see Beat Happening, and Fugazi when they'd come through, and Nirvana and Melvins and whatever, and we'd brag about our band. . . . So then we were like, 'What do we do? First of all, how do we get up there?'"[3]

Neuman bought a used car and transportation was taken care of. Robert Christie, of Some Velvet Sidewalk and Oswald 5-O, lent them rehearsal space, and advised them to listen to the Ramones for guidance. "I was like, 'Huh?'" Wolfe remarks. "We didn't have any Ramones records. I guess my first thought was, 'Awesome, thanks.' He totally helped us out. But my second thought was, 'Well, if some punk guy tells me to listen to the Ramones to be in a band, I'm gonna go do the opposite.' I've never owned a Ramones record. From that day on, I was like, 'I'm not listening to the Ramones!' 'Cause if every punk band sounds like the Ramones, I don't want to, you know? I want to be different. So it was sorta being, [or] trying to be, rebellious."[4]

Initially, Neuman would rotate between guitar and drums, contributing to their early spare sound. After a few sit-in performances by Christina Billotte (of Slant 6, Quix*o*tic, and the Casual Dots), Jen Smith (who worked with Neuman and Wolfe on *Riot Grrrl*), and other "special guests" in Olympia, the Bratmobile lineup became official: guitarist Erin Smith, lead vocalist Allison Wolfe, and drummer Molly Neuman. On a family visit to Washington, D.C., in 1991, Neuman was introduced to Erin Smith through Calvin Johnson at a show by Nation of Ulysses, another band often given credit for inspiring the beginnings of riot grrrl. An all-male outfit, D.C.-based Nation of Ulysses combined staunch, inflammatory political rhetoric with punk spontaneity, ideals that were sometimes lost in the mire of "mindless career-goal bands."[5] Neuman, Wolfe, and Smith, along with Hanna and Vail, spent the summer of 1991 in D.C., and began combining feminism and punk rock in earnest through their new 'zine, *Riot Grrrl*. Neuman once remarked, "I think it's cool for women to start playing any time. Dudes do it all the time and they wank and they suck and people go see them and if you're gonna wank and suck, you can be a girl, too."[6]

Bratmobile's first album, *Pottymouth*, was released on the Kill Rock Stars label in 1993. After seeing their 1991 Olympia, Washington, debut, Kill Rock Stars owner Slim Moon released their song "Girl Germs" on his first compilation. The band's official debut and Slim Moon's first official compilation both occurred at K Records' Internal Pop Underground Convention. *Pottymouth* was an assault of a different color. Bratmobile lost none of punk's writhing anger, but sang with urgent, echoing vocals combined with punk surf sounds. The album was an incredible accomplishment for a trio in which only a year and a half before, two of the members didn't know how to play. Bratmobile solidified their unique, spare sound in sixteen songs packed with succinct, witty lyrics that sounded like they were yelled through a megaphone. The girls gave the Runaways hit "Cherry Bomb" a searing makeover: The chorus was sung with a bloody scream that erased the double-entendre play of the original, creating a purely feminist call to arms. Consistent with the grrrl goal of bringing punk to feminism and feminism to punk, Bratmobile successfully put the fun back into both with songs like "Cool Schmool," "Girl Germs," and "Fuck Yr. Fans." Wolfe's taunting vocals bring to mind the nagging, insistent little sister interrupting her brother's garage band practice.

The most refreshing thing about Bratmobile is their ability to make feminism personal, bringing it down to the everyday happenings in a girl's life. They offer tangible examples of the overarching systemic oppression so railed against in much of political punk. Their sing-along songs make both feminism and punk accessible and real to all kinds of young women, not just activists. For fans still tuning in to the stale pop radio that had once offered '80s girl bands like the Go-Go's and the Bangles but had by the early '90s given way to bubblegum dance like Debbie Gibson and Paula Abdul, Bratmobile was an enlivening discovery. As a band they were able to create a space where feminism was malleable, and the listener was free to take away from it whatever meaning was needed.

The ladies toured with Sleater-Kinney founder Corin Tucker's early band Heavens to Betsy in 1992, bringing riot grrrl, still unfettered by mainstream media's filters, to teenage girls all over the country. Erin Smith told *Punk Planet*, "It was such a wonderful time in the life of so many of our friends' bands as well: Bikini Kill, Heavens to Betsy, Beat Happening, Kicking Giant, Tiger Trap, Huggy Bear, Heavenly, Fugazi, Autoclave, Nation of Ulysses. It was a wonderful time and they were great people to share it with. . . . Everyone was just starting out and just starting to learn how to do things like play shows and tour and we were all experiencing these things for the first time, together. There was a big sense of the Oly-D.C. connection in the community and in helping each other. This part of the underground was only just starting out and just getting attention and finding an audience, so it was really our first time for everything."[7]

Bratmobile's six-song EP *The Real Janelle* was released in 1994 on Kill Rock Stars. The three women somehow managed to hold the band together while living on separate coasts. Neuman and Wolfe initially remained in the Northwest for school, and Smith stayed in D.C. After graduation, Neuman relocated to Berkeley, California, and Wolfe split her time between Olympia and D.C. The difficulties of maintaining a long-distance band, as well as the increasing pressure of dealing with the attention that riot grrrl brought, came to a head onstage in New York City, and the band broke up in the middle of the show in 1994. Despite Joan Jett's presence backstage and her encouraging whispers to continue through a particularly difficult set, Bratmobile dissolved, and the women embarked on individual projects for a few years. Neuman worked her way up to general manager and co-owner of Berkeley-based Lookout! Records, and played with the Peechees. She cur-

rently manages both the Donnas and the Locust. Wolfe and Smith formed
Cold Cold Hearts with bassist Nattles (now of Flin Flon) and drummer
Katherine Brown. Smith now works at Lookout!, and Wolfe also played
with the band Deep Lust and initiated the first Ladyfest in Olympia in
2000, a weeklong women's festival of workshops, music, and discussions that
now takes place annually all over the country and around the world.

Bratmobile re-formed in 1998, releasing two scorching albums on
Lookout! as if not a day had gone by. *Ladies, Women and Girls* and *Girls Get
Busy* (the latter released in 2002) are evidence of the band's evolution, from
both a musical and an ideological standpoint. Jon Nikki added bass and
keyboards to *Ladies, Women and Girls*, and with the addition of keyboardist
Audrey Marrs and bassist Marty Violence, *Girls Get Busy*'s sound swells to
match Wolfe's fiery admonitions. Both albums contain timely, political,
fun feminist punk anthems like "I'm in the Band," and much-needed critical responses to the second Bush administration with songs like "Shop for
America" and "United We Don't." While the rest of the country pulled
forgotten flags out of attics in the wake of 9/11, Allison sharpened her
pencil and wrote:

> We won't fly your flag
> For the rights we never had
> We don't buy all your lies
> Your lies in disguise
> The Right side is crushing down
> And it doesn't make a sound.[8]

In "Gimme Brains," on *Ladies, Women and Girls*, Bratmobile ask for a
truly intelligent man:

> Gimme brains for breakfast baby
> And gimme more for lunch
> Throw me a bone for dinner yeah yeah
> A girl could starve on a boy like you
> With nothing left to offer so that means that we're through.[9]

These days riot grrrl is often brushed off as an underground, flash-in-
the-pan fad, and feminist dialogue is waved away as an outdated topic
within indie rock, but the same can't be said of Bratmobile. "How many
different ways can guys be sexist? And how many different ways can women

be feminist?" Wolfe once asked rhetorically. "As long as there's a myriad of ways to be sexist there's going to be myriad ways to respond to that or resist that—like feminism. They can call it a fad, like they did with riot grrrl. But as long as fucking lame ass losers exist, as long as sexism exists, women are going to fight back. And we're going to call it different things. I think it's important to have fresh ideas and fresh communities. But it's still feminism and that's really important."[10]

Chapter 28

TO THE ENEMIES OF DYKE ROCK

Team Dresch

"YOU MIGHT PLAY A SHOW IN PORTLAND," TEAM DRESCH bassist, singer, and songwriter Jody Bleyle told *Punk Planet* in 1997, "and people will say, 'Yeah, yeah, we know what they're about, whatever, blah, blah, blah,' and you go to Germany or anywhere else and there's only ten girls at the show and they've never seen an all-girl band before, let alone a dyke band, and they freak out. They want it so bad. We'll ask them, 'Who wants to come up and play this instrument, who wants to come up and play that instrument? Let's start a band right now.' Everybody will come up and play, and people get really excited—guys get excited, too. Most punk bands' politics are pretty dead, but everyone wants to be alive."[1]

All-girl, all-dyke Team Dresch's accessible, searing lyrics and complex guitar riffs helped garner them a rabid following over their brief tenure as queercore's most popular crossover band. Originally composed of Kaia Wilson, Jody Bleyle, Donna Dresch, and Marci Martinez, Team Dresch's throw-down, heart-on-the-floor rock was an integral part of the Northwest queercore movement that gained prominence in the early 1990s. The band released two albums with original co-lead Wilson, *Personal Best* (1995) and

Captain My Captain (1996), and then continued on without her after she left to join Tammy Rae Carland as co-owner of the now-defunct Mr. Lady Records. Wilson later released two solo albums on Mr. Lady Records before forming dyke punk outfit the Butchies. Dresch and Bleyle disseminated queercore, too, through their respective labels, Chainsaw and Candy-Ass Records. Team Dresch reunited for an Olympia show in August 2004.

***

All four members of Team Dresch were politically active and socially aware, as well as being masterful lyricists and songwriters. Donna Dresch, specifically, has been a constant promoter, supporter, and creator within the Northwest music scene, although she is almost entirely overlooked by the mainstream chronicles of punk. After launching her acclaimed *Chainsaw* 'zine in the mid- to late '80s, she began playing bass at age eighteen, when a friend asked her if she wanted to start a band. "He asked, 'What do you want to play?'" she once relayed. "I said, 'Bass.' I don't know why I said that. I just made it up. I didn't own a bass. I never even touched one. We went to the music store downtown and pretended that we were shopping for instruments and would 'jam' in the little back room they had. We were really, really bad."[2]

Dresch started Chainsaw Records in Olympia in 1991. After Dresch initially made a compilation tape of her favorite bands, Chainsaw officially released its first 7" (by the Frumpies), and has since released the work of Sleater-Kinney, Tracy + the Plastics, and Dresch's own bands, Team Dresch and Davies vs. Dresch. The band's first drummer, Marci Martinez, had been playing drums since the age of nine, taking lessons as a child, and was a member of her high school's marching band. "When I first started playing, I just practiced for hours," she told *Drummergirl*. "I listened to songs I that I liked and copied what the drums were doing."[3]

Kaia Wilson started playing music in her teens as well. "At fifteen, my mom taught me three chords on her acoustic guitar, and from there I taught myself how to play and wrote a gazillion tortured love songs about the girl I loved; it was totally like Lili Taylor in [the film] *Say Anything*. [Taylor's character wrote song after tortured love song for her ex.] I still write almost all my songs on my mother's guitar, which I did, in fact, steal, along with her Yamaha PSR-150 keyboards. Thanks, Mom!"[4] As more proof of the importance of 'zines in the emerging indie culture, Wilson discovered the alternative rock scene when she came across a punk rock 'zine at fourteen, and eventually stumbled over Dresch's *Chainsaw* through another queer 'zine, *Homocore*. Wilson knew drummer Marci Martinez from Portland's all-girl Calamity Jane, and met Jody Bleyle around the same time. "I think they call that fate," says Wilson.[5] "I think a little bulb went off in all of our heads saying that we all had to be in a band together," Dresch once explained. "We had one crappy practice and became a band. It was magical."[6]

The band formed in 1993, and was named to honor guitarist Donna Dresch, whom punk-folk dyke Phranc teasingly called "captain" (hence their second album's title, *Captain My Captain*). Dresch had already played with a score of other bands, including Dinosaur Jr., Dangermouse, and the Screaming Trees. Kaia Wilson was with Adickdid at the time, and Jody Bleyle was a member of Hazel. Team Dresch recorded *Personal Best* in 1995, and coreleased it on Candy-Ass and Chainsaw Records.[7] Marci Martinez left soon after, and master drummer Melissa York joined the band. *Captain My Captain* was also coreleased by the two labels in 1996.

Through Candy-Ass Bleyle assembled the *Free to Fight* compilation in 1995, to generate self-defense awareness and education. The album came with a booklet outlining self-defense strategies and included songs by Team Dresch, Excuse 17, Heavens to Betsy, all-dyke outfit Fifth Column, and others. Team Dresch kicked off their first tour with self-defense classes for the audience. After their first show, an incident involving a club owner had taken place, which, along with Bleyle's social conscience, inspired *Free to Fight*. The owner, who apparently regularly hosted events for the gay community, had a fight with Bleyle in the parking lot. His ring ended up cutting her face when the fight culminated with a blow to her head. "I just think it happened because he could tell I was a dyke and I was being assertive with him and he didn't like it and he snapped," she commented.[8]

Wilson and Bleyle wrote all of Team Dresch's lyrics, creating a healthy balance between Bleyle's concrete sense of expression and Wilson's more abstract approach. The band's first album is their most intimate release, but the group's vision has always embodied the personal and political, the enlightening and self-revelatory. Along with songs that served as expressions of love were angry ones, too. *Personal Best* contains "Hate the Christian Right!," a theme that never seems to go out of style, and "#1 Chance Pirate TV," which defended Sinead O'Connor's admonishment of the Catholic Church on *Saturday Night Live*. Other songs, like "Growing up in Springfield," told of Wilson's first love (whose protagonist happened to come from a fundamentalist Christian family), articulating the longing for a freer life of her younger queer self. More than addressing young dyke love and disseminating queer visibility, Team Dresch sought to make their plight, their pain, and their joy universal. As Bleyle once said, "Of course I'm speaking of where I come from; you have to be able to extrapolate from there and feel what anyone who's not [known] freedom or who's wanted to feel it has felt. I want anyone to be able to feel this sadness and these longings and elations from listening to these songs—otherwise, it doesn't mean anything."[9] Take a line from the song "Yes I Am Too, But Who Am I Really?" from *Captain My Captain*:

> Don't tell us we only care about the dykes and fags
> Don't try to find fake reasons to hate us
> Some people get it
> A lot more people need it
> Freedom.[10]

Team Dresch bridged the emotional isolation between queer and nonqueer audiences, gaining fans within queercore and the larger indie-rock communities. "There always were people who wanted to tell us that we were being exclusive, alienating straight audiences, that we were too this, too that, the whole 'Why do you gotta talk about it?' thing," Wilson commented. "But the positives always outweighed the negatives. At the very least, we felt embraced by the people we needed to feel embraced by."[11] From the content of their lyrics to queer activism and visibility in places dykes wouldn't otherwise find a home (like *Spin* or *Interview* magazines, in which they were profiled), Team Dresch was determined to offer something positive to young dykes and punks. Bleyle's lyrics in "Musical Fanzine" are some of the band's most cited and most inspiring ones—a prime example of Team Dresch's aim to liberate: "Queer sex is great, it's fun as shit/Don't kill yourself 'cause people can't deal with your brilliance."[12]

Captain My Captain goes even further to bridge gaps between the personal and political. Before recording the album, Bleyle suffered a nervous breakdown, and her songs on the resulting album document her coming to terms with the event—a rescue operation for herself and her audience. In a way, Bleyle's brutal honesty about her mental illness further cemented the band's ability to build bridges and celebrate all forms of liberation. As she told *Punk Rock Academy*, "I think talking about mental illness, especially, is far more taboo than talking about being gay or anything. I think it's one of the most taboo things left in U.S. society to talk about but I just feel like it's easy for me, at this point, to talk about being gay. It's totally easy. I know it's not easy for everyone, but for me, it's nothing. . . . I feel like even though [mental illness is] hard for me to talk about, that's the next thing I need to do."[13]

Although it may not be apparent from the socially responsible themes found in Team Dresch's songs, a sense of divide between political and artistic activism was endemic to the Northwest scene by the mid-'90s. The region was also vulnerable to exploitation; the indie-rock label was used as a career stepping stone for many bands hoping to follow in the successful footsteps of grunge luminaries. The scene was still recovering from its worldwide-hype hangover when Team Dresch wrote "To the Enemies of Political Rock." The song calls to task the indie rock community, and the larger musical audience, for its increasing complacency: "Do it yourself means do it for me/I don't give a shit/Just get my video on MTV."[14]

Luckily, the Northwest did not continue to fall victim to the exploitation of the mainstream record industry, though, and Team Dresch, among others, helped spawn a new generation of freer, less alienated, self-invented and self-sustaining young female musicians, straight and queer alike.

PATTI SMITH
Patti Smith takes a break from whirling dervishes.

THE RUNAWAYS
Battle axes: Joan Jett (left) and Lita Ford (right) in the Runaways.

TINA WEYMOUTH

Tina Weymouth, the bass muscle of the Talking Heads.

DEBBIE HARRY

Glamour girl Debbie Harry's other side.

© JENNY LENS PUNK ARCHIVE. JENNY LENS/DAN KESSEL PRODUCTIONS

THE GERMS

The Germs' "secret weapon": Lorna Doom, left, poses with Darby Crash, Donna Rhia, and Pat Smear.

© ANN SUMMA

EXENE CERVENKA
Exene Cervenka holds court at
the Masque in Los Angeles.

© ANN SUMMA

POISON IVY
The Cramps' Poison Ivy puts her
own stamp on psychobilly.

PENELOPE HOUSTON

Penelope Houston of the
Avengers re-envisions the
American female.

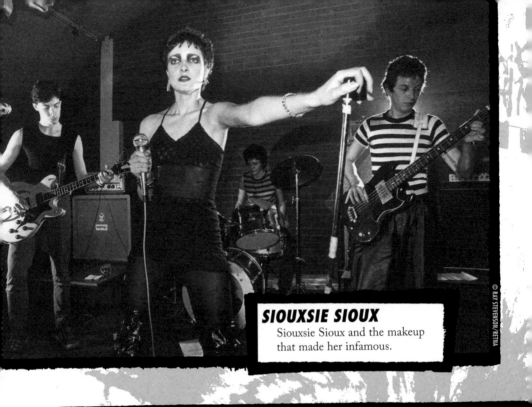

SIOUXSIE SIOUX
Siouxsie Sioux and the makeup that made her infamous.

THE SLITS
Viv Albertine (left) and Ari-Up (right) of the Slits eschewing expectations of "typical girls."

© 1978 EBET ROBERTS

POLY STYRENE
X-Ray Spex's Poly Styrene,
wild-eyed at CBGB.

© FRANCES PELZMAN LISCIO

THE RAINCOATS
The anti-posturing of the
Raincoats. Left–right: Gina Birch,
Ana da Silva, Vicky Aspinall, and
Ingrid Weiss.

WENDY O. WILLIAMS

The physical feminism of Wendy O. Williams.

© BOB FARINA, PLASMATICS MEDIA LLC

LYDIA LUNCH

Lydia Lunch blurs the line between the erotic and the disturbed.

© RAY STEVENSON/RETNA

© ALLISON C. WOLFE

LULU GARGIULO

Lulu Gargiulo jumps for joy with the Fastbacks.

KIM GORDON

Queen of noise: Sonic Youth's
Kim Gordon.

JENNIFER FINCH

L7's Jennifer Finch feminizes the classic metal god stance while rocking for choice.

BIKINI KILL

Bikini Kill, uniting girls and educating boys. Left–right: Kathi Wilcox, Kathleen Hanna, and Tobi Vail.

MIA ZAPATA

Mia Zapata sings the blues with the Gits.

© MARGARITA LA PUSSYGATA

TEAM DRESCH
Empowering dyke punks everywhere: Left–right: Donna Dresch, Kaia Wilson, Marci Martinez, Jody Bleyle.

SLEATER-KINNEY
Sleater-Kinney at Olympia's 2000 Ladyfest. Left–right: Corin Tucker, Carrie Brownstein, and Janet Weiss.

© 2004 CYNTHIA CONNOLLY

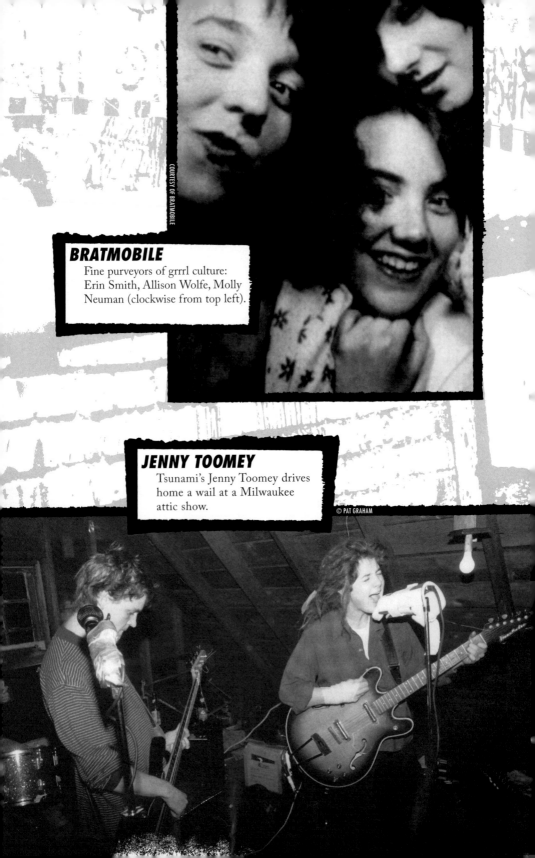

BRATMOBILE

Fine purveyors of grrrl culture:
Erin Smith, Allison Wolfe, Molly
Neuman (clockwise from top left).

JENNY TOOMEY

Tsunami's Jenny Toomey drives
home a wail at a Milwaukee
attic show.

THE BUTCHIES

Are we not hot? Left–right:
Kaia Wilson, Melissa York, and
Alison Martlew.

THE GOSSIP

Not in Arkansas anymore:
Kathy Mendonca, Nathan
Howdeshell, and Beth Ditto
(left-right).

© STATIA MOLEWSKI

LE TIGRE
Perfect protest pop. Left–right: Kathleen Hanna, Johanna Fateman, and JD Samson.

© HADLEY HUDSON

PEACHES
Peaches, the fatherfucker.

Part V

THE LATE 1990S–
EARLY 2000S

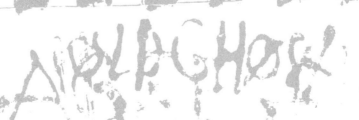

Introduction

FEMINISTS, WE'RE CALLING YOU. PLEASE REPORT TO THE FRONT DESK[1]

IF WE WERE TO BELIEVE THE HYPE, THEN NIRVANA SHOULD HAVE changed music forever. The laws that seem to govern politics, music, and culture in general have a pendulum-like momentum, though. A swing to the right inevitably means one back to the left, and music at once loud, messy, and populist has its moment only to be replaced by ordered, precise, and manipulated sounds the next. As the '90s came to a close, the decade's swing to the left, especially among young people, both in music and in politics, could only mean a dreaded swoop back in the other direction. When word got out that riot grrrls' affections could not be bought or co-opted easily and the record industry was stumped as to what to do with bands like the Lunachicks, mainstream music seemed to trip over its own version of the "angry girl." And out trotted a string of attractive young women armed with guitars and a softer, cleaner feminist bent that tidied up riot grrrl's grit. Enter: Jewel, Alanis Morissette, Fiona Apple, Tracy Bonham, Sheryl Crow, Joan Osborne, et al. The "women in rock" years were now under way—and the public devoured it.

Unlike the infamous riot grrrls, these women were not perceived in the

223

mainstream as witches corrupting the minds and CD players of young girls, but as ladies politely elbowing their way onstage with musical training under their belts and high production quality tightly intact. Riot grrrls' self-made communities, networks, shows, and lifestyles were viewed as "antisocial," while these more mainstream acts, existing within well-paved social and artistic avenues, were considered new and engaging. Girls with guitars, whose music L7 defined as "PMS fraud rock," worked within a commercial-based system rife with traditional notions of sellable females. They were polite and affable, they were always slender (almost frighteningly so), and for all their whispered "fuck you"s, they teetered on a feminist tightrope, revealing both their strongest and most stereotypical sides when it came to love and rejection.

Singer-songwriter Jewel commented in a 1997 issue of *Time* magazine, "People are hungry for emotiveness. They want bare honesty, emotional blood-and-bone honesty."[2] What the public so hungrily craved, apparently, was still only acceptable when packaged in typical forms of female expression (flowery, lovelorn lyrics) by commercially marketable (photogenic, heterosexual, and sexually available) women. While Lynn Breedlove of Tribe 8 demanded blow jobs from bound straight boys, Alanis Morissette cited *giving* a blow job as a symbol of brashness in her first hit single, "You Oughta Know." Instead of Breedlove's tool to unravel power, Morissette's rebellion is used to remind a wandering lover of what he's missing. Where Meredith Brooks' 1997 hit, "Bitch," proudly extolled women's tougher side, it also reinforced the typical female archetypes of wife, mother, and saint. (Kim Gordon allegedly wrote "Female Mechanic Now on Duty" as a response to this song.) Album covers like Fiona Apple's *Tidal* and Sarah McLachlan's *Fumbling Towards Ecstasy* offered softly lit portraits in the tradition of Hollywood circa 1940, lending the singers an air of ethereality. Behind the flawless packaging came reams of lyrics that loosely revealed the musicians' perspectives on life (Morissette's sunny "Hand in My Pocket" and Joan Osborne's philosophical "One of Us"), or entire albums that dealt almost exclusively with traditional approaches to relationships (Apple's *Tidal* or McLachlan's *Surfacing*). Whatever the formula, mainstream female rock sold a lot of records and got a lot of press. Morissette and Jewel were the most successful examples of the industry's favorite females: The former rang in the new century with eight Top 40 hits, the latter with four.

Proof of the artists' palatability was solidified on commercial radio,

MTV, and the perpetual harbinger of aspirational femininity, *Cosmopolitan*. More comfortable with "PMS fraud rock" acts than they ever were with riot grrrl, and never one to promote anything too heavy, angry, serious, ugly, deep, or brown, *Cosmo* lovingly doted praise on music's new women, whom they dubbed "Rockin', Ragin', and Female." In *Cosmo*'s eyes, women like Alanis Morissette, Jewel, and Tracy Bonham were "a revolution of rage and passion" and "guitar-wielding warriors."[3] "You Oughta Know," which *Cosmo* called the "nineties anthem of female empowerment," doesn't really allow for empowerment at all, but instead for commiseration over a relationship with a man.[4] Amid the heartsick clamor, though, Sleater-Kinney slammed through "Anonymous" on their 1996 LP *Call the Doctor*:

> Feel safe inside, inside those well-drawn lines
> Boyfriend, a car, a job my white girl life
> She swallowed a spider to catch, to catch that fly
> But I don't know why, why she swallowed that lie.[5]

With artists like Morissette, McLachlan, and others selling millions of albums, McLachlan was able to organize a mainstream answer to the boy-centric music festivals with the creation of her own estrocentric Lilith Fair in 1997. Named after Eve's predecessor from the Old Testament, a rare, stubborn, independent woman, Lilith Fair promoted female musicians and allowed a platform for feminist groups, yet Jewel's "emotional blood-and-bone honesty" pervaded the tour. The festival had a formulaic and uniform feel to it, with one quiet set after another performed before a relatively sedate audience. While Tracy Chapman provided some lyrical diversity with her blues and folk set, the majority of the festival was devoted to love or the lack thereof. One article reported that Lilith acts "reflect McLachlan's taste, concentrating on guitar-strumming, melody-loving songwriters rooted in folk, pop, and country music. . . . The main-stage headliners of the first Lilith show . . . are all pop-folk songwriters who, despite distinct styles, could also be a chapter of the Joni Mitchell fan club."[6] Lilith Fair, for all its good intentions, reinforced the idea of women writing, singing, performing, and appearing in a traditionally feminine way, without the angrier voices present to balance out the picture (and sound).

While most reporters opined that women were "finally" getting their due by the second half of the '90s, the issues initially raised by third-wave feminism, riot grrrl, punk, and indie music had been almost completely erased from the mainstream catalog, even though they had flooded it only four years earlier. One candid Atlantic Records executive, Val Azzoli, commented, "Honestly, we in the record business are not leaders. We are a bunch of sheep. When one kind of record does well, we all follow with more like it."[7]

"PMS fraud rock" prompted more than a few musings on the "arrival" of women in rock, but they were no match for the Spice Girls and their commodification of "Girl Power." This time, the feminist message would be appropriated with lamé go-go shorts, sculpted bodies, and saccharine dance songs. One positive side effect of the Spice Girls' meteoric yet short-lived success was the sudden appearance of quite a few ten-year-olds in T-shirts emblazoned with the words "Girl Power." The real impact of the Spice Girls, though, was in inadvertently raising the question of how to define "girl power." What does it really mean? The preening Spice Girls didn't seem all that different from the hundreds of novelty pop acts that came before. Shirley Manson of the band Garbage stated, "I don't see how wearing a bra and your knickers on the front cover of a magazine, with your breasts stuck up with your Wonderbra, holding up a peace sign and a pout, [has] anything to do with female equality."[8]

No Doubt earned a feminist gold star when vocalist Gwen Stefani penned "Just a Girl," a punk-influenced pop song about the social captivity of girlhood. Even for a more confrontational and interesting lady fronting a relatively raucous band, though, Stefani still pouted and posed like a rockabilly Betty Boop, not veering far enough from mainstream conventional beauty to shake it up. While "Just a Girl" reached number twenty-three on the Billboard charts, their breakup ballad "Don't Speak" hit number one. The band also detoured off the feminist road that handed them their first Top 40 hit, releasing subsequent singles that mimicked the more romantic vein of "Don't Speak" instead of the more unusual one of "Just a Girl."

Rolling Stone's laughable 2002 "Women in Rock" cover story featured Britney Spears, Michelle Branch, Mandy Moore, and Avril Lavigne, along with smarter, sounder choices like Sharon Osbourne, Mary J. Blige, Sleater-Kinney, Tori Amos, and Joni Mitchell. The story's letter from the editors, however, claimed that these women "think for themselves, calling their own shots."[9] One's left to wonder if that includes the megamachine behind Spears and her schoolgirl image.

This new coquettish face of feminism didn't begin and end with "Girl Power"—it became the catchall category for independent-minded women who shied away from the "f-word." For women unwilling to label themselves "feminist," there was now the gentler "postfeminist" moniker, apparently meant to imply that feminism was—or is—no longer relevant, the postfeminist label came to imply the new "free" woman who is in charge of herself sexually and who apparently embodies both the cultural feminine ideal and feminist independence. In other words, it meant women were free to embrace obsessing over their cellulite—as long as it was a "choice." While supposedly free to fret over personal flaws, rejecting typical beauty standards was still a problem for women, as made evident by the heckling the Gossip's Beth Ditto suffered, from audience members of both genders, when she proudly flaunted her larger body.

While some see the mainstream success of Nirvana as the death toll of the underground, indie rock alternately thrived and faltered throughout the late '90s and early years of the new century. Successful underground labels like Matador and Sub Pop aligned with majors for distribution or part ownership. The overexposure of grunge and, to a larger extent, the growth of the Internet offered high school students easier access to underground art and allowed the means for anyone to promote his or her own music. Beth Ditto recalls her hometown Searcy, Arkansas' introduction to the underground, courtesy of bandmate Nathan Howdeshell: "[W]e were all listening to Nirvana, and we were all listening to Hole, and we were getting as underground as we could, until Nathan discovered Sonic Youth. It started leading him more and more to the underground and to the punk scene that was going on. . . . Arkansas was so far away and so far removed and so behind the times, anyway, but we were ahead of our time for that town."[10]

Prior to Nirvana, the divide between towns like Searcy and those with an indie scene was rarely breached. Now young fans had Internet access to anyone selling records or MP3s online and desktop publishing made 'zine production infinitely easier. Even with this new unfettered access to counter cultural art forms and a flood of DIY activity, the lifting of radio ownership restrictions regulated by the Federal Communications Commission allowed large conglomerates to buy up more independent stations. The ensuing buyouts syndicated much of radio programming nationwide, making it more homogeneous, a fact that Jenny Toomey relayed to the Congressional Committee on Commerce, Science, and Transportation in 2003.[11] While a once invisible brick wall stood between mainstream and underground music, the major labels now had their hands on more subversive, diverse music, but nationally syndicated radio programming simultaneously limited the number of musicians receiving mainstream radio airplay. As if this didn't do enough to generate homogeneous playlists, the record industry suffered quite a few buyouts, and tended to save promotion budgets for its surefire blockbusters. *The Nation* reported that "some 250 bands were dropped to clear the roster for the latest trend, 'teen pop,'" in the 1998 merger of Polygram and Universal.[12]

Regardless of these changes in radio and among the major labels, truly independent scenes safe from mainstream interference existed (and still do), bolstered by this very exclusion from mainstream airplay. Revolution girl style lasted; there are just too many women playing basements, small clubs, and larger venues to list them all here. A short list includes Tracy + the Plastics, Quix*o*tic, Gravy Train!!!!, and Northern State. There are musicians like Glass Candy's Ida No, Chan Marshall of Cat Power, Michelle Mae of the Make-Up and the Scene Creamers, and the higher-profile Meg White of White Stripes, Karen O. of the Yeah Yeah Yeahs, and the Donnas. The list is endless, and the few covered in the following pages represent just a taste of what women are doing to subvert the status quo in underground rock today.

———————

As indie rock wound its way through the corporate world, another grassroots art form found itself there, too. Growing from an underground phenomenon to a lifestyle trend in urban communities, and emerging as a scapegoat for censorship during the '80s and early '90s, hip-hop exploded in the premillennial suburbs. Kids bought Jay-Z albums in the millions: He had five Top 40 hits between 1997 and 1999, and five of his nine albums went multiplatinum.[13] 50 Cent's *Get Rich or Die Tryin'* had netted $6.5 million by the end of 2003.[14] With the advent of hip-hop's mainstream popularity, MTV became the genre's biggest crossmarket promoter. Along with male artists like Jay-Z and 50 Cent came female rappers like Eve and Missy Elliott, and R&B singers Mary J. Blige and Lauryn Hill, all of whom were individual in style and substantive sound. Although these women didn't sell in the same volume as Jay-Z and other male acts, they certainly weren't apologetic or hypersexualized, either. The white pop mainstream, however more diversified, wasn't as prolific as either the underground or hip-hop when it came to stronger women. Enter: the angry young man.

Portending the conservative turn of the White House in 2000, the estrogen-influenced late '90s met the mother of all backlashes at the decade's end. Mainstream audiences opted for a return to sexual stereotyping when it backed white male-rage acts over girl rock. Following the chart successes of the female confessional, Limp Bizkit sold more than seven million copies of their 1999 album *Significant Other*, while Kid Rock's 1998 release, *Devil Without a Cause*, sold ten million.[15, 16] Acts like Korn and Limp Bizkit idealized the anger of rap without the sociopolitical context of the hip-hop community. The result was a combination of rap and alternative rock, music the bands had grown up on, matched, more often than not, with the vapid longings of frat boys. As Limp Bizkit proclaimed, they were doing it for the "Nookie." The male-rage arena became one where white boys haplessly searched for something they "deserved," while black rap artists conversely demanded respect long due. The only thing these new white acts seemed to demand was rampant, unchecked sexism, the right to freely appropriate black art forms, and the eternal sexual availability of women.

The comparatively wider emotional range portrayed by Alanis Morissette and Fiona Apple confronted the puerile longings and random aggression found in the form of Limp Bizkit's schoolyard bully, Fred Durst. In a 1999 interview for *Spin*, writer Zev Borow reported that Durst's oeuvre revolved around "a certain lying, cheating ex-girlfriend—the same muse that inspired much of the first album. 'There aren't enough records for me to make about her,' Durst says. 'She was this sweet innocent girl I was in love with, and she just turned into this swinging-ass bisexual, fucking my dirtiest friends.'"[17] The sentiment never wears thin or wears out, it just bubbles over into a general, sweeping misogyny. Kid Rock, a more cartoonish version of the male-rage phenomenon who promoted his own country-infused vision of pimp culture, offered songs early in his career like "Balls in Your Mouth" and "I Am the Bullgod."[18] Later, white rapper Eminem honed his talent for rhyme by verbally butchering his on-again, off-again wife Kim, channeling his hurt into a song about stuffing her into a trunk and drowning her with his daughter present. Testimony to his hatred of her is forever emblazoned on his stomach, in a tattoo that reads, "Kim: Rot in Pieces." However, Eminem's ensuing work deftly explored his celebrity status, his place in the world, and the contradictions of American culture (while still using puerile insults to make his points).

The new white male-rage acts sang about sexual violence without consequence, and at the 1999 Woodstock festival life imitated "art." Significantly, the festival occurred during Lilith Fair's last summer—and morphed into one of the worst possible examples of gang mentality and its ensuing behavior. Not unlike rap-rock itself, the mosh pit had grown into an unwieldy, blind behemoth of male aggression. To make matters worse, the mainstream acts that encouraged the most aggression were the main attractions of the weekend. *Spin* magazine's day-by-day coverage of the festival documented numerous sexual assaults, among them the following accounts: "Suddenly, Schneider [a Woodstock volunteer] saw a crowd-surfing woman get swallowed up by the pit; when she reemerged, two men had clamped her arms to her sides. 'She was giving a struggle,' said Schneider. 'Her clothes were physically and forcibly being removed.' Yet no one nearby seemed to react. Schneider said that the woman and one of the men fell to the ground for about twenty seconds; then, he said, she was passed to his friend, who raped her, standing from behind. . . . Finally, the woman was pulled from the pit by some audience members, who handed her to security. . . . Schneider said he watched in horror as five more women were pushed into the very same pit throughout Korn's set."[19] Although the grunge explosion, riot grrrl, and even the industry's "angry young women" encouraged cultural inclusion in their own ways, it seemed that what the mainstream was actually responding to was unbridled anger. Without thought to the context of anger (or perhaps due to empty media representations of it), Limp Bizkit seemed as appealing as Nirvana for young fans, and one pop phenomenon replaced another.

By the next day, during Alanis Morissette's show, a woman "surfed her way to the front of the stage. 'I don't know how they got me,' she said. 'There were about three guys on each arm and each leg, and then three or four right inside me with their hands. One guy put his hand inside my anus. Another guy was yelling, "Rip her apart!"' The woman finally managed to extricate herself from the pit by kicking some of her assailants in the head."[20] While *Spin* alone documented nine sexual assaults in one form or another, only five were officially reported to police.[21] One fan commented, "If you didn't want to be in a rough situation there, you shouldn't have been in the mosh pit. I'm tired of people making excuses for their own fucking stupidity. Limp Bizkit equals mosh pit. Duh."[22]

The end of 2000 brought the self-righteous Bush administration, and the new millennial guard justified entitlement without accountability through corporate corruption scandals, the hotly protested war in Iraq, and a host of infringements on civil liberties. The ultraconservative administration succeeded fairly quickly in reversing the relative liberalism that had infused the country during the Clinton years. Many indie fans hoped for a heavy influx of political dialogue as bittersweet comfort. Tobi Vail recently described the punk reaction to Reagan that she hoped to see resurface: "Even apolitical skate bands had songs against Reagan. We saw all this stuff as connected to our lives and starting dressing differently and building community via our scene as a means of taking a stance against injustice and war. And we got a whole lot of shit for it."[23]

Those waiting for the revolt saw little to nothing happen in the first few years of the new decade. Indie still had its politically ethical niche, just as it had a spot for pop sounds, experimentation, novelty acts, dance acts, noise, and so forth, but the general nonreaction of the indie rock community was as disappointing as the result of the election wrangle. The new underground, even that which divorced itself from the mainstream hype, became interminably hip and fashionable and no longer the refuge of outcasts. The popularity of indie rock in the '90s brought an influx of apathetic members, more interested in fitting in than in creating their own avenues of expression. It was as if riot grrrl had been enough; the discourse that had for so long unnerved the scene was at a standstill, devolving into musings about selling out, and politics took a back seat.

Even post-9/11, the indie underground sounded much as it did before—politically careless. Some acts and a lot of fans took the Bush administration to task for its rampant infidelities and blind patriotism through political actions, activism, and the loose alliances known as Bands Against Bush and Punk Voter, but the general feeling seemed to be one of apathy, until the threat of Republican reelection met a groundswell of grassroots activity in 2004. Even mainstream political strongholds like the Beastie Boys and members of the then-defunct Rage Against the Machine (save for guitarist Tom Morello) were either astoundingly mute or completely ignored by the media. Where the Beastie Boys had spent the '90s organizing events like

Free Tibet concert festivals and Rage Against the Machine promoted progressive (and sometimes radical) ideals, the highest-profile politically vocal musicians retreated as the culture's political climate changed. (The Beastie Boys did release *To the 5 Boroughs* in 2004, on which they finally took Bush to task.) Even U2, famous for political involvement, stayed out of the discourse on war and the Bush administration (even while lead vocalist Bono advocated for reducing Third World debt and fighting AIDS in Africa).

Punk Planet's March/April 2003 cover story asked, "Where Have All the Musicians Gone?" and discussed artistic and political responsibilities and the dearth of protest music in such a politically charged time. Writer Mike McKee's introduction reads: "As rock stars once again double as army recruiters and representatives (elected, appointed, and ballot-thieving alike) opt for paths of least resistance, much of the so-called indie and punk scenes dissolve into political ambiguity, taking flimsy refuge in disaffected irony and a privileged sense of entitlement. As the bombs drop, maybe it's worth reflecting on the idea of punk as a conscious rejection and a life-affirming alternative."[24]

With the emergence of a new conservatism in the larger culture and the subculture's continued political apathy, acts like Sleater-Kinney, Bratmobile, and Le Tigre became all the more potent for their tradition of onstage political rhetoric and high-spirited fun. Le Tigre, Kathleen Hanna's latest project, mixes catchy dance beats with Hanna's strong passion and political philosophy. Bratmobile released the anti-Bush anthem "Shop for America" on their 2002 album *Girls Get Busy*, taking the administration to task for its post-9/11 credit-card patriotism. Sleater-Kinney wrote "Combat Rock" for the 2002 album *One Beat*, a rousing and scathing antiwar song. Revealing the dearth of contemporary political protest songs, a 2002 article written for *CounterPunch* excitedly declared, "Our protest songs are here!"—then went on to report only on "Combat Rock" and another Sleater-Kinney song, "Far Away."[25]

As the administration censored safe-sex information on the Center for Disease Control's website, banned partial birth abortions, and proposed a constitutional ban on gay marriage, Peaches led the onstage revolution of blunt, female sexual expression and genderplay, while the Butchies offered a more complex representation of butch lesbian identity. And election year 2004 has showed signs of change for feminism (and postfeminism, too), and within the underground, as well. The Butchies and the Lunachicks played a show together the night before the million-strong March for Women's Lives on Washington in April. Fat Mike of NOFX released the punk compilations *Rock Against Bush Vols. I* and *II*, accompanied by a national tour. Techno DJ and electronica musician Moby helped to rally MoveOn.org, which seeks to expose the corruption of the Bush administration and the fallacies of the right-wing agenda, and thousands of suddenly politicized youth posted their websites, joined organizations, volunteered, and marched.

As of this writing, the decade's not even half over, and the election results are still unknown; political and artistic rebellion continues, proof not only that feminism is alive and well, but that politics in punk, and all its descendants, is, too.

Chapter 29

I WANNA BE YOUR JOEY RAMONE

Sleater-Kinney

SLEATER-KINNEY ARE A WORLD AWAY FROM THE MAINSTREAM'S "women in rock" category. Since their inception in 1994, they've surpassed the "grrrl band" ghetto in both underground circles and among mainstream rock critics. Their socially conscious yet personal lyrics are tempered by a technical prowess and a complex assault of guitars and vocals. Their sound is equal parts energetic rhythm patterns and layer upon layer of dueling guitars fused with thick, desperate vocals. Onstage the ladies are plainly themselves, playing their hearts out.

Sleater-Kinney formed from Corin Tucker's Heavens to Betsy and Carrie Brownstein's Excuse 17. Following a national tour with Bratmobile in 1992, Heavens to Betsy shared much of the underground riot grrrl spotlight (although they were often absent from the media's grrrl roster). Excuse 17 and Heavens to Betsy toured together once and both put out albums on the Kill Rock Stars label in the mid-'90s. Excuse 17 released their self-titled debut for Chainsaw and *Such Friends Are Dangerous* for Kill Rock Stars in 1995. Both LPs are filled with raw vocals and the burgeoning pop indie guitar sound Brownstein would hone with Sleater-Kinney. Heavens to Betsy released *Calculated* in 1994. Before joining a band, though, Corin Tucker was inspired by the sprinkling of female acts she uncovered in the Northwest while working on a school video project covering the local music scene. Tucker recounted in *She's a Rebel*, "[T]his was before riot grrrl had even started, but I could just see it. The things Bratmobile and Bikini Kill were saying instantly validated all these things that I felt."[1]

Tucker and Brownstein initially met at a Heavens to Betsy show in 1992; the two started Sleater-Kinney, named after a road in Olympia, after Brownstein moved to Olympia to attend college in the early '90s. Both of their earlier bands displayed distinct sounds that were sharpened when the ladies joined forces for what they thought would be a side project. After Sleater-Kinney's start, they ran through a few drummers, including Misty Farrell, Lora McFarlane, and Toni Gogin, before finding Janet Weiss, who hopped behind the kit in time to record their 1997 release, *Dig Me Out*.

Weiss played with numerous bands prior to Sleater-Kinney, and she continues to play in Quasi with Sam Coomes. In 1996, her band at the time was Jr. High, who shared a bill with Sleater-Kinney. Soon after the show, Weiss heard they were looking for a new drummer, and that was that. Weiss first began drumming with the Furies in San Francisco. "I indicated to them that I didn't know how to play the drums," she told Experience Music Project, "but they gave me a record, and they lent me a drum kit, and said they'd get back to me in two weeks to see if I could possibly handle the job. And I practiced in my room in the Haight every day and sort of got a basic understanding of how to play, just the most rudimentary things, which was all the band really required anyway, and then went on tour." After meeting Sam Coomes, the two moved to Portland and began jamming in their basement, which eventually evolved into the band Motorgoat, and Motorgoat became Quasi.[2]

In 1995, Sleater-Kinney released a self-titled debut album on Donna Dresch's Chainsaw label, followed by *Call the Doctor* in 1996. All of their subsequent releases have appeared on Kill Rock Stars. The band pointedly shies away from talking about "women in rock," claiming boredom with the topic. They don't, however, decry feminism or politics as part of their oeuvre; their lyrics tell personal stories of desire, restlessness, and sexism. Brownstein once said, "I think of ourselves as a band that has ideals that can be interpreted as political in a sense that they are outside the conventional way of being in a band. I think that choosing to be on an independent label and not work for a big corporation is a political decision. I don't think, though, that our songs are sloganistic. They're definitely not."[3] It's a stance often repeated in other interviews with the band. In a 2003 article, Brownstein told the *Tampa Tribune*, "As an artist, my only responsibility is to make good art. . . . No matter what you say, no matter what your message is, if it's not couched in a good album or a good song, it's sort of futile. . . . On the other hand, I think that I naturally want our music to have meaning to it. . . . Music is a way for me to process the external world and the interior world."[4]

If noting the gender of musicians might seem blasé today, Janet Weiss' comments stress that it's still an important distinction in some regions of the country: "When I'm in a community like Portland or Olympia, where we have just so many great women playing, I think, 'Wow, this has really come a long way.' This is the way it should be: everyone playing music together, nothing is segregated, no one's looked down upon, it's all people playing music. But then I go on tour and I realize, oh my God, there are just a few little pockets of this around the country. There are huge expanses where things are still in the dark ages. You hear things like, 'Wow! I've never seen a girl drummer, ever.' It's just a shock. It's easy to think that things have come so far, but we get letters from girls who grew up in the Midwest or are living in areas where the resources are not readily available. And there's no one for them to play with—they want to start a band with other girls or guys, and there's no one around."[5]

Sleater-Kinney's political sentiments seem more an intimate conversation than a call to action (which makes the injustices they describe all the more heartbreaking). On "Taking Me Home," from *Call the Doctor*, Tucker resists the measuring of personal worth based on physical perfection.

> This part of my body
> That you're pricing now
> I'm cutting it off
> I'm throwing it out.[6]

And on "The Professional" from *All Hands on the Bad One*, the band decries the music industry's fine-tuning and censorship of female voices, as well as the subsequently harsh criticism so many female musicians suffer. The now-classic "I Wanna Be Your Joey Ramone," on *Call the Doctor*, uses the images of Joey Ramone and Thurston Moore, two undisputed male icons of the indie underground, to express the group's longing for the same kind of status these men enjoy.

> I wanna be your Joey Ramone
> Pictures of me on your bedroom door
> Invite you back after the show
> I'm the queen of rock and roll.[7]

And in "You're No Rock n' Roll Fun" from *All Hands on the Bad One,* the girls brush this previous notion aside, caustically snubbing men who shy away from female bands.

> And all the boys in the band
> Know how to get down
> fill our Christmas socks
> with whiskey drinks
> and chocolate bars

> And when the evening ends we won't
> be thinking of you then
> Although the best man
> won't hang out with the girl band!

> You're no rock n' roll fun
> like a piece of art
> that no one can touch
> Your head is always up in the clouds
> writing your songs
> Won't you ever come down?[8]

While Sleater-Kinney make political statements through personal music, their 2002 album *One Beat* is their most overtly political to date, a rallying call against the rise of neoconservatism in America. In an interview for *Punk Planet,* Carrie Brownstein commented: "We consider ourselves a political band as well as many other things; I try not to define us using one word. We're a political band and a rock band and a punk band; they all sort of exist at once and our records seem to reflect that. . . . Certainly right now I think if you have a chance to stand on a stage with a microphone, and you have a chance to reach people or talk to people, there's really no reason not to be political. I definitely feel like it's [a] dark time. I don't think I can get on stage and not have that affect how I feel when I play or how intense it sometimes feels to be among a thousand or two thousand people. That is an intense feeling, and to be able to bring a sense of urgency, politics, or even joy, that to me is very important. To not have it at all reflect what's going on outside the doors of a venue, that's very bizarre to me."[9]

On *One Beat* their songs "Far Away," "Step Aside," and "Combat Rock" all address the way the country has changed, the latter being the most pointed and significant in its indictment. The song questions the censorship of antigovernment sentiment and the ensuing fear on the part of dissenters. "Combat Rock" makes a strong antiwar statement, accusing the Bush administration of ulterior motives in its march to war:

> Where is the questioning, where is the protest song?
> Since when is skepticism un-American?
> Dissent's not treason but they talk like it's the same
> Those who disagree are afraid to show their face
>
> Let's break out our old machine guns now
> It sure is good to see them run again
> Oh, gentleman start your engines
> And we know where we get the oil from.[10]

Six albums down the road, and Sleater-Kinney have invented sounds and songs so unique, they have yet to be replicated. They continue to evolve artistically, and with them, so does the perception of women in music.

Chapter 30

THE GALAXY IS GAY

The Butchies

LIPSTICK LESBIANS HAVE THEIR OWN CABLE NETWORK SERIES, *The L Word*. Madonna and Britney Spears' kiss was a marketing executive's dream, broadcast for the all world to see. Meanwhile, the controversy over gay marriage divides the country and has led to a push from the White House to rewrite the Constitution, specifically defining marriage as a union between a man and a woman. The emergence of the Butchies couldn't be better timed.

This trio of semi-manic dyke rockers is composed of bassist Alison Martlew, singer, songwriter, and guitarist Kaia Wilson, and drummer Melissa York (the latter two are Team Dresch alumni). The Butchies spend their stage time making tight, loud music and keeping mosh pits safe for young women. The band has not only reclaimed hard rock for lesbians but has succeed in making any club they play, if only for a few hours, a haven for lesbians. They've released four albums since 1998, toured with the likes of Sleater-Kinney and the Indigo Girls, and even opened for '70s rockers Cheap Trick once. One of their songs, "The Galaxy Is Gay," was even used as the soundtrack for a girl-on-girl kiss on Fox's popular teen drama *Party of Five*.

In addition to Wilson and Martlew's vocal harmonies and York's astounding drumming, the Butchies' gleeful, compulsive clowning can't be ignored. Their stage demeanor inadvertently chips away at the sexual barriers behind which the straight and queer worlds generally assemble. If their jokes don't cause a smile, then their raucous, catchy pop punk covers of songs like "Your Love," a cheesy '80s hit by the Outfield, should. (Their 2004 album *Make Yr Life* remakes the same song as an achingly slow and soft ballad.)

In 1998, Melissa York played drums on Kaia Wilson's solo *Ladyman* release. The two worked so well together they decided to look for a bass player, finding one in Alison Martlew while York was visiting Wilson in North Carolina.[1] Within three weeks of forming, the Butchies set to work on their first album, *Are We Not Femme?*, released the same year. The cover depicts the trio dolled up in red vinyl skirts and pink wigs, with pictures of them dressed butch on the back. The message is clear: The dresses are the costume, and in butch "drag" they are themselves. Wilson explains, "You know, we all do embody a sort of third gender. That's really what butch is in many ways, neither like a boy nor like a girl, although, of course, we do fall into what this world thinks of as more 'masculine.' So, in the real world, of course we'll be mistaken for boys sometimes, but what we want to see is tons of visibility to people who don't fit the masculine/feminine as assigned to their particular sex, and an opening up of space for all gender expressions to be honestly and lovingly accepted and recognized."[2]

Each subsequent album has revealed a new dimension of the Butchies' bighearted, rebellious soul. While some higher-profile underground bands ignore politics altogether, the Butchies sing (along with a local queer youth group) on *Population 1975*'s "More Rock More Talk" of their support for labor unions, pro-choice legislation, and the queer rights movement.

Wilson once told the *Lesbian News*, "All the shit we do is totally out. Everything we write is queer or feminist."[3] While magazines like *Billboard* speculate on the "marketability" of queer rock, Wilson says of politics and songwriting, "They are impossible to separate, and I think that actually that's the way it is for everyone, only with people who are more 'normal' or whatever, folks who go with the grain, that it's easy to not see that fact. No one ever talks about Bob Dylan 'sacrificing his musical integrity for his political views' like they talk about the Butchies doing—but we're really no different. You write songs about your life experience and your perception of the world around you, which is directly affected by how you exist in the world."[4] While the Butchies sometimes elicit cries of "separatism" from critics, the band's mission is to get their message to a larger audience, not just the lesbian and queer community. Their lyrics, while not intended to make the straight world comfortable per se, are universal, as on "Second Guess" from *Make Yr Life*, in which an empowered Wilson rises from the ashes of a failed relationship.

The band is committed to broadening their audience, but not at the risk of compromising themselves musically. According to Wilson, the press and mainstream culture in general are hindering queer music's crossover: "We get treated pretty well by queer mags and are pretty ignored by more 'mainstream' mags—like if they review Le Tigre or Sleater-Kinney they've already filled their 'woman quota.'" She continues, "I think the 'straight' world has issues with thinking they are excluded by the Butchies' world, but we are here to tell them otherwise. Lighten up, folks! We're just butch dykes, not serial murderers! I think the media and folks who are in charge of 'creating culture' have greatly underestimated the 'mainstream straight' world and what they want, and can handle being exposed to."[5]

The Butchies also break down boundaries within the queer community, not only through the immense scope of their sound and lyrical content, but also by covering dyke folk tunes like Cris Williamson's "Shooting Star" on *Are We Not Femme?*. "The whole perception of 'womyn's music' sucks," Wilson remarked in the *L.A. Weekly*. "Like punk girls or post–riot grrrls aren't supposed to like that kind of music because it's too old school, too lesbian, and too granola. We pay honor to those women, as *homage*."[6]

During live performances, York and Wilson mockingly act like metal stars. Wilson stretches her guitar from her crotch, hovering over the lip of the stage like a member of Kiss, playing directly to the front row of swarming fans. York occasionally raises her arm in the dramatic, chin-up pose made popular by Mötley Crüe's Tommy Lee. The Butchies' good-natured ribbing of metal allows a new, younger, and specifically female audience to revel in these dramatics. Perhaps other obstacles can be broken down, too—those old rockers might even love the Butchies back. Wilson relayed the following account of the Cheap Trick show in her tour diary: "Another guy made mention of how we were the 'lesbian band opening for Cheap Trick' and I said, 'Exactly right!' Honestly, I was just happy to know that everyone knew we were lezzians, as much as I guess that is obvious, sometimes I wonder if people will assume we're straight, or they might think we're boys. All in all, we were very warmly received and got nothing but praise from people there."[7] The Butchies' presence at mainstream venues creates a pro-queer, pro-woman space at shows unlikely to otherwise foster such social consciousness.

Rock and metal aren't the only areas the Butchies are attempting to reclaim. The Bush camp and others backing antigay legislation and sentiment are under the misguided notion that homosexuals needs to be saved or healed, and the Butchies counter this idea by encouraging their audiences to simply love themselves, accept differences, and resist oppression. This kind of message is vital to young queer youth (and older dykes, too) in places that lack a larger gay community. The Butchies are *fun*, first and foremost, and work to include their fans in ways that metal never attempted to. Besides the participation of queer youth on "More Rock More Talk," the band offered an open invitation for the "Make Yr Life" video shoot, which featured a Brooklyn club filled with their fans.

The Butchies aren't always as straightforward as their plainly stated politics on "More Rock More Talk" might intimate. Wilson's songwriting, as it did with Team Dresch, sometimes utilizes more obscure imagery. Her writing is nuanced and often, uncannily, takes the shape of the listener's world. This kind of subtlety leaves the responsibility of facing homophobic hang-ups to the listener, which is a good thing. The Butchies are too busy populating the mosh pit with joyful queer girls to explain.

Chapter 31

HOT TOPIC

Le Tigre

LE TIGRE SPEAK FOR TODAY'S POLITICALLY STARVED INDIE audience when they sing, "I went to your concert and I didn't feel anything."[1] While Bikini Kill attempted to reclaim the night, the bedroom, and the punk stage for women in the '90s, Le Tigre, composed of Kathleen Hanna on lead vocals and guitar, guitarist and keyboardist Johanna Fateman, and JD Samson on keyboards and sampler (although the three rotate depending on the song), capture electronic pop, often so lyrically shallow, infusing it with girl-group feminist ardor. "It's just nice to make dance music and create a space for a community of people who are otherwise oppressed," Samson once commented.[2]

"I do see a difference from when I first started playing music to how many women and queers in general are coming to shows," Hanna remarked in the same interview. "And that's not because of me; that's because of homo-core and Team Dresch and the Butchies and all the amazing bands and fanzine makers and promoters who've really been like, 'We want a girl-friendly and queer-friendly space to happen.' And maybe the world isn't that space yet, but we can turn a totally misogynist club into that space for one night."[3] Le Tigre's work is infused with Hanna's energetic hunger for political dialogue. Their music is replete with keyboards, electronic beats running under and around guitar chords, and vocals that conjure Devo's atonality one minute and a schoolgirl's taunts the next. During shows, the trio has been known to wear coordinated outfits and perform fun, choreographed dance moves in front of bright videos, exhibiting the band's political side along with their '80s video-pop consciousness. In contrast to the underground's overriding political apathy of recent years, Le Tigre have been engaged in a kind of fluorescent, five-year sit-in for leftist politics and pro-feminist/pro-queer art.

While Bikini Kill took a break in the mid-'90s, Hanna ended up in Portland, rooming with 'zine writer, artist, and musician Johanna Fateman. Fateman had played in the Mandy Sturgill Anti-Sex BMX Space War and had also penned a number of 'zines, some of which captured her passion for visual art. While in Portland, the two worked on a project together called the Troublemakers. As Bikini Kill began to wind down, Hanna embarked on a solo project called Julie Ruin and released a self-titled album on Kill Rock Stars in 1998. In an interview with Daniel Sinker for *We Owe You Nothing*, Hanna described Julie Ruin as an alter ego: "Some people think that anybody who is ever in the public eye becomes any object that they can banter about like you're not a person. That's why my new stage name is Julie Ruin—when people would say fucked-up things like 'Kathleen Hanna is this' or 'Kathleen Hanna is that' it was really disturbing. But when they say that about Julie Ruin, what the fuck do I care? She's just a character I created. . . . Julie Ruin was more confident than I am. She was able to say, 'I'm a fucking artist and people can't treat me this way anymore.'"[4]

After completing *Julie Ruin*, Hanna moved to New York and reconnected with Fateman, who had started art school there. With the addition of Sadie Benning in 1999, Le Tigre was born. Benning left to pursue videomaking in 2000, and Ohio-born JD Samson, already a filmmaker and projectionist for the band, took Benning's place as electronic beat conductor.

Around the same time Samson started what she described as a lesbian "conceptual dance troupe which choreographs dances that are performed unannounced, as interventions in New York City."[5] She also collaborated with photographer Cass Bird on *JD's Lesbian Calendar 2003*, a series of butch portraits Hanna curated for a SoHo gallery show in 2003.

With the help of Kaia Wilson and Tammy Rae Carland, then co-owners of Mr. Lady Records, Hanna, Fateman, and Benning released their self-titled debut album in 1999, with the *From the Desk of Mr. Lady* EP following in January 2001, and then the full-length *Feminist Sweepstakes* that October. In 2004 they signed to Universal imprint Strummer Records for *This Island*, an album produced by Ric Ocasek of the Cars.

Their songwriting uses the same clear expressiveness as punk with riot grrrl's pointed use of everyday language to simplify feminist concepts. And while Le Tigre have garnered their fair share of raves and even some commercial success, not all reviews of their work have been positive. One critic at Seattle's alternative paper *The Stranger* admitted: "While [Hanna's] confrontational vocal presence has always sounded bravely antagonistic throughout her career, it's been undermined by her tendency to veer into a screech that grates more than invigorates."[6] Some critics might find Hanna's delivery grating, but many fans appreciate Le Tigre's ability to simultaneously engage the listener's mind and body. And music fans who once shied away from political bands, viewing them as humorless, have been won over by a group that is creating pointedly feminist, queer-positive art.

The song "FYR," on the 2001 album *Feminist Sweepstakes*, refers to Shulamith Firestone's 1970 tome *The Dialectic of Sex*, in which Firestone argues that the feminist movement has suffered at the hands of "fifty years of ridicule." As Hanna told Jennifer Baumgardner in *Rockrgrl*, "The powers that be try to make us think that the art work we are going to make, and the music we are going to make, and the activism we are going to do has already been made and happened, so there is no point in making it. They trick you into thinking that everything you feel urgent about already happened."[7] This notion is reminiscent of the justification used in the transformation of feminist thought and action into the more ambiguous notion of postfeminism. Le Tigre use this "fifty years of ridicule" as a launching point for an anthem meant to counter the pervasive idea that feminism is dead:

> Ten short years of progressive change.
> Fifty fuckin' years of calling us names.
> Can we trade Title 9 for an end to hate crime?
> RU-486 if we suck your fuckin' dick?
> One step forward, five steps back.

One cool record in the year of rock rap.
Yeah we got all the power getting stabbed in the shower
And we got equal rights on ladies' nite.
Feminists we're calling you.
Please report to the front desk.
Let's name this phenomenon
It's too dumb to bring us down.
F.Y.R. Fifty years of ridicule.[8]

Le Tigre have effectively harnessed their growing popularity to promote outsider art and music. On a 2003 tour, the band flashed pictures of books and records by oppressed artists who had inspired them. (At a New York City show, the crowd exploded with cheers when they showed a slide of the Slits' album cover for *Cut*.) Le Tigre take pride in their political activism, and celebrate those who take action, proving that any art form, even pop, can be effectively wedded with politics. The following homage to some of the women who came before is offered by "Hot Topic" from their self-titled debut:

Hot topic is the way that we rhyme
Hot topic is the way that we rhyme
One step behind the drum style
One step behind the drum style
Carol Rama and Eleanor Antin
Yoko Ono and Carolee Schneeman
You're getting old, that's what they'll say, but
Don't give a damn I'm listening anyway
Stop, don't you stop
I can't live if you stop
Don't you stop.[9]

And while some may think *political* indie rock is "old," the ladies of Le Tigre beg to differ and, in doing so, have given it a facelift.

Chapter 32

BACK IT UP, BOYS

Peaches

BERLIN-BASED PERFORMER PEACHES THRIVES ON EXTREME contradictions. She mixes burlesque with gory rock and roll theatrics, and hardcore rap's stereotypically raw sexuality with starlet desire. During performances that offer exhibitionism or props like used tampons, Peaches meshes the typically reviled with the titillating. In the process, she helps reenvision cultural hang-ups as sexual fetishes.

As a music teacher of ten years, Merrill Nisker (AKA Peaches) approached her young students' creativity more radically than with the usual recitation of popular children's songs. These teaching experiences undoubtedly aided her own winding creative path. As a musician, she experimented with several genres, including jazz and folk, before settling on her current unique style. In 1996, Nisker formed the Shit, a rap project with Chilly Gonzalez, who collaborated with her on some work and with whom she first toured Europe as Peaches—a persona she developed in the late '90s. The character of Peaches allowed Nisker to explore and express her own sexuality, and to erase her inhibitions onstage.

She began by experimenting with a sampler, and then christened herself

Peaches, after a raging character she felt drawn to in Nina Simone's "Four Women." It should be of little surprise that Nisker picked Simone's toughest character after whom to name herself. Nisker recorded a demo in her bedroom and sent it to Berlin's Kitty-Yo Records. They signed her and released the *Lovertits* EP in 2000. Her first full-length album, released the same year in Europe, *The Teaches of Peaches*, sounds like phone sex performed over a dusty demo keyboard in the corner of an electronics store. Although spare in sound, the album is packed with wholly energizing, humorous rhymes. *The Teaches of Peaches* finally hit the more prudish shores of America in March 2002. Since her debut in the States, Peaches has toured extensively, with Queens of the Stone Age, . . . And You Will Know Us By the Trail of Dead, and as part of the 2002 Electroclash Festival. After seeing her perform, the White Stripes encouraged XL Recordings/Beggars Group to sign her next album, *Fatherfucker*, which was released in 2003.

Although Peaches might be seen by some as entirely decadent—or, as Britain's *Guardian* described her, "throwaway fun"—her ability to undo sexual stereotypes and cast off inhibitions makes her work provocative. The *Guardian* reviewer Dorian Lynskey yawned that porn rapper Lil' Kim had been doing the same thing for years.[1] But while Lil' Kim may talk as much trash as Peaches, she doesn't complicate female sexuality beyond the typically bawdy, nor does she display Peaches' gender fluidity—transforming from docile stripper one minute to bearded dildo-brandisher the next.

"I'm just trying to be inclusive," she told *Billboard*. "Some people find it angry or vindictive, as if I'm against males. But that happens a lot with my music. Artists like Busta Rhymes and 50 Cent get away with so much more lyrically, without being questioned. But because I'm a woman, there's that double standard."[2] Hence, the name *Fatherfucker*. "Motherfucker is a very mainstream word," Peaches told the 'zine *Venus*. "But if we're going to use motherfucker, why don't we use fatherfucker? I'm just trying to be even. Some of these songs are like 'Shake your tits, shake your ass,' so I'm trying to say 'Shake your tits, shake your dicks.' You know, guys get left out all the time. So, motherfucker, it's time for the fatherfuckers."[3]

Slithering around in her skivvies and bra, peering out from behind aviator frames, and donning wigs galore, Peaches is questioning the margins of sexuality in Western culture, and particularly in America. All of Peaches' controversial diddling means she's bound to hit a raw nerve, though. Despite her popularity, Sony dropped her when the video for her single "Set It Off" depicted the musician covered in hair.

Compared to her live show, excess body hair seems a tame reason to avoid her act. Onstage, she's been known to eat an entire loaf of bread, vomit fake blood, feign tampon removal, and dominate a sex slave. Light-years beyond this generation's interchangeable blond pop stars who are perpetually sexy and polished, Peaches represents much of what is left out of pop music—all things flawed, homegrown, spontaneous, and raunchy. The result is ultimately more entertaining and sensual than Britney's suggestive snake handling or Janet's Super Bowl revelation. Serendipitously, *Fatherfucker's* appearance in record stores in 2003 preceded the controversy over radio censorship, including the canceling of Howard Stern's show from six of Clear Channel's stations. This bearded mistress and girl-for-rent stands in stark opposition to the Tipper effect—which seeks to shelter everyone from that which offends a few. Peaches is a backdoor reminder that sexuality still exists as a cause for celebration in the face of those hell-bent on repressing it.

As subversive as she is, from album covers to promotional photos to her simulated onstage circus, there's no overlooking her tongue-in-cheek attitude toward her work. The illustration on the *Fatherfucker* disc is a case in point: Flames furl around the CD's center hole to form the shape of a vagina, with a microphone, meant to symbolize the clitoris, tipped on the edges of the flames. She also curates a crotch-shot gallery on her website (consisting of photographs taken by her fans at shows). While her entire aesthetic is meant to compel curious listeners toward sexual liberation, there's always plenty of fun to be had on the way.

Fatherfucker certainly displays a more refined production quality than *Teaches of Peaches*, yet her affectations and her lyrics—free of poetic or linguistic baggage—seem as improvised and as natural as her ever-morphing, unenhanced physique. An updated cover of the infectious "Bad Reputation" by Joan Jett, retitled "I Don't Give A . . . ", kicks off *Fatherfucker*. A sample of Jett singing the original chorus is followed by Peaches viciously responding with, "I don't give a fuck!" ad nauseam. In "I U She," she chants "I don't have to make the choice; I like girls and I like boys" over a frantic Casio keyboard-sounding beat.[5] By producing, writing, and performing all of her music, she embodies the DIY ethic, and if her work doesn't necessarily make the world a better place, it might at least make it a little more fun and a little less inhibited.

The audience reaction to Peaches has been predictably contentious but never ambiguous. "When she opened up for Queens of the Stone Age at the Fillmore," DJ Omar Perez remarked, "she played to a packed house. Half of them scurried away in fear and the other half fell in love."[6] Peaches' manager, Janice Gaffney, contends that although some reactions to the Queens of the Stone Age tour were mixed, the San Francisco audience was so receptive, Peaches walked out on top of the crowd. At Coney Island's ultra hip annual Siren Festival, her mic was pulled as she went over her allotted half hour and started to sing "Fuck the Pain Away." She relayed, "I picked up another mic and said, 'They're censoring me! They're making me get off the stage!' It turned out some mothers were complaining. They were like, 'Look, that girl's got her hands down her pants. *Make her stop!* She's masturbating!'"[7] This kind of narrow-mindedness is exactly what she hopes she can help change. Peaches confided to *Venus*:

> You really find out where people are at when you're putting your[self] way out there. I actually feel really good heckling my audiences. It usually doesn't happen in my audiences; it happens when I open for other people. Like when I opened for Queens of the Stone Age, someone shouted, 'Get off the stage, gay man' or 'You suck!' and I'm like, 'Yeah, and I swallow,' and they're like, 'Oh, she just got you at your own game, buddy.' I turn them around right there. So it's important for me to do that. . . . I opened for Björk in Europe [in 2003], Paris for two shows, and it was because she wanted me to. . . . So I did and then her audiences were really tough, too—they wanted their little angel, and rightly so. She's amazing, you know. I was upsetting them; they were screaming at me, 'Shut up!' Some of them. Of course there is always the half that is totally into it, giving signs like 'I love you.' So it's not all negative, and that's the point, that it's positive and negative. People are actually having a reaction, and that's important.[8]

Peaches hopes the controversy she inspires leads to a reconsideration of our narrow vision of sexuality and attraction. She told *The Observer*, "All people have sex, not just the Pamela Anderson look-alikes. . . . It's so dull, this idea that sexy is blond hair and big tits. Everyone is sexual, everybody has sex. And that's not to say everybody should be all rampant and fuck everybody. I'm just saying, 'Find your own, it's okay.'"[9] Or as she mutters on "Back It Up, Boys":

Technically, biologically, physically, psychologically . . .
Take a sabbatical
From your radical fanatical battle.
Sit on my saddle and rattle rattle rattle.[10]

In other words, loosen *up*.

Chapter 33

ARKANSAS HEAT

The Gossip

FOR ALL ITS CURRENT MUTATIONS THE UNDERGROUND STILL lacks one thing—old-style soul. The Gossip have it in spades, though. Marrying their childhoods in Southern choir with teenage years doused in the offerings of Kill Rock Stars, K Records, and Sonic Youth, Beth Ditto, Nathan Howdeshell, and Kathy Mendonca have formed a homegrown minimalist Southern ensemble. Mendonca's simultaneously spare and thunderous drums thud against Howdeshell's growling garage-pop guitar riffs and Ditto screams out her vocals in a gospel-cum-punk fusion, clawing open the underbelly of Southern rock. While dance-floor liberation is the band's highest priority, they have loftier goals, too—to reinvent the indie ideal of beauty. Instead of hiding her body, lead singer Ditto sexualizes the larger woman in desirous lyrics that are further eroticized by her bluesy drawl. Their Southern roots, too, are important to the band and inextricably linked, even more closely than the soulful twinges that loop through their music, to the Gossip's *faith*—faith in DIY culture, and, like Le Tigre's, faith that having fun is the best way to communicate their more serious political beliefs.

"We were all weirdos and just punks," Ditto recalls of the band member's teenage years in Arkansas in the '90s.[1] "[Feminism] was one of the things we really bonded on, because we were feminists in this small town where that wasn't very common," Mendonca adds.[2] However, it was Howdeshell who eventually introduced Searcy, Arkansas, to Sonic Youth, introduced Mendonca to riot grrrl, and cultivated an underground scene by starting his own bands and booking out-of-town acts like K Records' Dub Narcotic Sound System. "It was because of Nathan that the community started bumpin' in Searcy, but it's because of Kathy that we got the hell outta there," Ditto says. "She was like, 'I'm gonna do something—I'm not sticking around.' And we [said], 'We'll do that, too.'"[3] So in 1999, the future members of the Gossip hightailed it to Olympia, where Mendonca was attending Evergreen.

As with most punk bands, the formation of the Gossip was a happy accident. Mendonca, a self-taught drummer, remembers, "I had moved to Olympia about a year before [Beth and Nathan]. They probably lived there for a couple months, and we were all living in the same house. Nathan and I played music together a lot, just because we were always home. I just started playing drums. He was really good at guitar, so we'd just kind of play around. We were doing that one day, and Beth came downstairs into the basement, and started singing with us."[4]

"We just had like five minute-and-a-half-long songs, it was very punk and very pure," says Ditto. "Then Nathan [came] home one day, and said, 'Oh yeah, we have a show.' I was like, 'Oh, okay.'"[5] The band played basement shows on the weekends, and soon after, Calvin Johnson came knocking on their door and subsequently released their first, self-titled 7".

Ditto and Mendonca were working at a Subway shop in their neighborhood when Carrie Brownstein dropped by one day and, having seen a recent Gossip show, invited them to open for Sleater-Kinney on an upcoming tour in 2000. "It was really scary at first," Mendonca admits. "I remember the first show we played was probably the biggest on the tour—[it was] a thousand people, and the biggest audience we had up until that point was maybe twenty people. It was really just surreal. I barely even remember the show, I just remember looking out in the audience and being like . . . [she shudders]."[6] The band toured with no merchandise; the 7" from K Records was still forthcoming. "We didn't have anything," Ditto remembers, "no one knew who we were, we were just like, 'Hey, we're a band.' It was the most amazing experience."[7]

The Gossip have since moved to Portland and released two albums,

That's Not What I Heard in 2001 and *Movement* in 2003, as well as a 2002 EP, all on Kill Rock Stars. All of their recordings exude an urgent energy, speeding from song to song, laden with hypnotic riffs. In addition to the Gossip, Mendonca works on two 'zines, as does Howdeshell, and both also play with other bands. Howdeshell has also started his own label, Fast Weapons Records.

The Gossip's lyrics express sexual desire and love, politicization, and, particularly on the 2002 *Arkansas Heat* EP, the latent possibility of making or finding a community. The EP is dedicated to "all the kids and grownups alike stuck in a shitty small town."

Their lyrics empower all kinds of outcasts and their shows are nothing less than good old-fashioned hoedowns, but the band broadens the indie mindset in almost everything they do, both onstage and on record. Their most obvious contribution is their roots, the Southern voice being noticeably absent from much of indie rock (as well as, from the younger set, the Southern influence). There's always been an overarching insistence on acting and being urban (no matter how suburban an upbringing most fans have), as well as a crushing notion that anything else, especially the rural experience, is backward and provincial. For other Southern outcasts, the Gossip embody a way of being proudly Southern, radical, and creative all at once.

And then there is the matter of image. In a community of people who tend to, openly or not, revere flat, angular bodies, there's the obvious pride Ditto takes in her shape. Mendonca elaborates,

> I think [Beth]'s really changed a lot of minds about being fat, and almost every other show we play, a girl comes up to her and talks about how she's more accepting of her body because she's seen her perform, or how she really made them think about being fat, and how you can be fat and be sexy, and be outspoken. . . . I think that most of the people who are up front and really vocal at shows are really into her whole thing. They're obviously not going to heckle, but [about] a year or two ago, there had been boys in the audience [who] yelled not very nice things at her. Then there's this other weird thing where people yell at her to take off her clothes. . . . I could see, in one way, how it's kind of a good thing, but they're expecting her to do that every time she plays, and it's just kind of weird. That's a new development. This past tour we went on, she said, she refused to take off her shirt at all, just because it was getting really strange.[8]

Ditto's frenzied onstage antics force audience members to face some of their prejudices and even disdain for fat people. At least one show found her flailing around the stage in a miniskirt and garter belt, gnashing a bra with her teeth. Her performances aren't contrived, either—they're a celebratory extension of her fiery dialogue and activism. Ditto's abandon makes the Gossip's minimalist punk feel truly soulful, angry, and gleeful all at once.

Riot grrrl couldn't solve everything, and fatphobia and homophobia remain in indie culture. Ditto and Mendonca run up against them all the time. And it is these incidents that seem to feed the Gossip's determination to infuse the culture with social dialogue. "I've just been thinking about this a lot within the past year," Ditto says, "and I think that both [fat positivity and queer acceptance] have such a long way to go, in actually ingraining this in people's brains, or actually getting them to understand and not just agree, [but to] think something else. . . . There are ways to be homophobic and fatphobic all the time, and you can be the punkest, most radical person, and still not understand it, and you can tell. You can say, like, 'Yeah man, that's cool she's fat,' but are you going to date a fat person? Are you going to diet?

"Right now, I think the most important part is to get fat people empowered and inspired, as opposed to making thin people understand their privilege," she continues. "That's really important, too, but actually, making them feel, and even fat people too, making all of us feel, what's actually going on, that it's just turning us against each other and making another division. It's just another beauty standard; it's actually the Man coming down on you. . . . So right now, I think the most important thing is to empower fat people, so they can make it a part of their daily lives to live freely and feel as beautiful as possible, or to fight it—maybe not the same way I do or a lot of activists do—but to make activism a part of your daily life, just by being happy with yourself. That's revolution; that's a revolution inside of you."[9]

The Gossip are determined to liberate all bodies (and minds, for that matter) from self-consciousness. Regardless of what might hold you back, their infectious pulse makes it nearly impossible to stand still.

Chapter 34

CONTROLLED CHAOS

Erase Errata

GUITARIST SARA JAFFE, DRUMMER BIANCA SPARTA, LEAD SINGER
Jenny Hoyston, and bassist Ellie Erickson combine what seems like the
whole history of experimental noise with infectious rhythms, sporadic trumpet, and searing, abrupt vocals infused with obscure lyrical intelligence, creating the phenomenon that is Erase Errata. More than one listener has
compared them to Captain Beefheart, but no matter what influences the
girls draw from, they have a distinctly off-kilter, danceable sound and lovable intensity. A host of the band's musical roots collide at the outset of each
song—drums that echo with funk rhythm backing speedy, stark guitar riffs
combined with garage-rock vocals doused with glam inflection, and finished
off with improvised jazz trumpet.

The amount of virtuosity flooding Erase Errata's sound points to the
fact that all its members learned their instruments from an early age, all have
played in other bands, and three have been formally trained in some aspect
of music. Jaffe and Erickson were also co–music directors of their Connecticut
college radio station, WESU.

Once Erickson and Jaffe separately moved to San Francisco in 1999, they hooked up with neighbors Hoyston and Sparta and started playing live in 2000. Jaffe recounts, "Our first show was at a warehouse by Oakland's Embarcadero that felt like the New Orleans bayou, lots of flimsy shacks and mean-looking dogs wandering around. . . . We played four or six songs. It was mostly our friends; they were nice, but they probably would have been anyway. Our first club show was at Kimo's in San Francisco in spring 2000, where a lot of people we didn't know came up to us and told us they were into what we were doing and would like to hear more."[1]

Jaffe released their first single on her own Inconvenient label in August of that year, selling out of its initial pressing of five hundred copies. Erase Errata then signed to Troubleman Unlimited and recorded their first album, *Other Animals*, in a short two and a half days. The band quickly captivated audiences across the country, and released a series of split singles, including one with Sonic Youth in 2003. For the Sonic Youth split single both bands performed songs based on a theme: Mariah Carey. (Erase Errata's was "Shimmer on Into the Night"; Sonic Youth's was "Mariah Carey and the Arthur Doyle Hand Cream," later released on their *Sonic Nurse* album and retitled "Kim Gordon and the Arthur Doyle Hand Cream.") Jaffe officially announced her departure from the band after their second full-length effort, *At Crystal Palace*, was released in 2003. After a brief hiatus, the band performed a number of shows with Jaffe in the spring of 2004.

Their energetic spontaneity is spurred on by the songwriting itself. Although it's impossible to believe while picking your way through their highly strung and tightly wound songs, Erase Errata improvise as they write, something they've described as a "ready, set, go!" process. "We all have the technicalities down, and so we're all pretty comfortable just starting out like that," Hoyston once commented.[2]

"There is definitely the danger of never getting anything set permanently, when you never know where something's going," Jaffe says. "I think I'm the one who's most likely to say, 'Okay, that's a part, let's get it down and then move on to the next one.'" She later admits, "There are times when it's hard. . . . I think it has mostly to do with a person's mood or state of mind at the practice. If you're not feeling freed up and enthusiastic, it's really hard to come up with exciting, spontaneous ideas."[3] Hoyston writes most of the band's disjointed, slightly obscure lyrics: "Most of the lyrics are improv [that come] during practice. Normally, I've got a theme in my head of something I'm thinking about, and it just builds from there."[4]

Just because Erase Errata are female and their lyrics are sociopolitically based doesn't mean their work is steeped in a feminist dialogue. Hoyston told art and music journal *Swingset*, "From a lyrical standpoint, I've tried to stray from lyrical content that I would perceive as purely emotive or clichéd relationships or sex analysis, and focus more on ideas and stories involving paradigms, historical injustice, . . . class issues."[5] This is particularly clear on *Other Animals*, which contains the song "Other Animals Are #1," an analysis of the way technology is at odds with humanity and society. The urgency of their sound makes Erase Errata's catalog feel like an expulsion of the overwhelming stimuli we ingest daily. The result, though, has a sweatier beat, making it way more fun than just processing Orwellian advertising.

Despite their intentions, Erase Errata aren't immune from being pigeonholed with directly feminist bands. Jaffe says, "I think we've seen it most in the way journalists write about our band—assuming we must sound like or feel kinship with Le Tigre or Sleater-Kinney just because we're all girls, or assuming that we necessarily have a defined feminist agenda, or that that's the most salient aspect of our band. Of course, you can't divorce the fact that we're all women from the music we play, but that's only one of many factors that comprise both our personal and musical identities. There's this sort of reductionist outlook that assumes there's only one way to be a woman, or a woman musician."[6] Hoyston once explained: "There's a certain element of empowerment that can't be denied in our music and performance. We're strong women and creative women. It would be hard to narrow that down to how feminism or any other movement has helped us evolve. For one thing, we're all at different ages and stages in our lives, and we're not necessarily 'evolving' in any really traceable way as far as politics in relation to our music. I've been playing in all-female punk bands for a decade and I've come a long way, artistically, beyond the basic acknowledgment of my feminist and queer background, but I wouldn't seek to escape that influence."[7]

Embracing feminism, of course, isn't the only way to be political, as Jaffe told *Punk Planet*: "We're eschewing those [pop] channels and the frameworks that are laid out in order to do something different. But I also do think our band is 'pop,' and I think that calling the music we make pop *is* political, because it speaks to the fact that different things are catchy to different people."[8]

In addition to their obvious virtuosity, the real charm of Erase Errata comes from the irresistible rush of adrenaline that audiences experience from hearing just the band's first few opening notes. Erase Errata have an unassuming onstage presence, too, preferring the music to speak for them. There's no false showmanship in their spontaneous and uninhibited performances. They occasionally wear homemade costumes, but avoid makeup and upstaging. Indie music's modern-day propensity for apathetic pretension is picked clean by the band's accessible beats. As Jaffe once remarked, "We have never once thought about shaping our image, or our sound, to please anyone other than ourselves."[9] The studied way in which they perform is the antithesis of their music's propensity for chaos: Jaffe and Erickson calmly peer at their instruments while racing through riffs and bass lines that match Sparta's fierce beat, and Hoyston expels stuttering vocals that culminate with a controlled wail or shriek, forcing her voice through the barrage of sound. Somehow, they manage to convey the spontaneity of their songwriting, a truly collaborative experiment in improvisation, in taut live shows. Through it all, Erase Errata make impressive art and hyperactive fun out of chaos.

Conclusion

GIRLS GET BUSY

IN THIS NEW CENTURY WE'RE STILL LEARNING WHAT OUTSIDERS' voices sound like, and what we can say or whom we can reach by being (and supporting) women working outside major label and corporate censorship. No matter how varied the music or how much more there is to come, the lessons to take away from these women's work begins with what makes them better role models than those floating around in the mainstream abyss: their resistance to self-censorship. Regardless of what bikini-addled, smiling, submissive, starved, or eager-to-please decorations are held up as talented or worthy, there are far more interesting, engaging, and inspiring women—we just have to keep making the space, and praising each other for stepping into it. The truth is that emotionally expansive women who frown, yell, or demand more for themselves may never gain mainstream acceptance. But there is always something deeper out there, in the art that counters popular culture's shallower tendencies. These transgressive voices will always be marginalized by lack of equal time and voice, in print, onscreen, and onstage. But we just have to keep looking for them.

Punk rock began in order to give voice to the voiceless, to change the definition of art, and to alleviate the tedium of radio-friendly rock. In lyrics that shake the foundations of popular culture, in instruments wielded like weapons, in sounds that soothe boredom and monotony, the varied, vibrant, vivacious independent underground screams, whispers, teaches, preaches, throbs, and sings the moral of the story:

If you feel like an outsider, you aren't alone. If an idea grabs you by the collar and won't let go, someone, somewhere, will listen.

Anger, intelligence, and wit are ultimately more seductive than zero percent body fat.

Anyone can learn an instrument, sing a song, create a magazine or a film, write, paint, sculpt, take pictures, start a smart, successful, socially conscious business, and make greatness out of one lonely little vision. Fame, beauty, and money are fleeting, but truepunkrocksoul can last forever.

ROCK 'N' ROLL FIGHT SONGS

Discographies

ALL ALBUM AND EP DISCOGRAPHIES WERE COMPILED USING THE Library of Congress, allmusic, Artist Direct, *Trouser Press*, and individual artists' discography listings. Discographies are arranged in the order the artists appear in this work, and under each artist's project, in chronological order. Album/EP titles are followed by their U.S. label and release date. If more than one date is given for a specific title, the first is the original date of release, and the second is the album's reissue release date. When information allowed, imports were labeled as such, and compilations by various artists are not included.

PATTI SMITH

Patti Smith Group
Horses Arista, 1975
Radio Ethiopia Arista, 1976
Easter Arista, 1978
Wave Arista, 1979

Patti Smith
Dream of Life Arista, 1988
Gone Again Arista, 1996
Peace and Noise Arista, 1997
Gung Ho Arista, 2000
Trampin' Sony, 2004

THE RUNAWAYS
The Runaways Mercury, 1976
Queens of Noise Mercury, 1977
Live in Japan Mercury, 1977
Waitin' for the Night Mercury, 1977
Mama, Weer All Crazy Now Rhino, 1978
And Now . . . the Runaways Cherry Red, 1979 [Import]
Flaming Schoolgirls UK Cherry Red, 1980 [Import]
Little Lost Girls Rhino, 1981
The Best of the Runaways Mercury, 1987
I Love Playing with Fire Laker-Cherry Red, 1982
Neon Angels Special Music, 1991
Born to Be Bad Marilyn, 1993

Joan Jett
Joan Jett Blackheart, 1980
Bad Reputation Boardwalk, 1981; Blackheart, 1992
The Hit List Blackheart/CBS, 1990
Fetish Blackheart, 1990

Joan Jett and the Blackhearts
I Love Rock-n-Roll Boardwalk, 1981; Blackheart, 1998
Album Blackheart/MCA Records, 1983; Blackheart, 1993
Glorious Results of a Misspent Youth Blackheart/MCA, 1984; Blackheart, 1993
Good Music Blackheart/Epic, 1986
Up Your Alley Epic, 1988
Notorious Blackheart/Epic, 1991
Flashback Blackheart, 1993
Pure and Simple Warner Bros., 1994
Fit to Be Tied: Great Hits by Joan Jett and the Blackhearts
    Blackheart/Mercury, 1997
Fetish Blackheart, 1999

Evil Stig
Evil Stig Warner Bros., 1995

Lita Ford
Out for Blood Mercury, 1983

Dancin' on the Edge Mercury, 1984
Lita RCA, 1988
Stiletto RCA, 1990
Dangerous Curves RCA, 1991
Best of Lita Ford Dreamland, 1992
Greatest Hits RCA, 1993
Black ZYX Records, 1995
Greatest Hits BMG, 1999
Kiss Me Deadly: Best of Lita Ford BMG International, 2001

Cherie Currie
Beauty's Only Skin Deep Mercury, 1978
Messin' With the Boys Capitol, 1980
Unplugged in Hollywood Rocket City, 1996
Young and Wild Raven, 1998

TINA WEYMOUTH

Talking Heads
Talking Heads: 77 Sire, 1977
More Songs About Buildings and Food Sire, 1978
Fear of Music Sire, 1979
Remain in Light Sire, 1980
The Name of This Band Is Talking Heads Sire, 1982
Speaking in Tongues Sire, 1983
Stop Making Sense Sire, 1984
Little Creatures Sire, 1985
True Stories Sire, 1986
Sounds from True Stories Luaka Bop/Sire, 1986
Naked Fly, 1988
The Best Of: Once in a Lifetime EMI International, 1992
Popular Favorites 1976–1992: Sand in the Vaseline Warner Bros., 1992
Stop Making Sense (Special Ed. Live) Sire/Warner Bros., 1999

Tom Tom Club
Tom Tom Club Island Records, 1981
Close to the Bone Sire, 1983
Boom Boom Chi Boom Boom Red Eye, 1989
Dark Sneak Love Action Sire, 1991
The Good the Bad and the Funky Rykodisc, 2000
Live @ the Clubhouse Artist Direct BMG, 2002

LORNA DOOM

The Germs
(GI) Slash, 1979
What We Do Is Secret Slash, 1981
Germicide: Live at the Whisky ROIR, 1982; Bomp Records, 1998
Let the Circle Be Unbroken Gasatanka, 1985
Lion's Share Ghost o'Darb, 1985
Rock n' Rule XES, 1986
Media Blitz Cleopatra, 1993
Germs MIA: The Complete Anthology Slash/Rhino, 1993; Rhino, 2000
Cat's Clause Munster, 1996

DEBORAH HARRY

The Wind in the Willows
The Wind in the Willows Capitol, 1968

Blondie
Blondie Private Stock, 1976; Chrysalis, 1976
Plastic Letters Chrysalis, 1977
Parallel Lines Chrysalis, 1978
Eat to the Beat Chrysalis, 1979
Autoamerican Chrysalis, 1980
The Best of Blondie Chrysalis, 1981
The Hunter Chrysalis, 1982
Blonde and Beyond Chrysalis, 1993
The Platinum Collection Chrysalis/EMI, 1994
Remixed Remade Remodeled: The Remix Project Chrysalis/EMI, 1995
Picture This Live Chrysalis/EMI/Capitol, 1997
No Exit Beyond, 1999
Blondie Live Beyond, 1999
The Curse of Blondie Sanctuary, 2004

Debbie Harry
KooKoo Chrysalis, 1981
Rockbird Geffen, 1986; Geffen Goldline, 1997
Def, Dumb & Blonde Sire/Reprise, 1989
Debravation Sire/Reprise, 1993
Collection Disky, 2000

Debbie Harry and Blondie
Once More Into the Bleach Chrysalis, 1988
The Complete Picture: The Very Best of Deborah Harry and Blondie UK
    Chrysalis, 1991 [Import]

Jazz Passengers Featuring Debbie Harry
Individually Twisted 32 Jazz, 1996
"Live" in Spain 32 Jazz, 1998

EXENE CERVENKA

X
Los Angeles Slash, 1980; Rhino, 2001
Wild Gift Slash 1981; Slash/Rhino, 2001
Under the Big Black Sun Elektra, 1982; Rhino, 2001
More Fun in the New World Elektra, 1983; Rhino, 2002
Ain't Love Grand Elektra, 1985; Rhino, 2002
See How We Are Elektra, 1987; Rhino, 2002
Live at the Whisky A Go-Go on the Fabulous Sunset Strip Elektra, 1988
Hey Zeus! Big Life/Mercury, 1993
Unclogged Infidelity/Sunset Blvd., 1995
Los Angeles/Wild Gift (Combination Reissue) Slash, 1988; Uni/Slash, 1996
Beyond & Back: The X Anthology Elektra, 1997
Make the Music Go Bang Rhino, 2004

Knitters
Poor Little Critter on the Road Warner Bros., 1985
Poor Little Critters Rhino, 2000

Exene Cervenka and Wanda Coleman
Twin Sisters Freeway, 1985

Exene Cervenka
Old Wives' Tales Rhino, 1989
Running Scared Rhino, 1990
Wordcore, Vol. 7 Kill Rock Stars, 1994
Surface to Air Serpents Thirsty Ear, 1996

Exene Cervenkova
Excerpts from the Unabomber Manifesto Year One, 1995

Exene Cervenka and Lydia Lunch
Rude Hieroglyphics Rykodisc, 1995

Auntie Christ
Life Could Be a Dream Lookout!, 1997

Original Sinners
Original Sinners Nitro, 2002

PENELOPE HOUSTON

The Avengers

The Avengers EP Dangerhouse, 1977
The Avengers EP White Noise, 1979
The Avengers CD Presents, 1983
Died for Your Sins Lookout!, 1999
The American In Me DBK Works, 2004

Penelope Houston

Birdboys Subterranean Records, 1987
On Borrowed Time (Live in Frisco) id Records, 1990
500 Lucky Pieces id Records, 1992
The Whole World Heyday Records, 1993; Penelope.net Records, 2000
Silk Purse (From a Sow's Ear) Return to Sender/Normal, 1993
Karmal Apple Normal, 1994
Cut You Warner/Reprise Records, WEA Germany, 1996
Tongue WEA Germany, 1998 [Import]; Warner/Reprise, 1999
Once in a Blue Moon Orchard/Penelope.net Records, 2000
Loners, Stoners and Prison Brides Return to Sender/Normal, 2001
Eighteen Stories Down WEA, 2003

Penelope Houston and Pat Johnson

Crazy Baby Return to Sender/Normal, 1994
The Pale Green Girl DBK Works, 2004

Penelope Houston and the Maydays

Snap Shot Flare, 2003

POISON IVY

The Cramps

Lucky 13 Drug Fiend, 1978
Gravest Hits EP IRS, 1979
Songs the Lord Taught Us Illegal/IRS, 1980
Psychedelic Jungle IRS, 1981
. . . Off the Bone Illegal, 1983 [Import]
Smell of Female Big Beat, 1983; Capitol/Enigma, 1990; Restless, 1994
Bad Music for Bad People IRS, 1984, 1990
Date with Elvis Big Beat, 1986 [Import]; Big Beat/Capitol, 1990; Restless, 1994
Rockinnreelininaucklandnewzealandxxx Vengeance, 1987 [Import]; Vengeance/Restless, 1994
What's Inside a Ghoul Pow Wow, 1988
Psychedelic Jungle/Gravest Hits IRS, 1989

Stay Sick! Enigma, 1990; Dutch East Wax, 1991
All Women Are Bad EP Enigma, 1990 [Import]
Look Mom No Head! Restless, 1991
Most Exalted Potentates of Trash Taylordisco, 1993
Beyond the Valley of the Cramps LUX, 1993
Tales of the Cramps Cave, 1993
FlameJob Medicine Label/Warner Bros., 1994; Epitaph, 1994
Big Beats from Badsville Epitaph/Vengeance, 1997; Vengeance, 2001
Fiends of Dope Island Vengeance, 2003

SIOUXSIE SIOUX

Siouxsie & the Banshees
The Scream Polydor/Geffen, 1978; Geffen, 1990
Join Hands Polydor/Geffen, 1979; Polydor, 1989; Geffen, 1990;
    Universal, 2003
Kaleidoscope Geffen, 1980; Polydor, 1980; Geffen, 1990
Juju Polydor/ PVC, 1981; Geffen, 1984 and 1990
Arabian Knights EP PVC, 1981
Once Upon a Time/The Singles Polydor, 1981; Geffen, 1990
A Kiss in the Dreamhouse Polydor, 1982 [Import]; Geffen, 1984
Nocturne Wonderland, 1983
Hyaena Geffen, 1983; Wonderland, 1984
The Thorn EP Wonderland, Polydor, 1984
Cities in the Dust EP Geffen, 1985
Tinderbox Wonderland/Geffen, 1986
Through the Looking Glass Wonderland/Geffen, 1987
The Peel Sessions EP Strange Fruit, 1987 [Import]
Peep Show Geffen, 1988
The Peel Sessions Strange Fruit/Dutch East India Trading, 1991
Superstition Wonderland/Geffen, 1991
Twice Upon a Time: The Singles Wonderland/Geffen, 1992
The Rapture Wonderland/Geffen, 1995
The Best of Siouxsie and the Banshees Interscope, 2002
Seven Year Itch Sanctuary, 2003

The Creatures
Wild Things EP Polydor, 1981 [Import]
Feast UK Wonderland/Polydor, 1983
Boomerang Geffen, 1989
A Bestiary of Polygram International, 1998
Anima Animus Instinct, 1999
Hybrids Remixes Hydrogen Juke, 1999
US Retrace Remixer Instinct, 2000

Sequins in the Sun Sioux, 2001
Hái! Sioux, 2003; Artful, 2004

THE SLITS
Cut Antilles, 1979; Island, 2000
Retrospective Rough Trade/Y Records, 1980
Return of the Giant Slits CBS, 1981; Sony International, 2004
The Peel Sessions Strange Fruit, 1989; 1999 [Import]
In the Beginning: A Live Anthology (1976–1981) Cleopatra, 1997

New Age Steppers
New Age Steppers On-U Sound, 1980, 2000
Action Battlefield Statik, 1981; On-U Sound, 2000
Crucial 90 Statik, 1981
Foundation Steppers On-U Sound, 1983
Victory Horns On-U Sound, 1983
Massive Hits, Volume 1 Restless Records, 1994

New Age Steppers & Creation Rebel
Threat to Creation Cherry Red, 1981, 2002

LORA LOGIC AND POLY STYRENE

X-Ray Spex
Germ Free Adolescents EMI International, 1978; Silverline, 2002
Live at the Roxy Receiver, 1991
Obsessed with You Receiver, 1991
Conscious Consumer Receiver, 1995
The Anthology Castle Sanctuary, 2001

The Red Krayola
Soldier Talk Radar, 1979
Kangaroo? [The Red Krayola w/Art & Language] Rough Trade, 1981;
    Drag City, 1995

Essential Logic
Essential Logic EP Virgin, 1979 [Import]; 2001
Essential Logic 2 EP, 2002
Beat Rhythm News Rough Trade, 1979
Fanfare in the Garden Kill Rock Stars, 2003

Lora Logic
Pedigree Charm Rough Trade, 1982

Poly Styrene
Translucence UA, 1981; Receiver, 1990
Gods & Goddesses EP Awesome, 1986

JOY DE VIVRE AND EVE LIBERTINE

Crass
The Feeding of the 5000 Crass, 1978
Stations of the Cross Crass, 1979
Penis Envy Crass, 1981
Christ the Album Crass, 1982
Yes Sir, I Will Crass, 1983
Best Before Crass, 1986
10 Notes on a Summer's Day Crass, 1986
Christ the Bootleg EP No Idea, 1999
You'll Ruin It for Everyone Import, 2001

Eve Libertine and Penny Rimbaud
Acts of Love Crass, 1985

THE RAINCOATS
The Raincoats Rough Trade, 1980; DGC, 1993
Odyshape Rough Trade, 1981; DGC, 1994
Animal Rhapsody EP Rough Trade, 1983
The Kitchen Tapes ROIR, 1983
Moving Rough Trade, 1984; Geffen, 1994
Fairytales Tim/Kerr, 1995
Extended Play EP Smells Like Records, 1994
Looking in the Shadows DGC, 1996

The Red Krayola
Kangaroo? [The Red Krayola w/Art & Language] Rough Trade, 1981;
    Drag City, 1995

The Hangovers
Slow Dirty Tears Kill Rock Stars, 1998

Hefner
The Fidelity Wars Too Pure, 1999

LYDIA LUNCH
[Collaborations listings are partial]

Teenage Jesus and the Jerks
Pre-Teenage Jesus and the Jerks ZE, 1979
Everything Atavistic, 1995

8 Eyed Spy
Live ROIR, 1981
8 Eyed Spy Fetish, 1981 [Import]; Atavistic, 1997

Lydia Lunch
Queen of Siam ZE, 1980; Widowspeak, 1985; Triple X, 1991
13.13 Situation 2, 1982; Widowspeak, 1988
In Limbo EP UK Doublevision, 1984; Widowspeak, 1986
The Uncensored Lydia Lunch Widowspeak, 1984
Hysterie Rough Trade/Widowspeak, 1989
Oral Fixation Widowspeak, 1988
Drowning in Limbo Widowspeak, 1989; Atavistic, 1995
Conspiracy of Women Widowspeak, 1990
Crimes Against Nature Triple X, 1994; Atavistic, 1999
Universal Infiltrators Atavistic, 1996
Matrikamantra Atavistic/Figurehead, 1998
Widowspeak (Greatest Hits Compilation) New Millennium
     Communications, Ltd., 1998
The Devil's Racetrack Almafame Ltd., 2000
Hangover Hotel Widowspeak, 2001
Champagne, Cocaine, and Nicotine Stains Crippled Dick Hot Wax, 2002

Lydia Lunch and Rowland S. Howard
Shotgun Wedding Triple X, 1991
Some Velvet Morning EP 4AD, 1982
Transmutation/Shotgun Wedding: Live Insipid, 1994
Shotgun Wedding/Shotgun Wedding Live Atavistic, 1999

Lydia Lunch and the Birthday Party
The Agony Is the Ecstacy [sic; split EP with the Birthday Party's *Drunk on the
     Pope's Blood*] 4AD, 1982 [Import]

Lydia Lunch and Jim Thirlwell [AKA Clint Ruin, Foetus]
The Crumb EP Widowspeak, 1988
Stinkfist EP Widowspeak, 1988
Don't Fear the Reaper EP Big Cat, 1991 [Import]
Stinkfist and the Crumb Reissue Widowspeak, 1990
York [Foetus Symphony Orchestra Featuring Lydia Lunch] Thirsty Ear, 1997

Harry Crews
Naked in Garden Hills Big Cat, 1990

Lydia Lunch and Exene Cervenka
Rude Hieroglyphics Rykodisc, 1995

WENDY O. WILLIAMS

The Plasmatics

New Hope for the Wretched Stiff Records UK, Stiff, 1980

Beyond the Valley of 1984 Stiff Records UK, 1981; Plasmatics Media/WOW, 2000

Metal Priestess EP Stiff Records UK, 1981; Plasmatics Media/ WOW, 2001

Coup d'Etat Capitol, 1982; Razor and Tie, 2000

WOW Passport/WOW Records, 1984; Plasmatics Media/WOW Records, 2000

Kommander of Kaos JEM/Gigasaurus, 1986; Plasmatics Media/Gigasaurus/ WOW, 2000

Maggots: The Record Profile/WOW, 1987; Plasmatics Media/WOW, 2000

Deffest and Baddest: Ultrafly and the Hometown Girls Profile/WOW, 1987; Plasmatics Media/WOW, 2001

New Hope for the Wretched/Metal Priestess EP (Reissue) Plasmatics Media/ WOW, 2001

Coup de Grace Plasmatics Media/WOW, 2002

Final Days: Anthems for the Apocalypse Plasmatics Media/WOW, 2002

Put Your Love in Me: Love Songs for the Apocalypse Plasmatics Media/ WOW, 2002

KIM GORDON

Sonic Youth

Sonic Youth EP Neutral, 1982; SST, 1987

Confusion Is Sex Neutral, 1983; SST, 1987; DGC, 1995

Kill Yr Idols EP Ger. Zensor, 1983

Sonic Death: Early Sonic Youth 1981–1983 Ecstatic Peace!, 1985; SST, 1984

Bad Moon Rising Homestead, 1985; DGC, 1995

Death Valley 69 EP Homestead, 1985

EVOL SST, 1986; DGC, 1994

Sister SST, 1987; DGC, 1994

Master-Dik EP SST, 1987

Daydream Nation Blast First/Enigma, 1988; DGC, 1993

Daydream Nation EP Blast First/Enigma, 1988

Candle EP Blast First/Enigma, 1989

Goo DGC, 1990

Dirty Boots EP DGC, 1991

Dirty DGC, 1992; DGC, 2002

Whores Moaning EP Geffen, 1993

Experimental Jet Set, Trash and No Star DGC, 1994

Made in USA Rhino, 1995

Screaming Fields of Sonic Love DGC, 1995

Turn It Up! Turn It Up! Ruta 66, 1995

Washing Machine DGC, 1995
SYR1: Anagrama EP Sonic Youth, 1997
SYR2: Slaapkamers Met Slagroom EP Sonic Youth, 1997
SYR3: Invito el Cielo EP Sonic Youth, 1998
A Thousand Leaves DGC, 1998
Hold That Tiger Goofin, 1998
Silver Session for Jason Knuth Sonic Knuth, 1998
SYR4: Goodbye 20th Century Sonic Youth, 1999
NYC Ghosts & Flowers Geffen, 2000
Murray Street DGC, 2002
Kali Yug Express Geffen, 2002
Sonic Nurse Geffen, 2004

Ciccone Youth
The Whitey Album EP Blast First/Enigma, 1988
The Whitey Album Blast First/Enigma, 1988; Geffen, 1995

Harry Crews
Naked in Garden Hills Big Cat, 1990

Free Kitten
Call Now Ecstatic Peace!, 1992
Unboxed Wiiija, 1994 [Import]
Nice Ass Kill Rock Stars, 1995
Sentimental Education Kill Rock Stars, 1997

Sonic Youth and Eye Yamatsuka
TV Shit EP Ecstatic Peace!, 1993

KIM WARNICK AND LULU GARGIULO

Fastbacks
Fastbacks Play Five of Their Favorites EP No Threes, 1982
Every Day is Saturday EP No Threes, 1984
. . . And His Orchestra PopLlama, 1987
Bike-Clock-Toy-Gift Lucky, 1990
Very, Very Powerful Motor PopLlama, 1990
Never Fails, Never Works LP UK Blaster, 1991
The Question Is No Sub Pop, 1992
Gone to the Moon EP Sub Pop, 1993 [import]
Zücker Sub Pop, 1993
Answer the Phone Dummy Sub Pop, 1994
Alone in a Furniture Warehouse Scaring You Away Like a Hotel Mattress
    Munster, 1996
New Mansions in Sound Sub Pop, 1996

Here They Are: Fastbacks Live at Crocodile Café Lance Rock, 1996
Win or Lose Both EP PopLlama, 1998
The Day That Didn't Exist spinART, 1999
In America Lost & Found, 2000
Truth, Corrosion & Sour Biscuits Book Records, 2004

Visqueen

King Me Blue Disguise, 2003
Sunset on Dateland Blue Disguise, 2004

KIM DEAL

The Pixies

Come on Pilgrim EP 4AD, 1987 [Import]; Elektra, 1987; 4AD/Elektra, 1991
Surfer Rosa 4AD/Rough Trade, 1988; 4AD/Elektra, 1992
Surfer Rosa/Come on Pilgrim 4AD/Rough Trade, 1988
Doolittle 4AD/Elektra, 1989
Monkey Gone to Heaven EP 4AD/Elektra, 1989
Here Comes Your Man EP 4AD/Elektra, 1989
Dancing the Manta Ray EP 4AD, 1989
Bossanova 4AD/Elektra, 1990
Velouria EP Elektra, 1990 [Import]
Dig for Fire EP 4AD/Elektra, 1990
Trompe le Monde 4AD/Elektra, 1991
Planet of Sound EP 4AD, 1991 [Import]
Alec Eiffel EP Elektra, 1991
Death to the Pixies 4AD/Elektra, 1997
Pixies at the BBC 4AD/Elektra, 1998
Complete B-Sides 4AD, 2001 [Import]
The Pixies spinART, 2002
Wave of Mutilation 4AD, 2004

The Breeders

Pod 4AD/Elektra, 1990, 1992
Safari EP 4AD, 1992
Last Splash 4AD/Elektra, 1993, 1994
Head to Toe EP 4AD, 1994
Cannonball EP 4AD/Elektra, 1993
Live in Stockholm Breeders Digest, 1995
Title TK Elektra, 2002

The Amps

Pacer 4AD/Elektra, 1995

THE GITS

Frenching the Bully C/Z Records, 1992; Broken Rekids, 2003
Enter: The Conquering Chicken C/Z Records 1994; Broken Rekids, 2003
Kings and Queens Broken Rekids, 1996; Broken Rekids, 2003
Seafish Louisville Broken Rekids, 2000

Dancing French Liberals of '48

Scream Clown Scream Broken Rekids/Revenge, 1994
Powerline Broken Rekids/Revenge, 1995

Evil Stig

Evil Stig Warner Bros., 1995

JENNY TOOMEY

Tsunami

Deep End Simple Machines, 1993
The Heart's Tremolo Simple Machines, 1994
World Tour and Other Destinations Simple Machines, 1995
A Brilliant Mistake Simple Machines, 1997

Grenadine

Goya Shimmy Disc, 1992
Nopalitos Simple Machines, 1994

Liquorice

Listening Cap 4AD/Simple Machines, 1995

Jenny Toomey

Antidote Misra, 2001
Tempting: Jenny Toomey Sings the Songs of Franklin Bruno Misra, 2002

HOLE

Pretty on the Inside Caroline, 1991
Live Through This Geffen, 1994
Ask for It EP Caroline, 1995
First Session Sympathy for the Record Industry, 1997
My Body the Hand Grenade EP City Slang, 1997 [Import]
Celebrity Skin Geffen, 1998
Awful: Australian Tour EP MCA International, 1999 [Import]

Courtney Love

America's Sweetheart Virgin, 2004

Melissa Auf der Maur

Auf der Maur EMI International, 2004 [Import]

L7

L7 Epitaph, 1988
Smell the Magic EP Sub Pop, 1991
Bricks Are Heavy Slash, 1992
Hungry for Stink Slash/Reprise, 1994
The Beauty Process: Triple Platinum Slash/Reprise, 1997
L7 Live: Omaha to Osaka Man's Ruin, 1998
Slap-Happy Wax Tadpole/Bong Load, 1999
Best of L7: The Slash Years London/Slash, 2000

TRIBE 8

Allen's Mom Outpunk, 1994
By the Time We Get to Colorado EP Outpunk, 1995
Fist City Alternative Tentacles, 1995
Roadkill Café EP Alternative Tentacles, 1995
Snarkism Alternative Tentacles, 1996
Role Models for Amerika Alternative Tentacles, 1998

LUNACHICKS

Lunachicks Plan 9/Caroline, 1989
Babysitters on Acid Blast First, 1990
Binge and Purge Safe House, 1992
Sushi a la Mode EP Toys Factory, 1993 [Import]
Jerk of All Trades Go-Kart, 1995
Pretty Ugly Go-Kart, 1997
Drop Dead Live Go-Kart, 1998
Luxury Problem Go-Kart, 1999

Bantam
Bantam Heavy Nose Records, 2002

Theo Kogan
Theo self-released, 2003

PJ HARVEY

Demonstration Too Pure, 1992 [Import]
Dry Indigo, 1992
4-Track Demos Island, 1993
Rid of Me Island, 1993
To Bring You My Love Island, 1995
Is This Desire? Island, 1998
Stories from the City, Stories From the Sea Island, 2000
Uh Huh Her Island, 2004

PJ Harvey and John Parish
Dance Hall at Louise Point Island, 1996

BIKINI KILL (also see LE TIGRE)
Bikini Kill self-distributed cassette, 1991
Bikini Kill EP Kill Rock Stars, 1992
The CD Version of the First Two Records Kill Rock Stars, 1992
Pussy Whipped Kill Rock Stars, 1993
Reject All American Kill Rock Stars, 1996
The Singles Kill Rock Stars, 1998

The Fakes
Real Fiction Chainsaw, 1995

Julie Ruin
Julie Ruin Kill Rock Stars, 1998

The Frumpies
Frumpie One Piece Kill Rock Stars, 1998

The Casual Dots
The Casual Dots Kill Rock Stars, 2004

BRATMOBILE
Pottymouth Kill Rock Stars, 1993
The Real Janelle EP Kill Rock Stars, 1994
Peel Session EP Dutch East, 1994
Ladies, Women and Girls Lookout!, 2000
Girls Get Busy Lookout!, 2002

Peechees
Do the Math Kill Rock Stars, 1996
Games People Play Kill Rock Stars, 1997
Life Kill Rock Stars, 1999

Cold Cold Hearts
Cold Cold Hearts Kill Rock Stars, 1997

TEAM DRESCH (also see THE BUTCHIES)
Personal Best Chainsaw/Candy-Ass, 1995
Captain My Captain Chainsaw/Candy-Ass, 1996

Hazel
Are You Going to Eat That? Sub Pop, 1995
Toreador of Love Sub Pop, 1993
Airiana Candy-Ass, 1997

Kaia Wilson
Kaia Chainsaw, 1996
Ladyman Mr. Lady Records, 1998
Oregon Mr. Lady Records, 2002

The Vegas Beat
The Vegas Beat Candy-Ass, 1997

Infinite Xs
Infinite Xs Chainsaw, 2002

Davies vs. Dresch
Vs. Love EP Chainsaw, 2004

SLEATER-KINNEY

Sleater-Kinney Chainsaw, 1995
Call the Doctor Chainsaw, 1996
Dig Me Out Kill Rock Stars, 1997
The Hot Rock Kill Rock Stars, 1999
All Hands on the Bad One Kill Rock Stars, 2000
One Beat Kill Rock Stars, 2002

Heavens to Betsy
Calculated Kill Rock Stars, 1994

Excuse 17
Excuse 17 Chainsaw, 1995
Such Friends Are Dangerous Kill Rock Stars, 1995

Quasi
Early Recordings Key Op, 1996
R&B Transmogrification Up Records, 1997
Featuring Birds Up Records, 1998
Field Studies Up Records, 1999
The Sword of God Touch & Go, 2001
Hot Shit Touch & Go, 2003

Cadallaca
Introducing Cadallaca K Records, 1998
Out West EP Kill Rock Stars, 2000

Spells
The Age of Backwards EP International Pop Underground Records, 1999

THE BUTCHIES (also see TEAM DRESCH)

Are We Not Femme? Mr. Lady Records, 1998

Population 1975 Mr. Lady Records, 1999
3 Mr. Lady Records, 2001
Make Yr Life Yep Roc, 2004

LE TIGRE (also see BIKINI KILL)
Le Tigre Mr. Lady Records, 1999
From the Desk of Mr. Lady Mr. Lady Records, 2001
Feminist Sweepstakes Mr. Lady Records, 2001
Remix Mr. Lady Records, 2002
This Island Strummer Records, 2004

PEACHES
Lovertits EP Kitty-Yo Intl, 2000
The Teaches of Peaches Kitty-Yo Intl, 2000; Beggars XL, 2002
Fatherfucker Beggars XL, 2003

THE GOSSIP
That's Not What I Heard Kill Rock Stars, 2001
Arkansas Heat EP Kill Rock Stars, 2002
Movement Kill Rock Stars, 2003
Undead in NYC Dim Mak Records, 2003

ERASE ERRATA
Other Animals Troubleman Unlimited, 2001
At Crystal Palace Troubleman Unlimited, 2003
Dancing Machine Remix EP Troubleman Unlimited, 2003

Paradise Island
Lines Are Infinitely Fine Dim Mak Records, 2003

NOTES

INTRODUCTION

1. Leee Childers, *Please Kill Me: The Uncensored Oral History of Punk*, ed. Legs McNeil and Gillian McCain (New York: Penguin, 1997), 65.

2. Kristy Eldredge, "Chicks Rock: No Shit, Sherlock," *Glorious Noise*, www.gloriousnoise. com/arch/000774.php.

3. Joe Heim, "American Bandstand," *Salon* (4 March 1999), www.salon.com/ent/music/ feature/1999/03/04feature.html.

4. Jon Savage, *England's Dreaming: Anarchy, Sex Pistols, Punk Rock, and Beyond* (New York: St. Martin's Griffin, 2002), 516.

5. Paul Marko, "No Fun No Fun!! Politics," *Punk 77*, www.punk77.co.uk/groups/ womeninpunkpolitics.htm.

6. Wanda Jackson, *Country!*, Capitol Records ST-434, 1968.

7. Michael Azerrad, *Our Band Could Be Your Life: Scenes from the American Indie Underground* (Boston: Back Bay Books, 2002), 150.

8. Ibid.

9. Crass, "...In Which Crass Voluntarily 'Blow Their Own,'" on *Best Before 1984*, Crass Records 5, 1986.

10. Mark Paytress, liner notes for *The Anthology*, X-Ray Spex. Sanctuary/Castle CMDDD369, 2001.

11. Azerrad, *Our Band Could Be Your Life*, 152.

12. Kim Gordon, "Boys Are Smelly: Sonic Youth Tour Diary '87," reprinted in *Rock She Wrote: Women Write About Rock, Pop, and Rap,* ed. Evelyn McDonnell and Ann Powers (New York: Delta, 1995), 72.

13. Ibid.

14. Susan Faludi, *Backlash: The Undeclared War Against Women* (New York: Crown, 1991), 79.

PART I

AMERICA IN THE 1970S

1. Larry Starr and Christopher Waterman, *American Popular Music: From Minstrelsy to MTV* (New York: Oxford University Press, 2003), 308.

2. Don Breithaupt and Jeff Breithaupt, *Precious and Few: Pop Music in the Early Seventies* (New York: St. Martin's Griffin, 1996), 30.

3. Lester Bangs, *Psychotic Reactions and Carburetor Dung,* ed. Greil Marcus (New York: Anchor Books, 2003), 71-72.

4. The fear of lower profit margins led to paralysis on the part of the major labels and AM radio, which leaned on the Top 40 for its programming. And although FM grew considerably during the '70s, it focused on album-oriented hard rock. Starr and Waterman, 307.

5. Ibid., 306.

6. Harvey Kubernik, *We Got the Neutron Bomb: The Untold Story of L.A. Punk,* ed. Marc Spitz and Brendan Mullen (New York: Three Rivers Press, 2001), 5.

7. Gillian G. Gaar, *She's a Rebel: The History of Women in Rock & Roll* (New York: Seal Press, 2002), 145.

8. Ibid., 96.

9. Ibid., 145.

10. David Johansen, *Please Kill Me,* ed. Legs McNeil and Gillian McCain (New York: Penguin, 1997), 116.

11. Lester Bangs, "Sex and the Art of Rock and Roll," *Creem* 8, no.6 (1976): 38–42.

12. Hilly Kristal, "CBGB Omfug," CBGB, www.cbgb.com/history/history2.html.

13. Penelope Houston, interview by the author, 25 September 2003.

14. Calvin Johnson, *Songs for Cassavetes: An All Ages Film,* DVD, directed by Justin Mitchell.

15. Ed. Spitz and Mullen, *We Got the Neutron Bomb,* 13.

16. Ibid., 35.

17. When Fowley wasn't writing the lyrics, that is. Joan Jett, Sandy West, and Kari Krome wrote most of the Runaways songs themselves.

18. Gary Stewart, *We Got the Neutron Bomb,* ed. Spitz and Mullen, 53.

19. Nicole Panter, interview by the author, 9 September, 2003.

20. Spitz and Mullen, *We Got the Neutron Bomb,* 58.

21. Pleasant Gehman, liner notes for *We're Desperate: The L.A. Scene 1976–1979,* various artists. Rhino R271176, 1993.

22. Houston, interview, 2003.

23. Panter, interview, 2003.

24. Eileen Polk, *Please Kill Me,* ed. McNeil and McCain, 285.

25. Ivan Julian, *Please Kill Me,* ed. McNeil and McCain, 283.

26. Jena Cardwell, *Lexicon Devil: The Fast Times and Short Life of Darby Crash and the Germs,* ed. Brendan Mullen, Don Bolles, and Adam Parfrey (Los Angeles: Feral House, 2002), 101.

27. Hal Negro, *We Got the Neutron Bomb,* ed. Spitz and Mullen, 144.

28. Margot Olaverra, *We Got the Neutron Bomb,* ed. Spitz and Mullen, 234.

CHAPTER I

PATTI SMITH

1. Patti Smith, *Patti Smith Complete: Lyrics, Reflections, and Notes for the Future* (New York: Anchor Books, 1999), xxi.

2. Ingrid Sischy, "Because the Light," *Interview* (June 1996).

3. Leee Childers, *Please Kill Me,* ed. Legs McNeil and Gillian McCain (New York: Penguin, 1997), 98.

4. Sischy, *"Because the Light."* (June 1996).

5. Richard Hell, *Please Kill Me*, ed. McNeil and McCain, 114.

6. Caroline Coon, "Punk Queen of Sheba," *Melody Maker*, 15 January 1977: 22, 27.

7. Hilly Kristal, "CBGB Omfug," CBGB, www.cbgb.com/history/history9.html.

8. Smith, *Patti Smith Complete*, 7.

9. Patrick Goldstein, "Patti Smith: Rock 'n' Roll Pandora Unleashes Violence and Mayhem," Creem 8, no. 10 (1977): 42–45, 67–69.

10. Patti Smith, interview by Terry Gross, "Fresh Air," National Public Radio, 24 June 1996.

11. Smith, *Patti Smith Complete*, 68.

CHAPTER 2
THE RUNAWAYS

1. Joan Jett, *We Got the Neutron Bomb* ed. Marc Spitz and Brendan Mullen (New York: Three Rivers Press, 2001), 35.

2. The Official Site of the Runaways, www.ite.his.se/~c95chrha/bio.html.

3. Spitz and Mullen, *We Got the Neutron Bomb*, 45–46.

4. The Official Site of the Runaways.

5. Spitz and Mullen, *We Got the Neutron Bomb*, 47.

6. Cherie Currie and Neal Shusterman, *Neon Angel: The Cherie Currie Story* (Los Angeles: Price Stern Sloan, 1989), 52–53.

7. Chris Salewicz, "And I Wonder . . . Wah Wah Wah Wonder. . . ." *New Musical Express* (24 July 1976): 25.

8. Ibid., 26.

9. Currie and Shusterman, *Neon Angel*, 60.

10. Spitz and Mullen, *We Got the Neutron Bomb*, 54–55.

11. Lori Twersky, *Rock She Wrote*, ed. Evelyn McDonnell and Ann Powers (New York: Delta, 1995), 178.

12. Joe Garden, "Joan Jett," *The Onion AV Club* (26 February 1998).

13. Rick Johnson, review of *Queens of Noise* by the Runaways, Creem 8, no. 11 (1977): 62.

14. Spitz and Mullen, *We Got the Neutron Bomb*, 50.

15. Ibid., 48.

16. Ibid.

17. Patrick Goldstein, "The Runaways: Lissome Lolitas or Teenage Trash?," *Creem* (February 1997): 67.

18. Sandy West, *We Got the Neutron Bomb*, ed. Spitz and Mullen, 52.

19. The Official Site of the Runaways.

CHAPTER 3
TINA WEYMOUTH

1. Nick Kent, "Are These Guys Trying to Give Rock a Bad Name?," *New Musical Express* (25 June 1977): 7–8.

2. Tina Weymouth, www.talking-heads.net/tina.html.

3. Ibid.

4. Miles, "This is a Minimalist Headline," *New Musical Express* (23 April 1977): 18.

5. Scott Rowley, "Wot, No Sid? The 50 Best Basslines of Punk and New Wave," *Total Guitar* 2 (2004): 64.

6. Mikal Gilmore, "Psychodramas You Can Dance To," *Rolling Stone* 305 (1979): 23.

7. Gillian G. Gaar, *She's a Rebel* (New York: Seal Press, 2002), 212.

8. Ibid.

9. Miles, "This is a Minimalist Headline," 16.

10. David Byrne, interview by Bob Edwards, "Morning Edition," National Public Radio, 18 November 2003.

11. Walter Tunis, "To the Surprise of Its Founders, Tom Tom Club Is Still Going Strong," *Lexington Herald-Leader* (Kentucky) (22 September 2003).

12. Tom Tom Club, "History," www.tomtomclub.com/history.html.

13. David Bowman, "No One Knew What Held the Talking Heads Together," *Toronto Star* (6 December 2003).

14. Gilmore, "Psychodramas You Can Dance To," *Rolling Stone* 305 (1979): 23.

15. Legs McNeil, *Please Kill Me*, ed. Legs McNeil and Gillian McCain (New York: Penguin, 1997), 256.

16. Tina Weymouth, "My Bass Buddhas," *Bass Player* (January 2004): 112.

CHAPTER 4

LORNA DOOM AND NICOLE PANTER

1. Pleasant Gehman, liner notes for *We're Desperate*, various artists. Rhino R271176, 1993.

2. Pat Smear, *Lexicon Devil* ed. Brendan Mullen, Don Bolles, and Adam Parfrey (Los Angeles: Feral House, 2002), 46.

3. Ibid., 43.

4. Ibid.

5. Pat Smear, *We Got the Neutron Bomb* ed. Marc Spitz and Brendan Mullen (New York: Three Rivers Press, 2001), 108.

6. Nicole Panter, interview by the author, 9 September 2003.

7. Ibid.

8. Ibid.

9. Mullen, Bolles, and Parfrey, *Lexicon Devil*, 171.

10. Don Bolles, *Lexicon Devil*, ed. Mullen, Bolles, and Parfrey, 171.

11. *The Decline of Western Civilization*, directed by Penelope Spheeris (Nu-Image Film, 1980).

12. Mullen, Bolles, and Parfrey, *Lexicon Devil*, 293.

13. Ibid., 293.

CHAPTER 5

DEBBIE HARRY

1. Roy Cohn, "Blondie Cometh," *New Musical Express* (13 November 1976): 9.

2. Brian Harrigan, "Seeds, Doors, Giant Ants, and Blondie," *Melody Maker* (28 May 1977): 46.

3. Cohn, "Blondie Cometh," 9.

4. Toby Goldstein, "Blondie: High School Never Ends!," *Creem* 8, no. 12. (1977): 73.

5. Ibid.

6. Jon Tiven, "Blondie Was a Group: An Appreciation," liner notes for *The Platinum Collection, Blondie*. EMI/Chrysalis F2 31100, 1994.

7. Harrigan, "Seeds, Doors, Giant Ants, and Blondie," 46.

8. Miles, "Sex Kitten Sharpens Claws, Headline Writer Blunts Brain," *New Musical Express* (16 April 1977): 43.

9. Roy Carr, "Male Chauvinist Pigs' Corner Episodes 2 & 3: Listen Honey, I Can Make You a Star," *New Musical Express* (9 April 1977): 25.

10. ———, "Return of the Teen Nymphette," *New Musical Express* (19 February 1977): 35.

11. ———, "Blondie Cometh: The Sensuous Pout from CBGB," *New Musical Express* (13 November 1976): 9.

12. "Blondie Bombshell," Melody Maker (4 February 1978): 4.

13. Deborah Harry, "Blondie on Blondie," by Harry Doherty, *Melody Maker* (4 March 1978): 10.

CHAPTER 6

EXENE CERVENKA

1. Marc Spitz and Brendan Mullen, ed., *We Got the Neutron Bomb* (New York: Three Rivers Press, 2001), 97.

2. Ibid.

3. Ibid., 123.

4. Kristine McKenna, liner notes for *Wild Gift*, X. Slash SR-107, 1981; Slash/Rhino R2 74371, 2001.

5. ———, liner notes for *Los Angeles*, X. Slash SR-104, 1980; Rhino R274370, 2001.

6. Kara Moloney, "Post-Punk Women," *Mother Jones* 15, issue 7 (1990): 14.

7. Lydia Lunch, interview by the author, July 2004.

8. Exene Cervenka, *Search and Destroy #7–11: The Complete Reprint*, ed. V. Vale (San Francisco: Bel Search, 1997), 94–95; original emphasis, ellipses.

9. Amy Philips, "Exene Cervenka," *Furious*, September 2002, www.furious.com/perfect/exene.html.

CHAPTER 7

PENELOPE HOUSTON

1. Richie Unterberger, "Penelope Houston Interview," www.richieunterberger.com/houston.html.

2. Penelope Houston, interview by the author, 25 September 2003.

3. Jonathan Krop, "Penelope Houston: Purity of Intention," *Rockrgrl* (May/June 1995): 11.

4. Houston, interview, 2003.

5. Ibid.

6. Ibid.

7. Houston, interview, 2003.

8. Unterberger, "Penelope Houston Interview."

9. Greil Marcus, "Avenging the Past," *Interview* (May 1999).

CHAPTER 8

POISON IVY

1. Frank Reese, "The Cramps: An Interview with Lux Interior and Poison Ivy," *Stain*, 2000, www.stainmagazine.com/cramps.html.

2. Poison Ivy, *We Got the Neutron Bomb* ed. Marc Spitz and Brendan Mullen (New York: Three Rivers Press, 2001), 175.

3. Jas Obrecht, "Oooh! Poison Ivy: Cramps Vamp Talks Guitar," *Guitar Player* (August 1980), www.phnet.fi/public/godmonster/Cramps/poison.html.

4. Robert Gordon, "Cramps," *Spin* 6, no. 5 (1990): 55.

5. Cynthia Rose, "The Cramps in Conversation," www.state51.co.uk/hottips/crampsconv. html.

6. Miles Copeland, *We Got the Neutron Bomb*, ed. Spitz and Mullen, 175.

7. Blackhawk, "Cramps," ed., V. Vale, *Search and Destroy #7–11: The Complete Reprint* (San Francisco: Re/Search, 1997), 36.

8. Obrecht, "Oooh! Poison Ivy."

9. The Cramps' official bio, Epitaph Records.

PART II

BRITAIN IN THE 1970S

1. Crass, "Dry Weather," *Penis Envy*, Crass 321984, 1981.

2. Frank Oglesbee, "Suzi Quatro: A Prototype in the Archsheology of Rock," *Popular Music and Society* 23, no. 2 (1999): 29.

3. Ibid.

4. Mark Perry, *Sniffin' Glue: The Essential Punk Accessory* (England: Sanctuary Publishing, 2000), 5.

5. Oglesbee, "Suzi Quatro," 29.

6. Jon Savage, *England's Dreaming* (New York: St. Martin's Griffin, 2002), 496.

7. Chrissie Hynde, "Chrissie Hynde's Advice to Chick Rockers on How I Did It," reprinted on the Pretenders' "Night in My Veins" promotional single, Sire, 1994.

8. Savage, *England's Dreaming*, 241.

9. Ibid., 45–57.

10. Mark Paytress, *Siouxsie and the Banshees: The Authorised Biography* (London: Sanctuary Books: 2003), 39.

11. George Gimarc, *Punk Diary: 1970–1977* (New York: St. Martin's Press, 1994), 36–37.

12. Savage, *England's Dreaming*, 264.

13. Ari-Up, interview by the author, 29 October 2003.

14. Tom Forester, *The British Labour Party and the Working Class*, 31 (New York: Holmes & Meier, 1976), 31.

15. BBC Online, "BBC History: Strikes, Unemployment, and the Winter of Discontent 1978–1979," www.bbc.co.uk/history/timelines/england/pwar_strikes_winter_ discontent.shtml

16. Martin Pugh, *Women and the Women's Movement in Britain, 1914–1959* (New York: St. Martin's Press, 2000), 329.

17. Susan Brownmiller, *In Our Time: Memoir of a Revolution* (New York: Dial Press, 1999), 259.

18. Ibid.

19. Paytress, *Siouxsie and the Banshees*, 59.

20. Penny Rimbaud, *Shibboleth: My Revolting Life* (San Francisco: AK Press, 1998), 79.

21. Simon Reynolds and Joy Press, *The Sex Revolts: Gender, Rebellion and Rock 'n' Roll* (Cambridge: Harvard University Press, 1995), 67.

22. Savage, *England's Dreaming*, 310.

23. Ibid., 310–311.

24. Malcolm McLaren, *Please Kill Me*, ed. Legs McNeil and Gillian McCain (New York: Penguin, 1997), 264.

25. Perry, *Sniffin' Glue*, issue 1.

26. Ibid, issue 4, 2.

27. Savage, *England's Dreaming*, 332.

28. Perry, *Sniffin' Glue*, 38.

29. Paytress, *Siouxsie and the Banshees*, 32.

30. Savage, *England's Dreaming*, 102.

31. Ibid., 159.

32. Ibid., 124.

33. Paul Fryer, "Everybody's on Top of the Pops: Popular Music on British Television," *Popular Music and Society* 21, issue 3 (1997): 153.

34. Ibid.

35. Ibid.

36. Savage, 252.

37. Savage, *England's Dreaming*, 304.

38. Ibid., 255.

39. Ibid,. 256.

40. Ibid, 259.

41. Ari-Up, interview by the author, 29 October 2003.

CHAPTER 9

SIOUXSIE SIOUX

1. Gillian G. Gaar, *She's a Rebel* (New York: Seal Press, 2002), 202.

2. Stud Brothers, "Kiss of the Spider Woman," *Melody Maker* (11 May 1991): 30.

3. Jaan Uhelski, "Black Is Beautiful," *Women Who Rock* (January/February 2004), www.utiedundone.com/013104.html.

4. *Punk 77*, www.punk77.co.uk/groups/banshees.htm.

5. Mark Paytress, *Siouxsie and the Banshees* (London: Sanctuary Books, 2003), 133.

6. Uhelski, *"Black Is Beautiful."*

7. Paytress, *Siouxsie and the Banshees*, 23.

8. Ibid., 27.

9. Dave Simpson and Will Hodgkinson, "Punk: How Was It for You?," *The Guardian Unlimited* (10 August 2001), www.guardian.co.uk/friday_review/story/0,3605,534365,00.html.

10. Paytress, *Siouxsie and the Banshees*, 51.

11. Jon Savage, *England's Dreaming* (New York: St. Martin's Griffin, 2002), 219.

12. Charles Shaar Murray, "Sex Pistols: Screen on the Green," *New Musical Express* (11 September 1976): 41, original emphasis.

13. Simpson and Hodgkinson, "Punk: How Was It for You?"

14. Ibid.

15. Savage, *England's Dreaming*, 259.

16. Paytress, *Siouxsie and the Banshees*, 72.

17. Uhelski, "Black Is Beautiful."

CHAPTER 10

THE SLITS

1. Ari-Up, interview by the author, 29 October 2003.

2. Paloma McLardy, interview by the author, 13 January 2004.

3. Ari-Up, interview, 2003.

4. Mike Appelstein, "Interview with Palmolive," N-Stop, www.nstop.com/paloma/intervw.html.

5. Ari-Up, interview, 2003.

6. According to Palmolive, Ari-Up joined the band prior to Korus.

7. McLardy, interview, 2004.

8. Gregory Mario Whitfield, "Earthbeat: In the Beginning There Was Rhythm," *3AM Magazine* (November 2003), www.3ammagazine.com/musicarchives/2003/nov/interview_tessa_pollitt.html.

9. Ari-Up, interview, 2003.

10. Ibid.

11. Ari-Up, interview, 2003.

12. Ibid.

13. Bruce Smith, interview by the author, 8 December 2003.

14. McLardy, interview, 2004.

15. Mark Paytress, liner notes for *Cut*, The Slits. Island, 1979; Universal UICY-3232, 2000.

16. Ari-Up, interview, 2003.

17. Paytress, liner notes, *Cut*.

18. Smith, interview, 2003.

19. Ari-Up, interview, 2003.

20. Ibid.

21. Ibid.

CHAPTER 11

LORA LOGIC AND POLY STYRENE

1. Jon Savage, *England's Dreaming* (New York: St. Martin's Griffin, 2002), 327.

2. Ibid., 325.

3. Ibid., 326.

4. Lora Logic, interview by the author, November 2003.

5. Savage, *England's Dreaming*, 326.

6. Ibid.

7. Ibid.

8. Dave Simpson and Will Hodgkinson, "Punk: How Was It for You?," *The Guardian Unlimited* (10 August 2001), www.guardian.co.uk/friday_review/story/0,3605,534365,00.html.

9. Logic, interview, 2003.

10. Ed., "The 50 Most Essential Punk Records," *Spin* 17, no.5 (2001): 108–112.

11. Logic, interview, 2003.

12. *Punk 77*, www.punk77.co.uk/wip/polystyrene.html.

13. Savage, *England's Dreaming*, 495; Mark Paytress, liner notes for *The Anthology*, X-Ray Spex. Castle/Sanctuary CMDDD369, 2001.

14. X-Ray Spex, *The Anthology*, Castle/Sanctuary CMDDD369, 2001.

15. Logic, interview, 2003.

16. Ibid.

17. Ibid.

18. Greil Marcus, *In the Fascist Bathroom: Punk in Pop Music, 1977–1992* (Cambridge: Harvard University Press, 1999), 55–56.

19. Logic, interview, 2003.

20. Jason Gross, "Logically Essential," *Venus* no. 14 (2002).

CHAPTER 12

JOY DE VIVRE AND EVE LIBERTINE

1. Crass, *Love Songs* (Britain: Pomona, 2004), xix.

2. Crass, *The Feeding of the 5000*, Crass 621984, 1978.

3. Penny Rimbaud, *Shibboleth* (San Francisco: AK Press, 1998), 99.

4. Eve Libertine, letter to the author, 2004.

5. Joy de Vivre, letter to the author, 2004.

6. Libertine, letter, 2004.

7. De Vivre, letter, 2004.

8. Ibid.

9. Ibid.

10. Ruth Schwartz, "Crass," *Maximumrocknroll* 9 (1983).

11. De Vivre, letter to the author, 2004.

12. Crass, *The Feeding of the 5000*, 1978.

13. Ibid.

14. Rimbaud, *Shibboleth*, 127.

15. Libertine, letter, 2004.

16. De Vivre, letter, 2004.

17. Rimbaud, *Shibboleth*, 129.

18. Phil Free and Joy de Vivre, *Love Songs*, 138.

19. De Vivre, letter, 2004.

20. Libertine, letter, 2004.

21. Crass, liner notes for *Best Before*. Crass 5, 1986.

22. Libertine, letter, 2004.

23. De Vivre, letter, 2004.

24. Crass, *Best Before*, Crass 5, 1984.

CHAPTER 13

THE RAINCOATS

1. Artist Direct Indie Showcase, "The Raincoats," www.artistdirect.com/showcase//indie/raincoats.html.

2. Michael Appelstein, "How I Discovered Music," *Caught in Flux* 3, www.applestein.com/cif/interviews3.html.

3. Richie Unterberger, "Gina Birch," 12 December 1996, www.richieunterberger .com/birch.html.

4. Paloma McLardy, interview by the author, January 2004.

5. Unterberger, "Gina Birch."

6. Artist Direct, "The Raincoats."

7. McLardy, interview, 2004.

8. Ibid.

9. Kurt Cobain, liner notes for *Incesticide*, Nirvana. Geffen Records DGCD-24504, 1992.

10. Charles Taylor, "Natural One," *The Boston Phoenix*, 6 July 1998, www.weeklywire.com/ww/07-06-98/boston_music.html.

11. Greil Marcus, *In the Fascist Bathroom* (Cambridge: Harvard University Press, 1999), 113.

12. David Sprague, "DGC's Raincoats Prove Impermeable to Time," *Billboard* 108, issue 14 (1996): 18.

PART III

THE 1980S

1. Eagle Forum website, www.eagleforum.org.

2. Susan Faludi, *Backlash* (New York: Crown, 1991), 247.

3. Concerned Women for America, www.cwfa.org/history.asp.

4. Faludi, *Backlash*, 93.

5. Ibid., 170.

6. Ibid., 169-199.

7. Ibid., 100.

8. Ibid., 106.

9. Larry Starr and Christopher Waterman, *American Popular Music* (New York: Oxford University Press, 2003), 388–389.

10. Mikal Gilmore, "Bruce Springsteen," *Rolling Stone* 591 (1990).

11. Jay Cocks, "Rock Is a Four-Letter Word; A Senate Committee Asks: 'Have Lyrics Gone Too Far?,'" *Time* 126 (1985): 70.

12. W.A. Henry III, "Are Artists Godless Perverts?," *Time* 136, issue 11 (1990): 81.

13. Starr and Waterman, *American Popular Music*, 371.

14. Gillian G. Gaar, *She's a Rebel* (New York: Seal Press, 2002), 259.

15. Ibid., 260.

16. Greg Shaw, *We Got the Neutron Bomb*, ed. Marc Spitz and Brendan Mullen (New York: Three Rivers Press, 2001), 178.

17. Gaar, *She's a Rebel*, 261.

18. Naomi Wolf, *The Beauty Myth: How Images of Beauty Are Used Against Women* (New York: Anchor, 1992), 164.

19. John Skow, "Madonna Rocks the Land: Sassy, Brassy, and Beguiling, She Laughs Her Way to Fame," *Time* 125 (1985): 74.

20. Gaar, *She's a Rebel*, 266.

21. Jay Cocks, "These Big Girls Don't Cry," *Time* (4 March 1985): 74.

22. Ibid.

23. Jim Miller, "Rock's New Women," *Newsweek* 105, issue 9 (1985): 49.

24. Gaar, *She's a Rebel*, 266.

25. Cocks, "These Big Girls Don't Cry," 74.

26. Skow, "Madonna Rocks," 74.

27. Jon Savage, *England's Dreaming* (New York: St. Martin's Griffin, 2002), 295.

28. Ellis Conklin, "Is It Time to Consider 'De-punking and De-metalizing' Some Teens?," *San Francisco Examiner* (19 May 1985): B4.

29. X, *Wild Gift*, Rhino R274371, 2001. Original release, Slash SR-107, 1981.

30. Spitz and Mullen, *We Got the Neutron Bomb*, 196.

31. Ibid., 223.

32. Ibid., 222.

33. Penelope Houston, interview by the author, 25 September 2003.

34. Michael Azerrad, *Our Band Could Be Your Life* (Boston: Back Bay Books, 2002), 152.

35. Ibid., 141.

36. Lee Ving, *The Decline of Western Civilization*, directed by Penelope Spheeris (Nu-Image Film, 1980).

37. Azerrad, *Our Band Could Be Your Life*, 325.

38. Lynn Breedlove, interview by the author, October 2003.

39. Donna Dresch, *Rock She Wrote*, ed. Evelyn McDonnell and Ann Powers (New York: Delta, 1995), 74, original emphasis.

40. *Maximumrocknroll*, "Frightwig: Humans Making Noise!," *Maximumrocknroll* 23 (1985).

41. ———, "Gang Mentality," *Maximumrocknroll* 18 (1984).

CHAPTER 14
LYDIA LUNCH

1. Lydia Lunch, letter to the author, July 2004.

2. Alec Foege, *Confusion Is Next: The Sonic Youth Story* (New York: St. Martin's Press, 1994), 31.

3. Lunch, letter, 2004.

4. Jeremy Dean, "Lydia Lunch Interview, 1996," freespace.virgin.net/questing.beast/ llscrawl2.html.

5. Lunch, letter, 2004.

6. Dean, "Lydia Lunch Interview."

7. Theresa Stern, "Lydia Lunch," *Furious*, October 1997, www.furious.com/perfect/ lydialunch.html.

8. Lunch, letter, 2004.

9. Lydia Lunch, "Lydia Lunch," *Scrawl*, Summer 1997, www.scrawlmagazine.com/ lydialunch.html, original emphasis.

10. Lydia Lunch, *Crimes Against Nature*, Atavistic 114, 1999.

11. Stern, "Lydia Lunch."

CHAPTER 15
WENDY O. WILLIAMS

1. Rod Swenson, interview by the author, 14 April 2004.

2. Ibid.

3. Ibid.

4. Ibid.

5. Wendy O. Williams, unidentified television interview.

6. Ibid.

7. Courtesy of Rod Swenson.

8. Ibid.

9. Swenson, interview, 2004.

10. Ibid.

11. Ibid.

CHAPTER 16

KIM GORDON

1. Kim Gordon, "Boys Are Smelly," *Village Voice*, 12–18 October 1988, www.villagevoice. com/issues8842/gordon.php.

2. Carla DeSantis, "Kim Gordon: Sonic Warrior," *Rockrgrl* (March/April 2000): 23.

3. Michael Azerrad, *Our Band Could Be Your Life* (Boston: Back Bay Books, 2002), 240.

4. Kim Gordon, "Kim Gordon in Her Own Words," *Women, Sex, and Rock and Roll,* ed. Liz Evans (London: Pandora, 1994), 173.

5. Gordon, "Boys Are Smelly."

6. Azerrad, *Our Band Could Be Your Life,* 237.

7. David Browne, "Sonic Youth," *Entertainment Weekly* 699 (2003): 7.

8. Byron Coley and Jimmy Johnson, "Feelin' Up the Man Tit with Sonic Youth," *Forced Exposure* 7/8 (1985): 15.

9. Alec Foege, *Confusion Is Next* (New York: St. Martin's Press, 1994), 191.

10. Foege, *Confusion Is Next,* 191.

11. Sonic Youth, *Dirty*, Geffen 24485, 1992.

CHAPTER 17

KIM WARNICK AND LULU GARGIULO

1. Kathleen Wilson, "Set Me Free: Kim Warnick Says Goodbye to the Fastbacks," *The Stranger* 11, no. 22 (2002), www.thestranger.com/2002-02-14/music.html.

2. Lulu Gargiulo, interview by the author, 25 February 2004.

3. Ibid.

4. Ibid.

5. Ibid.

6. Evelyn McDonnell, review of *Zücker, Rolling Stone* 655 (1993): 63.

7. Gargiulo, interview, 2004.

8. Jon Cooper, "Up to Speed: Kurt Bloch and Kim Warnick," *Chin Music!* #4, www. chinmusic.net/fastbacks.html.

9. Wilson, "Set Me Free."

10. Gargiulo, interview, 2004.

CHAPTER 18

KIM DEAL

1. Karen Schoemer, "A Breed Apart," *Rolling Stone* 682 (1994): 88.

2. Helen Dalley, "Pixies," *Total Guitar* 58 (1999): 26.

3. Ibid.

4. Maddy Costa, "The Addict Family," *The Guardian Unlimited* (10 May 2002): 6.

5. Dalley, "Pixies," 27.

6. Marc Spitz, "Life to the Pixies," *Spin* 20, no. 9 (2004): 72.

7. Charles Aaron, "Raw Deal," *Spin* 11, no. 4 (1995): 41.

8. Ibid.," 40.

PART IV

THE 1990S

1. Ira Robbins, "The Alternative Underground," *Rolling Stone* 615 (1991): 20.

2. Michael Azerrad, *Our Band Could Be Your Life* (Boston: Back Bay Books, 2001), 487.

3. Ibid., 488.

4. Mark Andersen and Mark Jenkins, *Dance of Days: Two Decades of Punk in the Nation's Capital* (New York: Akashic Books, 2003): 321.

5. Ibid., 93.

6. Ibid., 94.

7. Ibid., 208.

8. Ibid., 259.

9. Jenny Toomey, interview by the author, 13 April 2004.

10. Azerrad, *Our Band Could Be Your Life*, 437.

11. Allison Wolfe, interview by the author, 10 January 2004.

12. Joe Ambrose, *Moshpit: The Violent World of Mosh Pit Culture* (New York: Omnibus Press, 2001), 53.

13. Ibid., 54, original emphasis.

14. Jennifer Baumgardner, "Kathleen Hanna's Eye of Le Tigre," *Rockrgrl* 36 (2000): 26.

15. Toomey, interview, 2004.

16. Kathleen Hanna, "Riot Grrrl Manifesto," reprinted in *Discorder: That Online Magazine from CiTR 101.9 FM*, www.ams.ubc.ca/citr/discorder/archive/2003-03/riot.html, original emphasis.

17. Andersen and Jenkins, *Dance of Days*, 336.

18. Wolfe, interview, 2004.

19. Leslie Mah, interview by the author, 17 November 2003.

20. Jim DeRogatis, *Milk It!: Collected Musings on the Alternative Music Explosion of the '90s* (Massachusetts: Da Capo Press, 2003), 110.

21. David Browne, "Go On, Grrrls," *Entertainment Weekly* 207 (1994).

22. Kim France, "Grrrls at War," *Rolling Stone* 660/661 (1993).

23. Farai Chideya and Melissa Rossi, "Revolution, Girl Style," *Newsweek* 120, no. 21 (1992): 85.

24. Ibid., 84.

25. Ibid.

26. Wolfe, interview, 2004.

CHAPTER 19

MIA ZAPATA

1. The Gits, *Enter: The Conquering Chicken*, C/Z CZ076, 1994; Broken Rekids Skip 106, 2003.

2. Steve Moriarty, interview by the author, 9 October 2003.

3. Ibid.

4. Peter Sheehy, liner notes for *Kings and Queens*, the Gits, Broken Rekids Skip 44, 2003.

5. Moriarty, interview, 2003.

6. The Gits, *Frenching the Bully*, C/Z CZ051, 1992; Broken Rekids Skip 103, 2003. [The actual lyric is "I tear myself apart and throw..."]

7. Moriarty, interview, 2003.

8. Ibid.

9. Emily White, "Dead Again," *Spin* 11, no. 5 (1995): 49.

10. Moriarty, interview, 2003.

11. The Gits, *Enter: The Conquering Chicken,* 2003.

12. Moriarty, interview, 2003.

13. The Gits, *Enter: The Conquering Chicken,* 2003; Joan Jett Official Website, www.joanjett.com.

14. Moriarty, interview, 2003.

CHAPTER 20

JENNY TOOMEY

1. Jenny Toomey, interview by the author, 13 April 2004.

2. Ibid.

3. Ibid.

4. Ibid.

5. Ibid.

6. Mike DeBonis, "The Future of Music Is Now," *Georgetown Voice*, 14 November 2002, www.georgetownvoice.com/news/2002/11/14/Cover/The-Future.Of.Music.Is.Now-322816.shtml.

7. Toomey, interview, 2004.

8. Jenny Toomey, *Antidote*, Misra MSR 010, 2001.

9. Jill Pesselnick, "Misra's Jenny Toomey Finds 'Antidote' for Pain," *Billboard* 113, no. 38 (2001): 11.

10. Toomey, interview, 2004.

11. Ibid.

12. Kristin Thomson and Jenny Toomey, "The Simple Machines Story," Simple Machines, www.simplemachines.net/story.html.

13. Toomey, interview, 2004.

14. Ibid.

CHAPTER 21
HOLE

1. Katherine Dunn and Peggy Sirota, "Courtney Love," *Rolling Stone* 773 (1997): 164.

2. Craig Marks, "Endless Love," *Spin* 10, no. 11 (1995): 47.

3. Pamela Des Barres, "Rock 'n' Roll Needs Courtney Love," in *Rock She Wrote,* ed. Evelyn McDonnell and Ann Powers (New York: Delta, 1995), 204.

4. David Goldman, "From Stripper to Singer to Star," *Biography* 1, no. 10 (1997): 66.

5. Ibid.

6. Des Barres, "Rock 'n' Roll Needs Courtney Love," 201.

7. Hole, *Live Through This,* Geffen DIDX 021847, 1994.

8. Goldman, "From Stripper to Singer to Star," 2004.

9. Des Barres, "Rock 'n' Roll Needs Courtney Love," 205.

10. Kurt Cobain, liner notes for *Incesticide,* reprinted on Digital Nirvana, www.digitalnirvana.net/discography/nirvana/incesticide_note.asp.

11. David Ansen, "'Bad' Courtney Is Back," *Newsweek* 131, no. 5 (1998): 60.

12. Marks, "Endless Love," 45.

13. Dunn and Sirota, "Courtney Love," 164.

14. Ibid.

15. Susan Hopkins, "Hole Lotta Attitude," *Social Alternatives* 18, no. 2 (1999): 11.

CHAPTER 22
L7

1. Daina Darzin, "Ah, the Smell of It: L7 Bask in the Sweet Stink of Success," *Rolling Stone* 688 (1994): 25–26.

2. Nsid Hajari, "Women on the Verge," *Entertainment Weekly* 236 (1994): 60.

3. Lorraine Ali, "Banding Together," *Rolling Stone* 692 (1994): 55.

4. Ibid.

5. Mah Sioman, "Livin' Large: L7 Gets Slap Happy with a New Album and a National Tour," *Synthesis,* www.thesynthesis.com/music/feature.php?bid=253.

6. Ibid.

7. Stuart Barr, "L7," www.obsolete.com/convulsion/interviews/convulse/frames.hmtl.

CHAPTER 23
TRIBE 8

1. *Rise Above: The Tribe 8 Documentary,* directed by Tracy Flannigan (Los Angeles: Red Hill Pictures, 2003).

2. Lynn Breedlove, interview by the author, 2 October 2003.

3. Leslie Mah, interview by the author, 17 November 2003.

4. Ibid.

5. Breedlove, interview, 2003.

6. Ibid.

7. Ibid.

8. Mah, interview, 2003.

9. Breedlove, interview, 2003.

10. Breedlove, interview, 2003.

11. Trish Deitch Rohrer, "Making Herself Heard," *The Advocate* (28 May 2002), www.theadvocate.com/html/books/864_breedlove.asp.

12. Tribe 8, *Role Models for Amerika*, Alternative Tentacles Virus 212CD, 1998.

13. Flannigan, *Rise Above*, 2003.

14. Gregg Shapiro, "The Next Chapter: An Interview with Lynn Breedlove," *Windy City Times*, 24 April 2002.

15. Flannigan, *Rise Above,* 2003.

16. Mah, interview, 2003.

17. Breedlove, interview, 2003.

18. Mah, interview, 2003.

19. Todd Wiese, "Tribe 8 Interview," *The Roc*, www.theroc.org/roc-mag/textarch/roc-18/roc18-08.htm.

CHAPTER 24
LUNACHICKS

1. Theo Kogan, interview by the author, 14 January 2004.

2. Ibid.

3. Gina Volpe, interview by the author, 29 December 2003.

4. Ibid.

5. Kogan, interview, 2004.

6. Volpe, interview, 2003.

7. Ibid.

8. Kogan, interview, 2004.

9. Volpe, interview, 2003.

10. Ibid.

11. Volpe, interview, 2003.

12. Ibid.

13. Ibid.

14. David Grad, "Lunachicks: Femmes Vitales," *Alternative Press* 88 (1995), www.altpress.com/sections/basement/10-25-1999/story.asp?story=1.

15. Volpe, interview, 2003.

CHAPTER 25
PJ HARVEY

1. David Cavanaugh, "Dark Star," *Q* (December 2001), original ellipses.

2. Robert Christgau, "The Ballad of PJ Harvey," *Spin* 11, no. 2 (1995): 52.

3. Charles Aaron, "Artist of the Year: PJ Harvey," *Spin* 11, no. 10 (1996): 58.

4. Kerry Lengel, "Inspired by Men, PJ's Her Own Woman," *Arizona Republic* (22 April 2001): E3.

5. Victoria Segal, "PJ Harvey, "Re-Introducing PJ Harvey," *New Musical Express* (October 2000).

6. Bill Wyman and David Antrobus, "PJ Harvey," *Trouser Press*, www.trouserpress.com/entry_90s.php?a=pj_harvey.

7. Leagues O'Toole, "PJ Harvey," *Muse* (2001), www.muse.ie/101100/interview/harvey.html.

8. Aaron, "Artist of the Year," 59.

9. Ibid.

10. Iain Shedden, "Pretty Polly," *The Weekend Australian* (13 January 2001): R14.

11. Ed Gonzalez, "PJ Harvey: Live in New York," *Slant Magazine* (2001), www.slantmagazine.com/music/features/pjharvey.html.

12. Segal, "Re-Introducing PJ Harvey."

CHAPTER 26
BIKINI KILL

1. Bikini Kill, *The CD Version of the First Two Records*, Kill Rock Stars KRS 204, 1994.

2. Mark Andersen and Mark Jenkins, *Jigsaw* excerpt reprinted in *Dance of Days* (New York: Akashic Books, 2001), 308.

3. Daniel Sinker, *We Owe You Nothing: Punk Planet: The Collected Interviews* (New York: Akashic Books, 2001), 60.

4. Andersen and Jenkins, *Dance of Days*, 331.

5. Ibid., 360–361.

6. Gillian G. Gaar, *She's a Rebel* (New York: Seal Press, 2002), 378.

7. Andersen and Jenkins, *Dance of Days*, 308.

8. Emily White, "Revolution Girl Style Now," in *Rock She Wrote*, ed. Evelyn McDonnell and Ann Powers (New York: Delta, 1995), 406. Originally published in *L.A. Weekly* (10–16 July 1992).

9. Andersen and Jenkins, *Dance of Days*, 318.

10. Kathleen Hanna, "Kathleen's Herstory," Le Tigre, letigreworld.com/sweepstakes/html_site/fact/khfacts.html.

11. Sinker, *We Owe You Nothing*, 63.

12. Tobi Vail, liner notes for *The CD Version of the First Two Records*, original ellipses.

13. Ibid. Original emphasis, original ellipses.

14. Bikini Kill, *The CD Version*, 1994.

15. Ibid.

16. Ibid.

17. Ibid. Original emphasis.

CHAPTER 27
BRATMOBILE

1. Allison Wolfe, interview by the author, 10 January 2004.

2. Ibid.

3. Ibid.

4. Ibid.

5. Mark Andersen and Mark Jenkins, *Jigsaw* excerpt reprinted in *Dance of Days* (New York: Akashic Books, 2003), 308.

6. Beth Fell, "Interview with Molly from Bratmobile," *Tablet*, www.tabletnewspaper.com/old%20tablet/vol2iss_13/webmolly.html.

7. Jessica Hopper, "Interview with Bratmobile," *Punk Planet* (spring 1999), www.killrockstars.com/bands/bratmobile/press/index.html.

8. Bratmobile, *Girls Get Busy*, Lookout! LK280CD, 2002.

9. Bratmobile, *Ladies, Women and Girls*, Lookout! LK252CD, 2000.

10. Jennifer O'Connor, "Getting Busy with Bratmobile," Knitting Factory (2002), www.knittingfactory.com/articles/bratmobile.cfm.

CHAPTER 28
TEAM DRESCH

1. Joel Schalit, "Jody Bleyle," in *We Owe You Nothing*, ed. Daniel Sinker (New York: Akashic Books, 2001), 229.

2. Experience Music Project, "Donna Dresch," www.experience.org/archives/index.asp?section=intv&id=97&pg1.

3. Chaia Milstein, "Beaucoup Marci," *Drummergirl* (2001), www.drummergirl.com/interviews/martinez.html.

4. Kaia Wilson, interview by the author, 2004.

5. Ibid.

6. Experience Music Project, "Donna Dresch."

7. Gillian G. Gaar, *She's a Rebel* (New York: Seal Press, 2002), 428.

8. Jody Bleyle, "Team Dresch," *Punk Rock Academy*, www.punkrockacademy.com/stm/int/dresch.html.

9. Schalit, "Jody Bleyle," 225.

10. Team Dresch, *Captain My Captain,* Chainsaw/Candy-Ass, 1996.

11. Kaia Wilson, "Remember Who They Are," *Seattle Weekly*, 28 July–3 August 2004.

12. Team Dresch, *Captain My Captain*, 1996.

13. Bleyle, *Punk Rock Academy*.

14. Team Dresch, *Captain My Captain*, 1996.

PART V
INTRODUCTION

1. Le Tigre, *Feminist Sweepstakes*, Mr. Lady, 2001.

2. Christopher John Farley, "Galapalooza!," *Time* 150, no. 3 (1997).

3. Jen Salvato, "Rockin', Ragin', and Female," *Cosmopolitan* 221, no. 6 (1996).

4. Ibid.

5. Sleater-Kinney, *Call the Doctor*, Chainsaw CHSW-13, 1996.

6. Ed.,"The Lilith Fair Showcases Female Musicians," *The News & Record* (17 July 1997): 5.

7. Farley, "Galapalooza!"

8. Lucy O'Brien, "The New Voices of Feminism: Rock Stars Stand Up as Role Models of Strength, Smarts, and Sexuality," *The Record* (5 January 1999).

9. *Rolling Stone,* "Women in Rock," *Rolling Stone* 908 (2002).

10. Beth Ditto, interview by the author, 3 November 2003.

11. Jenny Toomey, "Media Ownership: Statement of Jenny Toomey, Executive Director, Future of Music Coalition," FDCH Congressional Testimony to the Committee on Commerce, Science, and Transportation, 30 January 2003.

12. Johnny Temple, "Noise from Underground," *The Nation* 269, no. 12 (1999).

13. Roc-A-Fella Records, www.rocafella.com/artist.aspx?v=bio&key=1.

14. Andrew Dansby, "50 Cent Tops 2003," *Rolling Stone* (5 January 2004), www.rollingstone.com/news/story?id=5935283.

15. Limp Bizkit official website, www.limpbizkit.com/.

16. Kid Rock official website, www.kidrock.com/bio/bio_detail.asp?item_id=10&categoryid=87.

17. Zev Borow, "How to Succeed in Bizness . . . by Really, Really Trying," *Spin* 15, no. 8 (1999): 100.

18. Sacha Jenkins, "Pimpin' Ain't Easy." *Spin* 15, no. 10 (1999): 94, 96.

19. David Moodie and Maureen Callahan, "Don't Drink the Brown Water," *Spin* 15, no. 10 (1999): 103.

20. Ibid., 105.

21. Ibid., 114.

22. Ibid.

23. Tobi Vail, "From Rock Against Reagan, to Bands Against Bush," Bumpidee, www.bumpidee.com/From%20%20Rock%20Against%20Reagan.html.

24. Mike McKee, "Where Have All the Musicians Gone?," *Punk Planet* 54, (2003): 67.

25. Josh Frank, "Sleater-Kinney Rocks: Our Protest Songs Are Here," *CounterPunch* (9 November 2002), www.counterpunch.org/frank1109.html.

CHAPTER 29

SLEATER-KINNEY

1. Gillian G. Gaar, *She's a Rebel* (New York: Seal Press, 2002), 438.

2. "Janet Weiss," Experience Music Project, www.experience.org/archives/index.asp?section=intv&id=13&pg=1.

3. Joe Heim, "American Bandstand: Sleater-Kinney's Carrie Brownstein Talks About Politics, the President, and Simple Pop Songs," *Salon* (4 March 1999), www.salon.com/ent/music/feature/1999/03/04feature.html.

4. Curtis Ross, " Sleater-Kinney Backs Message With Meaningful Rock," *Tampa Tribune* (11 April 2003): 18.

5. Molly Wright Steenson, "Intensity and Hot Rock," *Maximag* (1999), www.maximag.com/imitate/sk.

6. Sleater-Kinney, *Call the Doctor*, Chainsaw *CHSW-13*, 1996.

7. Ibid.

8. Sleater-Kinney, *All Hands on the Bad One*, Kill Rock Stars KRS-360, 2000.

9. Kyle Ryan, "Sleater Kinney," *Punk Planet* 61 (2004): 39.

10. Sleater-Kinney, *One Beat*, Kill Rock Stars KRS-387, 2002.

CHAPTER 30

THE BUTCHIES

1. Gillian G. Gaar, *She's a Rebel* (New York: Seal Press, 2002), 429.

2. Kaia Wilson, "The Butchies in Search of World Domination," *Lesbian News* 29, no. 8 (2004): 24.

3. T.A. Gilmartin, "The Butchies Are Fightin' the Power," *Lesbian News* 26, no. 1 (2000): 42.

4. Kaia Wilson, interview by the author, 2004.

5. Ibid.

6. Vaginal Davis, "Femmes on Flames," *L.A. Weekly* (15–21 September 2000): www.laweekly.com/ink/00/43/music-davis.php.

7. Kaia Wilson, "The Butchies Tour Diary," 12 April 2004, www.thebutchies.com/diary.html.

CHAPTER 31
LE TIGRE

1. Le Tigre, "The The Empty," *Le Tigre*, Mr. Lady MRLR 07, 1999.

2. Jaime Buerger, "Le Tigre Dance to a Political Beat," *Las Vegas Weekly* (12 June 2003), www.lasvegasweekly.com/2003/06_12/music_noise1.html.

3. Ibid.

4. Daniel Sinker, "Kathleen Hanna," in *We Owe You Nothing* (New York: Akashic Books, 2001), 62.

5. JD Samson, "JD's Herstory," Le Tigre website, letigreworld.com/sweepstakes/html_site/fact.

6. Hannah Levin, "Torch Songs: Le Tigre Continue Carrying the Feminist Light," *The Stranger* 12, no. 39 (2003), www.thestranger.com2003-06-12/music3.html.

7. Jennifer Baumgardner, "Kathleen Hanna's Eye of Le Tigre," *Rockrgrl* 36 (2000): 26.

8. Le Tigre, *Feminist Sweepstakes*, Mr. Lady MRLR 19, 2001.

9. Le Tigre, *Le Tigre*, 1999.

CHAPTER 32
PEACHES

1. Dorian Lynskey, "Peaches, Fatherfucker," *The Guardian*, 12 September 2003: 16.

2. Michael Paoletta, "Peaches Seeks Equality on New Disc," *Billboard* 115, no. 36 (2003): 33.

3. Fred Sasaki, "The Teaches of Peaches," *Venus* 19.

4. Peaches, *Fatherfucker*, Kitty-Yo/XL XLCD171, 2003.

5. Ibid.

6. Neva Chonin, "Surging on the Scene: Electroclash Mixes Pop with Hip Fashion, Art," *San Francisco Chronicle*, 27 October 2002.

7. William Van Meter, "She's a Very Kinky Girl," *Spin* 19, no.2 (2003): 74.

8. Sasaki, "The Teaches of Peaches."

9. Kitty Empire, "Ripe for Stardom," *The Observer*, 17 August 2003.

10. Peaches, *Fatherfucker*, 2003.

CHAPTER 33
THE GOSSIP

1. Beth Ditto, interview by the author, 3 November 2003.

2. Kathy Mendonca, interview by the author, 3 November 2003.

3. Ditto, interview, 2003.

4. Mendonca, interview, 2003.

5. Ditto, interview, 2003.

6. Mendonca, interview, 2003.

7. Ditto, interview, 2003.

8. Mendonca, interview, 2003.

9. Ditto, interview, 2003.

CHAPTER 34
ERASE ERRATA

1. Sara Jaffe, interview by the author, 2004.

2. Jenny Tatone, "Erase Errata's Post–Riot Grrrl, Post-Feminist Post-Punk: The Bay Area Quartet Creates a New Kind of Noise," *NeuMu* (2001), www.neumu.com/inquisitive/erase_errata/erase_errata_02/shtml.

3. Jaffe, interview, 2004.

4. Tatone, "Erase Errata's Post–Riot Grrrl, Post-Feminist Post-Punk."

5. Laura Barcella, "Erase Errata," *Swingset* 2 (2002): 59.

6. Jaffe, interview, 2004.

7. Barcella, "Erase Errata."

8. Jessica Hopper, "Erase Errata," *Punk Planet* 61 (2004): 50, brackets added.

9. Ibid., 51.

BIBLIOGRAPHY

INTERVIEWS AND PERSONAL COMMUNICATION

Beech, Wes, 10 May 2004.
Breedlove, Lynn, 2 October 2003.
de Vivre, Joy, 2004.
Ditto, Beth, 3 November 2003.
Gargiulo, Lulu, 25 February 2004.
Houston, Penelope, 25 September 2003.
Jaffe, Sara, 2004.
Kogan, Theo, 14 January 2004.
Libertine, Eve, 2004.
Logic, Lora, November 2003.
Lunch, Lydia, July 2004.
Mah, Leslie, 17 November 2003.
McLardy, Paloma, 13 January 2004.
Mendonca, Kathy, 3 November 2003.
Moriarty, Steve, 9 October 2003.
Panter, Nicole, 9 September 2003.
Smith, Bruce, 8 December 2003.
Stotts, Richie, 3 March 2004.
Swenson, Rod, 14 April 2004.
Toomey, Jenny, 13 April 2004.
Ari-Up, 29 October 2003.
Volpe, Gina, 29 December 2003.
Wilson, Kaia, 2004.
Wolfe, Allison, 10 January 2004.

BOOKS

Ambrose, Joe. *Moshpit: The Violent World of Mosh Pit Culture*. New York: Omnibus Press, 2001.

Andersen, Mark, and Mark Jenkins. *Dance of Days: Two Decades of Punk in the Nation's Capital.* New York: Akashic Books, 2003.

Azerrad, Michael. *Our Band Could Be Your Life: Scenes from the American Indie Underground.* Boston: Back Bay Books, 2002.

Bangs, Lester. *Psychotic Reactions and Carburetor Dung.* Edited by Greil Marcus. New York: Anchor Books, 2003.

Bayton, Mavis. *Frock Rock: Women Performing Popular Music.* Oxford: Oxford University Press, 1998.

Bouchier, David. *The Feminist Challenge: The Movement for Women's Liberation in Britain and the USA.* London: MacMillan, 1983.

Breithaupt, Don, and Jeff Breithaupt. *Precious and Few: Pop Music in the Early Seventies.* New York: St. Martin's Griffin, 1996.

Brownmiller, Susan. *In Our Time: Memoir of a Revolution.* New York: Dial Press, 1999.

Caine, Barbara. "The Postwar World," chap. 6 in *English Feminism 1780–1980.* Oxford: Oxford University Press, 1997.

Cashmore, E. Ellis. *No Future: Youth and Society.* London: Heinemann, 1984.

Crass. *Love Songs.* Britain: Pomona Press, 2004.

Crompton, Rosemary. *Women and Work in Modern Britain.* Oxford: Oxford University Press, 1997.

Currie, Cherie, and Neal Shusterman. *Neon Angel: The Cherie Currie Story.* Los Angeles: Price Stern Sloan, 1989.

DeRogatis, Jim. *Milk It!: Collected Musings on the Alternative Music Explosion of the '90s.* Massachusetts: Da Capo Press, 2003.

Evans, Liz, ed. *Women, Sex, and Rock and Roll.* London: Pandora, 1994.

Faludi, Susan. *Backlash: The Undeclared War Against Women.* New York: Crown, 1991.

Foege, Alec. *Confusion Is Next: The Sonic Youth Story.* New York: St. Martin's Press, 1994.

Forester, Tom. *The British Labour Party and the Working Class.* New York: Holmes and Meier, 1976.

Gaar, Gillian G. *She's a Rebel: The History of Women in Rock & Roll.* New York: Seal Press, 2002.

Gimarc, George. *Punk Diary 1970–1979.* New York: St. Martin's Press, 1994.

LeBlanc, Lauraine. *Pretty in Punk: Girls' Gender Resistance in a Boys' Subculture.* New Jersey: Rutgers University Press, 1999.

Lunch, Lydia, and Exene Cervenka. *Adulterers Anonymous.* San Francisco: Last Gasp, 1996. Previously published by Evergreen, 1982.

Marcus, Greil. *In the Fascist Bathroom: Punk in Pop Music, 1977–1992.* Cambridge: Harvard University Press, 1999.

McAleer, Dave, ed. *The Warner Guide to UK & US Singles Charts.* London: Carlton/Little, Brown, 1994, 1996.

McDonnell, Evelyn, and Ann Powers, eds. *Rock She Wrote: Women Write About Rock, Pop, and Rap.* New York: Delta, 1995.

McNeil, Legs, and Gillian McCain, eds. *Please Kill Me: The Uncensored Oral History of Punk.* New York: Penguin, 1997.

McRobbie, Angela, and Simon Frith. "Rock and Sexuality," chap. 6 in *Feminism and Youth Culture*, 2nd ed. New York: Routledge, 2000.

Mullen, Brendan, Don Bolles, and Adam Parfrey, eds. *Lexicon Devil: The Fast Times and Short Life of Darby Crash and the Germs.* Los Angeles: Feral House, 2002.

Paglia, Camille. *Sex, Art, and American Culture.* New York: Vintage Books, 1992.

Paglia, Camille. "Madonna in the Shallows: Madonna's *Sex*," *Vamps and Tramps: New Essays.* New York: Vintage, 1994, 367–374. Previously published in *Us Weekly*, December 1992.

Paytress, Mark. *Siouxsie and the Banshees: The Authorised Biography.* London: Sanctuary Books, 2003.

Perry, Marc. *Sniffin' Glue: The Essential Punk Accessory.* England: Sanctuary Publishing, 2000.

Pugh, Martin. *Women and the Women's Movement in Britain 1914–1999*, 2nd ed. New York: St. Martin's Press, 2000.

Reynolds, Simon, and Joy Press. *The Sex Revolts: Gender, Rebellion and Rock 'n' Roll.* Cambridge: Harvard University Press, 1995.

Rimbaud, Penny. *Shibboleth: My Revolting Life.* San Francisco: AK Press, 1998.

Rolling Stone, ed. *The Best of Rolling Stone: 25 Years of Journalism on the Edge.* New York: Doubleday, 1993.

Savage, Jon. *England's Dreaming: Anarchy, Sex Pistols, Punk Rock, and Beyond.* New York: St. Martin's Griffin, 2002.

Sinker, Daniel, ed. *We Owe You Nothing: Punk Planet: The Collected Interviews.* New York: Akashic Books, 2001.

Smith, Patti. *Patti Smith Complete: Lyrics, Reflections, and Notes for the Future*. New York: Anchor Books, 1999.

Somerville, Jennifer. "The New Right: Anti-Feminism in Power?" chap. 5 in *Feminism and the Family: Politics and Society in the UK and the USA*. New York: St. Martin's Press, 2000.

Spitz, Marc, and Brendan Mullen, eds. *We Got the Neutron Bomb: The Untold Story of L.A. Punk*. New York: Three Rivers Press, 2001.

Starr, Larry, and Christopher Waterman. *American Popular Music: From Minstrelsy to MTV*. New York: Oxford University Press, 2003.

Vale, V., ed. *Search and Destroy #7–11: The Complete Reprint*: *The Authoritative Guide to Punk Culture*. San Francisco: Re/Search, 1997.

Whitburn, Joel. *Billboard Top 10 and Singles Charts, 1955–2000*. Wisconsin: Record Research, Inc., 2001.

Whitburn, Joel. *The Billboard Book of Top 40 Hits: Complete Chart Information About the Artists and Their Songs, 1955–2000*, 7th ed. New York: Billboard Books, 2000.

Wolf, Naomi. *The Beauty Myth: How Images of Beauty Are Used Against Women*. New York: Perennial, 2002.

ARTICLES AND SELECT LINER NOTES

Aaron, Charles. "Artist of the Year: PJ Harvey." *Spin*, January 1996.

Aaron, Charles. "Raw Deal." *Spin*, July 1995.

Adams, Sam. "Great Day for Up." *Philadelphia City Paper*, 14–21 February 2002. www.citypaper.net/articles/021402/mus.ariup.shtml.

Aitch, Iain. "Country House Anarchy." Originally published in *The Guardian*, 5 January 2001.

Ajeman, Jerry. "Jerry Falwell Spreads the Word: The Fundamentalist Leader Wages Political War on Immorality." *Time*, 2 September 1985.

Alarcon, Michael. "Interview with Lux and Ivy of The Cramps: The Devil Makes 'Em Do It." Originally published on OCNow.com, 12 October 1998. www.michaelalarcon.com/ocnow_Cramps.html.

Ali, Lorraine. "Banding Together." *Rolling Stone*, 6 October 1994.

Anderman, Joan. "Quiet Riots: The Girls from the North[west] Country." *The Boston Phoenix*, 3 November 1997.

Anderson, Brett. "Sharps & Flats." *Salon*, 6 October 1999. www.salon.com/ent/ music/review/1999/10/06/fastbacks/print.html.

Anderson, Sunny. "The Life and Times of Wendy O. Williams." *Girlyhead*. www. girlyhead.com/past_issues/issue03.htm.

Ansen, David. "'Bad' Courtney Is Back." *Newsweek*, 28 February 1998.

Appelstein, Michael. "How I Discovered Music." *Caught in Flux* 3. www.appel-stein.com/cif/interviews3.html.

Appelstein, Michael. "Interview with Palmolive." *N-Stop*. www.nstop.com/pal-oma/intervw.html.

Applestein, Michael. "The Raincoats." *Net* 12. www.appelstein.com/cif/raincoat-snet.html.

Armstrong, Gene. "Worth Talking About: Powerful and Fiery, The Gossip Leaves Small Towns and Pop Fluff in the Dust." *Tucson Weekly*, 13–19 June 2002.

Arnold, Gina. "Built for Speed: Fastbacks: Punk in the Present Tense." *L.A. Weekly*, 30 January–5 February 1998.

Arnold, Gina. "Outside the Loop." *Metroactive*, 16–22 November 2000. www. metroactive.com/papers/metro/11.16.00/harvey-0046.html.

Bangs, Lester. "Sex and the Art of Rock 'n' Roll: Q: Does Sex Sell Records?" *Creem*, November 1976.

Barcella, Laura. "Erase Errata." *Swingset* 2, 2002.

Barr, Stuart. "L7." www.obsolete.com/convulsion/interviews/convulse/frames. hmtl.

Barrington, Judith. "Women's Lib Hits London, 1972," *The Gay and Lesbian Review*, May/June 2003.

Baumgardner, Jennifer. "Kathleen Hanna's Eye of Le Tigre." *Rockrgrl*, November/ December 2000.

BBC. "History: Timelines: Post WWII." http://www.bbc.co.uk/history/timelines/ england/pwar_opportunity_all.shtml.

Bell, Geoff. "Space I Believe In." Reprinted from *Rock a My Soul* 2. www.sydonia. hypermart.net/pixiesweb/kimdeal.htm.

Berger, George. "Killing Time with Crass." *3AM Magazine*, 1 August 2002. www.3ammagazine.com/berger/2002_aug_1.html.

Bessman, Jim. "Jett Enlists Riot Grrrls for Blackhearts' Warner Debut." *Billboard*, 7 May 1994.

Bessman, Jim. "ROIR Brings Its Punk-Era Rarities to CD." *Billboard*, 30 January 1999.

Biafra, Jello. "Pandoras." *Maximumrocknroll*, January 1985.

Bir, Sara. "Radical Adults." *Metroactive*, 8–14 August 2002. www.metroactive.com/papers/sonoma/08.08.02/sonicyouth-0232.html.

Blackwell, Mark. "Do You Believe in Pixies?" *Spin*, October 1991.

Board, Mykel. "Columns." *Maximumrocknroll*, October/November 1983.

Borow, Zev. "How to Succeed in Bizness. . . . by Really, Really Trying." *Spin*, August 1999.

Brazier, Chris. "The Resurrection of Patti Smith." *Melody Maker*, 18 March 1976.

Brennan, T. Corey. Review of *Love Between Women: Early Christian Responses to Female Homoeroticism* by Bernadette J. Brooten. *Bryn Mawr Classicial Review*, 7 May 1997. http://ccat.sas.upenn.edu/bmcr/1997/97.05.07.html.

Browne, David. "Go On, Grrrls." *Entertainment Weekly*, 1 January 1994.

Browne, David. "Sonic Youth," *Entertainment Weekly*, 7 March 2003.

Buerger, Jamie. "Le Tigre Dance to a Political Beat." *Las Vegas Weekly*, 12 June 2003.

Calhoun, Ada. "Art Rocker: Radical-Feminist Powerhouse Kathleen Hanna has a New Gig—as a Soho Curator." *New York Metro*. www.newyorkmetro.com/nymetro/news/culture/n_8004/.

Carr, Roy. "Blondie Cometh: The Sensuous Pout from CBGB." *New Musical Express*, 13 November 1976.

Carr, Roy. "Male Chauvinist Pigs' Corner Episodes 2 & 3: Listen Honey, I Can Make You a Star." *New Musical Express*, 9 April 1977.

Carr, Roy. "Return of the Teen Nymphette." *New Musical Express*, 19 February 1977.

Catamero, Maria. "The Gossip." *Skyscraper Magazine*. www.skyscrapermagazine.com/features/gossip.html.

Cavanaugh, David. "Dark Star." *Q*, December 2001.

Chideya, Farai, and Melissa Rossi. "Revolution, Girl Style." *Newsweek*, 23 November 1992.

Chonin, Neva. "Surging on the Scene: Electroclash Mixes Pop with Hip Fashion, Art." *San Francisco Chronicle*, 27 October 2002.

Christgau, Robert. "The Ballad of Polly Jean Harvey." *Spin*, May 1995.

Christgau, Robert. "Sonic Elders: Sonic Youth." *Rolling Stone*, 25 June 1998.

Cobain, Kurt. Liner notes for Nirvana, *Incesticide*. Geffen Records DGCD-24504, 1992.

Coble, Margaret. "Hot Gossip." *The Advocate*, 13 February 2001.

Cocks, Jay. "Rock Is a Four-Letter Word; A Senate Committee Asks: 'Have Lyrics Gone Too Far?'" *Time*, 30 September 1985.

Cocks, Jay. "These Big Girls Don't Cry." *Time*, 4 March 1985.

Cohn, Roy. "Blondie Cometh." *New Musical Express*, 13 November 1976.

Coley, Byron, and Jimmy Johnson. "Feelin' Up the Man Tit with Sonic Youth." *Forced Exposure*, summer 1985.

Conklin, Ellis. "Is It Time to Consider 'De-punking and De-metalizing' Some Teens?" *San Francisco Examiner*, 19 May 1985.

Coon, Caroline. "London's Swinging Again—and the Whole World Is Watching." *Melody Maker*, 31 May 1977.

Coon, Caroline. "Punk Queen of Sheba." *Melody Maker*, 15 January 1977.

Cooper, Dennis. "Love Conquers All." *Spin*, May 1994.

Cooper, Jon. "Up to Speed: Kurt Bloch and Kim Warnick." *Chin Music!* 4. www.chinmusic.net/fastbacks.html.

Cost, Jud. "Exene Cervenka." *Magnet*. www.magnetmagazine.com/interviews/exene.html.

Costa, Maddy. "The Addict Family." *The Guardian Unlimited*, 10 May 2002.

Cuda, Heidi Siegmund. "The Hole Truth." *Entertainment Weekly*, 10 January 1997.

Cvetkovich, Ann, and Gretchen Phillips. "Revenge of the Girl Bands: The Dyke Music Scene Blends Feminist Values and 'Do It Yourself' Punk Culture." *The Nation*, 10 July 2000.

Dalley, Helen. "Pixies." *Total Guitar*, July 1999.

Dalton, Stephen. "Peaches." *The Times* (UK), 20 September 2003.

Daly, Steve. "The Original Riot Grrrl: Joan Jett Lives Up to Her Reputation." *Rolling Stone*, 24 March 1994.

Daniels, Keith. "Interview with Carrie Brownstein." *Aversion*. www.indiedarlings.20m.com/articlepages/suicidegirls.html.

Dansby, Andrew. "50 Cent Tops 2003." *Rolling Stone*, 5 January 2004.

Dansby, Andrew. "Gits Reenter with Reissues." *Rolling Stone*, 26 February 2003.

Darzin, Daina. "Ah, the Smell of It: L7 Bask in the Sweet Stink of Success." *Rolling Stone*, 11 August 1994.

Dauphin, Edouard. "Wendy and the Plasmatics: 1984 Will Be a Little Bit Early." *Creem*, September 1981.

Davis, Vaginal. "Femmes on Flames." *L.A. Weekly*, 15–21 September 2000.

Dean, Jeremy. "Lydia Lunch Interview, 1996." http://homepage.virgin.net/questing.beast/llscrawl2.htm.

DeBonis, Mike. "The Future of Music Is Now." *Georgetown Voice*, 14 November 2002.

DeRogatis, Jim. "The Nirvana Wars." *Spin*, June 2002.

DeSantis, Carla. "Kim Gordon: Sonic Warrior." *Rockrgrl*, March/April 2000.

DeSantis, Carla. "Le Tigre: Feminism is a Hot Topic." *Rockrgrl*, spring/summer 2002.

Doherty, Harry. "Blondie on Blondie." *Melody Maker*, 4 March 1978.

Doherty, Harry. "The Arrival of ABBA." *Melody Maker*, 13 February 1977.

Dunn, Katherine, and Sirota, Peggy. "Courtney Love." *Rolling Stone*, 13 November 1997.

Edwards, Bob. Interview with David Byrne. "Morning Edition," National Public Radio, 18 November 2003.

Edwards, Bob. 2004. Interview with Jenny Toomey. "Morning Edition," National Public Radio, 11 February, 2004.

Ehrenreich, Barbara. "Sorry, Sisters, This Is Not the Revolution." *Time*, fall 1990.

Empire, Kitty. "Ripe for Stardom." *The Observer*, 17 August 2003.

Experience Music Project. "Donna Dresch." www.experience.org/archives/index.asp?section=intv&id=97&pg1.

Experience Music Project. "Janet Weiss." http://www.experience.org/archives/index.asp?section=intv&id=13&pg=1.

Experience Music Project. "Punk Chronology: Lydia Lunch." www.emplive.com/explore/punk_chron/allthisandmore.asp?sa=story&vid=852.

Farley, Christopher John. "Galapalooza!" *Time*, 21 July 1997.

Farren, Mick. "Fascism in the U.K. '77!" *New Musical Express*, 22 January 1977.

Felder, Rachel. "The Creatures." *Alternative Press*, November 1990.

Fell, Beth. "Fat Trashy Southern Rock." *Tablet* 9. www.tabletnewspaper.com/old%20tablet/vol12iss9/thegossip.htm.

Fell, Beth. "Interview with Molly from Bratmobile." *Tablet* 13. www.tabletnewspaper.com/old%20tablet/vol2iss_13/webmolly.html.

Fontana, Paul. "Stay Sick! The Cramps' Degeneracy Continues." *The Stranger*, 5–11 June 2003.

Fouratt, Jim. "Tank Girl Comes Out with 'Godspeed.'" *Gay City News*. www.gaycitynews.com/GCN5/Breedlove.html.

France, Kim. "Grrrls at War." *Rolling Stone*, 8 July 1993.

Frank, Josh. "Sleater-Kinney Rocks: Our Protest Songs Are Here." *CounterPunch*, 9 November 2002. www.counterpunch.org/frank1109.html.

Frey, Hillary. "Kathleen Hanna's Fire." *The Nation*, 13 January 2003. www.thenation.com/doc.mhtml?I=20030113&s=frey.

Freydkin, Donna. "Fierce Feminists L7 Rant on with Live Album." CNN Interactive, 11 December 1998. www.cnn.com/SHOWBIZ/Music/9812/11/l7/index.html.

Fricke, David. "Krist Noveselic." *Rolling Stone*, 13 September 2001.

Fricke, David. "Slick, Sweet, and Dangerous." *Rolling Stone*, 1 October 1998.

Fricke, David. "The Rolling Stone Interview with Sonic Youth's Thurston Moore." *Rolling Stone*, 22 September 1994.

Friedrich, Otto. "Freed from Greed? The Past Decade Brought Growth, Avarice, and an Anything-Goes Attitude. But the '90s Will Be a Time to Fix Up, Clean Up, and Pay Up." *Time*, 1 January 1990.

Fryer, Paul. "Everybody's on Top of the Pops: Popular Music on British Television." *Popular Music and Society*, fall 1997.

Future of Music Coalition. "Media Ownership: Statement of Jenny Toomey, Executive Director, Future of Music Coalition." FDCH Congressional Testimony to the Committee on Commerce, Science, and Transportation, 30 January 2003.

Future of Music Coalition. "The Future of Music Manifesto." Future of Music Coalition, 1 June 2000. www.futureofmusic.org/manifesto.

Gaines, Donna, and various. "Let's Talk About Sex." *Rolling Stone*, 13 November 1997.

Gale Research. "Assimilation of the Counterculture in the 1970s." *Discovering U.S. History*. Gale Research, 1997. Reproduced in the History Resource Center. Michigan.

Gale Research. "Media in the 1970s: An Overview." *Discovering U.S. History*. Gale Research, 1997. Reproduced in the History Resource Center. Michigan: Gale Group.

Gale Research. "Pop-Music Stars (1980s)." *American Decades CD-ROM*. Gale Research, 1998. Reproduced in the History Resource Center. Michigan: Gale Group.

Gale Research. "Social Trends in the 1970s: An Overview." *Discovering U.S. History*. Gale Research, 1997. Reproduced in the History Resource Center. Michigan: Gale Group.

Gale Research. "Underground Music Trends of the 1980s." Gale Research, 1997. Reproduced in the History Resource Center. Michigan: Gale Group.

Gale Research. "Women's Liberation in the 1970s." *Discovering U.S. History*. Gale Research, 1997. Reproduced in the History Resource Center. Michigan: Gale Group.

Garden, Joe. "Joan Jett." *The Onion AV Club*, 26 February 1998.

Gehman, Pleasant. Liner notes for various artists, *We're Desperate: The L.A. Scene 1976–1979*. Rhino Records R271176, 1993.

Giles, Jeff. "Courtney's Second Coming." *Newsweek*, 21 October 1996.

Gilmartin, T.A. "The Butchies Are Fightin' the Power." *Lesbian News*, August 2000.

Gilmore, Mikal. "Bruce Springsteen." *Rolling Stone*, 15 November 1990.

Gilmore, Mikal. "Psychodramas You Can Dance To." *Rolling Stone*, 29 November 1979.

Gladden, Mendy. "Tempting Antidote: Jenny Toomey Discusses Music, Activism, and Passion." *Iris: A Journal About Women*, fall 2003.

Glover, Tony. "Sweet Howling Fire: Patti Smith." *Creem*, January 1976.

Goldman, David. "From Stripper to Singer to Star." *Biography*, October 1997.

Goldstein, Patrick. "Patti Smith: Rock 'n' Roll Pandora Unleashes Violence and Mayhem." *Creem*, March 1977.

Goldstein, Patrick. "The Runaways: Lissome Lolitas or Teenage Trash?" *Creem*, February 1977.

Goldstein, Toby. "Blondie: High School Never Ends!" *Creem*, May 1977.

Gonzalez, Ed. "PJ Harvey: Live in New York." *Slant Magazine,* 2001. www.slant-magazine.com/music/features/pjharvey.html.

Goodman, Fred. "Nirvana Box Set on Hold." *Rolling Stone,* 16 August 2001.

Gordon, Kim. "Boys Are Smelly." *Village Voice,* 12–18 October 1988.

Gordon, Kim. "Erase Errata." *Index,* April/May 2003.

Gordon, Kim, and Kim Deal. "The Two Kims." *Interview,* November 1995.

Gordon, Robert. "Cramps." *Spin,* August 1990.

Grad, David. "Lunachicks: Femmes Vitales." *Alternative Press.* www.altpress.com/sections/basement/10-25-1999/story.asp?story=1. Previously published in *Alternative Press,* December 1995.

Greer, Jim. "Kool Things." *Spin,* September 1990.

Gross, Jason. "Logically Essential." *Venus,* winter 2002.

Hajari, Nsid. "Nirvana's Helping Hand." *Entertainment Weekly,* 4 November 1994, 71.

Hajari, Nsid. "Women on the Verge." *Entertainment Weekly,* 19 August 1994.

Hanna, Kathleen. "Riot Grrrl Manifesto." Reprinted in *Discorder: That Online Magazine from CiTR 101.9 FM.* www.ams.ubc.ca/citr/discorder/archive/2003-03/riot.html.

Harrigan, Brian. "Seeds, Doors, Giant Ants, and Blondie." *Melody Maker,* 28 May 1977.

Harvard, Joe. "Pixies." *Boston Rock Storybook.* www.rockinboston.com/pixies.html.

Hay, Carla. "L7 Returns to Roots on Wax Tadpole/Bong Load's 'Slap Happy.'" *Billboard,* 17 July 1999.

Heck, Mike. "The Cramps." *The Roc.* www.theroc.org/roc-mag/textarch/roc-09/roc09-4b.htm.

Heim, Joe. "American Bandstand: Sleater-Kinney's Carrie Brownstein Talks About Politics, the President, and Simple Pop Songs." *Salon,* 4 March 1999. www.salon.com/ent/music/feature/1999/03/04feature.html.

Heim, Joe. "An Interview with Sleater-Kinney's Carrie Brownstein." *Washington Post,* 13 October 2002. www.washingtonpost.com/wp-srv/entertainment/new_features/music/sleaterkinney.htm.

Henry III, W.A. "Are Artists Godless Perverts?" *Time,* 10 September 1990.

Hernandez, Eric. "The Cramps." *The Bee's Kneez Zine.* www.hhbtm.com/beesknees/int/cramps.html.

Hirshey, Gerri. "The Backstage History of Women Who Rocked the World." *Rolling Stone*, 13 November 1997.

Hirshey, Gerri. "The Eighties: Wild Things, Boy Toys, and Fierce MC's." *Rolling Stone*, 12 November 1997.

Hopkins, Susan. "Hole Lotta Attitude." *Social Alternatives*, April 1999.

Hopper, Jessica. "Emo: Where the Girls Aren't." *Punk Planet*, July/August 2003.

Hopper, Jessica. "Erase Errata." *Punk Planet*, May/June 2004.

Hopper, Jessica. "Interview with Bratmobile." *Punk Planet*, spring 1999. www.killrockstars.com/bands/bratmobile/press/index.html.

Hopper, Justin. "Jenny Toomey, Revolutionary Rocker." *Alternet*. www.alternet.org/story.html?StoryID=17607. Originally printed in *Pittsburgh City Paper* (Pittsburgh, Pennsylvania), 28 October 2003.

"Interview of PJ Harvey and Björk on Dutch TV." home.concepts.nl/bj2.html.

Jackson, Blair. "Talking Heads' 'Psycho Killer.'" *MIX*, August 2002. www.mixonline.com.

Japenga, Ann. "Punk's Girl Groups Are Putting the Self Back in Self-Esteem." *The New York Times*, 15 November 1992.

Jenkins, Sacha. "Pimpin' Ain't Easy." *Spin*, October 1999.

Johnson, D.J. "Talkin' Axes and Amps with the Queen of the Cramps." *Cosmic Debris* 29, October 1997. members.shaw.ca/thecramps/cosmicdebrisivy.htm.

Johnson, Rick. Review of *Queens of Noise* by the Runaways. *Creem*, April 1977.

Kahn, Brenda. "Says Le Tigre." *WomanRock*. www.womanrock.com/features/le_tigre.html.

Kahn, Brenda. "Sleater Kinney: No Censorship." *WomanRock*. www.womanrock.com/features/sleater_kinney.html.

Kemp, Mark. "The Greatest Albums Ever Made." *Rolling Stone*, 28 November 2002.

Kent, Nick. "Are These Guys Trying to Give Rock a Bad Name?" *New Musical Express*, 25 June 1977.

King, Brad. "The Indie Queen of Digital Music." *Wired*, 10 July 2000.

Klinge, Steve. "Le Tigre Hot Topics, or, the Le Tigre Hit Parade." *Stomp and Stammer*, Feburary 2002. www.stompandstammer.com/cover0202.shtml.

Knoth, Brian. "Jen and the Art of Activism." *Glide Magazine*, 4 May 2003. www.glidemagazine.com.php?ar_id=28.

Koether, Jutta. "Kim Gordon and Thurston Moore, 1998." *Index*. www.indexmaga-zine.com/interviews/kim_gordon_thurston_moore.shtml.

Kristal, Hilly. "CBGB Omfug." CBGB, www.cbgb.com/history/history2.html.

Krop, Jonathan. "Penelope Houston: Purity of Intention." *Rockrgrl*, May/June 1995.

Lang, Dave. "The Screamers." March 2000. www.furious.com/perfect/screamers.html.

Leckman, Phil. "Rock Band the Gossip Gets It On at Solar Culture." *The Arizona Daily Wildcat Online*, 6 February 2001. www.wildcat.arizona.edu/papers/94/93/04_3_m.html.

Lee, Chris. "Kelley Deal." Originally published in *Monstro Glammo*, September 1996. www.bychrislee.com/ppt/kelleydeal.html.

Lee, Michelle. "Oh Bondage: The Early Punk Movement—and the Women Who Made it Rock." *Off Our Backs*, November/December 2002.

Lengel, Kerry. "Inspired by Men, PJ's Her Own Woman." *Arizona Republic*, 22 April 2001.

Leroy, J.T. "Checking In: J.T. Leroy Talks with Lydia Lunch About 'Johnny Behind the Deuce.'" *Filmmaker*, winter 2001. www.filmmakermagazine.com/winter2001/short_reports/checking_in.html.

Levin, Hannah. "Lesbionic Action Figure: Kaia Wilson's New Team Strategy." *The Stranger*, 19 April 2001.

Levin, Hannah. "Torch Songs: Le Tigre Continue Carrying the Feminist Light." *The Stranger*, 12 June 2003.

Lippens, Nate. "Getting Bent: Planning a Queer Rock Festival." *The Stranger*, 16 August 2001.

Lopez, Antonio. "Sonic Youth's Thurston Moore." *Thirsty Ear*, December 1999/January 2000. www.thirstyearfestival.com/interviews/sonic.html.

Lotta, Tess. "Second Skin: The Gits Rewrite History by Knowing How to Live with It." *The Stranger*, 19 October 2000.

Love, Courtney. "Summer of Love," *Spin*, December 1995.

Lustig, Jay. "Patti Smith Fails to Make This Year's Slate of Rock and Roll Hall of Fame Inductees." *The Star-Ledger* (Newark, New Jersey), 13 December 2000.

Lustig, Jay. "Rock 'n' Roll Survivor: Patti Smith Pushes On." *The Star-Ledger* (Newark, New Jersey), 26 March 2001.

Lynskey, Dorian. "Peaches, Fatherfucker." *The Guardian*, 12 September 2003.

Mackin, Bob. "Abandoning the Beauty Process." *North Shore News*, 17 May 1999.

Maerz, Melissa. "Come On, Feel the Noise." *City Pages*, 3 July 2002.

Mah, Sioman. "Livin' Large: L7 Gets Slap Happy with a New Album and a National Tour." *Synthesis*, www.synthesis.net/music/feature.php?bid=253.

Marcus, Greil. "America's Best Artists and Entertainers: Rock Band: Sleater-Kinney." CNN, 2001. www.cnn.com/SPECIALS/2001/americasbest/pro.skinney.html.

Marcus, Greil. "Are You Ready to Fly?" *The Guardian*, 9 May 2003.

Marcus, Greil. "Avenging the Past." *Interview*, May 1999.

Marks, Craig. "Endless Love." *Spin*, February 1995.

Maximumrocknroll. Letters sections, scene reports, and columns. 1983–1985.

Maximumrocknroll. "Frightwig: Humans Making Noise!" March 1985.

Maximumrocknroll. "Gang Mentality." October 1984.

McDonnell, Evelyn. Review of the Fastbacks, *Zücker. Rolling Stone*, 29 April 1993.

McDonnell, Evelyn. "The Olympia Spirit." *Rolling Stone*, 8 September 1994.

McGrath, Kathryn. "The Dykes Are Back! Interview with Team Dresch." *The Online Daily of the University of Washington*, 14 November 1996. archives.thedaily .washington.edu/1996/111496/team111496.html.

McGuigan, Cathleen, and Shawn D. Lewis. "Showdown in Cincinnati." *Newsweek*, 8 October 1990.

McKenna, Kristine. Liner notes for X, *Los Angeles*. Slash SR-104, 1980. Reissue Rhino R274370, 2001.

McKenna, Kristine. Liner notes for X, *Wild Gift*. Slash/Rhino SR-107, 1981. Reissue Rhino R2 74371, 2001.

Mehr, Bob. "Grand Royal." *Seattle Weekly*, 12–18 February 2003.

Miles. "Sex Kitten Sharpens Claws, Headline Writer Blunts Brain." *New Musical Express*, 16 April 1977.

Miles. "This is a Minimalist Headline." *New Musical Express*, 23 April 1977.

Millea, Holly, and Joshua Rich. "Love Is a Battlefield." *Entertainment Weekly*, 29 March 2002.

Miller, Jim. "Rock's New Women." *Newsweek*, 4 March 1985.

Milstein, Chaia. "Beaucoup Marci." *Drummergirl*, 2001. www.drummergirl.com/ interviews/martinez.html.

Moloney, Kara. "Post-Punk Women." *Mother Jones*, November/December 1990.

Molyneaux, Libby. "Smell Tha Noise: L7: You Can Take White Thrash Anywhere." *L.A. Weekly*, 19–25 November 1999.

Moodie, David, and Maureen Callahan. "Don't Drink the Brown Water." *Spin*, October 1999.

Morris, Chris. "L7 Readies the Beauty Process." *Billboard*, 25 January 1997.

Morris, Chris. "Toomey, Thomson Hit 'Off' On Simple Machines." *Billboard*, 21 Feburary 1998.

Muhlke, Christine. "Incoming: Peaches." *Spin*, June 2001.

Mullen, Brendan. "Annihilation Man: How Darby Crash Lost Control. Of the Germs. Of Circle One. Of Everything." *L.A. Weekly*, 29 December 2000–4 January 2001.

Murray, Charles Shaar. "Sex Pistols: Screen on the Green." *New Musical Express*, 11 September 1976.

Murray, Charles Shaar. "Welcome to the Monkey House." *New Musical Express*, 23 October 1976.

Neely, Kim. "The Fight for the Right to Choose: L7 and Friends Rock for Reproductive Freedom." *Rolling Stone*, 18 March 1993.

Nelson, Sean. "Saint Mia." *The Stranger*, 16 January 2003.

New Musical Express eds. "Blondie Bombshell." *Melody Maker*, 4 February 1978.

Newman, Melinda. "In an Anything-Goes Year, Girl Power Sticks, Vets Score, Teens Are Triumphant." *Billboard*, 27 December 1997.

Newman, Melinda. "Talents Old and New Make News in '96; Female Artists Repeat Last Year's Success." *Billboard*, 28 December 1996.

Noise for Heroes. "The Fastbacks." www.nkvdrecords.com/fastback.htm. Originally printed in 1991.

Obrecht, Jas. "Oooh! Poison Ivy: Cramps Vamp Talks Guitar." *Guitar Player*, August 1990.

O'Brien, Lucy. "The New Voices of Feminism: Rock Stars Stand Up as Role Models of Strength, Smarts, and Sexuality." *The Record* (Bergen County, New Jersey), 5 January 1999.

O'Connor, Jennifer. "Getting Busy with Bratmobile." Knitting Factory, 2002. www.knittingfactory.com/articles/bratmobile.cfm.

O'Dair, Barbara, and Brigitte Lacombe. "Kim Gordon." *Rolling Stone*, 13 November 1997.

Oglesbee, Frank. "Suzi Quatro: A Prototype in the Archsheology of Rock." *Popular Music and Society*, summer 1999.

O'Hara, Gail. "Janet Quasi/Sleater-Kinney." *Chickfactor*, 1999.

Ostling, Richard. "Jerry Falwell's Crusade: Fundamentalist Legions Seek to Remake Church and Society." *Time*, 2 September 1985.

O'Toole, Leagues. "PJ Harvey." *Muse*, 2001. www.muse.ie/101100/interview/harvey.html.

Page, Mike Flood. "Rock's Next Generation?" *Creem*, October 1977.

Paoletta, Michael. "Peaches Seeks Equality on New Disc." *Billboard*, 6 September 2003.

Parcellin, Chris. "Girls Interrrupted: The Controversial New Runaways Documentary." *Film Threat*, 21 December 2003.

Parker, Kat. "Feminist/Queer Entrepreneurs: Mr. Lady Music and Videos." *The Independent Weekly* (Durham, North Carolina), 27 June 2001.

Parsons, Tony. "Seventh Vertebra During the Seventh Number. . . ." *New Musical Express*, 5 February 1977.

Partridge, Robert. "Punk Rock: There's Money in Anarchy." *Melody Maker*, 23 April 1977.

Paytress, Mark. Liner notes for the Slits, *Cut*. Island Records, 1979. Universal Records UICY-3232, 2000.

Plagens, Peter, and Shawn D. Lewis. "Mixed Signals on Obscenity." *Newsweek*, 15 October 1990.

Perry, Claudia. "Reunited, Blondie Rides a New Wave." *The Star-Ledger* (Newark, New Jersey). 22 February 1999.

Pesselnick, Jill. "Misra's Jenny Toomey Finds 'Antidote' for Pain." *Billboard*, 22 September 2001.

Philips, Amy. "Easter: An Interview with Patti Smith." *Next*. www.nextnyc.com/features/pattismith.html.

Philips, Amy. "Exene Cervenka." *Furious*, September 2002. www.furious.com/perfect/exene.html.

Picture, Bill. "Get With the Gits." *San Francisco Examiner*, 26 June 2003.

Piedmont Triad. "The Lilith Fair Showcases Female Musicians." *Piedmont Triad* (North Carolina), 17 July 1997.

Pressler, Charlotte, and Miriam Linna. "Patti Smith in Her Own Lights." *Creem*, July 1976.

Punk 77. www.punk77.co.uk.

Punk and Oi. "Adverts." punkandoi.fre.fr/adverts_biography.htm.

Punk Rock Academy. "Team Dresch." www.punkrockacademy.com/stm/int /dresch.html.

Quindlen, Anna. "Still Needing the F Word." *Newsweek*, 20 October 2003.

Raine, Allison. "Poison Girls: Richard Famous and Vi Subversa." *Maximumrocknroll.*

Rayner, Ben. "Absence Builds Craving for Peaches." *Toronto Star*, 17 October 2002.

Reese, Frank. "The Cramps: An Interview with Lux Interior and Poison Ivy." *Stain*, 2000. www.stainmagazine.com/cramps.html.

Robbins, David. "Jenny Toomey of Liquorice." *Rational Alternative Digital*, 1995. www.radcyberzine.com/text/interviews/liquorice.int.j.html.

Robbins, Ira. "The Alternative Underground." *Rolling Stone*, 17 October 1991.

Robinson, Lisa. "Girls Will Be Boys." *New Musical Express*, 14 August 1976.

Robinson, Lisa. "Magic and Loss." *Spin*, July 1996.

Robinson, Lisa. "The Runaways: Naughty Nymphets Leave Lisa Cold." *Creem*, November 1976.

Robinson, Sara. "Jenny Toomey: Executive Director, Coalition for the Future of Music." *Interactive Week*, 12 March 2001.

Rogers, Ray. "Queens' Reich." *Rolling Stone*, 18 May 1995.

Rohrer, Trish Deitch. "Making Herself Heard." *The Advocate*, 28 May 2002.

Rolling Stone. "Women in Rock." *Rolling Stone*, 31 October 2002.

Rose, Cynthia. "The Cramps in Conversation." www.state51.co.uk/hottips/ crampsconv.html.

Rosen, Craig. "Epic 'Home Alive' Compilation Comes to Women's Defense." *Billboard*, 20 January 1996.

Rosen, Jody Beth. "Exene Cervenka." *Southside Callbox.* southsidecallbox.com/ exene_cervenka_interview.html.

Rowley, Scott. "Wot, No Sid? The 50 Best Basslines of Punk and New Wave." *Total Guitar*, April 2004.

Royer, Jeff. "Joan Jett: Still Loves Rock and Roll." *Fly*, June 2003. www.flymaga-zine.net/archive_bands_article.cfm?id=7ae77adf.

Salewicz, Chris. "And I Wonder . . . Wah Wah Wah Wonder . . . ." *New Musical Express*, 24 July 1976.

Salvato, Jen. "Rockin', Ragin', and Female." *Cosmopolitan*, December 1996.

Sasaki, Fred. "The Teaches of Peaches." *Venus* 19.

Schoemer, Karen. "A Breed Apart." *Rolling Stone*, 19 May 1994.

Schoemer, Karen. "Playing the Game of Love." *Newsweek*, 6 February 1995.

Schwartz, Ruth. "Crass." *Maximumrocknroll*, October/November 1983.

Seattle Post-Intelligencer. "Hole's New Album an Ode to Life and Times of Courtney Love." 9 September 1998.

Shapiro, Gregg. "The Next Chapter: Interview with Lynn Breedlove." *Windy City Times*, 24 April 2002.

Sheehy, Peter. Liner notes to the Gits, *Kings and Queens*. Broken Rekids Skip 44, 2003.

Shepherd, Julianne. "Erase You: Spazzy, Tough Ladies Kick No Wave Ass." *The Portland Mercury*, 11 October 2001.

Sidey, Hugh. "The Right Rev. Ronald Reagan." *Time*, 21 March 1983.

Siegler, Dylan. "Kathleen Hanna: The Quintessential Riot Grrrl Riffs on the State of Women Fans in Rock." *Ms. Magazine*, August/September 2000.

Simpson, Dave, and Will Hodgkinson. "Punk: How Was It for You?" *The Guardian Unlimited*, 10 August 2001.

Sinclair, Tom. "Viva Zapata." *Entertainment Weekly*, 1 August 2003.

Sioman, Mah. "Livin' Large: L7 Gets Slap Happy with a New Album and a National Tour." *Synthesis*. www.thesynthesis.com/music/feature.php?bid=253.

Skow, John. "Madonna Rocks the Land: Sassy, Brassy, and Beguiling, She Laughs Her Way to Fame." *Time*, 27 May 1985.

Smith, Eric J. "Interview with Kim Deal." www.jericsmith.com/Interviews/dealint.htm.

Smith, Ethan, and Jeff Gordinier. "Love's Hate Fest." *Entertainment Weekly*, 28 July 1995.

Spencer, Lauren. "Grrrls Only." *Washington Post*, 3 January 1993.

Spin. "The 100 Sleaziest Moments in Rock." October 2000.

Spitz, Marc. "Life to the Pixies." *Spin,* September 2004.

Sprague, David. "L7 Still Hungry for Punk Lifestyle." *Billboard,* 6 June 1994.

Sprague, David. "Simple Machines: A Well-Oiled Indie." *Billboard,* 4 November 1995.

Sprague, David. "DGC's Raincoats Prove Impermeable to Time." *Billboard,* 6 April 1996.

Steenson, Molly Wright. "Intensity and Hot Rock." *Maximag,* 1999. www.maximag.com/imitate/sk.

Steinbacher, Bradley. "Holy Cow: It's a Sad Day for the Fastbacks." *The Stranger,* 8 March 2001.

Stern, Theresa. "Lydia Lunch." *Furious,* October 1997. www.furious.com/perfect/lydialunch.html.

Stoval, Natasha. "Kicking Against the Pricks." *Spin,* March 1995.

Strachota, Dan. "Gang of Four." *San Francisco Weekly,* 11 July 2001.

Stud Brothers. "Kiss of the Spider Woman." *Melody Maker,* 11 May 1991.

Sturges, Fiona. "Return of the Creature." *The Independent,* 24 October 2003.

Sutherland, Steve. "Caught in the Act: Keep Off the Crass." *Melody Maker,* 20 June 1981.

Tatone, Jenny. "Erase Errata's Post–Riot Grrrl, Post-Feminist Post-Punk: The Bay Area Quartet Creates a New Kind of Noise." *NeuMu,* 2001. www.neumu.com/inquisitive/erase_errata/erase_errata_02/shtml.

Taylor, Charles. "Natural One." *Boston Phoenix,* 6 July 1998.

Temple, Johnny. "Noise from Underground." *The Nation,* 18 October 1999.

Thomson, Kristin, and Jenny Toomey. "The Simple Machines Story." Simple Machines. www.simplemachines.net/story.html.

Thompson, Stephen. "The Joy of Pop." *The Onion AV Club,* 4 November 1999. www.theavclub.com/avclub3540/bonusfeature13540.html.

Time, "Musical Milestones of the 1980s." *Time,* 1 January 1990.

Tiven, Jon. "Blondie Was a Group: An Appreciation." Liner notes to Blondie, *Blondie: The Platinum Collection.* EMI Records/Chrysalis F2 31100, 1994.

Toomey, Jenny. "Empire of the Air." *The Nation,* 23 December 2002.

Tran, Lionel. "Interview Lydia Lunch." perso.wanadoo.fr/markus.leicht/lylunch2.htm.

Tsunami. "Tour Diary: Tsunami Across America." *Washington City Paper*. www.washingtoncitypaper.com/archives/indc/td/tsunami/tsunam1.html.

Tunis, Walter. "To the Surprise of the Founders, Tom Tom Club Is Still Going Strong." *Lexington Herald-Ledger* (Kentucky), 22 September 2003.

Turman, Katherine. "Chicks with Picks: A New Breed of Women Rockers Is Ready to Lead the Way." *Billboard*, 24 June 2000.

Uhelski, Jaan. "Black Is Beautiful." *Women Who Rock*, January/February 2004.

Ula. "Queen of Shock Rock: Wendy O. Williams of the Plasmatics." *Painproof Rubber Girls*. painproofrubbergirls.com/writing/wow/index.php.

Unterberger, Richie. "Gina Birch." 12 December 1996. www.richieunterberger.com/birch.html.

Unterberger, Richie. "Penelope Houston Interview." www.richieunterberger.com/houston.html.

Vaid, Urvashi. "Separate and Unequal." *The Advocate*, 29 October 2002.

Vail, Tobi. "From Rock Against Reagan, to Bands Against Bush." *Bumpidee*. www.bumpidee.com/From%20%20Rock%20Against%20Reagan.html.

Vail, Tobi. Liner notes for Bikini Kill, *The CD Version of the First Two Records*. Kill Rock Stars KRS 204, 1994.

Vale, V. "Tomata du Plenty, R.I.P. 1948–2000." *RE-Search*. www.researchpubs.com/latest/tomatafeat.shtml.

Van Meter, William. "She's a Very Kinky Girl." *Spin*, February 2003.

Villepique, Greg. "Brilliant Careers: Patti Smith." *Salon*, 9 November 1999. www.salon.com/people/bc/1999/11/09/smith/.

Von Furth, Daisy. "Hole Lotta Love." *Spin*, October 1991.

Vote, Robin. "Sex and Violence." *Maximumrocknroll*, December 1985.

Wallis, Claudia. "Onward, Women!" *Time*, 4 December 1989.

Webb, Susy. "After the Riot." *Discorder: That Online Magazine from CiTR 101.9 FM*. www.ams.ubc.ca/citr/discorder/archive/2003-03/riot.html.

Weeks, Laurie. "Kathleen Hanna, 2000." *Index*. www.indexmagazine.com/interviews/kathleen_hanna.html.

Weisbach, Eric. "Laugh, Riot." *Spin*, August 1996.

Weiss, Philip. "The Love Issue." *Spin*, October 1998.

Weymouth, Tina. "My Bass Buddhas." *Bass Player*, January 2004.

White, Cliff, and Tony Parsons. "On the Town." *New Musical Express*, 9 October 1976.

White, David. "A Home for Homocore." *The Advocate*, 19 June 2001.

White, Emily. "Dead Again." *Spin*, August 1995.

White, Emily. "Revolution Girl-Style Now!" *Chicago Reader*, 25 September 1992.

Whiteside, Johnny, and Poison Ivy. "The Way He Walked." *L.A. Weekly*, 19–25 January 2001.

Whitfield, Gregory Mario. "Earthbeat: In the Beginning There Was Rhythm." *3AM Magazine*, November 2003.

Whitman, Allen. "Lydia Lunch Does It Her Way—Or Else." *Mediacast*. mediacast.com/Calendar/97-06-12/Erotic_Salon.editorial/LL-001-aw.html.

Wiese, Todd. "Tribe 8 Interview." *The Roc*. www.theroc.org/roc-mag/textarch/roc-18/roc18-08.htm.

Wilkinson, Kathleen. "Traveling with Godspeed: Lynn Breedlove Spreads Butch Culture." *Lesbian News*, May 2002.

Williamson, Nigel. "The Big Interview: Siouxsie Pseud?" *The Times Metro Music*, 10 October 1998.

Wilson, Kaia. "The Butchies Tour Diary." 12 April 2004. www.thebutchies.com/diary.html.

Wilson, Kathleen. "Set Me Free: Kim Warnick Says Goodbye to the Fastbacks." *The Stranger*, 14 February 2002.

Wolk, Douglas. "Grrrl Talk: Kathleen Hanna Resurfaces as Julie Ruin." *The Boston Phoenix*, 28 September 1998.

Worrell, Denise. "Now: Madonna on Madonna." *Time*, 27 May 1985.

Wyman, Bill, and David Antrobus. "PJ Harvey." *Trouser Press*. www.trouserpress.com/entry_90s.php?a=pj_harvey.

Yohannon, Tim. "The Avengers." *Maximumrocknroll*, August 1985.

FILMS AND VIDEOS

The Cramps Live at the Napa State Mental Hospital, 1978, DVD. Pennsylvania: Music Video Distributors, Inc., 2003.

The Decline of Western Civilization. Directed by Penelope Spheeris. Nu-Image Film, 1980.

Punk: The Early Years, DVD. Pennsylvania: Music Video Distributors, 2003.

Rise Above: The Tribe 8 Documentary. Directed by Tracy Flannigan. Los Angeles: Red Hill Pictures, 2003.

Songs for Cassavetes: An All Ages Film, DVD. Directed by Justin Mitchell. Pennsylvania: Music Video Distributors, Inc., 2001.

Williams, Wendy O., and the Plasmatics, compiled footage of television appearances. Origin unknown.

OTHER INFORMATION

Biographical information was aided by various databases, including All Music Guide, www.allmusic.com; Artist Direct, www.artistdirect.com; Experience Music Project, www.emplive.com; MTV, www.mtv.com; VH1, www.vh1.com; Punk 77, www.punk77.co.uk; and artist and label websites.

INDEX

A

ABBA: 59, 60, 72, 85

Abdul, Paula: 152

absence of women in punk: 155–157

absurdist indie: 154

Adam and the Ants: 75

Adams, Bryan: 152–153

Advert, Gaye: 35, 69

Adverts, The: 68–69, 71

AIDs: 163, 164

Akron: 9

Albini, Steve: 116, 199

albums: *A Brilliant Mistake* 173; *Allen's Mom* 189; *All Hands on the Bad One* 236; *America's Sweetheart* 179; *...And His Orchestra* 141; *Animal Rhapsody* 102; *Anthology, The* 88, 91; *Antidote* 173; *Are We Not Femme?* 240; *Arkansas Heat* 254; *As Nasty as They Wanna Be* 108; *At Crystal Palace* 257; *A Thousand Leaves* 138, 139; *Auf der Maur* 179; *Avengers, The* 50; *Babysitters on Acid* 194; *Bad Moon Rising* 136; *Beauty Process Triple Platinum, The* 183; *Big Lizard in My Backyard* 154; *Bikini Kill* 205; *Binge and Purge* 193, 195; *Blondie* 40; *Blondie Live* 40; *Bobbing for Pavement Rathouse Compilation* 168; *Boomerang* 77; *Bricks Are Heavy* 183, 184; *By the Time We Get to Colorado* 189, 190; *Calculated* 235; *Call the Doctor* 225, 235; *Captain My Captain* 216, 217, 218; *CD Version of the First Two Records, The* 205, 206; *Celebrity Skin* 179; *Colour and the Shape, The* 36; *Come on Pilgrim* 145; *Confusion Is Sex* 136; *Conscious Consumer* 91; *Coup d'Etat* 128; *Crimes Against Nature* 125; *Curse of Blondie, The* 40; *Cut* 81, 83–84; *Dance Hall* 199; *Daydream Nation* 136; *Deep End* 172–173; *Died for Your Sins* 50; *Dig Me Out* 235; *Dirty* 138; *Document* 147; *Dream of Life* 21; *Dry* 198, 199, 200, 201; *Easter* 20–21; *Enter The Conquering Chicken* 165; *Everglade* 184; *Experimental Jet Set* 138; *Extended Play* 103; *Far Away* 232; *Fatherfucker* 248, 249; *Fear of Music* 29; *Feeding of the 5000, The* 93, 95–96, 97–98; *Feminist Sweepstakes* 245; *Fetish* 205; *Fist City* 189, 190; *Free to Fight* 217; *Frenching the Bully* 165; *From the Desk of Mr. Lady* 245; *Fumbling Towards Ecstasy* 224; *Funky Kingdom 101*; *Germ Free Adolescence* 87, 88; *Get Rich or Die Tryin'* 228; *(GI)* 35; *Girls Get Busy* 213, 232; *Gone Again* 21; *Goo* 138; *Go to the Sugar Altar* 146; *Gung Ho* 21; *Hey Zeus!* 43; *Horses* 11, 19, 20; *Hungry for Stink* 183; *Hysterie* 125; *Is This Desire?* 201; *Jerk of All Trades* 195; *Joshua Tree, The* 148; *Julie Rain* 244; *Kill Rock Stars* 154; *Kill Yr Idols* 136; *King Me* 143; *Kings and Queens* 166; *Kitchen Tapes, The* 102; *Kommander of Kaos* 128; *Ladies, Women and Girls* 213; *Ladyman* 240; *Last Splash* 146; *Life Could Be a Dream* 44; *Little Creatures* 30; *Live Through This* 36, 177–178, 179; *Looking in the Shadows* 103; *Los Angeles* 43, 45; *Lovertits* 248; *L7* 184; *Luxury Problems* 197; *Make Yr Life* 240, 241; *Milk It!* 161–162; *More Fun in the New World* 43; *More Songs About Buildings and Food* 29; *Morrison Hotel* 6; *Movement* 254; *Moving* 102; *Murray Street* 138; *Naked* 30; *Nevermind* 183; *Nice Ass* 137; *No Exit* 40; *No Star* 138; *Odyshape* 102, 103; *Old Wives' Tales* 44; *One Beat* 232, 237, 238; *Other Animals* 257, 258; *Parallel Lines* 40; *Peace and Noise* 21; *Peel Sessions* 81; *Peep Show* 77; *Penis Envy* 68, 94, 95, 96–97; *Personal Best* 215–216, 217; *Pig Bitch* 189; *Platinum Collection* 40; *Population 1975* 240; *Pottymouth* 211; *Pretty on the Inside* 137, 177, 178; *Pretty Ugly* 197; *Private Lubs* 166; *Pussy Whipped* 205; *Radio Ethiopia* 20; *Raincoats, The* 102, 103; *Real Janelle, The* 212; *Reject All American* 205; *Remain in Light* 29; *Retrospective* 81; *Return of the Giant Slits* 81; *Rid of Me* 199, 200, 201; *Rock Against Bush Vols. I and II* 233; *Roe vs. Wade* 151;

Rude Hieroglyphics 46; *Running Scared* 44; *Safari* 146; *Scream, The* 76; *Seafish Louisville* 166; *Second Coming* 154; *Sgt. Pepper* 101; *Significant Other* 229; *Silk Purse* 10; *Sister* 136; *Slap-Happy* 183, 184; *Slow Dirty Tears* 103; *Smell the Magic* 183, 184; *Snarkism* 189, 190; *Songs About Fucking* 148; *Sonic Death* 136; *Sonic Nurse* 138, 257; *Soul Kitchen* 43; *Speaking in Tongues* 30; *Stories from the City, Stories from the Sea* 201; *Stukas over Dickieland* 154; *Such Friends Are Dangerous* 234; *Sunset on Dateland* 143; *Surface to Air Serpents* 44; ; *Talking Heads 77* 29; *Teaches of Peaches, The* 248, 249; *That's Not What I Heard* 254; *Theo* 197; *There's a Dyke in the Pit* 164; *This Island* 245; *Tidal* 224; *Tinderbox* 73; *Title TK* 146; *To Bring You My Love* 199, 201; *To the 5 Boroughs* 232; *Trampin'* 21; *Trash* 138; *Uh Huh Her* 201; *Uncensored Lydia Lunch, The* 123; *Unclogged* 43; *Under the Big Black Sun* 43, 44; *¡Viva Zapata!* 168; *Warehouse Songs and Stories* 148; *Washing Machine* 138; *Wave* 21; *We're Desperate* 32; *Wild Gift* 43, 45; *WOW* 128; *Yes, Please* 31; *Zücker* 142

Ambrose, Joe: 157
America: 5
American Bandstand: 70
Andersen, Mark: 155
anger: 15, 153–154, 262
anorexia: 14
Apple, Fiona: 223, 229
Arista: 11
Ari-Up: 64, 72, 79–85
art shows: 158
Ashford, Chris: 34
Aspinall, Vicky: 101
Avengers, The: 11, 14, 15, 47–51; "American in Me" 49; *Avengers, The* 50; break up 49–50; *Died for Your Sins* 50; England 50; Furious, Danny 48; gender issues 49; Houston, Penelope 11, 13, 47–51; 115, 152, 153, 154; Ingraham, Greg 48; Lookout! 50; Mabuhay Gardens 48; musical style 49, 50–51; "Open Your Eyes" 49; personal history 47–48; politics 49; Postal, Jonathan 48; punk scene 47; Sex Pistols, The 47, 49; songwriting 48, 50; "Uh-Oh" 49; "We Are the One" 49; "White Nigger" 49; Wisley, Jimmy 48

Axl Rose: 163
Azerrad, Michael: 115–116, 154
Azzoli, Val: 226

B

Babes in Toyland: 153, 177, 183, 196
Bacharach, Burt: 4, 5, 59
Back in Control Training: 114
Bad Brains: 163
Bag, Alice: 14
Bags, The: 14
Balkan rape victims: 157
Bananarama: 147
Bands Against Bush: 231, 232
Bangs, Lester: 4–5, 10
Banshees, The: 72
Bassey, Shirley: 51
Bay Area punk scene: 47
Beastie Boys: 231–232
Beat Happening: 11, 117, 154
Beat, Nickey: 33
Beatles, The: 5
Beefeater: 155
Beefheart, Captain: 199
Belew, Adrian: 29
Bello, Elissa: 14
Big Black: 116–117, 147
Bikini Kill: 154, 158, 159, 160, 164, 184, 203–208; abuse 207; Andersen, Mark 204; *Bikini Kill* 205; *Bumpidee* 206; *CD Version of the First Two Records, The* 205, 206; *Dance of Days* 204; development of riot grrrl movement 205–207, 208; feminism 205–207; *Fetish* 205; Hanna, Kathleen 203, 204–205, 207; Jenkins, Mark 204; Jett, Joan 205; *Jigsaw* 203, 205; *Julie Ruin* 206; Karren, Billy 203, 205, 206; *L.A. Weekly* 205; March for Women's Lives 204; Nation of Ulysses 204, 205; negative attention 204; Neuman, Molly 205; "New Radio" 205; oppression 203; personal history 204–205; *Punk Planet* 204, 206; *Pussy Whipped* 205; "Rebel Girl" 205, 207; *Reject All American* 205; Reko Muse 205; riot grrrl invasion 203; sexism in punk 204; sexuality 207; Sinker, Daniel 204; Smith, Erin 205; Smith, Jen 205; songwriting 205; "Star Bellied Boy" 207; "Suck My Left One" 207; Team Dresch 205; Vail, Tobi 203, 205, 206; Viva Knieval 205; *We Owe You Nothing* 204;

"White Boy" 207; Wilcox, Kathi 203, 206; Wolfe, Allison 205
Bingenheimer, Rodney: 12–13
birth of punk: 7–8
Bizarros, The: 9
Bjelland: 183
Black Flag: 35, 37, 114–116
Blige, Mary J.: 228
Blondie: 13, 38–41, 53, 60, 70, 71, 109–110; beauty 40; *Blondie* 40; *Blondie Live* 40; break up of band 40; Burke, Clement 39; "Call Me" 41, 71; Capitol Records 39; CBGB 38, 39, 40; Chrysalis Records 40; *Curse of Blondie, The* 40; Destri, Jimmy 39; "Dreaming" 41; film work 40; *Hairspray* 40; Harry, Debbie 38–41; "Heart of Glass" 40, 41, 71; "In the Flesh" 40; Jazz Passengers 40; "Kung Fu Girls" 40; mainstream radio 40; media coverage 41; *Melody Maker* 40; New York sound 39, 40; *No Exit* 40; "One Way or Another" 40, 41; *Parallel Lines* 40; personal background 39; *Platinum Collection* 40; Playboy 39; Private Stock 40; punk pop 39; "Rapture" 41; reunion 40; "Rip Her to Shreds" 39, 41; sexuality 40–41; songwriting 41; Stein, Chris 39; Stilettos, The 39; Television 39; Tiven, Jon 40; Top 40 41; "Union City Blue" 41; Valentine, Gary 39; Waters, John 40; "X Offender" 39, 41
Bolan, Marc: 9
Bolles, Don: 33, 36
Bonebrake, D.J.: 33, 42
Bonham, Tracy: 223, 225
Bono: 232
books: *A Beer on Every Page* 44; *Adulterers Anonymous* 43–44, 45–46; *Backlash: The Undeclared War Against Women* 107–108, 159, 160; *Beauty Myth, The* 111, 159; *Christ's Reality Asylum* 96; *Confusion is Next The Sonic Youth Story* 121; *Courtney Love: Queen of Noise* 180; *Dance of Days* 155, 159, 204; *Decline of Western Civilization, The* 35, 42, 116; *Dialectic of Sex, The* 245; *England's Dreaming* 63, 67, 69, 75, 87, 113; *Godspeed* 189; *Incesticide* 103, 180; *JD's Lesbian Calendar 2003* 245; *Just Another War* 44; *Last Exit to Brooklyn* 122; *Love Songs* 92–93; *Mechanics Guide to Putting Out Records, The* 174; *Mr. Right On and Other Stories* 36–37; *Neon Angel The Cherie Currie Story* 23; *Our Band Could Be Your Life* 115–116, 156; *Paradoxia A Predator's Diary* 123; *Please Kill Me* 14, 30, 67; *Popular Music and Society* 62; *Precious and Few* 4; *Rock She Wrote* 118, 178; *Scream Quietly or the Neighbors Will Hear* 65; *Sex Revolts, The* 66; *She's A Rebel* 6, 112, 235; *Shibboleth* 93, 96; *Virtual Unreality* 44; *We Got the Neutron Bomb* 5, 12, 14, 22, 34
Boone, Debbie: 5
Born in the U.S.A.: 108
Borow, Zev: 229
Bovell, Dennis: 83
Bowie, David: 8–9, 12, 29, 33, 61, 63, 93
Boyz II Men: 153
Bratmobile: 154, 156, 160, 205, 209–214, 232, 234 ; Beat Happening 209, 210; Billotte, Christina 211; break up 212–213; Brown, Katherine 213; Calamity Jane 209; "Cherry Bomb" 211; Cold Cold Hearts 213; "Cool Schmool" 211; Deep Lust 213; DIY spirit 209–210; Donnas, The 213; feminism 211–212, 214; "Fuck Yr. Fans" 211; "Gimme Brains" 213; *Girl Germs* 210; *Girls Get Busy* 213; "I'm in the Band" 213; individual projects 212–213; Internal Pop Underground Convention 211; *Jigsaw* 210; K Records 211; Kill Rock Stars 211; *Ladies, Women and Girls* 213; Ladyfest 213; Locust, The 213; Lookout! Records 212; Marrs, Audrey 213; musical style 209, 210–211; Neuman, Molly 209–213; Nikki, John 213; 9/11 213; Oly-D.C. connection 212; Oswald 5-O 210; Peechees 212; personal history 210–211; politics 211; pop escapism 209; *Pottymouth* 211; *Punk Planet* 212; Ramones, The 210–211; *Real Janelle, The* 212; reunion 213; riot grrrl 212, 213–214; *Riot Grrrl* 210; sexism 213; "Shop for America" 213; Smith, Erin 209–213; Smith, Jen 211; Some Velvet Sidewalk 210; "United We Don't" 213; Tucker, Corin 213; Vilence, Marty 213; Viva Knieval 209; Wolfe, Allison 209, 210–214
Breedlove, Lynn: 117–118, 224
Breithaupt, Don and Jeff: 4
Britain: 59–72
British press: 64

British punk vs. American punk: 71–72
Bromley Contingent, The: 64
Brooklyn's Shirts: 14
Brooks, Meredith: 224
Browne, David: 162
Brownstein, Carrie: 234, 235–236, 237–238
Bush Sr., George: 151
Butchies, The: 232–233
butch lesbian identity: 232
Butthole Surfers: 154, 163
Buzzcocks: 64, 70

C
cable television: 109
Cadena, Dez: 35, 36
Caffey, Charlotte: 14
Candi, Staton: 61
Candy-Ass: 164
Canzoneri, Ginger: 14
Cardwell, Jenna: 14
Carey, Mariah: 152, 153
Carland, Tammy Rae: 156–157, 205, 216
Carlisle, Belinda: 12, 14, 33, 36
Carpenters, The: 5, 6, 60
Casual Dots: 206, 211
Caucasian rock: 4
CBGB: 10–11, 12, 27, 28, 53–54, 71
CD Presents: 50
censorship: 108
Cervenka, Exene (Christine): 15, 42–46, 47,
    111–112
Chainsaw: 164
Chalk Circle: 117, 155
Chapman, Tracy: 225
Charles, Tina: 61
Chideya, Farai: 162
Childers, Leee: 17, 67
Chilton, Alex: 54
Choir, The: 9
Chris Spedding and the Vibrators: 64
Circle Jerks: 37
Clague, Leslie: 171
Clash, The: 63, 64, 65, 67, 71, 72, 80, 85
classism: 160
Cleveland: 9
Coachmen, The: 134
Cobain, Kurt: 36, 67, 134, 157
cock rock: 4, 7, 9
Cocks, Jay: 112
Cola, Casey: 67
Collins, Judy: 61
Color Me Badd: 153

Concerned Women for America (CWA): 107
Conflict: 118
Connolly, Cynthia: 171
conservative government: 231
conservative movement: 107
Cook, Paul: 63
Coomes, Sam: 235
Coon, Caroline: 28
Cooper, Alice: 23
Copeland, Mike: 54
Cop Killer: 108
corporate rock: 154
Cramps, The: 15, 42, 52–55; androgyny 54;
    Del Mar, Candy 55; Gregory, Bryan
    53; *Guitar Player* 55; Interior, Lux 52,
    53; IRS Records 54; Ivy, Poison 52–55;
    Max's Kansas City 52; musical style
    53–54, 55; New York punk 52, 53;
    personal history 53–54; psychobilly 52;
    rockabilly 53, 54; sexuality 53, 54; *Smell of
    Female* 54; *Songs the Lord Taught Us* 54;
    Stay Sick! 55; Vengeance Records 54;
    Wallace, Kirsty 53; West Coast punk
    scene 54
Crash, Darby: 67
Crass: 65, 66, 68, 72, 92–99, 118; anarchy
    93; antiwar movement 92; artistic
    contributions 92; break up 98; British
    Secret Service 98; Christianity 96;
    Christ's Reality Asylum 96; communes
    92, 94; controversy 96–97, 98; Crass
    Agenda 98; criticism of punk 93; de
    Vivre, Joy 68, 92–99; Dial House 94;
    Duffield, Mick 95; *Feeding of the 5000,
    The* 93, 95–96, 97–98; female only
    album 96–97; feminism 94, 95–96; Free,
    Phil 93, 96, 98; Ignorant, Steve 93; jazz
    98; legal problems 97–98; Libertine,
    Eve 68, 92–99; *Love Songs* 92–93;
    new projects 98–99; "Our Wedding"
    97; Palmer, N.A. 93; *Penis Envy* 94,
    96–97; philosophy 99; political punk
    93, 94, 96–97; "Punk Is Dead" 93;
    "Reality Asylum" 96, 97–98; Rimbaud,
    Penny 92–93, 96; sexism 94, 95–96;
    Shibboleth 93, 96; Southern Records
    96; Stormtrooper 93; Thatchergate
    98; Vaucher, Gee 93; Women 95–96;
    Wright, Pete 93
Crime: 47
Crow, Sheryl: 223
crystal meth: 14

Culture Club: 109
Cure, The: 74, 76

D

Damned, The: 64, 69, 71
Dangermouse: 217
da Silva, Anna 100–104
Davis, Clive: 19
Dawn: 5
DCeats: 155
D.C. scene: 155, 171–172
Dead Kennedys: 118
Deadly Nightshade: 12
Dead Milkmen: 154
Deal, Kim: 144–148
deregulation in radio: 175
DeRogatis, Jim: 161
de Vivre, Joy: 68, 92–99
Devo: 9
Devoto, Howard: 50, 64
Diamond, Neil: 5
Dickies, The: 154, 163
dieting: 14
Dils, The: 13
Dinosaur Jr.: 148, 217
disco: 61
Ditto, Beth: 227, 252–253, 254, 255
Division, Joy: 73
DIY ethic: 131, 156, 160, 227
DNA: 122
Doe, John: 42, 43, 44
Dogs, The: 12, 34
Doors, The: 5, 6
Drano, Jane: 14
Dresch, Donna: 215–219
Durst, Fred: 229
Dylan, Bob: 5, 10, 18

E

East Coast punk: 13
eating disorders: 160
Echo: 73
Eddie and the Hot Rods: 63
Electric Eels, The: 9
Elliott, Eve: 228
Elliott, Missy: 228
Eminem: 229
EMI Records: 64
English Disco: 12, 13
English punk: 34
Entertainment Weekly: 162
Equal Rights Amendment (ERA): 107

Erase Errata: 256–259; *At Crystal Palace* 257;
  Erickson, Ellie 256–257, 259; feminism
  258; Hoyston, Jenny 256, 257, 258, 259;
  Inconvenient 257; Jaffe, Sara 256–257,
  258, 259; lyrics 257–258; musical style
  256, 258–259; personal history 256;
  politics 258; *Other Animals* 257, 258;
  "Other Animals Are #1" 258; *Punk
  Planet* 258; songwriting 257–258; *Sonic
  Nurse* 257; Sonic Youth 257; Sparta,
  Bianca 256, 257, 259; Troubleman
  Unlimited 258; WESU 256
Essential Logic: 72
exclusion by mainstream radio: 227
Experience Music Project: 235

F

Faltskog, Agnetha: 60
Faludi, Susan: 107–108, 159, 160
Fanny: 12
Fastbacks, The: 62, 117, 140–143, 156–157;
  ... And His Orchestra 141; Bird, The
  141; Bloch, Kurt 140–143; breaking
  up 143; bubblegum punk 141, 142;
  Cheaters, The 141; concerts 140–141;
  Enemy, The 141; Flotard, Rachel 143;
  Gargiulo, Lulu 140–143; gender themes
  142–143; Girlschool 141; Hooker, Ben
  143; Jett, Joan 140, 141; *King Me* 143;
  McDonnell, Evelyn 142; Musberger,
  Mike 140; musical style 140–142;
  No Threes 141; Pearl Jam 140–141;
  personal history 141; PopLlama
  140; pop punk 140; Radios, The 141;
  Seattle sound 140; Seaweed and the
  Supersuckers 140; sexism 142–143;
  sexuality 143; songwriting 140, 142–
  143; spinArt 140; *Stranger, The* 140–141,
  142, 143; Sub Pop 140; *Sunset on
  Dateland* 143; Visqueen 143; Warnick,
  Kim 62, 140–143; *Zücker* 142
Fat Mike: 197, 233
FCC: 175
Fear: 116, 117
Federal Communications Commission: 227
female indie rock fans: 158
female perspective in punk: 157
female reality: 154
female singer-songwriters: 60
feminism: 7, 107, 112, 153, 157, 159, 160,
  223, 224, 232, 233
feminist authors: 159

feminist politics and males: 157
Fifth Column: 164
50 Cent: 228
films: *Butch Cassidy and the Sundance Kid* 4;
   By Hook or By Crook 189; *Edgeplay* 26;
   Foxes 25; *Gang Girls* 197; *Gits, The* 16;
   Hairspray 40; *Kurt and Courtney* 180;
   L7: The Beauty Process 183; *Man on the
   Moon* 179; *People vs. Larry Flynt, The*
   179; *Rise Above* 190; *Sid and Nancy* 178;
   Songs for Cassavetes 11; *Stop Making
   Sense* 30
Fire Party: 117, 155–156, 172
Firestone, Shulamith: 245
Fishbone: 117, 163
Flowers of Romance: 79
Flucts, The: 135
Foege, Alec: 137
folk musicians: 5
Foo Fighters, The: 36
Fowley, Kim: 12
Franklin, Aretha: 110
Free Tibet: 232
Friedan, Betty: 160
Frightwig: 117, 118
Fryer, Paul: 70
Fugazi: 117, 118, 155, 159, 164
Furies, The: 235

G
Gaar, Gillian: 6, 28, 29, 112
Galas, Diamanda: 164
garage bands: 7-8, 11
Garbage: 226
Gargiulo, Lulu: 140–143
Geek: 153, 170–176; *A Brilliant Mistake* 173;
   activism 175–176; *Antidote* 173; Beat
   Happening 172; *Billboard* 173; Bloody
   Mannequin Orchestra 171; D.C. punk
   170; *Deep End* 172–173; feminism 171–
   172, 173; Future of Music Coalition
   (FMC) 170, 175–176; *Georgetown
   Voice* 172; Government Issue 171;
   Grenadine 173; "The Heart's Tremolo,"
   173; "Herasure" 172; "In a Name" 173;
   Liquorice and Grenadine 170, 173;
   Littleton, Dan 173; lyrics 172–173;
   McCaughan, Mac 172; *Mechanics Guide
   to Putting Out Records, The* 174; musical
   style 172–173; 9:30 Club 171; Pamer,
   John 172; "Patsy Cline" 173; personal
   history 171; political impact 171, 175–
176; Positive Force 171, 172; Robinson,
   Marc 173; Scrawl 174; Seaweed 172;
   Sigal, Brad 170, 173; Simple Machines
   170, 173–175; Superchunk 172; Teen
   Beat Records 173; think tank 170;
   Thomson, Kristin 170, 172–176;
   Toomey, Jenny 153, 155–156, 158,
   170–176, 205, 227; Tsunami 170–172;
   Unrest 173; Webster, Andrew 172;
   Working Holiday series 174
Gehman, Pleasant: 13, 32
gender issues: 236
genderplay: 232
Genet, Jean: 17
Germs, The: 12–15, 32–37, 42, 205; *Back
   Door Man* 34; Beahn, Jan Paul 33; chaos
   35; Crash, Darby 33; decline of band
   36; *Decline of Western Civilization, The*
   35, 116; Doom, Lorna 33; "Forming"
   34; *(GI)* 35; Jett, Joan 35; L.A. sound
   34; lyrics 254; *Mr. Right On and Other
   Stories* 36–37; Panter, Nicole 34, 35,
   36–37; Panter's writing 36–37; *Pee-Wee's
   Playhouse* 36; personal history 32–35;
   politics 36; punk 'zines 34; Rhia, Donna
   33; Ruthenberg, Georg 33; *Slash* 33, 34;
   Smear, Pat 33; Spheeris, Penelope 35;
   We're Desperate 32; What? Records 34;
   women playing instruments 35
Gibson, Debbie: 147
Ginn, Greg: 114–115
girl mosh pit: 159, 164
Gits, The 165–169; Agnew, Valerie 167–168;
   Antioch College 166; "Beauty of the
   Rose" 168; bisexual 169; blues 165;
   Broken Rekids 166; Dancing French
   Liberals of '48 166; DC Beggars
   168; Dresdner, Matt 166; *Enter The
   Conquering Chicken* 165; Evil Stig
   166, 168; Farm, The 167; *Frenching the
   Bully* 165; hardcore fans 167; Holiday,
   Billie 165; Jett, Joan 166; lyrics 168;
   Moriarity, Steve 166; musical style
   168–169; personal history 166–167;
   political beliefs 168, 169; *Private
   Lubs* 166; "The Rathouse" 168; RL
   C/Z Records 165; Seattle 167–168;
   7 Year Bitch 167–168; Sheehy, Peter
   166; Smith, Bessie 165; songwriting
   168–169; "Spear and Magic Helmet"
   168–169; Spleen, Joe (Andy Kessler)
   166; Sub Pop 167; Vigil, Selene 168;

¡Viva Zapata! 168; Zapata, Mia 165–169; Zapata's murder 165–166
glam: 8–9
Glitter, Gary: 61
Gloria Estefan and the Miami Sound Machine: 147
God Is My Co-Pilot: 164
Go-Go's, The: 12, 14, 36, 47
Golden, Annie: 14
Goldstein, Patrick: 20, 25
Gordon, Kim: 115, 133–139
Gossip, The: 227, 252–255; *Arkansas Heat* 254; body image 254–255; Brownstein, Carrie 253; Ditto, Beth 227, 252–253, 254, 255; DIY 252; Dub Narcotic Sound System 253; empowerment 255; fat phobia; 255; feminism 253; homophobia 255; Howdeshell, Nathan 252, 253, 254; indie beauty 252; indie rock 254; Kill Rock Stars 254; Mendonca, Kathy 252, 253, 254, 255; *Movement* 254; musical style 252, 254; Olympia 253; riot grrrl 253; sexuality 252; Sleater-Kinney 253; soul music 252; Southern influence 252, 254; *That's Not What I Heard* 254
Graham, Bill: 49
Gregory, Pam "Balam": 53
groupie culture: 7
Grundy, Bill: 71, 76
grunge: 156, 157, 227
Guns N' Roses: 163

H
Hanger, Cliff: 33
Hangovers, The: 103
Hanna, Kathleen: 156–157, 232, 243–244, 245
hardcore punk: 114–118
hard rock: 7
Harrigan, Brian: 40–41
Harris, Rolf: 59
Harrison, Jerry: 29, 31
Harron, Mary: 63
Harry, Debbie: 38–41
Harvey, PJ (Polly Jean): 198–202; Antrobus, David 200–201; "A Perfect Day Elise" 201; Automatic Dlamini 199; Bologna 199; "Catherine" 201; "Dress" 200; Ellis, Robert 199; evolution 201; Feldman, Eric Drew 199; "50 Ft Queenie" 200, 202; gender issues 199–200, 201–202; Gonzalez, Ed 202; Gore, Joe 199; "Hair" 200; Hynde, Chrissie 202; image 201; Island Records 199; "Joy" 201; lyrics 199, 200–201; mainstream success 201; musical style 198, 199–202; "My Beautiful Leah" 201; *NME* 200, 202; "Oh My Lover" 200; Parish, John 199; personal history 199; philosophy 199–200; "Plants and Rags" 200; *Q* 199; sexuality 201, 202; "Sheela-Na-Gig" 200, 202; *Slant* 202; Smith, Patti 202; Too Pure 199; *Trouser Press* 200–201; Vaughn, Steve 199; "The Wind" 201; Wyman, Bill 200–201
Hazel: 27
Heartbreakers, The: 17
Heavens to Betsy: 154, 212
heavy metal culture: 163
Hell, Richard: 11, 20, 63
Hendrix, Jimi: 5
Henley, Rob: 33, 36
Hermosa Beach: 114, 115
Hill, Lauryn: 228
hip-hop: 228
Hole: 153, 157, 177–181, 183, 227; *America's Sweetheart* 179; "Asking for It" 179; *Auf der Maur* 179; Auf der Maur, Melissa 179; Bjelland, Kat 177; break up 179; Broomfield, Nick 180; Caroline Records 177; *Celebrity Skin* 179; Cobain, Kurt 178, 179–180; Corgan, Billy 179; *Courtney Love: Queen of Noise* 180; Des Barres, Pamela 178, 180; Emery, Jill 178; Erlandson, Eric 178; Eugene, Oregon 178; feminism 177, 179, 181; film acting 178, 179; Finch, Jennifer 177, 183; Hanna, Kathleen 181; hate victim 180; influences 178; "I Think That I Would Die" 179; "Jennifer's Body" 177, 179; *Kurt and Courtney* 180; *Live Through This* 177–178, 179; Lollapalooza tour 181; Love, Courtney 36, 67, 154, 157, 162, 177–181, 183; *Man on the Moon* 179; "Miss World" 179; molestation 179; musical style 177, 179; *Newsweek* 180; Ono, Yoko 178, 180; *People vs. Larry Flynt, The* 179; personal history 178–179; Pfaff, Kristin 178; *Pretty on the Inside* 177, 178, 179; public misconduct 181; *Rock She Wrote* 178; *Rolling Stone* 181; Rossi, Melissa 180; Rue, Caroline 178; Schemel, Patty 178;

sexuality 177; *Sid and Nancy* 178; Smashing Pumpkins 179; songwriting 179; *Spin* 178; Sugar Baby Doll 177; "Teenage Whore" 178, 179; themes 177–178; Virgin Records 179

Holstrom, John: 34

homophobia in punk: 116, 160, 163, 164

Hopper, Jessica: 162

Houston, Penelope: 11, 13, 47–51, 115, 152, 153, 154

Howdeshell, Nathan: 227

Huggy Bear: 204, 205

Hüsker Dü: 148

Hynde, Chrissie: 89

IJ

Idol, Billy: 64, 75, 109

Iggy Pop: 8, 33, 63

indie rock: 117, 118, 157, 227, 228, 231

indie underground: 151

International Pop Underground Convention (IPU): 154, 155, 159

Internet: 227

Ivy, Poison: 52–55

Jackson, Janet: 152

Jackson, Michael: 109

Jackson, Wanda: 54–55

Jagger, Mick: 6, 12

Jam: 84

Jane's Addiction: 117

Jarecke, Kenneth: 44

Jay-Z: 228

Jenkins, Mark: 155

Jett, Joan (Larkin): 12, 22–26, 74, 115

Jewel: 223, 224, 225

Johansen, Dave: 8

Johnson, Calvin: 11, 154, 205, 209

Johnson, Rick: 24

Jones, Steve: 63, 71, 75, 79

Joplin, Janis: 6, 10

Jr. High: 235

Julian, Ivan: 14

K

Kaye, Lenny: 17

Kent, Nick: 27

Kid Rock: 229

Kill Rock Stars: 103

King, Carole: 5

Knox, Nick: 53

Korn: 230

Kristal, Hilly: 10, 19

KROQ: 13

Kubernik, Harvey: 5

L

L.A. punk: 37

Lauper, Cyndi: 111–113, 114, 119

Le Jardin: 18

Lennon, John: 21

Lennox, Annie: 110

lesbian queercore: 153

Le Tigre: 158, 232, 243–246; Baumgardner, Jennifer 245; Benning, Sadie 244; Bikini Kill 244; Bird, Cass 245; electronic pop 243; Fateman, Joanna 243, 244, 245; feminism 243, 244, 245–246; *Feminist Sweepstakes* 245; *From the Desk of Mr. Lady* 245; FYR 245; Hanna, Kathleen 156–157, 232, 243–244, 245; "Hot Topic" 246; indie rock 243–246; *JD's Lesbian Calendar 2003* 245; *Julie Rain* 244; leftist politics 244; lesbian dance troupe 244–245; musical style 244; Ocasek, Rick 245; oppressed artists 246; political activism 246; pro-queer art 244; riot grrrl 245; *Rockrgrl* 245; Samson, JD 243, 244–245; Sinker, Daniel 244; songwriting 245; *Stranger, The* 245; Strummer Records 245; *This Island* 245; Troublemakers 244; *We Owe You Nothing* 244

Letts, Don: 84

Libertine, Eve: 68, 92–99

Lilith Fair: 225, 230

Limp Bizkit: 229, 230

Linna, Miriam: 53, 55

Lisa Lisa: 147

Living Colour: 163

Logic, Lora: 86–91

London Weekend Show: 71

Los Angeles glam scene: 12

Los Angeles punk: 32

Love, Courtney: 36, 67, 154, 157, 162, 177–181, 183

Love Rock Revolution Girl Style Now: 154

L7: 153, 154, 177, 182–5, 196; abortion rights 183–184; *Beauty Process Triple Platinum, The* 183; "Beaver" banner 197; "Everglade" 184; feminism 182–185; Feminist Majority Foundation 182, 183; Feminists of the Year 182; films 183; Finch, Jennifer 182, 183; Gardner, Suzi 183, 184; Greenwood,

Gail 183; *Hungry for Stink* 183; *L7* 184; "Ms. 45" 184; musical style 182; Novoselic, Krist 183; Ono, Yoko 185; Plakas, Dee 183; political activism 183–184; record label 182; Rock for Choice 182, 183; *Slap-Happy* 183, 184; Slash/Reprise 183; Slash/Warner 182; *Smell the Magic* 183, 184; Sparks, Donita 183, 184–185; Tanaka, Janis 183; "Wargasm" 185; Warped Tour 183; Wax Tadpole 182, 183, 185

Lucy Stoners: 164

Lunachicks: 153, 193–197, 223, 232–233; acting 197; *Babysitters on Acid* 194; Bantam 197; *Binge and Purge* 193, 195; "Bitterness Barbie" 195; Blast First 194; CBGB 197; current activities 197; Del Mar, Katrina 197; Destroy, Helen 194, 197; Devil's Kit 197; Dinosaur Jr. 194–195; DIY spirit 194; English, Chip 194, 197; Fallopian Rhapsody 195; feminism 193, 195–196; FlyRite Tattoo 197; Fusaro, Mike 194; *Gang Girls* 197; Go-Kart Records 197; Gordon, Kim 194; Heavy Nose Records 197; image 196; influences 194; *Jerk of All Trades* 195; Kogan, Theo 193–195, 197; L7 197; *Luxury Problems* 197; March for Women's Lives 197; Moore, Thurston 194; musical style 193; Offspring 197; paintings 197; "Plugg" 195; political outlook 195–196; *Pretty Ugly* 197; pro-choice 195; queercore 197; Rancid 197; Silver, Sidney 193–194; Sindi B 193–194, 196; Squid 193–194; Suicide King 197; Superstrong 195; *Theo* 197; touring 194–195; Vans Warped Tour 197; Volpe, Gina 193–194, 195–196, 197; Wreck, Becky 194

Lunch, Lydia: 115, 121; Beirut Slump 121, 122, 125; Birthday Party 123; books 123; Cave, Nick 123; CBGB 122; Cervenka, Exene 123; "Conspiracy of Women" 125; *Crimes Against Nature* 125; "Daddy Dearest" 125; "Death Valley '69" 123; 8 Eyed Spy 121–122, 125; Einstürzende Neubaten 123; emotional intimacy 123–125; feminism 125–126; films 123; Foetus 123; Genet, Jean 122, 123; Gira, Michael 123; *Hysterie* 125; James Chance and the Contortions 122; Miller, Henry 122, 123; musical style 121, 122–124; New York Dolls 122; no wave movement 121; *Paradoxia A Predator's Diary* 123; personal history 121–122; political statements 125–126; pornography 126; recording company 123; Rollins, Henry 123; Rowland, Howard S. 123; Sclavunos, Jim 121; *Scrawl* 124–125; sexual abuse 125; songwriting 122; Suicide 122; Swans, The 123; Teenage Jesus and the Jerks 121, 122, 125; Thirlwell, Jim 123; *Uncensored Lydia Lunch, The:* 123; Velvet Underground, The 122; Widowspeak 123

Lyngstad, Anni-Frid: 60

M

MacKaye, Ian: 155

Madonna: 119, 151–152, 162, 187

Maffeo, Lois: 205

magazines: *Back Door Man* 34; *Billboard* 4, 173, 240, 248; *Boston Phoenix* 103; *Bumpidee* 206; *Carrie* 154; *Chainsaw* 216, 217; *Cosmopolitan* 161, 225; *CounterPunch* 232; *Cowboy Mouth* 18; *Crawdaddy* 19; *Creem* 10, 11, 19, 24, 25, 39, 62; *Critical List* 155; *Daily Mail* 70; *Entertainment Weekly* 162, 183; *Forced Exposure* 135; *Georgetown Voice* 172; *Girl Germs* 158, 210; *Good Housekeeping* 108; *Guardian Unlimited, The* 75, 145, 248; *Guitar Player* 28; *I "Love" Amy Carter* 156; *Jigsaw* 158, 203, 205, 210; *Julie Ruin* 206; *L.A. Weekly* 183, 205, 241; *Lesbian News* 240; *Loving* 97; *Maximumrocknroll* 50, 95, 118, 136; *Melody Maker* 19, 28, 40, 69, 87, 204; *Moshpit* 157; *Ms.* 112; *Nation, The* 228; *New Musical Express (NME)* 23, 27, 29, 41, 69, 75, 200, 202; *Newsweek* 108, 162, 180; *Observer, The* 250; *Penthouse* 62; *Playboy* 131; *Popular Music and Society* 70; *Punk* 11, 63; *Punk Planet* 204, 206, 212, 215, 232, 237; *Punk Rock Academy* 218–219; *Q* 199; *Riot Grrrl* 210; *Rockrgrl* 135, 157, 235; *Rolling Stone* 19, 108, 181, 226; *Sassy* 162; *Scrawl* 124–125; *Search and Destroy* 46; *Slant* 202; *Slash* 33, 34; *Sniffin' Glue* 62, 68, 69; *Spin* 146, 147, 157, 178, 229, 230; *Stranger, The* 140–141, 142, 143, 245; *Tales from the Crypt* 53; *Time* 112, 113; *Total Guitar* 145; *Trouser Press* 200–201;

Venus 248, 250; *Village Voice, The* 34, 134, 137; *We Owe You Nothing* 204, 244; *Who Put the Bomp* 4
Mah, Leslie 161, 187, 188, 189, 190, 191
mainstream: acceptance 261; female vs. punk female 224; feminism 159, 160; music 59, 114, 152–153, 224–225; sexism 152; values 69
Malanga, Gerard: 17
male-rage: 229–230
Mansfield, Jayne: 74
Manson Family: 123
Manzarek, Ray: 5
Mapplethorpe, Robert: 17, 21, 109
March for Women's Lives: 160, 232–233
Marcus, Greil: 50–51
Marquee Club: 64
Mars: 122
masochism: 115, 116
Masque, The: 43
MC5: 8
McGovern, Maureen: 5
McKee, Mike: 232
McLachlan, Sarah: 224, 225
McLaren, Malcolm: 63, 67, 69
McLean, Don: 5
McNeil, Legs: 30, 34
MDC: 118
Meat Puppets: 117
Mecca Normal: 154
Melvins, The: 209
Mendonca, Kathy: 252, 253, 254, 255
Mercer Arts Center: 18
Mercury, Freddie: 33
Minor Threat: 116, 155
Miro, Jennifer: 13
Misfits: 193
misogyny: 117
Mitchell, Joni: 5
Moby: 233
Modern Lovers: 29
Moon, Slim: 154
Moore, Thurston: 236
Morello, Tom: 231
Morissette, Alanis: 223, 224, 225, 229, 230
Morris, Keith: 115
Morrison, Jim: 5, 8
mosh pit: 184, 230
Motels, The: 12, 34
Motorgoat: 235
MoveOn.org: 233
MRR: 118

MTV: 72, 109, 110, 111–152, 157, 187, 225, 228
Mudhoney: 157
Mullen, Brendan: 43, 115
Murphy's Law: 193
music sales: 109
My New Boyfriend: 205

N
National Endowment for the Arts (NEA): 109
National Public Radio (NPR): 20
Nattles: 213
Negro, Hal: 14
Neuman, Molly: 158
New Right: 108
Newton-John, Olivia: 10, 15, 60, 61
new underground: 231
new wave: 109
New York Dolls, The: 8, 33, 53, 54, 63
nihilism: 69
Nirvana: 36, 137, 157, 183, 184, 223, 227, 230
No Doubt: 226
NOFX: 197, 233
nonconservative thinking: 108
Novselic, Krist: 157
Nuns, The: 13, 15, 47
Nurses, The: 155

O
O'Connor, Sinead: 152
Oglesbee, Frank: 62
Olaverra, Margot: 14
Olympia scene: 156
100 Club Punk Festival: 64, 75
Ono, Yoko: 21
Osborne, Joan: 223
Osmonds, The: 15, 60
Outpunk: 164
overexposure: 114

P
Pandoras, The: 117, 141
Pansy Division: 164
Panter, Nicole: 34, 35, 36–37
parental advisory warning: 108–109
Parents' Music Resource Center (PMRC): 108, 151
Patti Smith Group: 9, 11, 12, 16–21, 30, 47, 48, 63, 68, 71, 89; Arista Records 19; artistic androgyny 18–20; beat poetry 18; "Because the Night" 21, 71;

CBGB 19; *Cowboy Mouth* 18; Daugherty, Jay Dee 19; *Dream of Life* 21; *Easter* 20–21; family 21; gender issues 18–20; "Gloria" 19–20; *Gone Again* 21; *Gung Ho* 21; "Hey Joe" 19; *Horses* 19, 20; Kaye, Lenny 19, 21; Kral, Ivan 19; last concert 21; Mapplethorpe, Robert 17; Max's Kansas City 17; MC5 21; Nader, Ralph 21; *Peace and Noise* 21; "People Have the Power" 21; personal history 17–8; physical style 20; "Piss Factory" 17; *Radio Ethiopia* 20; rock journalism 19; "Rock n Roll Nigger" 16, 21; Smith, Fred "Sonic" 21; spine fracture 20; Television 21; *Trampin'* 21; underground scene 19–20; Verlaine, Tom 21; vocal style 18; *Wave* 21

Payne, Freda: 61

Paytress, Mark: 88

Peaches: 232, 247–251; audience reaction 250; "Back It Up, Boys" 250–251; Berlin 247, 248; *Billboard* 248; censorship 250; crotch-shot gallery 249; DIY ethic 249; Electroclash 248; *Fatherfucker* 248, 249; "Four Women" 248; "Fuck the Pain Away" 250; Gaffney, Janice 250; Gonzales, Chilly 247; *Guardian* 248; "I Don't Give A ..." 249; "I U She" 249; Kitty-Yo Records 248; Lil' Kim 248; *Lovertits* 248; Lynskey, Dorian 248; lyrics 248, 249; musical style 247; Nisker, Merrill (AKA Peaches) 247; *Observer, The* 250; Perez, Omar 250; Queens of the Stone Age 248, 250; "Set It Off" 249; sexuality 247, 248–249, 250–251; Shit, The 247; Simone, Nina 248; Siren Festival 250; *Teaches of Peaches, The* 248, 249; theatrics 249; *Venus* 248, 250; White Stripes 248; XL Recordings/Beggars Group 248

Pearl Jam: 157

Pedersen, Candice: 154, 209

Pere Ubu: 9, 199

Perroni, Marco: 75

Perry, Mark: 62, 68

physical abuse: 160

Pixies, The: 144–148; Amps, The 146; break up 145–146; Breeders, The 145, 146; "Cannonball" 146; *Come on Pilgrim* 145; Deal, Kelley 145; Deal, Kim 144–148; Donelly, Tanya 146; "Do You Love Me Now?" 146; feminism 147; 4AD Records 145, 146; *Go to the Sugar Altar* 146; *Guardian Unlimited, The* 145; "I Just Wanna Get Along" 146; indie bands 144; *Last Splash* 146; Lovering, David 145; MacPherson, Jim 146; mainstream music 146, 147; MTV 147; musical style 144, 145, 146, 147; personal history 145; reunion 145; *Safari* 146; Santiago, Joey 145; sexuality 149; songwriting 147; *Spin* 146, 147; Thompson IV, Charles (aka Black Francis) 145; Throwing Muses 146; *Title TK* 146; *Total Guitar* 145; "Wave of Mutilation" 146; Wiggs, Josephine 144

Plant, Robert: 7, 12

Plasmatics, The: 15

Pleased to Meet Me: 148

PMS fraud rock: 224, 225, 226

Poetry Project: 17, 18

Poison Girls: 68, 71, 72

Poison Ivy: 15, 35

Police, The: 109

politics and punk: 65, 151–152, 153

Polk, Eileen: 14

Polydor: 76

Poneman, Jonathan: 156

pop divas: 152, 153

Pop!, The: 12, 34

Positive Force: 153

post-feminism: 227, 232

Presley, Elvis: 7, 72

Press, Joy: 66

Prince: 110–111, 153

Prince Buster: 101

pro-feminist backlash: 151

protest songs: 232

Public Image Ltd: 79, 88

pub rock: 63

punk issues: anarchy 68; beauty 14; fem 160; gay culture 163–164; metal fusion 25, 156; philosophy 92, 262; racism 115–116; rock movement 3–15, 261–262; sexism 68–69, 158; sexualitiy 62; violence 72

Punk Voter: 231

punk 'zines: 46

QR

Quasi: 235

Quatro, Suzie: 12, 61–62

Queen: 33

queercore: 164

Quix*o*tic: 211

Radio Free Hollywood movement: 12

radio station buyouts: 227
Rage Against the Machine: 231, 232
Raincoats, The: 72, 82, 100–104; *Animal Rhapsody* 102; Aspinall, Vicky 100–104; Au Pairs, The 101; Birch, Gina 100–104; *Boston Phoenix* 103; break up 102–103; Cobain, Kurt 103, 104; da Silva, Anna 100–104; Delta 5, The 101; Essential Logic 101; *Extended Play* 103; feminism 104; Gordon, Kim 103, 104; Kinks, The 104; *Kitchen Tapes, The* 102; Kleenex 101; Liliput 101; "Lola" 104; *Looking in the Shadows* 103; Marcus, Greil 103–104; *Moving* 102; musical style 101–104; new projects 103–104; Nirvana 103; "No One's Little Girl" 104; *Odyshape* 102, 103; O'Loughlin, Shirley 101; "Only Loved at Night" 10; Palmolive 101–102; personal history 101; *Raincoats, The* 102, 103; Reach Out International Records 102; Red Krayola 103; reunited 103; Rough Trade 102; Shelley, Steve 103; *Slow Dirty Tears* 103; Smells Like Records 103; Sonic Youth 103; Weiss, Ingrid 102; world music sound 100
Ramone, Dee Dee: 14
Ramone, Joey: 7, 8, 11, 12, 13, 20, 71, 128, 236–237
Ramones, The: 28–29, 53, 70
rape: 160, 162
rap music: 108–109, 117
Reagan, Ronald: 107, 117
Recording Industry Association of America: 108
record labels: Alternative Tentacles 189; Arista Records 19; Atlantic Records 226; Blackheart Records label 25; Blast First 194; Bong Load Records 182; Broken Rekids 166; Candy-Ass Records 216; Capitol Records 39; Caroline Records 177, 178; Chainsaw 216, 234; Chrysalis Records 40; C/Z Records 165; Elektra Records 43; EMI Records 64; Epitaph 183; Go-Kart Records 197; Harp Label 189; Heavy Nose Records 197; Inconvenient 257; IRS records 14, 54; Island Records 199; Kill Rock Stars 153, 205, 206, 211, 234, 235, 254; Kitty-Yo Records 248; K Records 11, 154, 156, 209–210, 211; Matador 227; Mercury Records 23; Mer label 19; Mr.

Lady Records 156, 216; Outpunk 189; Rathouse, The 168; Simple Machines 153, 170, 173–175; Sire Records 28–29; Slash Records 43; Slash/Reprise 183; Slash/Warner 182; Strummer Records 245; Sub Pop 156, 227; Teen Beat Records 173; Too Pure 199; Virgin Records 179; Wax Tadpole 182, 183; What? Records 34; XL Recordings/ Beggars Group 248
Red C: 155
Reddy, Helen: 6
Red Hot Chili Peppers: 117
Reed, Lou: 48
Reinstein, Erika: 159
Reko Muse (art gallery): 156–157
religion: 107–108
R.E.M.: 117, 148
Reynolds, Simon: 66
Rhode Island School of Design: 28
Richard Hell and the Voidoids: 14
Richards, Keith: 18
Richman, Jonathan: 63
Rimbaud, Arthur: 10
Rimbaud, Penny: 66, 92, 93, 96
riot grrrl: 36, 155, 158–159, 160–164, 223–224; manifesto 158–159; white movement 163
rockabilly: 15, 42
Rocket from the Tombs: 9
Roessler, Kim: 115
Roessler, Kira: 35
Rogers, Kenny: 72
role models: 261
Rolling Stones, The: 5, 7, 18, 30, 59
Ronstadt, Linda: 10, 15, 61
Ross, Diana: 60
Rossi, Melinda: 162
Rotten, Johnny: 49, 63, 64, 65, 67, 75, 88
Rough Trade: 81
Roxy Music: 9, 33, 74–75
Rudimentary Peni: 118
Runaways, The: 12, 22–26, 34, 54, 62, 68; Blackheart Records label 25; Blue (Tischler), Vicki 25, 26; "Cherry Bomb" 23; *Creem* 24, 25; Currie, Cherie 12, 23, 25; "Don't Abuse Me" 24–25; *Edgeplay* 26; *Foxes* 25; Fox, Jackie 23, 25–26; Ford, Lita 23, 25; Fowley, Kim 22–23, 25; Germs, The 25; "I Love Rock 'n' Roll" 25; jailbait image 24–25; Jett, Joan (Larkin) 12, 22–26, 74, 115;

Krome, Kari 23, 25; male worship of female musicians 23–24; media critics 24; Mercury Records 23; "My Buddy and Me" 25; national tour 23; personal background 22–23; Quatro, Suzi 23; *Queens of Noise* 24; *Runaways, The* 23; sexuality issues 24–25; stage show 23; Steele, Micki 23, 25; teen glam 23; teen lust 24–25, 26; Top 40 hits 25; verbal abuse 25; West, Sandy 23, 25, 26

Ryan, Terri: 33

S

Salt-N-Pepa: 152

San Francisco Art Institute: 47–48

Savage, Jon: 69, 70, 75, 113

scene violence: 118

Schock, Gina: 14

Screamers, The: 13, 34, 37, 42, 48

Seattle scene: 156

"second wave" of feminism: 160

Seeds, The: 7–8

Seger, Bob: 20

Selby Jr., Hubert: 122

7 Year Bitch: 154, 164

Severin, Steve: 64, 66, 74, 76

sexism: 14, 15, 115–119, 155, 158, 229

Sex Pistols, The: 10, 11, 15, 33, 63, 64, 65, 67, 68, 70, 71, 73, 75, 85, 100, 187

Sex shop: 63, 64, 69

sex symbol: 62

sexual abuse: 150, 230

sexuality: 5, 6, 11–12, 13, 15

Shepard, Sam: 18

Shirkers, The: 155

Silverhead: 9

Simmons, Gene: 7

Simon, Carly: 5, 6

Simon and Garfunkel: 5

Sioux, Siouxsie: 63, 64, 64, 66, 70, 71, 72, 73–78

Siouxie and the Banshees: 63, 64, 64, 66, 70, 71, 72, 73–78; antiglamour 74; *Boomerang* 77; break up 77; Budgie 77; Creatures, The 77; goth image 73; Grundy, Bill 76; *Guardian Unlimited* 75; "Kiss Them for Me" 73–74; "Lord's Prayer, The" 75; McKay, John 76; Morris, Kenny 76; Murray, Charles Shaar 75, 76; musical style 77; new wave punk 78; 100 Club Punk Festival 75; "Peek-A-Boo" 77; *Peep Show* 77;

personal history 74; religion 75; reunite 77; *Scream, The* 76; Seven Year Itch tour 77; Severin, Steve 74–75; sexuality 74, 75–76, 77; Sioux, Siouxsie 63, 64, 64, 66, 70, 71, 72, 73–78; Smith, Robert 74, 76; "Standing There" 77

Sir Mix-A-Lot: 153

Sister Double Happiness: 183

skinheads: 118

Skunk Anansie: 163

slam pits: 115

Slant 6: 211

Sleater-Kinney: 232, 234–238; *All Hands on the Bad One* 236; anti-government 238; Brownstein, Carrie 234, 235–236, 237–238; "Combat Rock" 238; *Dig Me Out* 235; Excuse 17 234; Farrell, Misty 235; feminism 235; Gogin, Toni 235; grrrl band 234; Heavens to Betsy 234–235; "I Wanna Be Your Joey Ramone" 236; McFarlane, Lora 235; *One Beat* 237, 238; politics 235–236, 237–238; "The Professional" 236; *Punk Planet* 237; *She's a Rebel* 235; "Step Aside" 238; "Taking Me Home" 236; Tucker, Corin 234, 235; Weiss, Janet 235, 236; "You're No Rock n' Roll Fun 237

Slickee Boys: 155

Slits, The: 64, 66, 67, 68, 71, 72, 79–85; Albertine, Viv 79–85; Ari-and the True Warriors 84; Ari-Up 64, 72, 79–85; band changes 82–83; beauty 84; born again Christian 84–85; Budgie 82; Castrators, The 79; Clash, The 80, 84; current activity 84–85; *Cut* 81, 83–84; discrimination 84; feminism 81–82; Gutsy, Suzi 79; Korus, Kate 79, 81–82; musical style 81–84; New Age Steppers 84; New Town 83; Number One Enemy 85; Palmolive 79–84; *Peel Sessions* 81; personal history 79, 80; Pollitt, Tessa 79–85; Pop Group 82–83; reggae 83; *Retrospective* 81; *Return of the Giant Slits* 81; rhythm 82–83; Smith, Bruce 83; "Typical Girls" 82, 85; White Riot Tour (1977) 84

Smear, Pat: 14

Smith, Robert: 74, 76

Smith, T.V.: 69

Snakepit: 205

Social Distortion: 37

social problems: 59

soft rock: 5–6

Sohl, Richard: 18, 21

Solid Gold: 70

Sonic Youth: 117, 121, 133–139, 227; "alternative nation" 138; anarchy 135; Arcadians, The 135; *A Thousand Leaves* 138, 139; Azerrad, Michael 135; *Bad Moon Rising* 136; Bert, Bob 135; "Bone" 138; Boredom, The 137; "Boys Are Smelly" 137; Branca, Glenn 135; Cafritz, Julie 137; Chuck D 138; Ciccone Youth 136; "Cinderella's Big Score" 138; CKM 134; *Confusion Is Sex* 136; Crews, Harry 137; *Daydream Nation* 136; *Dirty* 138; DIY 135; Edson, Richard 135; *Experimental Jet Set* 138; "Female Mechanic on Duty" 138–139; feminism 136; *Forced Exposure* 135; Free Kitten 137; Geffen Records 137; *Goo* 138; Gordon, Kim 133–139; Graham, Dan 135; Hahn, Christine 135; Hill, Anita 138, 160; "The Ineffable Me", 139; "I Wanna Be Your Dog" 136; Ibold, Mark 137; "Into the Groove(y)" 136; *Kill Yr Idols* 136; "Kool Thing" 138; Lunch, Lydia 137; Moore, Thurston 134–139; MTV 138; *Murray Street* 138; musical style 133–134, 135–138; *Nice Ass* 137; Noise Festival 135; *No Star* 138; O'Rourke, Jim 138; Pavement, The 137; personal history 134–135; political statements 138–139; *Pretty on the Inside* 137; "Protect Me You" 136; Public Enemy 138; Pussy Galore 137; P-We, Yashimi 137; Ranaldo, Lee 134–139; "Revlon Liberation Orchestra" 137–138; *Rockrgrl* 135; Sclavunos, Jim 135; sexism 138–139; sexuality 133–134; "Shaking Hell" 136; Shelley, Steve 135; *Sister* 136; Smith, Patti 135–136; songwriting 137, 138; *Sonic Death* 136; *Sonic Nurse* 138; Stanton, Miranda 135; "Swimsuit Issue" 138; *Trash* 138; "Tunic (Song for Karen)" 138; UCLA 134; underground "cred" 138; *Village Voice* 134; *Washing Machine* 138; "Youth Against Fascism" 138

soul music: 51

Soundgarden: 157

space-age: 8–9

Spheeris, Penelope: 42

Spice Girls: 226

Spinanes, The: 154

Springsteen, Bruce: 21, 71, 108

Spungen, Nancy: 67–68

Squip, Tommy: 155

SST Records: 115

stage diving: 115

Stefani, Gwen: 226

Stern, Howard: 249

Stewart, Gary: 12

Stewart, Rod: 72

Stiff Records: 68–69

Stinky Toys, The: 64

St. Mark's Church: 17

St. Martin's Art College: 64

St. Martin's Press: 190

Stooges, The: 8, 9, 33, 54, 63

Stranglers, The: 63

Strummer, Joe: 63, 64, 75

Styrene, Poly (Elliot, Marion): 62, 74, 86–91

Subversa, Vi: 68

Subway Sect: 64, 71, 84

Sugar Baby Doll: 183

Sugar Shack: 23

Summer, Donna: 60

swastika use: 69

T

Take Back The Night March: 157

Talking Heads: 12, 13, 17, 27–31, 35, 53, 62, 71; albums 29; background 27–28; Bizadi 28; break up 30, 31; "Burning Down the House" 30; Byrne, David 27, 29; "Don't Worry About the Government" 29; emotion in songs 30; *Fear of Music* 29; Frantz, Chris 27–28; "Genius of Love" 30; *Guitar Player* 28; inspiration to women 30; *Little Creatures* 30; mainstream music 30; *More Songs About Buildings and Food* 29; musical style 28–30; *Naked* 30; *New Musical Express* 27, 29; New York City 27; "Once in a Lifetime" 30; personal history 27–28; politics 29; "Psycho Killer" 29; punk philosophy 30–31; *Remain in Light* 29; Revelation 28; "Road to Nowhere" 30; Rock and Roll Hall of Fame 31; *Rolling Stone* 28; sexuality 30; Sire Records 28–29; *Speaking in Tongues* 30; *Stop Making Sense* 30; synth-pop 29; Tom Tom Club 29, 30, 31; underground 31; Weymouth, Tina 27–31, 35, 62; *Yes, Please* 31

Taylor, James: 4–5

Taylor, Vince: 67

Team Dresch: 118, 164, 215–219; Bleyle, Jody 215, 217, 218–219; break up 216; Butchies, The 216; Candy-Ass Records 216; *Captain My Captain* 216, 217, 218; Carland, Tammy Rae 216; *Chainsaw* 216, 217; Chainsaw (record label) 216; Dresch, Donna 215–219; dyke band 215; Excuse 17 217; Fifth Column 217; *Free to Fight* 217; Frumpies, The 216; "Growing Up in Springfield" 217–218; "Hate the Christian Right!" 217; Heavens to Betsy 217; lyrics 216, 217; Martinez, Marci 215, 216; mental illness 218; Musical Fanzine 218; musical style 215; Northwest 219; Northwest queer movement 215–216; "#1 Chance Pirate TV" 217; *Personal Best* 215–216, 217; personal history 216–217; Phranc 217; political activism 216, 218–219; *Punk Planet* 215; queercore 215, 216; reunion 216; self-defense awareness 217; social responsibility 219; songwriting 216; "To the Enemies of Political Rock" 219; Wilson, Kaia 215, 216–218; "Yes I am Too, But Who Am I Really?" 218; young lesbian love 217–218

television: 10–11, 12, 53, 63

"third wave" of feminism: 159–160

Thomas, B.J.: 4, 5, 59

Thunders, Johnny: 14

Tiny Desk Unit: 155

TLC: 152

Toomey, Jenny: 153, 155–156, 158, 170–176, 205, 227

Toots and the Maytals: 101

Top 20 hits: 59, 60, 61, 70

T. Rex: 9, 61

Tribe 8: 117–118, 153, 161, 163, 164, 186–192; Acker, Kathy 189; *Allen's Mom* 189; Alternative Tentacles 189; "Barnyard Poontang" 190; Bellum, Slade 188; Biafra, Jello 189; Black and Blue Tattoo 189; Breedlove, Lynn 187, 188–189, 190–191; *By Hook or By Crook* 189; *By the Time We Get to Colorado* 189, 190; censorship 191; Denver scene 187; dildo castration 190; dyke punk rock 186; "Estrofemme" 190; fellatio stunt 190–191; feminism 190, 192; "Femme Bitch Top" 190; *Fist City* 189, 190; Flannigan, Tracy 190; Flipper's café 187–188; "Frat Pig" 189; gang castrate 189–190; gender issues 187; *Godspeed* 189; Harp Label 189; heterosexism 190; Howard, Silas 187–188, 189; lesbian scene 186, 188–189, 190; "Lezbophobia" 190; Lickety Split All-Girl Courier 189; lyrics 186, 188, 189; Mah, Leslie 161, 187, 188, 189, 190, 191; Mama T 188; Michigan Women's Music Festival 191–192; musical style 191; "Neanderthal Dyke" 190; "Old Skool, New Skool" 190; Outpunk 189; Payne, Lynne "Tantrum" 188; penile punishment 189; *Pig Bitch* 189; poetry 188; political agenda 186, 187, 189, 190, 191–192; queercore 186, 187; rape 189–190, 192; Red Dora's Bearded Lady café 187–188; *Rise Above* 190; Role Models for Amerika 189, 190; sadomasochism 190; sexual abuse issues 191–192; sexuality 187, 188–189; Slits, The 190; *Snarkism* 189, 190; "Tranny Chaser" 190; tribade 188; vigilantism 189–190; Wiese, Todd 192

Tru Fax and the Insaniacs: 155

Tsunami: 153

Tucker, Maureen: 31

Turner, Tina: 110

Twersky, Lori: 24

UV

"ugly girl": 154

United Kingdom: BBC 70; British media 69–72; classism 67; domestic violence 65; Equal Pay Act 65; feminist movement 65–66; labor issues 65–66; *Olde Grey Whistle Test* 69, 70, 71; Pizzey, Erin 65; politics 65; *Popular Music and Society* 70; racism 67; rape 65; *Scream Quietly or the Neighbors Will Hear* 65; sexism 67; *Top of the Pops* 70

Unterberger, Richard: 50

Urban Verbs: 155

U2: 148, 232

Vail, Tobi: 158, 231

Van Morrison, Jim: 19

Vedder, Eddie: 157

Velvet Mafia: 164

Velvet Underground, The: 8, 31

Vicious, Sid: 67–68, 75, 79

Vietnam war: 60, 65

Vig, Butch: 183

Vincent, Gene: 42

Ving, Lee: 116
Violent Femmes: 50, 117

W

Waits, Tom: 50, 199
Warhol, Andy: 17
Warnick, Kim: 62, 140–143
Warwick, Dionne: 61
Weirdos, The: 13, 34, 37, 42
West Coast punk: 12, 13
Westwood, Vivienne: 63, 69
Weymouth, Tina: 27–31, 35, 62
Whisky A Go-Go: 23
white pop mainstream: 228–229
white power: 116
White Riot tour: 67
Who, The: 7
Wiedlin, Jane: 12, 14
Williams, Wendy O.: 15
Wilson Center show: 155
Wilson, Kaia: 215, 216–218
Wings: 72
Winterland, The: 15, 47, 49
Wobble, Jah: 88
Wolfe, Allison: 156, 158, 160
Wolf, Naomi: 159, 162
Woodstock (1999): 230

XYZ

X: 15, 37, 42–46, 47, 114; *A Beer on Every Page* 44; *Adulterers Anonymous* 43–44, 45–46; Auntie Christ 44; books 43–44, 45; Cervenka, Exene (Christine) 42–46, 111–112; current projects 44; "Dancing with Tears in My Eyes" 44; *Hey Zeus!* 43; "I'm Coming Over" 43; "Johnny Hit and Run Paulene" 43; *Just Another War* 44; *Life Could Be a Dream* 44; literary talents 42, 43–44, 45; *Los Angeles* 43, 45; Lunch, Lydia 45–46;

More Fun in the New World 43; musical style 44–45; "Night Our Love Passed Out on the Couch" 44; *Old Wives' Tales* 44; personal history 42, 43; rockabilly and punk 42–43; *Rude Hieroglyphics* 46; *Running Scared* 44; "Sex and Dying in High Society" 44; Slash Records 43; solo albums 44; *Surface to Air Serpents* 44; *Unclogged* 43; *Under the Big Black Sun* 43, 44; *Virtual Unreality* 44; "We're Desperate" 44; *Wild Gift* 43, 45
X-Ray Spex: 62, 66, 86–91; *Anthology, The* 88, 91; antimaterialism 91; Cells 90; *Conscious Consumer* 91; "The Day the World Turned Day-Glo" 87; Essential Logic 90; family 91; feminist influence 89; formation of X-Ray Spex 88; *Germ Free Adolescence* 87, 88; Hare Krishna spirituality 90–91; "I Am a Cliché" 87; individualism 90; Logic, Lora 86–91; Mann, Geoff 90; Marcus, Greil 90; materialism 86–87; musical style 88–90; new wave 87; "Oh Bondage, Up Yours!" 87, 89; "Plastic Bag" 91; personal history 87; reunite 91; Roxy, The 88; sexuality 88–89; Styrene, Poly (Elliot, Marion) 62, 74, 86–91; Tea, Rich 90; 25th anniversary of punk 87
Yes: 7
Yoko factor: 158
Young, Toni: 155
You're Living All Over Me: 148
Y Records: 81
Zapata, Mia: 165–169
Zappa, Frank: 29
Zeppelin, Led: 7, 18, 59
Ziggy Stardust: 8–9
Zolar X: 9
Zoom, Billy: 42, 43

ACKNOWLEDGMENTS

WITHOUT ALL FORMS OF INDIE AND PUNK ROCK, MY RECORD collection, friendships, and this book wouldn't be. Keep it comin'! Warm thanks and love to my parents, John and Jackie Raha, for their lifelong acceptance and support of unbridled creativity and self-exploration. Thanks to my stalwart editor, Ingrid Emerick, for a year of sound advice, wit, intelligence, patience, and support, and to everyone at Seal Press and Avalon Publishing Group for making this a (sur)reality—especially Jane Musser for all manner of production assistance, Maggie Friedland for her critical help with permissions, and Adem Tepedelen for his excellent copyediting. Special thanks to Patrick Barber and Steve Connell for taking the time to read and provide thoughtful comments on the manuscript. Also, thanks to Patrick for his inspired cover design and interior layout work. To Lisa Corson—I couldn't ask for a kinder or more knowledgeable photo researcher. To all of the people I interviewed, I'm humbled and happy to have your input, thoughts, and warm support (and photos!): Wes Beech, Lynn Breedlove, Joy de Vivre, Beth Ditto, Lulu Gargiulo, Penelope Houston, Sara Jaffe, Theo Kogan, Eve Libertine, Lora Logic, Lydia Lunch, Leslie Mah, Paloma McLardy, Kathy Mendonca, Steve Moriarty, Nicole Panter, Bruce Smith, Richie Stotts, Rod Swenson, Jenny Toomey, Ari-Up, Gina Volpe, Kaia Wilson, and Allison Wolfe. To everyone who connected me with the artists: Alex Steininger at In Music We Trust, Brian Pearl, Jessica Hopper and Hopper PR, Kurt Bloch, Maggie Vail at Kill Rock Stars, Janice Gaffney, and lastly, to Penny Rimbaud, for making sure my letter looking for Eve and Joy made it safely to their helpful hands. A special thanks to Phil Free and Joy de Vivre for a wonderful Zen Palate lunch, to Ari-Up for tolerating my voice at rehearsal, and to Allison Wolfe for a flood of photos and a nice afternoon in D.C. To Ira Robbins and

Trouser Press, for kindly allowing me to model the discographies after their own. Love to my family: Lorraine Raha, Matthew, Jacqueline Sr., Jacqueline Jr., and Gabriella Gaynor, Camille Gagliano, Theresa Gagliano, Mike, Cynthia, and Stephanie Raha, Angela and Ralph Tomaccio, and all extended, honorary, or immediate members of the Raha, Gagliano, Tomaccio, and Varney clans, for a lifetime of laughs and support. To the freaky, smart, and sassy Ithaca Snack Bar Posse (you know who you are!), especially Brian Greyard, Anthony Pacifico, Peter Pagano, Becky Reitzes, Todd Skoglund, and Jennie Zappa. I'm grateful to everyone at *Vibe* and *Spin* magazines, particularly Renee Donatien, Paul Familetti, Beth Gillies, Steve Lowenthal, Enrico Mowatt, and Michelle Timmons, who provided support, contacts, smokes, drinks, concerts, CDs, and coffee. To my sistas, Holly Drawbaugh and Kyra Condo, and their equally cool husbands, Jon Drawbaugh and Brennan Condo, thank you for being who you are. Big smoochies to Johna de Pasquale and Keri Kaminskey, who have always been there. Thanks to kindred spirit Peatla, for friendship, for an unparalleled record collection, and for introducing me to Crass. To all the women of Hedgebrook, without whom I wouldn't have finished the second half of this work. And an extra-special thanks to Delaney Fong—for being infinitely patient and supportive, and for being an intrepid transcriber and co-discographer. I couldn't have done it without you.

ABOUT THE AUTHOR

MARIA RAHA has written for *Bitch: Feminist Response to Pop Culture* and *Time Out New York*, as well as dozens of small press journals and 'zines. Her essays have been published in the anthologies *Young Wives' Tales: New Adventures in Love and Partnership* and *The W Effect: Bush's War on Women*, and she has coproduced and cowritten two 'zines of her own. For the past six years she has worked at *Vibe* and *Spin* magazines, funding a towering record collection and countless rock shows in New York City, where she resides.